A MANUAL

OF THE

ART OF PROSE COMPOSITION:

FOR THE USE OF

COLLEGES AND SCHOOLS.

BY

J. M. BONNELL, D. D.
PRESIDENT WESLEYAN FEMALE COLLEGE, MACON, GA.

LOUISVILLE, KY:
JOHN P. MORTON AND COMPANY.
1867.

Entered, according to Act of Congress, in the year 1867, by

JOHN P. MORTON AND COMPANY,

In the Clerk's Office of the District Court of the United States for the District of Kentucky.

STEREOTYPED BY
JOHN P. MORTON AND COMPANY,
LOUISVILLE, KY.

PREFACE.

In the preparation of this work, it has been no part of the compiler's aim to be original. He has sought rather to select from the various treatises on this subject those rules and exercises which have been approved by the experience of teachers, and to combine them into one consistent whole, arranged with reference to the progressive development of the learner's powers.

The plan of the work does not contemplate that the study of it shall be accomplished in only one year. Even high-school and college classes, relieved by previous training from the necessity of going through the Preliminary Exercises in Parts I. and II. of Book First, could not do justice to the exercises prescribed in this Manual by devoting to it less than two years. Still better would it be to distribute its lessons over the space of three years or more.

The compiler acknowledges his obligations to Dr. E. A. Grant of Louisville for valuable assistance in the revision of the work. Similar aid has been afforded by Professors N. Butler and P. A. Towne.

Leave has kindly been granted to use some of the matter of Quackenbos's *Advanced Course of Composition and Rhetoric* and of *Boyd's Composition*, two of the best works in this department published in America. The publishers of *Lynd's Etymology* have allowed the valuable table of Synonyms found in that work to be inserted as an appendix in this.

If any apology is needed for introducing such amusing errors as are found in Chapters V. and VI. into a text-book, it may be found in the fact that such pleasantry beguiles many a young pupil into fondness for a study which otherwise he might consider dry.

It is hoped that American teachers may not find this Manual inappropriate to their use.

J. M. B.

CONTENTS.

BOOK SECOND.

PART I.—Invention—Resumed.

PART II.—Expression—Resumed.

BOOK THIRD.

PART I.—INVENTION—RESUMED.

PART II.—EXPRESSION—RESUMED.

PART III.—INVENTION—RESUMED.

PART IV.—EXPRESSION—RESUMED.

PART V.—INVENTION—RESUMED.

PART VI.—EXPRESSION—RESUMED.

BOOK FOURTH.

PART I.—Invention—Argumentation.

PART II.—Expression—Resumed.

PART III.—Invention—Resumed.

PART IV.—Expression—Resumed.

A MANUAL

OF THE

ART OF PROSE COMPOSITION.

GENERAL DIRECTIONS TO THE TEACHER.

There are two things indispensable to the attainment of excellence in the use of language; *originality in all the didactic exercises enjoined, and the actual correction of all errors in those exercises.*

Never accept an exercise or a composition from a pupil that you have reason to suspect is not original. If the pupil needs direction or assistance, let it be afforded by yourself, and no one else.

The most effectual method to secure this originality is to require every exercise to be written by the class in the presence of the teacher—*coram præceptore.* When the time assigned for the exercise arrives, require the class to be seated, and all ready to write. Whatever explanations and exemplifications may be needed should then be given, so that all the class may get the benefit. Then allow a brief space for questions from those who want further information; after which, command and enforce silence, and let the writing begin. While this is going on, no distracting noises, such as conversation or audible recitation, should be allowed. After the requisite time has elapsed, the teacher requires all the performances to be closed, names signed, and exercises handed to him for revision.

It is acknowledged that this plan is open to the objection that many pupils find it impossible, at first, to *think* in the school-room or recitation-room. But it has been found that this inability will yield to honest and repeated effort. Pupils must learn to think and write in the school-room, just as men have learned to think in every conceivable situation in which thinking is necessary. No other exercise than those thus prepared, *coram præceptore*, should be accepted by the teacher during all the novitiate of the pupil in this art. After he has acquired some facility in composition, and some confidence in his own powers, then, if the exercises demand more time than the teacher can devote to presiding over the class while writing them, the pupil may be permitted to prepare them elsewhere. The pleasure derived from originality and the moral repugnance to deception will be very effective in preventing plagiarism. But whenever there is any suspicion of plagiarism, or of having received undue help, there should be a prompt return to the *coram præceptore* system.

Another essential condition to the highest improvement in this art is the rigid and faithful correction of every error, and the repeated transcribing of every production, until it is faultless, or nearly so. This, it is granted, imposes a heavy labor upon the teacher—*at first.* But let every teacher be assured that the most economical expenditure of time and pains upon a pupil is that which requires on each effort the best that he can do at the time, and permits him not to leave it until all its faults have been corrected. As a means both of improving the pupil and lessening the labors of the teacher, it is recommended that the first draughts of each exercise be exchanged among the members of the class for mutual criticism, and then handed back, each one to its author, to be re-written and corrected. Let these second draughts be handed to the teacher for his revision. This work should be done by him very thoroughly. All those violations of rules that have been the subject of previous study may be corrected by a simple reference to the number of the paragraph or article containing the rule. As to all others, the teacher should carefully indicate what phraseology or form is proper; and then require *another* transcription by the pupil, with all these errors amended. And it should be understood, in every case, that no exercise or production is to be passed by until it is fully or very nearly correct. Perseverance in this course will bring abundant reward.

BOOK FIRST.

PART FIRST.

PRELIMINARY EXERCISES.

CHAPTER I.

TERMINAL PUNCTUATION.

[IT is presumed that the student into whose hands this Manual is placed, has acquired a correct orthography, and considerable facility in penmanship, such as is imparted in all good schools by what are called *dictation exercises.* If this is not the case, let him at once be set to work in such exercises, and continued in them, until he can, with accuracy and dispatch, write down whatever is dictated to him.

In the course of such exercises, the pupil will soon feel the need of some directions as to the use of capitals and points. Let the teacher, therefore, require him to memorize, and teach him to apply, the following rules:]

§ 1. The termination of every complete sentence is, in written or printed discourse, indicated by a *full stop.*

There are three full stops; viz.:

The period (.);

The interrogation point (?);

The exclamation point (!).

§ 2. The period is placed at the end of declarative and imperative sentences.

§ 3. The period is also placed after every abbreviation; as, Jas. Clarke, Esq. Sep. 16th, A. D. 1860.

§ 4. The interrogation point is placed after every question.

§ 5. The exclamation point is placed after every exclamation, whether it be a complete sentence, a phrase, or only one word.

THE USE OF CAPITALS.

§ 6. The first word of every separate and complete sentence should commence with a capital.

§ 7. The first word of every line of poetry should begin with a capital.

§ 8. All proper nouns, and words used as proper nouns, and adjectives derived from proper nouns, should begin with capitals.

§ 9. If a proper name consists of a phrase, every noun and adjective in the phrase should begin with a capital.

§ 10. The subject of the discourse, and a technical term when introduced to be explained, are written with capital initials.

§ 11. The pronoun I and the vocative interjection O are always capitals.

EXAMPLES.

It was customary to crown the kings of France at Rheims; but this place, at the death of Charles VI, being in possession of the English, his son, the Dauphin, could not go there to be crowned.

When Romance had reached this part of her story, the mother smiled, and History tittered aloud.

In the next year Burke published his "Essay on the Sublime and Beautiful."

"Brown Exercise rejoiced to hear,
And Sport leaped up, and seized his beechen spear."

"True prayer
Has flowed from lips wet with Castilian dews."

(For examples under § 10 see §§ 30, 31, 32.)

QUOTATIONS.

§ 12. When one writer introduces into his composition the exact language of another, the expression is called a quotation.

If merely the words are used, but it is not stated whose words they are, the quotation is said to be *informal*.

But if it is expressly stated that a person has spoken or used the words, the quotation is said to be *formal*.

If it is stated that a person uttered the sentiment cited, but the exact words are not given, the expression is sometimes called an indirect quotation, but it is, properly, no quotation at all.

§ 13. A quotation, whether formal or informal, must be indicated by quotation marks; thus: "——".

A formal quotation should also commence with a capital.

An indirect quotation requires no distinguishing mark whatever.

EXAMPLES.

INFORMAL QUOTATIONS.—In all your intercourse with the world remember that "evil communications corrupt good manners."

Afterwards they formed, or undertook to form, "a more perfect union."

FORMAL QUOTATIONS.—And when he saw their faith he said unto the sick of the palsy, "Man, thy sins are forgiven thee."

"Let me make the ballads of a nation," said Fletcher of Saltoun, "and I care not who makes its laws."

INDIRECT QUOTATIONS.—Wesley said that the world was his parish.

Boswell has remarked of Oglethorpe, that even the great Johnson did not hesitate to acknowledge the value of his patronage.

CHAPTER II.

INFLECTIONAL ORTHOGRAPHY.

§ 14. Many words are formed from other words of the language by adding letters to them, or otherwise changing their spelling. This method of forming one word from another is called *Derivation*. A word thus formed from another is called a *derivative* word. A word that is not thus formed is called a *primitive* word.

§ 15. Every derivative word consists of two parts: the *root* or *radical*, and the *added part*. The added part is called a *prefix* if placed at the beginning of the radical, and a *suffix* if placed at the end of it.

The radical is the part to which the prefix or suffix is joined. It may be a primitive word, or a derivative, capable of being analyzed into a simple radical and its added part.

The process of placing prefixes to radicals in English is so simple, requiring little or no change in the spelling, that no rules need be laid down for it. But the annexing of suffixes is more difficult, and requires some directions to be given.

§ 16. Derivation by suffixes is of two kinds. In one kind, the meaning of the word, and generally, its office as a part of speech, are altered, as well as the spelling, or form of the word. In the other kind, the meaning of the word is altered only so far as its grammatical properties or accidents are concerned. This kind of derivation is called *Inflection*.

The inflectional or grammatical suffixes used in English are the following: ——s ——'s ——ed ——er ——est ——eth ——ing.

§ 17. The suffix *s* has two uses:

1. It is added to common nouns to form their plural regularly.

2. It is added to the first radical of a verb to form the third person singular of the present tense.

§ 18. The suffix *'s* has two uses:

1. It is added to nouns in the singular to form the possessive case.

2. It is added to letters, marks, figures, and sometimes to proper names, when it is desired to express them in the plural.

§ 19. The suffix *ed* is added to the first radical of regular verbs to form their second radical, which is the form of the past tense and the perfect participle.

§ 20. The suffix *er* is added to the root of monosyllabic and some dissyllabic adjectives to form their comparative degree.

§ 21. The suffix *est* has two uses:

1. It is added to the radical of monosyllabic and dissyllabic adjectives to form their superlative degree.

2. It is added to the first or second radical of a verb when it has for its subject the pronoun *thou.*

§ 22. The suffix *eth* was in former times used to form the third person singular of the present tense of verbs, as we now use the suffix *s.*

§ 23. The suffix *ing* is added to the first radical of verbs to form their imperfect (present) participle.

RULES FOR CHANGES.

§ 24. When the suffix *s* is to be added to a radical, it is not in every instance immediately joined to the last letter, but takes an intervening *e* as a uniting vowel, thus converting the suffix *s* into *es.* This occurs in the following cases:

1st. When the last letter of the radical is such as to obscure the sound of *s* following it. In this case the suffix *es* forms an additional syllable; as, box, box-es; church, church-es; wash, wash-es.

2d. When the final letter of the radical is *o* or *y,* preceded by a consonant; as, negro, negroes; potato, potatoes.

To this rule there are some exceptions in usage, but the rules are gradually reducing all to a uniformity.

The following words change *f* into *v* and then take the intervening *e:*

Sheaf	sheaves	Leaf	leaves
Loaf	loaves	Beef	beeves
Thief	thieves	Calf	calves
Half	halves	Elf	elves
Shelf	shelves	Self	selves
Wolf	wolves	Life	lives
Knife	knives	Wife	wives
Staff	staves (*sticks*) staffs (*officers*)	Wharf	wharfs wharves

§ 25. When the final syllable of a radical is accented, and ends in a consonant preceded by a single vowel, if a suffix is to be added which begins with a vowel, the final consonant of the radical must be doubled.

Monosyllables are included in this rule; for, having only one syllable, the accent must, of course, fall upon it.

The final consonant is doubled after a vowel preceded by *qu*, as if it were a single vowel preceded by a consonant.

The letters *x* and *k* are never doubled in English.

The word *gas* does not double its final *s* in the plural, ***gases***.

EXAMPLES.

Beget	begetting	Red	redder
Compel	compelled	Flat	flattest
Expel	expelling	Begin	beginning
Forbid	forbiddest	Omit	omitting
Unpin	unpinned	Forget	forgettest
Quit	quitting	Mix	mixed

The final consonant of a radical, when not preceded by a single vowel, or when the accent is not on the last syllable, remains single when a suffix is added.

EXAMPLES.

Toil	toiling	Cheat	cheated
Spoil	spoilest	Shout	shouting
Travel	traveled	Level	leveler
Worship	worshiper	Equal	equaled
Cavil	caviling	Envelop	enveloping

§ 26. When a radical ends with silent *e*, and a suffix is to be added which begins with *e* or *i*, then the final *e* of the radical is dropped in the derivative.

EXAMPLES.

Live	living	Come	coming
Cure	cured	Fine	finer
Twine	twinest	Enslave	enslaved
Abase	abasing	Awake	awakest
Disgrace	disgraced	Lodge	lodging
Judge	judgeth	Service	services
White	whiter	Make	maker

When the final *e* of the radical is preceded by *o*, *e*, or *y*, it is retained in the derivative before the suffix *ing*.

The final *e* is also retained in the participles *singeing* (from singe), *tingeing* (from tinge), and *swingeing* (from swinge), to distinguish them from the corresponding participles of the verbs *sing*, *ting*, and *swing*.

§ 27. When the final letter of a radical is *y*, preceded by a *consonant*, and a suffix is to be added beginning with *e*, then the *y* is to be changed into *i* in the derivative.

EXAMPLES.

Pity	pitied	Copy	copiest
Comply	complied	Dirty	dirtier
Weary	wearied	Busy	busiest
Signify	signified	Purify	purifieth

§ 28. When the final letter of a radical is *y*, preceded by a vowel, the *y* is retained before any suffix that may be added.

EXAMPLES.

Gay	gayer	Pay	payest
Pray	prayed	Play	playing
Survey	surveyeth	Delay	delayed

Layed, *payed*, and *stayed* are generally contracted into *laid*, *paid*, and *staid;* and *said* is always used for *sayed.*

When the suffix *ing* is to be added to a radical ending in *ie*, this termination must be changed into *y* in the derivative.

EXAMPLES.

Die	dying	Tie	tying
Vie	vying	Untie	untying
Lie	lying	Outvie	outvying

§ 29. When the suffixes *ed* and *est* are both to be added to a radical, they are contracted into *edst.*

EXAMPLES.

Ordain	ordainedst	Laugh	laughedst

PART SECOND.

DIVISION OF THE SUBJECT—INVENTION.

CHAPTER III.

ELICITATION OF THOUGHT BY QUESTIONS.

§ 30. The Art of Composition is the combination of the two subordinate arts,—the Art of Invention and the Art of Expression.

§ 31. Invention is that art by which thoughts are produced and arranged in a natural and impressive order.

§ 32. Expression is the art by which thought is communicated in an accurate and pleasing manner.

These subordinate arts, though so distinguishable in the results at which they aim, and in the training exercises which they require, must, nevertheless, be studied in connection with each other; as no proficiency can be acquired in the one without corresponding attainments in the other.

For the manner in which the subsequent contents of this Manual are to be used, so as to secure the proper combination of Invention and Expression, see the Directions to the Teacher on page 11.

The most successful method of teaching young persons to put their thoughts on paper is the following. When they are ready to write, announce some easy, familiar subject, and proceed to ask questions upon it, calling for such replies as you know they can give. After a dozen or more of such questions have been proposed and answered, require them to write down as much of the substance of their answers as they can recollect, but avoid any approach to the question-and-answer form of expression.

If the teacher prefer it, he can write the questions all out on the blackboard, and keep them before the pupils while they are writing. But while this course may be pursued with mere beginners, it is advisable that the pupils should early be trained to recollect the thoughts which the questions may have suggested, and to produce them according to their natural associations, and independent of their connection with the questions.

The following composition, actually produced in this way by a little girl of ten years of age, is a fair specimen of the exercises here required.

MY DOG.

1. Did you ever have a dog?
2. What kind of a dog was he?
3. What was his color?
4. What was his name?
5. Why was he so named?
6. Was he playful?
7. Was he an intelligent dog?
8. How did he usually employ himself?
9. Did he ever go away from home?
10. What became of him?

COMPOSITION.

I once had a dog. He was a very little dog when I got him, but grew as he advanced in age. My brother brought him to me from Lexington. He was nearly all black, with a white stripe down his nose, and with brown tips to his paws. His name was Rip Van Winkle. He was named after that Rip Van Winkle who slept twenty years. I named him so because he slept so much. He was very playful and intelligent, as well as very active. He usually passed his time carrying people's shoes away. When you woke up in the morning you were sure to miss your shoes, and after a while you would find one on the staircase, or some other place in the house, and the other in the yard. He frequently went to make visits to his neighbors and friends, even after I had forbidden him to do so. He was punished for this, because disobedience is always punished. One day he started to market without my permission, and stopped to see some of his friends. I suppose they enticed him off, for he has never been heard of since.

CHAPTER IV.

REPRODUCTION.

To THE TEACHER.—The exercises prescribed in the foregoing section are not meant to be continuous, but performed at intervals as the class advances in those parts of the Manual devoted to Expression. After some facility in them has been acquired, they should give place to the form of exercise styled Reproduction.

This differs from the former, not only in the mode of eliciting thought, but also in the additional particular that the information is communicated by the teacher previous to writing. To do this, the teacher should prepare himself, and then deliver to the pupils a short, plain lecture on some interesting subject, on a level with their capacity. On no account should the lecture exceed fifteen or twenty minutes: less than that would be sufficient for young pupils. At its close, allow a few minutes for the asking of questions on points which may not have been fully apprehended. Then let silence be commanded, and require each pupil to reproduce so much of the substance of the lecture as he may recollect. These productions should be subjected to all the revisions and corrections recommended in the "General Directions to the Teacher."

The following is a specimen of the kind of lecture proper to be delivered for such a purpose. But be careful to avoid the mere *reading* of any piece to be reproduced by the pupils. Prepare your mind as thoroughly as you please, but deliver the lecture in a natural, conversational style, speaking very deliberately, and using all the aids that gestures, intonations, and looks can impart, to make the remarks impressive. Let this exercise be repeated at intervals of a week or two, as the class progresses through the parts devoted to Diction.

SPECIMEN OF LECTURE DELIVERED FOR REPRODUCTION.

Life in Seeds.—A dry seed looks as if it were dead. But there is life in it, shut up as in a prison house. It is very quiet as long as it is shut up. But once let it out, and it does wonderful things.

An apple-seed, with its stout brown covering, is a very little thing. It does not look as if any thing could ever come from it. But if it gets into the ground, the moisture softens and swells it, the covering bursts, and an apple-tree comes from that little seed. And you know that the Bible tells us that a tree, large enough for the fowls of the air to rest on, comes from the little mustard-seed.

The life in the dry seed is asleep. Put it into moist ground, and this life wakes up. This sleep of seeds sometimes lasts a great while. Commonly we keep them only from one year to another. And it is wonderful to think that the life can sleep through all the winter months and yet not die, but be ready at the call of Spring, when the sun warms the ground a little, to set in motion all the particles of the seed, and cause it to put on a new form, and change itself into a new being, as it were.

How beautifully does St. Paul compare the resurrection of the dead to the springing of a plant from the seed! "That which thou sowest, thou sowest not that body that shall be," not the stalk with its blades and nodding ear, "but bare grain; it may chance of wheat, or of some other grain. But God giveth it a body as it hath pleased him, and to every seed his own body." "So also is the resurrection of the dead. It is sown in corruption, it is raised in incorruption. It is sown in dishonor, it is raised in glory. It is sown in weakness, it is raised in power. It is sown a natural body, it is raised a spiritual body."

Commonly, I have said, seeds are kept only from one year to another, and the most of them will keep the life in them only that long; so that if they are not planted and permitted to sprout in the next year after they have been produced they will die. But sometimes they have been kept for a long time alive in their state of sleep. I will tell you a story to illustrate this.

Nearly eighteen hundred years ago an eruption occurred from the volcano Vesuvius. At first the heaving mountain belched forth fine ashes mingled with sand in such vast quantities, and to such an incredible height, that the rays of the sun were obscured, and it was dark for many miles around the base of the mountain. The ashes descending overwhelmed two great cities, and even entered and filled up the houses and shops of the people. This flood of ashes was so sudden that it arrested men in the streets, women in their houses, and children at play, instantly smothering and burying them and their beautiful cities in the same vast grave. Then a great stream of lava belched from its crater and rolled down its sides. It was all on fire, and looked like a stream of melted iron. It rolled over these already buried cities. When the lava cooled, not a trace of these cities could be found. The lava which buried them had hardened into a great rock above them, and the two cities and all they contained seemed lost forever.

But a few years ago learned and curious men took it into their heads to dig down through the rock, and see what they could find of the buried cities. And they have found one of the cities, called *Pompeii*, and have opened up some of its streets, and entered and explored many of its houses. They have found things just as they were left. Among other things, some *seeds* were found there. These were planted, and they sprang up just as seeds do that have been kept only from one year to another. The life in these seeds, then, had been asleep for nearly eighteen hundred years.

How *many* seeds come from one when it is planted! From a single grain of corn come one, two, three, or even four ears, each containing hundreds of grains. How many hills of corn could be planted from the produce of one grain in a single year! We use most of the produce for food, for we need to keep but a small portion for seed. As you look into a full corn-crib, you would hardly think that it holds what will cover hundreds of acres with the tall, rustling, deep green corn. There is a good deal of life asleep in a corn-crib.

Most of the seeds that drop from plants and trees are killed; they decay on the ground with the leaves, or insects devour them. It is only now and then that a seed finds its way into the ground and takes root. If all seeds were to live and spring up, we should have too many things growing about us. But the hand of God is every-where, and He doeth all things well. DR. W. HOOKER.

Exercises in Invention of a different character will be given after those parts of the Manual that treat of Diction. Those of the foregoing description will be sufficient for occasional diversions from the regular exercises in Expression.

PART THIRD.

THE ART OF EXPRESSION.

CHAPTER V.

STYLE—DICTION.

§ 33. *The Art of Expression* is the practical application of the rules of Grammar and Rhetoric. The proper cultivation of this art is the only way to secure a good *style.*

§ 34. *Style* is the mode of expression which one habitually adopts in giving utterance to his thoughts.

§ 35. Individuals necessarily differ very much in their modes of expression, and it is desirable that this variety should exist. But with all the freedom that should be given to differences of character, there are certain properties which the style of every one should possess. These are called the *Essential Properties of Good Style.*

These essential properties may be arranged under two general heads, according as they have reference either to the words and phrases which a person uses, or to the manner in which his words are connected and arranged in sentences. The first of these general heads is called *Diction*, the second *Structure.*

§ 36. *Diction* is that element of style which has reference to the words employed by a writer or speaker. Its four essential properties are: 1. *Purity;* 2. *Propriety;* 3. *Simplicity;* 4. *Precision.*

PURITY OF DICTION.

§ 37. The diction of a writer is said to be pure when he employs no words except such as belong to the English language, as it is at present used by the best writers and speakers.

Violations of purity in diction are called Barbarisms; and they are of four kinds, viz.:

1. *Provincialisms.*
2. *Obsolete words.*
3. *Unauthorized words.*
4. *Foreign words.*

PROVINCIALISMS.

§ 38. The English language is now spoken, not only in England, but in all those countries that have been settled by colonies from England, or that have been subjected to the English government. Hence, it is the vernacular of the greater part of Scotland, Wales, and Ireland, of the south-eastern provinces of British America, of the United States, and of the various British colonies in other parts of the world. In all these countries and places there is a great uniformity in the diction of well-educated people, and this constitutes the *standard* by which all English style is to be judged.

But in different sections of these countries, certain words and forms of speech come into use which are not recognized as belonging to that language which is used by well-educated people through the English-speaking world. These are called *Provincialisms.*

§ 39. This term is also applied to pure English words that have been, among certain classes of vulgar or ill-educated people, forced to assume a meaning not in accordance with the standard.

The pupil will perceive that the sole reason why words of this class are not as good as other words is that they are only partially used. Thus, *chores* is a barbarism, because it is used only in New England. *Tote* is a barbarism, because it is confined to the Southern States. *Hugger-mugger* is a barbarism probably peculiar to England.

As it is *partial* usage that stamps any word as a barbarism, all those *slang* words that come into use among men of a certain trade or profession are to be included in this class. But these must not be confounded with *technical* terms, which, as they describe certain substances, implements, or operations peculiar to any occupation, are very proper in their place. Under the condemnation of partial usage fall those words that are used only by the lower classes; but these have also an air of vulgarity about them, which is far worse than can be said of a mere provincialism.

§ 40. List of Provincialisms, including words used in a peculiar sense by certain classes.

Ambeer—*tobacco spit.*
Bamboozle—*cozen, outwit.*
Bender—*drunken frolic.*
Bogus—*spurious.*
Bosh—*nonsense, trash.*
Boss—*head-workman, employer.*
Booger—*supernatural monster.*
Buncombe—*the popular favor sought by a demagogue.*
Buss—*kiss.*
Bust (burst)—*a drunken frolic.*
Buster—*a huge fellow.*
Cahoot—*copartnership.*
Cantankerous—*contentious, irascible.*
Cavort (curvet)—*prance.*
Chores—*little jobs of daily work.*
Chunky—*short, thickset.*
Contraption—*contrivance.*
Darky—*negro.*
Dodger—*a cake of bread or dough.*
Dumps—*low spirits.*
Faize—*graze, scratch.*
Fice (perhaps Foist)—*a little dog.*
Flare-up—*a sudden manifestation of anger.*
Fornenst—*opposite, over against.*
Fuddle—*intoxicate.*
Gallivanting—*gallanting.*
Gammon—*insincere or deceitful talk.*
Gaum—*daub, besmear.*
Grab—*seize.*
Gump—*a blockhead.*
Gumption—*common sense, ingenuity.*
Hait—*a little bit.*
Harum-scarum—*in a wild, disorderly manner.*
Helter-skelter—*in a loose, irregular manner.*
Higgledy-piggledy—*in great confusion.*
Highfalutin—*bombastic, grandiloquent.*
Hobble—*difficulty.*
Hocus-pocus—*sleight of hand.*
Hugger-mugger—*secretly, mean.*
Hum-and-haw—*hesitate.*
Humbug—*a cheat, a pretense.*
Humdrum—*monotonous.*
Hypped—*affected with low spirits.*
Jabber—*to talk incessantly.*
Kerslosh—*splash.*
Larrup—*whip, flog.*
Lingo—*language, diction.*
Loggerheads—*variance, quarrel.*
Mulligrubs—*sullenness.*
Muss—*confusion, disarrangement.*
Palaver—*idle or deceptive talk.*
Pesky—*troublesome, provoking.*
Pickaninny—*a negro child.*
Pone—*a loaf of bread.*
Potter—*to trifle or delay.*
Primp—*to arrange one's self for show.*
Peert (corruption of pert)—*quick-motioned, lively.*

Rambunctious—*headlong, rough, and violent.*
Riff-raff—*low and vulgar people.*
Rigmarole—*a long and worthless account.*
Rippet } *a disturbance, disorderly noise.*
Rumpus }
Savagerous—*rude and fierce in manner.*
Shilly-shally—*in a hesitating manner.*
Shote—*a half-grown pig.*
Shackly—*loose, crazy.*
Skedaddle—*retreat in disorder.*
Slewed—*intoxicated.*
Splurge—*a dashing appearance.*
Spondulics—*coin piled for counting.*
Spree—*drunken frolic.*
Topsy-turvy—*upside down.*
Tote—*carry.*
Trampoose—*saunter, ramble.*
Vamose—*vanish, retire.*
Whopper—*a huge specimen.*

EXERCISE.—PROVINCIAL AND SLANG WORDS TO BE CORRECTED.

Having finished my chores, I trampoosed to the river bank.

I am not such a gump as to be bamboozled by a darky.

Boss went on a bender, and came home slewed. He gave me so much of his gab that we had a flare-up; so I picked up my traps and vamosed.

It is no wonder that I have the dumps, for I have not had a bait to eat since yesterday.

He must think that we have very little gumption not to perceive that he is speaking for buncombe.

Then there came along a chunky fellow, who had razors, and combs, and all sorts of contraptions to sell. I could not understand his lingo, and as I wanted very much to buy one of his razors, I was in a great quandary for a while.

Right fornenst me sat a Tennessee drover, a real buster, spitting amber on every side of him, and talking savagerously to all the passengers.

I had no sooner dropped the pone than the pesky fice grabbed it, and vamosed in less than no time.

"Tote out the chist! tote out the chist!" screamed somebody from the inside: and then there was sich a rumpus as you never did see.

OBSOLETE WORDS.

§ 41. This class of barbarisms is composed of those words that were formerly in good use, but have long been *laid aside* by reputable writers. Some of them, however, are still allowed in poetry.

§ 42. As the Sacred Scriptures were translated into English while yet many of these now obsolete terms were in common use, we find such expressions in the sacred text; but that does not justify their use in modern writing, except in quotations from scripture.

LIST OF OBSOLETE WORDS.

Agog—*eager, excited.*
Albeit—*although.*
Bedight—*bedecked.*
Behest—*command.*
Bedizen—*deck, adorn.*
Behoof—*benefit, advantage.*
Belike—*probably.*
Boot—*profit.*
Bewray—*betray.*
Companible—*affable, agreeable.*
Digne—*worthy.*
Dissimuler—*dissembler.*
Eftsoons—*presently, soon afterward.*
Eke—*also.*
Enow—*enough.*
Ensample—*example.*
Erst—*formerly.*
Een or eyen—*eyes.*
Fetise—*neat.*
Fro—*from.*
Gage—*wager, pledge.*
Greaten—*enlarge, grow.*
Heft—*handle or weight.*
Hight—*named.*
Holpen—*helped.*
Irks—*wearies.*
Let—*hinder, prevent.*
Lorn—*forsaken.*
Leasing—*deceit.*
Methinks—*I think.*
Nathless—*nevertheless.*
Pate—*head.*
Plight—*pledge.*
Quoth—*saith or said.*
Selfsame—*very same.*
Se'ennight—*week.*
Sheen—*brightness.*
Sith—*since.*
Sooth—*truth.*
Thereat—*at which.*
Therefor—*on that account.*
Thrall—*slave or slavery.*
Trow—*believe, trust.*
Twain—*two.*
Troth—*truth, faith.*
Vavasour—*landlord.*
Ween—*imagine.*
Wis—*think.*
Wight—*person.*
Wit—*know.*
Whilom—*some time since.*
Ycleped or cleped—*called.*
Ye—*you* (objective).
Yea—*yes.*

EXERCISE.—OBSOLETE WORDS TO BE TRANSLATED INTO THEIR EQUIVALENTS IN PRESENT USE.

All these things have happened as ensamples, and naught should let us from following them.

Anon this holy man wot the leasing of the fiend, and how he would have withdrawn fro to do well.

Thou, haughty lord! thou shalt be bewrayed by thine own thralls.

A train-band captain eke was he.

Erst we all had bread enow; but now, methinks, there 's many a wight doth go to bed supperless.

Belike, quoth he, ye wit not my name, and therefor will not accost me fair.

Richard the Third was a deep dissimuler, outwardly companible where he inwardly hated.

His pate hath not been beholden to a comb for a se'ennight.

The vavasour is fuddled, I ween, when he goes a gallivanting to the tap-room maids.

I 'll gage that this pickaninny gets a larruping if it do not eftsoons get out of the mulligrubs.

Nathless, I plight my troth that your behest shall be fulfilled.

In sooth the sheen of her twain eyen hath gleamed in all my dreams this night.

For all that he jabbers such highfalutin lingo, I take him to be a humbug.

UNAUTHORIZED WORDS.

§ 43. The introducing of a word for the first time is called *coining* a word. The privilege of coining a word is accorded only to him who has discovered or invented something new to which it is to be applied. Of course, it would be deemed presumptuous in any young person to attempt to exercise such a privilege.

§ 44. When it becomes necessary to make a new word, there are certain principles and usages that must be followed, or the resulting word will be rejected as a barbarism. To understand these principles requires a thorough knowledge of certain other languages, and the laws of what is called *Philological Etymology*. But, in a general way, it may be laid down as a maxim that *no word should be compounded of elements drawn from different languages.* Of course this does not forbid the subjection of a word that is once fairly Anglicized* to all the inflections and

* Anglicized means brought into the English tongue.

additions that belong to our language. But it clearly discountenances the use of such words as *happify*, *minify*, *mobocracy*, *negrophilism*, etc.

Even when all the requirements of etymology have been strictly followed, unless the word has found its way into use among reputable writers, the adoption of it by any young person would constitute a great blemish in his style.

From the above remarks, it will be seen that the class of unauthorized words is divisible into two kinds: 1st. Words rejected by good writers, though properly formed; 2d. Words rejected because not rightly formed.

REJECTED WORDS.

Acception—*for acceptation, the current meaning.*
Acclivious—*sloping upward.*
Adorement—*adoration.*
Affectuous—*pathetic.*
Amiableness—*amiability.*
Aspection—*aspect.*
Awakenment—*awakening.*
Candidness—*candor.*
Collaud—*to unite in praising.*
Conject—*to guess.*
Cruciate—*to torture.*
Disremember—*to forget.*
Dispensate—*to grant a dispensation.*
Dissimule—*to dissemble.*
Effectuate—*to accomplish.*
Effray—*to frighten.*
Eventuate—*result.*
Embracement—*for embrace.*
Explorate—*to explore.*
Fashiondom—*the fashionable world.*
Finitude—*limitation.*
Gladship—*gladness.*
Horally—*hourly.*
Hurryment—*hurry.*
Inconsumptible—*indestructible.*
Inexpected—*unexpected.*
Influencive—*influential.*
Latrociny—*robbery.*
Numerosity—*number.*
Particulate—*to mention by name.*
Pecunious—*pecuniary, or having money.*
Philosophism—*sophistry.*
Postable—*portable.*
Pravitude—*depravity*
Productivity—*productiveness.*
Quarrelous—*quarrelsome.*
Quiritation—*a crying for help.*
Reviction—*resuscitation.*
Risky—*hazardous.*
Sedation—*a calming.*
Sophomorical—*turgid or florid.*
Squalidness—*squalor.*
Unctuation—*anointing.*
Undull—*to clarify.*
Unshunnable—*unavoidable.*
Wonderment—*astonishment.*
Wrathy—*wroth.*
Unbeknown—*unknown.*

ILL-FORMED WORDS.

ABSQUATULATE—*to remove one's residence away;* as if *squat* were a Latin root, from which were formed *squatulare* and *absquatulare.*

ANNOYFUL—*annoying;* as if *annoy* were a substantive.

ARGUFY—*argue;* as if *argu-* were a Latin substantive root.

BETTERMENT*—*improvement;* as if *better* were naturally a verb.

BETWEENITY—*indecision;* as if there were such a Latin noun as *betweenitas*, or a French *betweenité.*

BIRTHDOM—*birthright;* as if *birth* were not an abstract noun.

BOTHERATION—*annoyance;* as if the verb were *botherate.*

CIRCUMBENDIBUS—*circuit* or *circuitous;* as if *bend* were a Latin root.

CONNEXITY—*connectedness;* as if there were such a Latin word as *connexitas.*

COME-AT-ABLE—*accessible;* as if *come-at* were a simple verb.

DAREFUL—*daring;* as if *dare* were a substantive.

FUNERALIZE—*perform funeral services for;* as if the person, and not the occasion, were the object of the verb.

GASEITY—*nature of gas;* as if the adjective were *gasey*, and not *gaseous.*

GO-AHEAD-ITIVE—*impulsive, enterprising;* as if *go-ahead* were a simple verb, and could be regarded as a Latin root.

GONENESS—*emptiness;* as if *gone* were naturally an adjective.

HAPPIFY—*beatify;* as if there were such Latin words as *happy* and *happifacere.*

JEOPARDIZE—*endanger;* as if there were not already the verb *jeopard.*

JOLLIFICATION—*noisy festivity;* as if there were such Latin words as *jollifacere* and *jollificatio.*

JUDGMATICAL—*judicious;* as if *judge* were a Greek word.

MELANCHOLIOUS—*melancholy;* as if it were from the Latin.

MINIFY—*reduce in size;* as if there were such a Latin verb as *minifacere.*

MOBOCRACY—*the rule of mobs;* as if *mob* were a Greek word.

NEGROPHILISM—*fanatical regard for the negro;* as if *negro* were a Greek word.

OUGHTNESS—*obligation;* as if *ought* were naturally an adjective.

PLUMPTITUDE—*plumpness;* as if there were such a Latin word as *plumptitudo.*

POCKETUALLY—*pecuniarily;* as if there were such a Latin word as *pocketualis*, or *pocket* were a Latin root.

* "*Betterments*" has been used in legal documents.

PREVENTATIVE—*preventive;* as if there were such an English verb as *preventate.*

RESIDENTER—*resident;* as if the verb were *resident* and not *reside.*

RETIRACY—*retirement;* as if there were such an English adjective as *retirate.*

STRATEGETICAL—*strategic;* as if the noun were *strateges*, and not *strategos.*

TRANSMOGRIFY—*transform;* as if there were such a Latin root as *mogr-.*

UNCONSCIONABLE—*enormous, unjustifiable;* a word built up of etymological blunders.

§ 45. Under the head of Ill-formed Words may properly be included those barbarisms that arise from violation of the rules of Grammatical Etymology. Such are the following:

Oxens	Talismen	Littlest	Bursted
Cupsfull	Cherubims	Worser	Alit
Aid-de-camps	Genuses	Hisself	Overseed
Knight-errants	Apparatuses	Theirselves	Shoed
Mussulmen	Lesser		

EXERCISE.—UNAUTHORIZED WORDS TO BE CORRECTED.

Mr. Ward's buggies have a good deal of goity about them.

The Rev. Mr. Scott will funeralize Mrs. Strong on this day three weeks.

If the house is come-at-able at all, it is only by a circumbendibus.

The neighborhood is much less troubled with latrociny since the Spensers have absquatulated.

I disremember the exact date of his embracement of religion, but it is certain that he has attended none of our jollifications since that event.

With his foolish hurryment, he jeopardized the lives of the whole family.

It was a strategetical movement, but it was not performed in a judgmatical manner.

Moral law always involves the idea of oughtness.

What external circumstances can happify an unforgiven sinner?

A sense of goneness in the visceral region is one of the most annoyful symptoms of the disease.

He is too go-ahead-ative ever to be found in a state of betweenity as to different courses of action.

This venerable residenter has come forth to-day from his retiracy, in answer to a very inexpected call.

Argufy the question how it will affect us pocketually.

FOREIGN WORDS AND PHRASES.

§ 46. It is a violation of purity to use in discourse a word or phrase borrowed from some other language, when the same idea could be expressed by an English term. He who is guilty of such a practice may justly be suspected of the contemptible fault called pedantry. Sometimes this pedantry is displayed by the unnecessary use of Latin and Greek terms, but far more frequently it is French that is dragged in to give an air of elegance and fashion to style. These French words are called *Gallicisms;* a word derived from the ancient name of France. A few of these French phrases are useful additions to our vocabulary, because they express ideas that no English word will express so well: but the following list contains those for which this apology can not be advanced.

LIST OF GALLICISMS.

Affaire du cœur—*a love affair.*
Agremens—*ornaments.*
Alamode—*according to the fashion.*
Amende honorable—*satisfaction, apology.*
Apropos—*to the purpose.*
Au fait—*skillful, adept.*
Au fond—*to the bottom.*
Au naturel—*to the life.*
Bagatelle—*a trifle.*
Beau monde—*the fashionable world.*
Beaux arts—*fine arts.*
Bizarre—*singular, striking.*
Bonmot—*witticism.*
Brusque—*blunt.*
Canaille—*rabble.*
Chateau*—*country-seat.*
Chef d'œuvre—*master-piece.*
Ci-devant—*former or formerly.*
Coup d'essai—*an attempt.*
Coup de grace—*a finishing stroke.*
Coup d'œil—*a glance.*
Dernier ressort—*the last resort.*
Élève—*pupil.*

* Chateau would be proper in speaking of a house in France.

École—*school.*
Empressement—*earnestness (in manner).*
Embonpoint—*corpulence.*
En masse—*in mass*
En passant—*in passing.*
Faux pas—*misconduct, error.*
Fête—*an entertainment.*
Finesse—*cunning.*
Hauteur—*haughtiness.*
Haut ton—*high life.*
Jeu d'esprit—*a display of wit.*
Malapropos—*unseasonable.*
Mauvaise honte—*false shame.*
N'importe—*no matter.*
Nous verrons—*we shall see.*
On-dit—*a common report.*
Outré—*eccentric, odd.*
Penchant—*inclination.*
Petit-maitre—*fop, dandy.*
Politesse—*politeness.*
Qui vive—*on the alert.*
Sang-froid—*with indifference.*
Soi-disant—*self-styled.*
Vis-à-vis—*face to face.*

EXERCISES.—CORRECTION OF GALLICISMS INTO PURE ENGLISH.

All the élevès of that école have a penchant for the beaux arts.

The emperor seems to have embonpoint, but I do not like the hauteur of his manner.

The chateau of the senator was soon surrounded by the canaille, but he went forth, and spoke to them in a very brusque manner.

The entire beau monde have been for a week on the qui vive to hear the denouement of the matter.

The young men gave us quite a jeu d'esprit; but, under the circumstances, it was condemned as malapropos.

Just as he was about to cut off the tough wing with a coup de grace of his knife, the goose slipped from under his fork, out of the plate, and landed in the lap of a lady just opposite. "Madam," said he, with the utmost sang-froid, "I will thank you for that goose."

Her dress is very outré, and there is always something bizarre about her head. Moreover her agremens are too glaring for the rest of her dress.

There I met my ci-devant governess, who, with a great deal of empressement, bade me welcome to the occasion.

MISCELLANEOUS EXERCISES.—CORRECTION OF BARBARISMS OF DIFFERENT KINDS.

I have got myself into a hobble about this brat of yours, and I want you to take the jackanapes away.

In sooth I wis she looks lorn enow, if looks will bring any boot to her.

He that was so remarkable for candidness has at last learned to dissimule.

The dernier ressort of the emperor will be to make the amende honorable, but nous verrons.

He repeated a rigmarole of nonsense in a humdrum manner, and cruciated us for three full hours.

For whose behoof will this petit-maitre accompany the party?

I defy you to conject all the on-dits that we have heard sith our arrival hither.

This affaire du cœur between the young people brought the two families to loggerheads, and eventuated in transmogrifying the whole neighborhood into a quarrelous community.

Every thing goes helter-skelter and topsy-turvy when the boss gets on a spree.

Sooth to say, it irks me to hear such a man hold forth for an hour.

The gaseity of his style totally unfits his sermons for the awakenment of the irreligious.

This painting is merely a coup d'essai, but the scene is drawn au naturel.

CHAPTER VI.

PROPRIETY.

§ 47. The words and phrases of a piece of composition must not only be such as belong to the language, but they must be the *right* words to convey the meaning intended. This property of good style is called Propriety. It may be considered under two subordinate heads; *Lexical Propriety* and *Decorous Propriety*. The former is generally violated through ignorance; the latter, through ill-breeding or bad taste.

I. LEXICAL PROPRIETY.

§ 48. Lexical Propriety is violated when a word is used in a sense which good usage does not give to it.

Strictly speaking, Lexical Propriety would include the proper use of synonyms; but that topic is, by most writers on Rhetoric, referred to the head of Precision, and will be most conveniently treated in that connection.

§ 49. Lexical Propriety may be divided, for the sake of convenience, into three subordinate heads; (1) *the dis-*

crimination of paronyms, (2) *the proper use of prepositions*, and (3) *the proper use of words generally*.

I. THE DISCRIMINATION OF PARONYMS.

§ 50. Words are said to be Paronyms when they are derived from the same root, whether that root belongs to the original English (Anglo-Saxon) stock, or has been introduced into the language from some other tongue.

For instance, the following words are paronyms, being all derived from the Latin root, signifying to *put* or *place: compose*, *depose*, *interpose*, *oppose*, *dispose*, *impose* *expose*, *repose*, *transpose*, *propose*, and *suppose*.

In many cases, the derived words retain a very close connection with the common radical; so that the cognate paronyms have a very perceptible relation in meaning. But in other cases, one or both of the paronyms have changed their signification so much that scarcely any trace of the relation is left, except what exists in the form of the words.

On this and the following pages, lists of paronymous words are given, arranged in cognate pairs. The pupil is required to acquaint himself with their meaning, if he does not already know it; and in reciting, give, in his own language, as nearly as he can, the precise difference between the words of each pair.

PARONYMS TO BE DISCRIMINATED.

College	colleague	Regimen	regiment
Conceit	conception	Scholar	schoolman
Domain	dominion	Scribe	scribbler
Genius	genus	Suit (noun)	suite
Jurist	juror	Specter	spectator
Mechanics	mechanism	Tenet	tenant
Memory	memoir	Tenor	tenure
Populace	population	Testament	testimony
Premier	primate	Specie	species
Partner	partisan	Treatise	treatment
Physic	physics	Rate	ratio
Produce (noun)	product	Pedestal	pedestrian
Idiot	idiom	Memorial	memorandum
Trope	tropic	Remission	remittance

IMPROPRIETIES FOR CORRECTION.

For more full information on this matter, I refer you to my college, who is a ripe schoolman, and thoroughly conversant with the whole subject.

Tasso is full of conceptions, points of epigrams, and witticisms.

Who was it that inherited the dominion of Washington?

What genus presides in such a place as this?

By diligent study of his profession, he came at last to rank among the first jurors of the country.

I can not explain to you the mechanics of a watch, unless you understand the principles of mechanism.

I have read the memory of the late primate, and now understand the foreign policy of the English government during the last ten years.

Have you been studying physics now for a year, and can not tell me why a regiment of salt food will bring on the scurvy?

The product of this valley will barely support the populace.

His unprincipled partisan had taken all the species out of the vault and eloped.

Have you found a tenet for your suit of rooms yet?

The story was called "The Lost Will and Testimony of Poor Puss," but I have no idea of the tenure of it.

At what ratio is this corn growing?

His dim figure, away in the dark, looked like a spectator.

PARONYMS TO BE DISCRIMINATED.

Tangent—*tangible.*
Temporal—*temporary.*
Ostensible—*ostentatious.*
Continual—*continuous.*
Pertinent—*pertinacious.*
Terraqueous—*terrestrial.*
Tolerant—*tolerable.*
Turbid—*turbulent.*
Reverend—*reverential.*
Sectarian (adj.)—*sectional.*
Sensual—*sensuous.*
Sensible—*sentient.*
Consequent (adj.)—*consequential.*
Insoluble—*insolvent.*
Spirituous—*spiritual.*
Responsive—*responsible.*
Distinct—*distinguished.*
Constant—*constituent.*
Instant (adj.)—*instantaneous.*
Sumptuous—*sumptuary.*
Supernal—*supernatural.*
Primary—*primitive.*
Roman—*Romish.*
Sage (adj.)—*sagacious.*

The teacher can invent and dictate exercises containing words in the foregoing list, improperly used, to be corrected by the pupil. Or, he may require the pupil to produce sentences, in which one paronym of each pair is clearly misused for the other.

PARONYMS TO BE DISCRIMINATED.

Salutary—*salubrious.*
Sanguine—*sanguinary.*
Imperious—*imperial.*
Fanciful—*fantastical.*
Luxuriant—*luxurious.*
Miserly—*miserable.*
Momentary—*momentous.*
Notable—*notorious.*
Numeral (adj.)—*numerous.*
Infinite—*indefinite.*
General (adj.)—*generic.*
Ingenious—*ingenuous.*
Graceful—*gracious.*
Human—*humane.*
Literal—*literary.*
Beneficent—*beneficial.*
Capable—*capacious*
Civic—*civil.*
Credible—*credulous.*
Politic—*political.*
Intent (adj.)—*intense.*
Virtual—*virtuous.*
Harmonic—*harmonious.*
Honorary—*honorable*

Exercises as before recommended.

PARONYMS TO BE DISCRIMINATED.

Affect—*effect.*
Commemorate—*remember.*
Confess—*profess.*
Deface—*efface.*
Emigrate—*immigrate.*
Expect—*suspect.*
Formalism—*formality.*
Propose—*purpose* (verb).
Complement—*compliment.*
Inquest—*inquisition.*
Nutriment—*nutrition.*
Organization—*organism.*
Observance—*observation.*
Pleasantry—*pleasantness.*
Process—*procession.*
Rote—*rotation.*
Remission—*remittance.*
Immature—*premature.*
Conscience—*consciousness.*
Barbarism—*barbarity.*
Coherence—*Cohesion.*
Duration—*endurance.*
Intellect—*intelligence.*
Policy—*polity.*

Exercises as before recommended.

II. THE PROPER USE OF PREPOSITIONS.

§ 51. No kind of impropriety is so common as the wrong use of prepositions. As the relations they express are often similar in a general sense, and yet quite distinct when narrowly examined, it is very natural that they should sometimes be misapplied.

Let the pupil learn the following discriminations among prepositions.

§ 52. *About*, referring to place or time, is less precise than *at* or *around.*

Compare "*about* the house" with "*around* the house."
Compare "*about* the gate" with "*at* the gate."
Compare "*about* the sixth hour" with "*at* the sixth hour."

§ 53. *Between* has reference to two objects; *among* to more than two.

Example.—"Between two stars;" "among the stars."

§ 54. *By* directs the mind to the agent or cause; *with* to the accompaniment. *By* and *with* may both refer to the means: *by* to the remoter means; *with* to the more immediate.

Examples.—The cow was killed by a butcher, with the intention to sell the beef.

I write with a gold pen, by candle-light.

§ 55. When the sense of a transitive verb is expressed by an abstract noun, the agent is put under the government of the preposition *by*, and the object generally under the government of *of*.

Example.—James corrected the essay. The correction of the essay by James.

§ 56. *In* and *at* are both used in reference to places. The former is applied to countries and large cities; the latter to single houses, small places, or distant cities.

§ 57. *To*, *into*, *in*, all refer to a boundary. *To* approaches it from without; *into* crosses it; *in* does not pass out beyond it.

Examples.—I am going to Louisville, in Kentucky, and shall put up at the Galt House. But I may remain in Portland a day or two, before I enter into the city itself.

§ 58. As a general rule, derivatives from Latin, Greek, or French compound words, which contain a preposition in their structure in the original language, require a corresponding preposition after them in English.

Thus we say, *expel from*, because the word *expel* is derived from a Latin word, one of the elements of which is the preposition *ex*, *from*.

This rule, however, often fails from the fact that the English word loses wholly or in part the meaning of its original elements.

§ 59. The following list indicates the prepositions that good usage requires after certain words.

Abhorrence OF—whatever is abhorred.

Abound IN or WITH—what is abundant.

Abridge OF—what is taken away.

Absent FROM—a place.

Accommodate TO—what we can not help.

Accommodate WITH—things desired.

Accord WITH—agree with.

Accuse OF—a crime.

Acquaint WITH—objects to be known.

Acquit OF—a charge.

Acquiesce IN—a sentiment or proposal.

Admonish OF—a fault or its consequences.

Admission TO—a person.

Admission INTO—a place.

Advantage OVER—a rival or adversary.

Advantage OF—what benefits us.

Affinity TO or WITH—any thing.

Affection FOR—a person.

Agree WITH—a person.

Agree TO—a proposition.

Agree UPON—a settlement or course.

Agreeable TO—a person.

Alter TO—some other form.

Alteration IN—the thing changed.

Amerce IN or OF—the penalty.

Analogy TO—some other thing.

Analogy BETWEEN—two things.

Antipathy TO (rarely AGAINST)—a thing.

Approve (with or without OF)—a thing.

Array WITH or IN—apparel, etc.

Ascendant OVER—a person.

Ask OF—a person.

Ask FOR—a thing.

Ask AFTER—what we seek to know.

Associate WITH—a person.

Assure OF—a fact.

Averse TO or FROM—the thing disliked.

Believe (transitive)—an assertion or its author.

Believe IN—a principle or a character.

Believe ON—a deliverer.

Bereave OF—what is taken away.

Bestow ON or UPON—the beneficiary.

Betray TO—an adversary or pursuer.

Betray INTO—a course not intended.

Boast OF—what we glory in.

Blush AT—what we are ashamed of.

Border ON or UPON—what is adjoining.

Call ON—a person.

Call AT—a place.

Capacity FOR—what can be done or contained.

Careful OF—the object of care.

Change FOR—a substitute.

Change TO or INTO—something different.

Charge ON—what is attacked.

Charge WITH—a commission.
Compare WITH--in order to judge.
Compare TO—in order to illustrate.
Composed OF—the components.
Concede TO—a person or a request.
Concur WITH—a person.
Concur IN—a measure.
Concur TO—an effect.
Condescend TO—a person or thing.
Confer ON or UPON—a beneficiary.
Confer WITH—a counselor.
Confide IN—a person or principle.
Conformable TO (seldom WITH) a pattern or rule.
Congenial TO—a person.
Congratulate ON or UPON—good experienced.
Consist OF—ingredients.
Consist IN—its equivalent.
Conversant WITH—men.
Conversant IN—things.
Convict OF—a crime charged.
Copy AFTER—a person.
Copy FROM—a thing.
Correspond WITH—what is consistent.
Correspond TO—what is suitable or analogous.
Cured OF—a disease or fault.
Defend (others) FROM.
Defend (ourselves) AGAINST.
Depend ON or UPON—a person or thing.
Deprive OF—what is taken away.
Derogate FROM } that which is lessened in some respect.
Derogatory TO } that which is lessened in some respect.
Devolve ON—a person.
Die OF—a disease.
Die BY—a means or method.
Difficulty OF—an action, as one.
Difficulty IN—a course of action.
Diminution OF—the thing lessened.
Disagree WITH—a person.
Disagree TO—a proposal.
Disagreeable TO—a person or thing.
Disappointed OF—what we fail to get.
Disappointed IN—what we have gotten.
Discourage FROM—any course of action.
Discouragement TO—the person discouraged.
Disgusted AT or WITH—a thing.
Dispose OF—a thing.
Disposed TO—a course of action
Dispossess OF—a thing.
Disqualify FOR—an action.
Divested OF—a thing.
Divide BETWEEN—two.
Divide AMONG—more than two.
Enamored WITH—a person or thing.
Encroach ON or UPON—a space.
Endeavor AFTER—a thing.
Engage IN—a work.
Engage FOR—a time.
Enjoin UPON—a person.
Equal TO or WITH—a person or thing.
Equivalent TO—a thing.
Espouse TO—a person.
Estimate AT—a price.
Exception FROM—a number.
Exception TO—a rule or statement.
Exception AT—what is offensive.
Exclusive OF—what is left out.

Expert AT—(before a noun).
Expert IN—(before a participle).
Fall FROM—an elevation.
Fall INTO—a lower place.
Fall UNDER—disgrace or censure.
Fall TO—what is done eagerly.
Fall UPON—an enemy, etc.
Familiar—a thing is familiar **TO** us.
Familiar—we are familiar **WITH** things.
Fawn ON or UPON—a person.
Followed BY—the follower.
Fond OF—a person or thing.
Foreign FROM or TO—a thing or person.
Found ON—what lies under the foundation.
Found IN—what surrounds the foundation.
Free FROM—what is absent.
Fruitful IN—what is produced.
Full OF—what fills.
Glad OF—something good for ourselves.
Glad AT—the good fortune of another.
Grateful TO—a person.
Grateful FOR—what is bestowed.
Hanker AFTER—a thing.
Hinder FROM—doing.
Incorporate substances **INTO** a whole.
Incorporate one **WITH** another.
Inculcate ON—a person.
Independent OF—a person or thing.
Indulge WITH—a thing not habitual.
Indulge IN—a thing habitual.
Indulgent TO—a person.
Inform OF or ABOUT—a subject.
Initiate INTO—a place.
Initiate IN—an art.
Inoculate WITH—an influence or substance.
Inroad INTO—a region.
nseparable FROM—a person or thing.
Insinuate INTO—a thing.
Insist UPON—a thing.
Instruct IN—a thing.
Inspection (prying) INTO—a thing.
Inspection (superintendence) OVER—a person or thing
Intent ON or UPON—a thing.
Interfere WITH—a person or thing
Introduce INTO—a place.
Introduce TO—a person.
Intrude INTO—a place inclosed.
Intrude UPON—a person or place not inclosed.
Inured TO—a thing.
Invested IN—apparel.
Invested WITH—rights or power.
Level WITH—a line or grade.
Listen TO—a person or sound.
Long FOR or AFTER—a thing.
Look ON—what is present.
Look FOR—what is absent.
Look AFTER—what is distant.
Made OF—the material.
Marry TO—a person.
Martyr TO or FOR—a cause.
Militate AGAINST—a thing or person.
Mistrustful OF—a person or thing.
Need OF—a thing.
Obedient TO—a person or command.
Object TO or AGAINST—a person or thing.

Obtrude ON or UPON—a person or thing.

Occasion OF—an event.

Occasion FOR—a measure.

Offensive TO—a person.

Operate ON or UPON—a person or thing.

Opposite TO—a thing.

Participate IN—a thing.

Partake OF—a thing.

Penetrate INTO—a place or thing.

Persevere IN—a work.

Pour IN—a substance or quality.

Prefer (promote) ABOVE—another.

Prefer (elect) one TO—another.

Preferable TO—another.

Prefix TO—a word.

Prejudice AGAINST—a person or thing.

Preside OVER—an assembly or nation.

Prevent FROM—doing something.

Prevail (persuade) WITH, ON, or UPON—a person.

Prevail (overcome) OVER or AGAINST—an opponent.

Prey ON or UPON—a thing.

Productive OF—the substance produced.

Profit BY—a thing.

Protect. (See Defend.)

Pronounce AGAINST—a person.

Pronounce ON—a thing.

Provide WITH—provisions.

Provide FOR—an emergency.

Proud OF—a person or thing.

Quarrel WITH—a person.

Reckon ON or UPON—a favorable contingency.

Reconcile a person TO another or TO a thing.

Reconcile WITH—what seems inconsistent.

Reduce (subdue) UNDER—power.

Reduce TO—the ultimate condition.

Reflect ON or UPON—a thing.

Regard (esteem) FOR—a person.

Regard TO—the part considered.

Rely UPON or ON—a person or thing.

Replete WITH—what is abundant.

Reproach FOR—a fault.

Resemblance TO—a person or thing.

Resolve ON—a course.

Respect TO (sometimes OF)—a person or thing.

Restore TO—a person or condition.

Rich IN—a substance or quality.

Rob OF—possessions.

Rule OVER—subjects.

Satisfied WITH—what satisfies.

Share IN or OF—a thing.

Sick OF—a disease, or what disgusts.

Significant OF—the meaning.

Similar TO—something.

Sink INTO—what receives.

Sink BENEATH—what overwhelms.

Skillful IN (before a noun).

Skillful AT (before a participle).

Strip OF—what is taken off or away.

Submit TO—a person or thing.

Swerve FROM—a course.

Taste OF—what is actually enjoyed.

Taste FOR—what we can enjoy.
Tax WITH—a charge or a burden.
Tax FOR—a purpose.
Thankful FOR—what has been received.
Unite (transitive) TO } some person or thing.
Unite (intransitive) WITH } some person or thing.
Unison WITH—a thing.
Useful FOR—a purpose.
Value ON or UPON—merits.
Vest IN—the possessor.
Vest WITH—the thing possessed.
Wait ON or UPON—a person or event.
Witness OF—a transaction.
Worthy OF—award.

EXERCISE—IMPROPRIETIES TO BE CORRECTED.

The sultry day was followed with a heavy storm of rain.
The case has no resemblance with the other.
Congress consists in a Senate and House of Representatives.
Of what does happiness consist?
The government is based in republican principles.
The Saxons reduced the Britons to their own power.
Said client believes that said judge is prejudiced to his cause.
Religion and membership may differ widely with each other.
The judge is disqualified from deciding in this case.
He was accused with acting unfairly.
Colonel Washington was very ill with a fever.
You may rely in what I say, and confide on his honesty.
This is a very different dinner to what we had yesterday.
The bird flew up in the tree.
What is my grief in comparison of that which she bears?
I find no difficulty of keeping up with my class.
There is constant hostility between these several tribes.
About two months ago he walked out of a fine morning by a bundle in his hand.
After an interesting conversation for an hour's length, we participated of a light repast.
She is bereft from all her children.
I do not concur in my wife with her puritanical notions.
This remark is founded with truth.
He concurred with recommending the measure to his fellow-citizens.
I find great difficulty of writing now.
Not every change is a change to the better.
Changed for a worse shape, it can not be.
It is important, at times of trial, to have a friend to whom you can confide.

You may rely in the truth of what he says.

Many have profited from good advice who have not been grateful of it.

I have no occasion of his services.

Favors are not always bestowed to the most deserving.

This article is very different to that.

Virtue and vice differ widely with each other.

We rode into a carriage drawn with four horses.

Such conduct can not be reconciled to your profession.

Go, and be reconciled with thy brother.

A man had four sons, and he divided his property between them.

I am now engaged with that work.

This measure will be productive in incalculable evils.

If he will be obedient under his instructions he will not be punished.

I listened at him for more than an hour, but could not understand him.

III. THE PROPER USE OF WORDS GENERALLY.

§ 60. From ignorance or carelessness, it comes to pass that some words are used in ordinary conversation in a signification which is not authorized by good usage. Sometimes these misapplied words find their way into newspapers, or even books: but every young person should be taught carefully to abstain from using any word in a sense that is not authorized by the practice of the best writers of the language.

§ 61. The following is a list of the words most frequently misapplied:

1. Above—for *foregoing;* as if above were an adjective.
2. Allow—for *expect* or *intend;* as, "I allow to go this afternoon.
3. Alone—for *sole*, *single*, or *only;* as if alone could be used before its noun; as, "His alone purpose was to maintain the law."
4. Ambition—for *spirit*, *resentment*, *pluck;* "His ambition was roused, and he was determined to fight."
5. Applicant—for *student;* as if *apply* always meant to apply *one' self.*
6. Awful (or Dreadful)—for *disagreeably* or *excessively;* as if it were an adverb, and as if the feeling of *discomfort* could ever amount to *awe.*

7. BACKWARD—for *bashful;* "My second daughter is quite backward."
8. BAD OFF—for *ill;* "I found the patient very bad off."
9. BAD OFF FOR—for *greatly in want of;* "I am very bad off for fodder."
10. BALANCE—for *remainder* or *rest;* "The balance of the hogs will die." *Balance* is what is wanting to make equal; *remainder*, what is left.
11. BETTER—for *more*, in speaking simply of quantity; "Better than a week."
12. BEING AS—for *inasmuch as* or *seeing that;* "Being as it is you, you may have it for nothing."
13. BE OF A MIND TO—for *have a mind to;* "I am of a mind to go myself."
14. BIT—for *while;* "I 'll come after a bit."
15. BRANCH—for *brook. Branch* is proper in speaking of the tributary of a large stream, but not as synonymous with *brook* or *rivulet.*
16. CALCULATE—for *design* or *intend;* "I calculate to plant a large crop."
17. CALL—for *recall, repeat,* or *pronounce;* "I can not call his name now."
18. CARRY—for *take* or *lead;* "Carry your wagon to the shed." *Carry* properly means to bear in the arms or hands.
19. CHANCE—for *quantity;* "He made a smart chance of wheat."
20. CIRCULATE—for *travel round about,* not strictly in circuit. *Circulate* is not properly applied to the movements of persons.
21. COME OF—for *outgrow;* "He will come of that ailment at last."
22. CONCEIVED—for *expressed;* "This sentiment was conceived in the following words."
23. CONSIDERABLE OF—for *a considerable* or *somewhat of;* "He is considerable of a politician."
24. CONVENIENT—for *near* or *at a convenient distance from;* "The house is convenient to church."
25. CREATURE (pronounced CRITTER)—for *horse* or *steed.*
26. CROWD—for *assembly* or *collection* of persons. An assembly is not a crowd unless it is packed into a small space.
27. DEMEAN—for *debase.* To *demean* is to behave in any way, properly or otherwise; to *debase* is to degrade or vitiate.
28. DESPERATE—for *exceedingly*
29. DIFFICULTED—for *put to inconvenience;* as if *difficult* were a verb.

30. DIGGINGS—for *region* or *neighborhood;* a California word; miners' slang.
31. DOES NOT BEGIN TO BE—for *is not near;* "This cloth does not begin to be as good as that."
32. EFFORT—for literary *work;* as, "He is the author of many dramatic efforts."
33. EMBLEM—for *motto, sentiment,* or *meaning;* generally applied to flowers. "The emblem of this flower is, '*I live for thee.*'" In this case the flower itself is the emblem: "*I live for thee*" is the meaning given to it.
34. ENJOY—for *experience;* "He enjoys very poor health."
35. EXPECT—for *suspect;* We *expect* what is future: we *suspect* what is not manifest.
36. FELLOWSHIP—for *affiliate* or *fraternize;* as if fellowship were a verb.
37. FILL—for *supply,* where there is no allusion to space; "They have filled our academies with incompetent teachers."
38. FIX—for *condition, predicament;* as if it were a noun.
39. FIX—for *repair, set in order;* an Americanism, creeping into good use.
40. FIXINGS—for *fixtures, appendages,* or *dressing.*
41. FOR—for *sort of;* "What for a preacher is he?"
42. FUNERAL—for *funeral sermon.*
43. GROW—for *multiply. Grow* means increase in size; *multiply,* increase in number.
44. HAVE GOT—for *am obliged;* as, "I have got to work."
45. HAVE—for *must* before a passive infinitive; "This work has to be done at night." It would be correct to say, "I have to do this work at night."
46. HATE—for *dislike;* too strong, or misapplying to things a word that properly is applied to persons.
47. HEALTHY—for *healthful* or *wholesome.* Healthy is *having* health; healthful, *causing* health.
48. HEAP—for *deal, much,* or *quantity;* "I think a heap of him."
49. HUMAN—for *person;* as if it were a noun.
50. IDENTIFY—for *connect* or *associate with;* "In this journey, Silas was identified with Paul."
51. IDLE—for *indolent.* Idle means not at work; indolent, not disposed to work.
52. IMPROVEMENTS—for *buildings.* Buildings are properly styled improvements, with reference to the land they stand on; but not in any other sense.

53. IMPRACTICABLE—for *impassable.*
54. IN—for *within*, used adverbially; "Is your father in?"
55. INCIDENT—for *liable;* "The trials to which human life is incident." Properly, the trials are incident to the life.
56. INTERFERE WITH—for *molest* or *disturb.* Not strong enough. We interfere with *matters;* we molest *persons.*
57. ITEM—for *information* or *hint;* "Give me some items of the party."
58. JUST SO—for *provided;* "You may stay all the afternoon, just so that you get home before night."
59. KIND O'—for *rather* or *somewhat;* "His breeches were kind o' brown."
60. LAY, LAID, LAID—for *lie, lay, lain;* "He lays as still as death.'
61. LEAVE—for *depart;* as if it were intransitive; "I will leave to-morrow."
62. LESS—for *fewer. Less* refers to size; *fewer* to number.
63. LET ON—for *admit* or give sign of perception; "She kept hinting that it was time to retire, but I did not let on." (A provincialism that has some claim to adoption on account of its conciseness.)
64. LICK—for *blow, stroke,* or *exertion;* "It is the licks laid on it, that makes it so costly."
65. LIFT—for *take up;* as, "We will lift a collection for the poor."
66. LIKE—for *disposed to;* or *as if, as it were;* "I don't feel like singing." "I feel like I'm on my journey home."
67. LOSS—for *lose.* The noun for the verb.
68. LOTS—for *great quantities;* "There are lots of chestnuts on this tree."
69. LOVE—for *like.* Too strong; applying to things a word that properly belongs to persons.
70. MAD—for *angry, vexed, provoked.*
71. MAKE OUT—for *succeed;* "How did you make out planting cotton?"
72. MAKE OUT LIKE—for *pretend;* "Simon made out like he was a deserter."
73. MIDDLING—for *moderately* or *tolerably.*
74. MIND—for *remember;* "I don't mind to have seen the word before."
75. MISERY—for *pain* in the body; "Doctor, I have a great misery in my back."
76. MIXED UP—for *promiscuous, confused.*
77. MONSTROUS—for *very* or *enormously.*

78. MOVE—for *remove;* "When are your folks going to move?"
79. NAME—for *mention;* "I never named the circumstance to any one."
80. NEVER—for *not;* applied to a limited time; "I never spoke a word the whole evening."
81. NO-ACCOUNT—for *worthless;* as if it were a compound word; "This is a no-account gun." "This gun is *of no account*," would be proper.
82. OBLIGED—for *must.* Obliged implies compulsion, *moral* or physical. If the necessity is only *logical*, obliged is not proper; as, "This bill is obliged to be correct."
83. OF (corruption in pronunciation)—for *have*, in conjugate verbs; "He would of done it, if I had of let him alone.
84. OPAQUE—for *obscure* (used figuratively). An object is obscure that we can not see distinctly; but an opaque object may be very plainly seen.
85. PAIR (of stairs)—for *flight.*
86. PEOPLE—for *we*, or *one*, or any indefinite subject; "People plant corn in March." "People go to church on Sunday."
87. PITCH IN—for *fall to, commence upon.*
88. PLUNDER—for *baggage.*
89. POORLY—for *weakly* or *sick.*
90. POWER—for *deal* or *great quantity;* "This field will bring a power of corn."
91. POWERFUL—for *very* or *exceedingly.*
92. PREDICATE—for *found* or *base;* "This argument is predicated on the plainest dictates of reason." "These notes are predicated on good security."
93. PROUD—for *glad* or *gratified.*
94. RAISE—for *rear* or *bring up*, in speaking of children. We *raise* corn and hogs.
95. RECKON—for *suppose* or *conjecture*, where no calculation is implied.
96. RISE OF—for *more than;* "The rise of a hundred bushels."
97. ROCK—for *pebble* or *stone. Rock* is more properly applied to a large mass.
98. RUN—for *leak*, speaking of vessels.
99. SCARED—for *afraid. Scared* seems to imply something *done* by the terrifying object.
100. SENSATION (noun)—for *emotion.* The former is felt *in* the body, and is caused by some material object; the latter is wholly in the mind, and is caused by some conception or belief of the mind.

101. SENSATION (adjective)—for *exciting; intended for effect;* as, "sensation sermons." It is never an adjective.
102. SIGN—for *vestige* or *track*, in hunters' slang.
103. SIGHT—for *great quantity.*
104. SHUT OF—for *rid of.*
105. SMART—for *considerable;* "A right smart chance, as they say in Maryland."
106. SOMETHING—for *somewhat* (adverbial); "This land is something better than mine."
107. SOON—for *early.*
108. SPELL—for *while* or *time;* "First, we plowed a spell, and then we knocked off and went a fishing."
109. SPLENDID—for *very fine;* applied without any discrimination; as, "A splendid pair of boots," etc.
110. SPOIL OUT—for *rub out* or *erase.*
111—STEREOTYPE—for *type* or *fac-simile.* The peculiarity of stereotype is its unchangeableness.
112. STUMP—for *hustings* or *electioneering.* An Americanism coming into use, supplanting, on this continent, the English word *hustings.*
113. STUMPED—for *confounded, non-plused.*
114. SUCCESS—used instead of the adjective *successful;* as, "The fair was a great success."
115. SURE-ENOUGH—for *real, veritable;* as, "This table is sure-enough mahogany;" "Is this a sure-enough diamond?"
116. SUSPICION—for *suspect;* the noun for the verb.
117. TAKE ON—for *make an ado*, or behave in some unusual manner; "I would not take on so just about a dog."
118. TIGHT—for *close* at a bargain.
119. TYPIFY—for *represent* otherwise than as a type.
120. TRAVEL—for *penitential experience.*
121. USED UP—for *exhausted.*
122. VERBIAGE—for *phraseology.*
123. WITHOUT—for *unless.*

EXERCISE.—IMPROPRIETIES TO BE CORRECTED.

I allow to circulate all through the country, and find out where they are worst off for Bibles.

The house is convenient to a splendid spring

The whole crowd were now invited into the dining-room, where they soon pitched into the good things provided. Some of them must have been dreadful hungry, to judge from the speed in which the eatables disappeared.

A monstrous polite fellow asked me to except a flower with its emblem.

I never ate any cake, the whole evening: I do n't think it is healthy.

Some one asked Miss G—— to sing, but she said she did n't feel like it, as she had been sort o' sick for a day or two.

My companion told me that was a stereotype of all the parties in these diggings.

Set up straight, and do not lay on your next companion.

I calculate to ditch this branch next spring.

He is considerable of a lawyer, but what for a judge he 'll make, I can not say.

My creature is desperate sick, and if he dies, I shall be difficulted to get home.

I have enjoyed very bad health ever since I moved from Carolina: I expect the bad water in these diggings is the cause of it.

I looked through all the improvements, but did not find a single human about the place.

I never hated to strike a lick at any job so bad in my life.

He made out like he knew all about the affair; and as I did not wish to make him mad, I never let on but that I believed him.

The verbiage of the letter is very good, but its tone is offensive.

You need not take on so about the writing on your slate. I can soon spoil it out again.

People demean themselves when they give way to such feelings.

Without I see that his ambition is roused, I intend to talk to him very plainly.

II. DECOROUS PROPRIETY.

§ 62. Decorous propriety requires that all the words and phrases of a piece of composition should be decent, and sufficiently dignified to be put upon paper. In this respect, there is some difference between what is proper for books, periodicals, and dignified correspondence, and what is allowable in conversation, popular oratory, and familiar epistles. Many an expression that would contribute to the vivacity of the latter would greatly disfigure the former. Those violations of decorous propriety that are sometimes allowable in conversation, oratory, and letters are called *colloquialisms.*

As to the extent to which a writer may indulge in colloquialisms in the lighter forms of literature, no definite rule can be given. All that can be done is to lay down the requirements of propriety with regard to all forms of serious and dignified composition; leaving it to the good sense of each individual to prescribe how far he may, in familiar discourse, deviate from those requirements.

§ 63. All violations of decorous propriety are called *vulgarisms*, and they are separable into three classes; viz.:

1. *Familiar abbreviations;*
2. *By-words;*
3. *Low expressions.*

§ 64. *Familiar abbreviations* should not appear in written discourse, except in dialogue, where the object is to give an exact representation of life and manners.

Such abbreviations are the following:

I 'm—for I am.
'T is—for it is.
'T is n't—for it is not.
I 'll—for I will.
Won't—for will not.
Do n't—for do not.
Gi' me—for give me.
Le 's—for let us.
'd—for would.

§ 65. But, on the other hand, many abbreviations, proper in writing, must, in oral reading, be expanded to the full expression. For example: A. D. must be read "Anno Domini," or "in the year of our Lord;" *inst.* must be read instant; *ult.*, ultimo; *Co.*, company, etc.

§ 66. But let the pupil observe that when any one of the cardinal or ordinal numbers is to be introduced into the body of a sentence, it must be written in full, and not by the Arabic figures, unless the number exceeds one hundred. Thus we write, "Nouns have three (not 3) cases;" "There are twenty-four (not 24) hours in a day;"

"It is half-past ten o'clock," etc. $10\frac{1}{2}$ *o'clock* is allowable only in notices, advertisements, etc.

§ 67. *By-words* are those expressions that are frequently uttered from the mere force of habit. They seldom appear on paper, but the rules of Expression condemn them even in ordinary conversation.

§ 68. *Low expressions* are words or phrases which, on account of some quaintness or spice of wit contained in them, become current among those who affect vivacity or smartness in their style. They have all a certain grossness about them that betrays their low origin. Good taste strongly condemns their introduction into all serious, dignified, or elegant discourse.

§ 69. The style of many newspapers, both in their editorials and correspondence, is exceedingly reprehensible in this particular. Many of the scribblers who put themselves in print seem to have learned their language in the bar-room, at the race-ground and cock-pit, from circus clowns and negro minstrels. Let all people of good taste and pure morals set their faces against such degradation of the language.

§ 70. The following list is humiliating to every person of good taste that loves the English language.

Brass—for self-confidence.
Brick—for rake.
Chawed—for mortified.
Chisel—for cheat.
Fast—for reckless.
Gent—for gentleman.
Green—for unsophisticated.
Jew—for beat down.
Kick—for jilt.
Loaf—for lounge.
Spec—for speculation.
Specs—for spectacles.
Sheepskin—for diploma.
Slope—for elope.
Spot (verb)—for mark or remember.
Streaked—for embarrassed or agitated.
Tight—for tipsy.
The ready, The rhino, The dust, The tin, The dimes—for money.
Whaler—for huge one.
Wallop—for whip.

Acknowledge the corn—all to pieces—anyhow you can fix it—bark up the wrong tree—like blazes—blow out at—brick in the hat—can't come it over—cave in—choke off—not a circumstance to—the clean thing—get one's dander up—deadhead—to be death on—to go one's death for—dyed in the wool—in for it—set by the ears—see with half an eye—cock-and-bull story—a mare's nest—wild-goose chase—throw into one's teeth—have a finger in the pie—go the whole hog—stir one's stumps—thrust one's nose into—fingers itching—like peas on a cowhide—beat him all hollow—one-horse concern—keep shady—keep a stiff upper lip—done up brown—bred in the bone—a nobody—runs in the blood—let her slide—stiff as a poker—as sure as you are born—full tilt—knock under—sing small—take a peg lower, or a button-hole lower—take the starch out—play second fiddle to one—have a screw loose—get the hang of—know the ropes—on one's own hook—in a horn—cut out (for be gone)—draw in one's horns—cast sheep's eyes—lean as a May shad—Hobson's choice—give it the go-by—old as the hills—be on pins and needles—turn one's stomach—fork over—cock of the roost—in clover—go to the dogs—poor as a church mouse—poor as Job's turkey—ride a high horse—dog cheap—cracked up—wet one's whistle—pop the question—let the cat out of the bag—catch a Tartar—cut up shines—the main chance—the gift of the gab—under one's thumb—mum 's the word—ugly as sin—set up a hulla-balloo—smell a rat—plain as the nose on your face—rain cats and dogs—make no bones of—give one a puff—blow one's own trumpet—spread like wild-fire—worm one's self into—keep one's eye skinned—face the music—give one fits, or particular fits—not by a jugful—go it blind—go it with a looseness—he 's a goner—good as wheat—sound on the goose—get the hang of—dry up.

If the teacher desire to do so, he can give exercises in the correction of such slang, but it is probable that quite enough will occur in the utterances of the pupils themselves to practice them in its correction.

EXERCISE.—MISCELLANEOUS BARBARISMS AND IMPROPRIETIES TO BE CORRECTED.

I got in such a botheration that I made the box all crank-sided, and shackly at that.

Nathless, for her behoof these self-same hands shall labor so long as life's ruby current courses in their veins.

If your theme be affectuous, do not attempt to dissimule your own interest on it; but never adopt the style sophomorical in order to rouse your auditors.

We traveled all day vis-à-vis, and I saw not the least faux pas in all her deportment.

As soon as I alit from my critter, I seed that I was not welcome.

Her natural powers of intelligence are of no ordinary gradation.

Do not be too fastidious to condescend with honest people in humble rank.

My horse has too much ambition for me to use a spur, and I have learned him to go the faster the more I pull upon the bit.

He 's a regular whig, dyed in the wool, and he' ll go his death on the nominees of his party.

He is encroaching into my lot, and I will have to go to law before I prevail over him to do the fair thing. I 'm of a great mind to sue him to-morrow.

Suppose you leave your plunder here, but carry your buggy to the other side of the branch.

I had no conscience of being in pain while the tooth was drawing.

The verbiage of the letter is correct, but its tone is offensive.

Samuel made out like he was an A No. 1 performer.

I set on pins and needles the whole evening, and was scared of the whole company.

The gal is smart, but she has too much brass to be lovable.

If you yield to the dictates of passion, you will demean yourself even in your own esteem.

An affected fop is not only a risible, but a contemptuous character.

These words do not convey even an opaque idea of the author's meaning.

I disremember the cause of his hurryment, but it had some strategetical end in view.

In two contagious sentences, he has repeated the same observance.

In sleep we lose all conscience of surrounding objects.

The gals went up stairs to primp, and I trampoosed to the stable-lot.

Erst we all had bread enow, but sith the war be waging, many a wight doth go to bed lacking his supper.

I am afraid I will be much difficulted about the matter, but if you stir your stumps I will succeed.

He 's done made a big speech, and if he do n't go it with a rush you can take my hat.

He was always fast, and often got tight; but I did not think he would chisel a green one out of his bottom dollar.

CHAPTER VII.

SYNONYMS.

Before proceeding to discuss the third essential property of good diction, which is simplicity, it is proper to learn the nature and use of synonyms.

§ 71. Words that are exactly or nearly alike in meaning, so that in some cases one can be used for the other without impropriety, are called *synonyms* or *synonymous* words. Instances of these are remarkably abundant in our language, owing to the fact that it has derived its words from so many different tongues. This quality of the language is called its *richness*, and it has justly been made a subject of admiration and pride. It is highly important that every student be initiated into the capacities of his vernacular to express every shade of thought.

In Appendix No. II will be found an alphabetical arrangement of the most common synonyms grouped together. That appendix can be advantageously used as follows: Let the teacher select some piece of composition, say one of the selections in the reading book used by the class, and require each pupil to write it off, with as many of the words changed into their synonyms as he may be able to change, without destroying or perverting the meaning of the original. Let this exercise be repeated on different selections in every variety of style, until a considerable degree of facility in it is acquired by the pupils. The teacher will find it to be an exceedingly improving exercise. The following is given as a sample.

EXTRACT.

He who is best educated for the world to come, is best educated for the world that now is. I would not displace any book necessary; I would not substitute the Bible for every thing else, but I would have it the groundwork and companion of the whole course. We talk of the expansive power of other studies, of their discipline, scope, and elevation; and true it is that the mind grows dwarfish or gigantic according to the subjects with which it is familiar. If, then, you would set to your seal, and give the world assurance of a man, set him to span the disclosures of revelation, to scale the altitudes of eternal truth, to explore the depths of infinite wisdom, and soar amid the glories of immortality, unveiled and spiritual; and then he shall descend, like Moses from the mount, radiant with the light of high communion. BP. PIERCE.

THE SAME, WITH SYNONYMS SUBSTITUTED.

That man who is best instructed for the future life, is best trained for the present state of existence. I do not wish to discard any book requisite. I would not put the Holy Scriptures in the place of every thing else, but I would have it the foundation and ally of the entire curriculum. We speak of the developing influence of other mental pursuits, of their training power, their drift, and their exaltation; and true it is that the intellect becomes puny or stalwart according to the themes with which it is conversant. If, then, you would add your attestation, and give mankind your voucher for a *man*, direct him to grasp the developments of revelation, to climb the heights of absolute truth, to search the profundities of boundless wisdom, and fly aloft amid the splendors of everlasting life, without concealment, and refined from grossness; and then he shall come down, like Moses from Sinai, beaming with the radiance of exalted intercourse.

CHAPTER VIII.

SIMPLICITY OF DICTION.

§ 72. It must not be supposed that, because propriety requires the exclusion of all undignified expressions, the diction should be pompous, stilted, and difficult to be understood by people of ordinary intelligence. On the contrary, simplicity is one of the first requisites of good style. The more readily a discourse is understood, the better its style; provided, of course, that all vulgarisms are excluded. Hence the following directions are to be observed by those aiming to form a good style.

§ 73. I. Avoid abstract or general terms, derivatives from the Latin or Greek, and all such words as require ordinary persons to consult a dictionary, provided simpler and easier words can be found to express the meaning.

The terms that represent common and familiar objects are more simple than those that refer to what is rare or remote. The terms that indicate what we know by our senses are simple, and generally have come down to us from the homely, but pleasant old Saxon. So are the expressions of our familiar emotions and energies. *Sun*, *star*, *sky*, *earth*, *hill*, *river*, *field*, *tree*, *house*, *bread*, *water*, *fire*, *love*, *hate*, *fear*, *hope*, *will*, *want*, *work*, *walk*, etc.—such as these are all plain and simple, and can be used to make a style both strong and sweet. Such words as these the poets all prefer, and so does every one who wants to find his way direct to the mind and heart of men.

On the other hand, the more general a term is, the more difficult it is to apprehend. *Hill*, *hillock*, *mountain*, *ridge*, *peak*, etc., are all simpler than the term *elevation*, which is applied to the whole class. And when the abstraction is carried still further, and the word is made to represent a quality only, the departure from simplicity is yet more obvious; as in *length*, *extension*, *weight*, *fluidity*, *attraction*, *intelligence*, *instinct*, *temperance*, etc.

The opposite of *abstract* is *concrete*. An *abstract* term expresses quality alone; a *concrete* term is one that is applied to objects that contain the quality. Now, it is often possible to express a general truth in terms that are really concrete. Thus,

"Atheism is folly," is abstract.

"He is a fool who denies that there is a God," is in terms concrete.

"Learning is generally confessed to be desirable." (Abstract.)

"Most persons grant that it is well to be learned." (Concrete.)

"The *understanding* of this *truth* will preclude that great source of human *misery*, groundless *expectations*." If the italicized abstract nouns in this sentence be converted into verbs and adjectives, which are concrete, the sentence becomes much simpler. "If we clearly *understand* that this is *true*, we shall be saved from what often makes us *miserable;* namely, *expecting* what there is no ground to hope for."

The style of Johnson was often faulty for want of simplicity. He was affected by the taste, prevalent in his day, for the use of Latin derivatives, in connections where Saxon words would have been equally expressive. Speaking on one occasion of a certain drama called "The

Rehearsal," he said, "It has not wit enough to keep it sweet." Then after a pause, he repeated the assertion in his assumed, but less natural style: "It has not sufficient virtue to preserve it from putrefaction."

A recent critic has exposed the stilted diction of some newspaper reporters in the following manner:

Was hanged—Was launched into eternity.

When the halter was put round his neck—When the fatal noose was adjusted about the neck of the unfortunate victim of his own unbridled passions.

A great crowd came to see—A vast concourse was assembled to witness.

Great fire—Disastrous conflagration.

The fire spread—The conflagration extended its devastating career.

House burned—Edifice consumed.

The fire was got under—The progress of the devouring element was arrested.

Man fell—Individual was precipitated.

A horse and wagon ran against—A valuable horse, attached to a vehicle, driven by J. S., in the employment of J. B., collided with.

The frightened horse—The infuriated animal.

Sent for the doctor—Called into requisition the services of the family physician.

The mayor of the city, in a short speech, welcomed—The chief magistrate of the metropolis, in well chosen and eloquent language, frequently interrupted by the plaudits of the surging multitude, officially tendered the hospitalities.

I shall say a few words—I shall, with your permission, beg leave to offer some brief observations.

A bystander advised—One of those omnipresent characters who, as if in pursuance of some previous arrangement, are certain to be encountered in the vicinity when an accident occurs, ventured the suggestion.

He died—He deceased; he passed out of existence; his spirit quitted its earthly habitation, winged its way to eternity, shook off its burden, etc.

§ 74. II. Avoid scientific and technical terms, those that belong to profound erudition, or that contain allusions to facts or personages not known to your readers.

The folly of violating this rule is manifest in the following examples:

"God begins his cure by caustics, by incisions, and instruments of vexation, to try if the disease that will not yield to the allectives of cordials and perfumes, frictions and baths, may be forced out by deleterics, scarifications, and more salutary, but less pleasing physic."

"To-day peering into the Golden Gardens of the Sun at Cuzco; to-morrow clambering over Thibet glaciers, to find the mystic lake of Yamuna; now delighted to recognize in Teoyamiqui (the wife of the Aztec God of War) the unmistakable features of Scandinavian Valkyrias; and now surprised to discover the Greek Fates sitting under the Norse tree Ygdrasil, deciding the destinies of mortals, and calling themselves Nornas; she spent her days in pilgrimages to moldering shrines, and midnight often found her groping in the classic dust of extinct systems."

"When so posited and become objects of meditation, they are subjective, and when its own orgasmic in its animalistic impulsions and psychical psytations, and its own self-conscious action, on or through these, are subjected to ratiocinative processes—the contemplation or analysis of these direct acts, passions, or affections is the reflex action of the self, which can only occur upon the reproduction of sensation, impulsion, or psytation, as an imaginate, and this through the intervention and use of concepts, opinions, notions, intuitates, and ideates, at every step involving the correlations—the action and reaction of the forces woven into nature and life."

§ 75. III. Avoid pompous circumlocutions, in which individuals or places are designated by some attribute or circumstance, which may not be generally accorded to them.

This rule is violated by Shaftsbury, when in writing of Aristotle he calls him "the master critic," "the mighty genius and judge of art," "the prince of critics," "the grand master of arts," etc. Also when he alludes to Homer as "the grand poetic sire;" to Socrates as "the philosophical patriarch," etc.

A ridiculous departure from simplicity was perpetrated by him who thus paraphrased the beautiful Twenty-third Psalm:

"Deity is my pastor. I shall not be indigent. He maketh me to recumb on the verdant lawns; he leadeth me beside the unrippled liquidities; he re-installeth my spirits, and conducteth me in the avenues of rectitude, for the celebrity of his appellations. Unquestionably, though I perambulate the glen of the umbrages of the sepulchral dormitories, I will not be perturbed by appalling catastrophes; for thou art present, thy wand and thy crook insinuate delectation.

"Thou spreadest a refection before me, in the midst of inimical scrutations; thou perfumest my locks with odoriferous unguents, my chalice exuberates.

"Indubitably, benignity and commiseration shall continue all the diuternity of my vitality; and I will eternalize my habitance in the metropolis of nature."

EXERCISE.

Let the pupil be required to translate the following passage into simple and natural diction.

"Every child must have observed how much more felicitous and beloved some juvenile individuals are than others. There are some youthful personages whom it always delights you to accompany. They are in a state of complacent beatitude themselves, and they assimilate you to them. There are others whose companionship you eschew. The very aspect of their facial features superinduces disagreeable emotions. Apparently they are destitute of amicable acquaintances. It is impossible that any individual should be in a state of mental satisfaction without friendly associates. The emotional part of our nature was constituted for affection, and is unable to maintain a pleasurable existence without opportunities of bestowing and receiving sympathetic fondness. But it is impossible for you to become the recipient of affectionate regard unless you will also bestow it. You will not be able to prevail upon others to entertain feelings of affection for you unless you will also reciprocate the feeling. Love is to be obtained in no other manner than by bestowing the same tribute of the heart upon others. Hence it is a matter of moment to cherish an amiable and benevolent temper of mind."

The teacher may continue these exercises at option, by selecting some pieces written in a very easy and simple style, and first privately translating them into such labored and stilted diction as the foregoing, and, having dictated this to the pupils, requiring them, without access to the original, to re-translate it, as well as they can, into simple style. Of course it would be impossible for them to hit upon the identical words of the original, but that is not necessary for the purpose. For specimens of simple diction the teacher is referred to the writings of Locke, Addison, Goldsmith, Cowper, Irving, and Abbott.

CHAPTER IX.

PRECISION.

§ 76. This property of correct diction consists in the use of such words as exactly convey the intended meaning, and nothing more. It is violated in two ways:

1. By the use of unnecessary words and phrases;
2. By the want of accuracy in the use of synonyms.

I. REDUNDANCY AND TAUTOLOGY.

§ 77. Words that are unnecessary in a sentence are said to be superfluous or *redundant.*

§ 78. Sometimes the writer intentionally uses expressions that are, strictly speaking, redundant, for the purpose of enforcing or emphasizing an idea. It is then called a *pleonasm* or *pleonastic* exp ression.

§ 79. Young writers are very apt to use such redundant expressions as the following:

Advance forward.
Return again.
Return back.
Predict beforehand.
Transcript copy.
False traitor.
Standard pattern.
Sylvan forest.
This here.
From hence.
A sight to behold.
Widow woman.
Try an experiment.
Formed out of.
Substitute in the place of.
Equally the same.
Filled full.
Fixed fact.
Both met together.
Retreat backward.
Repeat again.
First aggressor.
Latter end.
Old Veteran.
Verdant-green.
Umbrageous shade.
Another one.
That there.
From whence.
Fainted away.
Twice over.
Shrink smaller.
Since the time when.
Free gratis.
Mention over again.
These six months past.
No other person besides.
Last final.

Leisure on one's hands.
Universal—of all men.
Marry a wife.
New beginner.
Have got.
Deliciously happy.
More preferable.
Joyous bliss.
Gleeful merriment.
Throughout the whole of.
Universal panacea.
Must necessarily.
Most principal.
Both—same.

§ 80. *Tautology* is the repetition of the same word, or of the same idea, in different words. Unless used as a pleonasm, for the sake of clearness or strength,† it is a serious fault, and should be rigidly rejected from a composition. The following are examples:

Acknowledge and confess.
Bounds and limits.
Clear and obvious.*
Plain and evident.*
Advise and counsel.
Confused and disordered.
Effects and consequences.
Fears and apprehensions.
Assemble and meet together.
Dissemble and cloak.*
Friendly and amicable.
Governed and conducted.*
Intents and purposes.*
Mild and meek.*
Obliged and indebted.*
Obviate and prevent.
Pleasure and satisfaction.
Safe and secure.
Special and particular.
Support and stay.*
Wavering and unsettled.
Worship and adore.
Support and bear up.
Positive and peremptory.
Certain and confident.
Mutual to each other.
Just and upright.
Vice, sin, and immorality.
Agony and suffering.
Solemn and pathetic.*
Ruin and destruction.
Anguish and grief.
Temperance and abstinence.
Acquiesce in and be satisfied with.
Question minutely and examine at length.*

EXERCISES.—TAUTOLOGY AND REDUNDANCY TO BE CORRECTED.

Hence, consequently, he must necessarily, therefore, be in error.

At the sonorous sound of the last final trump, all the inanimate dead shall rise up into life again.

The subject-matter of his discourse was excellent, but his style and manner of expressing himself were confused, disordered, and obscure.

† See § 347.

* These are not always tautological.

I will freely give you my advice and counsel gratis, and charge nothing.

It is clear and obvious that he has no use for any of the laws and rules of versification.

He appears to enjoy the universal esteem of all men.

Alfred the Great, of England, was one of the most remarkable and distinguished men that we read of in the historical records of past ages.

The man of probity and honesty will be trusted, and esteemed, and respected, and relied upon.

The mind and temper of him who is always continually in the bustle and turmoil of the world, will often be ruffled and frequently disturbed.

This great politician always and in every case desisted from his designs and renounced them, when he found them to be impracticable or incapable of performance.

Thought and language act and react upon each other mutually.

I am certain and confident that the account I have given is correct and true, and in accordance with the facts.

The effects and consequences of such corruption and degeneracy are lamentable and deplorable.

Another old veteran of the cross has fallen and departed this life.

Our intercourse and association were all friendly and amicable until he married and became the husband of a wife.

She writes very well for a new beginner; I think she must take especial and particular pains to improve.

II. THE DISCRIMINATION OF SYNONYMS.

§ 81. As before noticed, words are said to be synonymous even when they are not exactly, but only *nearly* alike in meaning. A number of words that in some connections may be interchanged for each other is called a *group* of synonyms. Each member of such a group has, in most instances, some peculiarity of signification, derived from its root, that makes it appropriate in some connections and not in others.

For instance, the two words, *defend* and *protect*, have a very similar signification. But when we come to look at their etymology we find some difference between them. To *defend* is *to ward off;* to *protect* is *to put a cover over*. The one is seen to imply an exertion of power; the other a simple position or situation. A house does not defend, but protects us from the inclemency of the weather; but a soldier defends his country when attacked. Hence it is clear that although in many instances one of these words would answer as well as the other, yet in some cases one of them would be correct, and not the other.

§ 82. No other feature of style so fully exhibits accuracy of scholarship and skill in the use of language as the proper selection, among a group of synonyms, of the word that exactly conveys the idea. Hence the space devoted to the following exercises, in which the pupil is required, first, to recite the distinctions between the grouped synonyms, then, to embody them properly in sentences of his own composition, and lastly, to correct the sentences that contain them improperly used, stating the reasons for his corrections.

§ 83. SYNONYMS DISCRIMINATED.*

ARTISAN—a person who practices one of the useful or mechanical arts.
ARTIST—a person who pursues one of the fine or ornamental arts.

EXPECT—to look forward to, to regard as probable.
HOPE—to look forward to *with desire*.

FERTILE—having the power of producing in abundance (applied to soil.)
FRUITFUL—actually producing in abundance (applied to plants and animals as well as soil.)

PEACEABLE—inclined to peace (a moral quality.)
PEACEFUL—generally in a state of peace.

ROBBER—one who takes unlawfully by violence or compulsion.
THIEF—one who takes unlawfully in secret.

SOCIAL—relating to society; when applied to persons, the word has reference to their nature, habits, etc.
SOCIABLE—disposed to cultivate intercourse; it is rarely applied to things, but then means *promotive of intercourse*.

* If the class consists of very young pupils, it would be better to postpone the remaining exercises of this chapter until they shall have gone through Book Third.

SERVANT—one who serves, whether voluntarily or involuntarily.
SLAVE—one compelled to serve, or liable to be so compelled.

TRUTH—the conformity of statements or opinions to the actual state of things.
VERACITY (a personal quality)—the predominant intention to tell the truth.

TEACH—to impart instruction.
LEARN—to receive instruction.

EXERCISE.

Travelers in the mountains of Italy are frequently stopped by thieves and stripped of all their property.

I am afraid I shall not succeed, but I ardently expect to do so.

As his truth has never been called in question, we have no reason to doubt the veracity of his assertion.

Hast thou not learned me how to distinguish a fertile from a barren tree?

The fertility of our orchard is owing partly to the natural fruitfulness of the soil, and partly to the favorable seasons.

The young king, thus finding himself in peaceable possession of the throne, directed his attention to the arts which embellish and refine human nature.

Man appears to have been made a sociable being in order that he might attain the highest glory within reach of a creature.

Haydn, Mozart, and Beethoven were the greatest musical artisans that the world ever produced.

The British government has exerted itself strenuously to put down this inhuman traffic in servants.

The peaceable valley was inhabited, not by bands of thieves, but by busy artists.

§ 84. SYNONYMS TO BE DISCRIMINATED.

AUTHENTIC—worthy of belief (applied to history, memoirs, intelligence, etc.)
GENUINE—what it professes to be; not spurious.

CAUSES—exist in the nature of things.
REASONS—exist in the mind. A cause produces one event which we call an *effect;* a reason induces us to form an opinion or to perform an action.

Cultivation—the act of cultivating (applied to what is produced).
Culture—The state of being cultivated (applied to that which produces). Culture, with regard to persons, expresses the effect of cultivation.

Custom—the repetition of an act; it is more frequently applied to communities.
Habit—the effect of repetition on the character; it is more frequently applied to individuals.

Deity—the person of God, or of a god.
Divinity—the nature or attributes of God, or of a god.

Example—a thing or person; generally cited to instruct or to incite.
Instance—a fact or case; generally cited to illustrate or to prove.

Belief—refers primarily to propositions, and is produced by evidence.
Faith—refers primarily to persons and character; secondarily to testimony as based on the faith in character.

Healthy—enjoying health; abounding in health; consistent with health.
Wholesome—tending to preserve or to restore health.

Strength—The latent quality of agents, which may be exerted actively or passively.
Force—strength exerted; it is always active, and known from its results.

EXERCISE.

Those excellent seeds, implanted at an early age, will, by culture, be most flourishing in production.

The doctrine of the deity of Christ is said to be most distinctly learned in the Gospel according to John.

He conducts himself in every respect so properly that he is an instance to all the other servants on the plantation.

I have no belief in the truth of his character, and hence I can not accept his testimony in a case where his own interests are involved.

The pier had not sufficient force to resist the strength of the waves, and by morning the whole structure was a miserable wreck.

He never thought proper to explain the cause of his acting in this extraordinary manner; but I expect that the real reason was a partial and temporary insanity.

The books give a true account of the wars of the republic, but are they authentic? Did Julius Cæsar write them? That is the question.

Healthy food, pure air, and regular exercise will preserve both the bodily and the mental powers in a wholesome state.

The habit of early rising contributes to the formation of industrious customs.

§ 85. Synonyms to be Discriminated.

Alone—accompanied by no other.
Only (as an adjective)—this, and no other.
Only (as an adverb)—in this wise, and no other; to this extent, and no further.

Avenge—to take vengeance for another.
Revenge—to take vengeance for ourselves.

Excite—to stir up feelings generally.
Incite—To stir up feelings unto a certain purpose or action.

Exert—to put forth power; implying force.
Exercise—to put forth power repeatedly; implying the regulation of force or discipline of power.

Receive—to take, voluntarily or involuntarily
Accept—to receive voluntarily; implying an offer.

Remember—to retain in the memory, or to recall without effort.
Recollect—to recall before the attention, perhaps with difficulty

Satisfy—to furnish with enough, producing pleasure.
Satiate—to furnish with more than enough, tending to disgust.

Weary—to tire with repetition of things that act upon us.
Fatigue—to tire by the continuance of our own exertions.

EXERCISE.

The alone car that escaped damage from the collision was found standing only on the track.

I scorn to avenge myself on such a miserable man; God will, in due time, revenge me.

A hungry man will always be satiated with plain food; but the pampered epicure will scarcely relish the most costly viands.

"I have been trying to remember," said he, "all the circumstances of that eventful day; but I recollect nothing more than what I have already told you."

I have just accepted your letter, and hasten to assure you that I will receive the present that you say will be sent to me, with emotions of pride and satisfaction.

He exercised himself violently, and, not being accustomed to much exertion, he was prostrated.

I am fatigued with her continual banging on the piano; I actually weary myself with walking abroad to avoid hearing it.

She was powerfully incited by the sudden arrival of her brother.

§ 86. Synonyms to be Discriminated.

Approval—the act of approving, expressed.
Approbation—the feeling of approving, not necessarily expressed.

Defend—we defend one that is actually attacked; it implies exertion.
Protect—we protect one that is liable to be attacked; it implies posture rather than exertion.

Neglect—an act of omission.
Negligence—a habit of omission; a disposition to neglect.

Difficulty—that which renders any work hard to be done, inherent in the work itself.
Obstacle—that which opposes any attempt, extrinsic to the work.

Impracticable—that which can not be performed, owing to the limited powers of man.
Impossible—that which can not be, owing to the very nature of things.

Particular—numerically distinct from others.
Peculiar—unlike all others; belonging to an individual.

Rational—possessed of reason.
Reasonable—applied to persons, exercising reason well; applied to things, that for which good reason can be given.

Sufficient—as much as one needs.
Enough—as much as one desires.

Empty—simply having nothing within.
Vacant—wanting something within to put it in its proper condition; without occupant.

EXERCISE.

Custom is a kind of law, enacted, not by the formal consent of councils, but by the tacit approval of society.

Though the men were very weary with the night's march, they declared themselves ready to protect the castle from the coming attack.

The obstacles that pertain to the undertaking are so great that it has been pronounced impossible.

By repeated acts of negligence, he acquired such habits of neglect as to render his character a very particular one.

Since man is a reasonable animal, nature has furnished him with no weapons with which to protect himself. His reason is enough to provide him with all the defense that he needs.

We found the house utterly vacant, and concluded it must have been empty for some time previous.

I receive this gift as a token of your approval of my course; the sight of it will ever excite me to the performance of duty, no matter what difficulties may have to be overcome, or what evils may tax my powers of duration.

§ 87. Synonyms to be Discriminated.

Abstinence—the refraining from what is injurious.
Temperance—the moderate partaking of what is good.

Ease—the state of a person; implying absence of pain or disturbance.
Facility—refers to the doing of a thing; implying that it is wholly within the power of the doer.

New—opposed to old; something that did not exist before.
Novel—opposed to the known; something that we had not experienced before.

Occasion—comes unsought to us, and sometimes imposes obligation.
Opportunity—is desired, and allows to do what we desire.

Safety—absence of actual danger.
Security—a condition beyond the reach of danger, present or future.

Punishment—a generic term; the infliction of suffering for wrong done, for the sake of justice.
Chastisement—a particular kind of punishment; it is inflicted by a superior, and aims at the reformation of the culprit.

Repentance—sorrow for wrong done (a general term).
Contrition—a state of mind produced by repentance, long continued.

Tyranny—the abuse of arbitrary power.
Oppression—the effect of tyranny upon the objects of it.

EXERCISE.

Those who cultivate the virtue of abstinence will enjoy the reward of a wholesome body.

He has read a good deal, but he has not studied enough to have acquired ease in profiting by what he reads.

This physician has a particular fondness for trying new remedies with his patients; hence he makes prescriptions such as were never heard of before, and he seizes every occasion to test whatever conjecture may have last entered his mind.

On several opportunities the father had punished his son so severely that the neighbors were obliged to interfere.

His contrition was not the mere dread of chastisement; it was the sincere expression of his sorrow for his crimes.

What safety can we have from tyranny, if judges are removable by the executive?

The sociable nature of man is his best safety against lawlessness and crime.

I doubt the veracity of the above proposition.

The teacher should not content himself with requiring only the sentences given in these exercises to be corrected. He should invent some of his own, dictate them to the class, and require them to criticise and correct them.

§ 88. Synonyms to be Discriminated.

Actual—that which exists as the effect of actions.

Real—that which exists as an object of thought, but not necessarily as an effect; opposed to imaginary.

Conciliate—to gain the good will of another for ourselves.

Reconcile—to gain the good will of another toward some third party.

Confute—to overcome one argument by another, showing it to be unreasonable.

Refute—to prove an assertion to be false, but not necessarily unreasonable.

Contented—a state of mind resulting from our own moderation.

Satisfied—a state of mind resulting from what Providence or others have done for us.

Miserable—he is miserable who is to be pitied on account of his mental distress.

Wretched—he is wretched who is to be pitied on account of his external circumstances.

INCLINATION—a positive tendency toward a particular act.
DISPOSITION—a readiness to receive an impulse in some general direction.

PRIDE—a false feeling of superiority to others, involving contempt.
VANITY—a desire to be esteemed superior to others, not involving contempt.

TRUST—to put confidence in with respect to the future.
CREDIT—to put confidence in with respect to the past.

TRY—with or without desire to succeed.
ATTEMPT—with desire to succeed.
ENDEAVOR—to attempt continuously or repeatedly.

EXERCISE.

Such a crime is more imaginary than actual; for you may search the past history of our country in vain for any real example of it.

It must be confessed a happy attachment which can conciliate the Laplander to his freezing snows, and render the African satisfied beneath the scorching sun of Guinea.

The arguments employed on the opposite side were so weak and inconclusive that we found no obstacle in refuting them.

Julius Cæsar is said to have been a man of most amiable inclination; his first care after gaining a victory was to spare the vanquished; and on all opportunities he showed more disposition to mercy than to severity.

Robinson Crusoe, when wrecked on his uninhabited island, was wretched at the thought of being cut off from all sociable intercourse with his species; and the idea of his miserable and forlorn condition frequently excited him to expressions of the bitterest grief.

Vanity is increased by solitude; it loves to live only; it seeks desert places, away from the haunts of men. Pride, on the contrary, could not exist out of society; praise and flattery are the food it lives on; and where is it to find these in the desert?

This man is, I confess, a skillful artist; his workmanship is excellent. But he has deceived me so often that I can no longer put the least credit in his promises, nor give any trust to his statements.

I tried to escape from his grasp, but the trial only made him hold the faster.

I have the pride to think that I have discovered a novel machine; has the like ever been constructed before?

§ 89. Synonyms to be Discriminated.

Obtain—to get possession of, whether to keep or not.
Acquire—to get possession of in order to retain.
Attain—to get possession of by reaching or arriving at a thing.

Acquit—To release from criminal charge as innocent.
Absolve—to release from penalty or from any legal obligation.
Exonerate—to release from any burden, including criminal charges and suspicions.

Abate—to lessen in violence, intensity, or demand.
Diminish—to lessen in size or quantity.
Subside—to lessen in agitation.

Abettor—one who encourages or incites to crime.
Accomplice—one who takes an active or equal part in a bad action.
Accessory—a subordinate or less prominent actor; not necessarily criminal.

Divide—to put into parts; to keep one part from another.
Separate—to remove one part or thing from another, *in space.*
Distinguish—to separate *in the mind;* to show to be different.

Discover—to find out what existed before, but was not known.
Invent—to originate what did not before exist.

EXERCISE.

England is divided from France by the English Channel, which, you will observe, abates toward the east into a narrow passage, called the Strait of Dover.

I can not absolve him of the crime when the testimony is so strong; but I will acquit him from the penalty when I invent that he is penitent.

I pray you let your fears diminish; the fever is rapidly diminishing.

We tried to obtain the testimony of his abettor, in order to invent the precise facts of the occurrence.

By practice, one may obtain the power to separate between the original speaker and him who repeats the utterances of others.

I acquit him of all the blame except that which pertains to his negligent customs.

We absolve him from the suspicion of being an accessory in the foul deed.

I observed that he was endeavoring to diminish the demands of his copartner on their penniless debtor.

When the rage for glaring jewelry diminishes, I hope some habit more compatible with pure taste will prevail.

By the persistent habit of early rising, he saved time to make some valuable inventions in his favorite science.

§ 90. Synonyms to be Discriminated.

Adjacent—lying near to, without touching.

Adjoining, Contiguous } lying next to—actually touching.

Avow—to declare openly, perhaps with some pride.
Acknowledge—to declare with some slight degree of shame.
Confess—to declare what we know will be considered blameworthy.

Whole—with none of the parts wanting.
Entire—not divided into parts.
Complete—with no part or appendage wanting.

Falsehood—the quality of untrue assertions.
Falsity—the quality of unsound reasoning.
Falseness—the quality of a treacherous character or of a spurious thing.

Grieve—to feel sorrow, not implying expression.
Mourn—to feel and express sorrow, either in word or act.
Lament—to express sorrow audibly.

Estimate—to judge of the worth or measure of a thing.
Esteem—to set a high value on one.
Appreciate—to value fully up to the merits, impliedly good.
Prize—to value highly for our own sake.

EXERCISE.

Brooklyn is contiguous to New York, the East River lying between.

The complete matter of his discourse is disfigured with falseness.

I avow that I have sometimes coveted my neighbor's field, seeing that it was adjacent to mine, and could so easily be inclosed with it as to make one pasture-field of the two.

I have looked through the complete house, and have not found one whole apartment.

The lad had such a custom of uttering falsities that no person would give trust to his assertions.

I found her pacing the hall, and filling the house with her loud grief.

What do you esteem this ring to be worth?

He died, acknowledging his adherence to the principles of Mohammed, and no one had any cause to charge him with falsity of character.

I purchased the vehicle, thinking it to be not only complete, but entire; and, as such, fully worth the price at which it was prized and sold.

I estimate her none the less because she laments her loss in secret and silence.

I confess myself opposed to war for any cause; yet I avow that I lay myself liable to sarcasm for my opinions.

I estimate the kindness which prompted you in attempting to rally your friend on account of his foolish superstition.

§ 91. Synonyms to be Discriminated.

Antipathy—the opposite of sympathy; a feeling against a person or thing.

Aversion—a stronger feeling, causing one to turn from or avoid its object; that object may be an employment.

Repugnance—the resistance of the feelings, caused by an effort to run counter to an aversion.

Admit—to suffer to enter; to receive as true.

Permit, Allow } to suffer to be done; not to hinder; allow, tacitly; permit, formally.

Calculate—the process by which we arrive at a certain result, mathematical or otherwise.

Reckon, Compute } to calculate arithmetically. (*Reckon* is also used in the sense of *conjecture.*)

Conception—the power of recalling or realizing an object before the mind.

Imagination—the power of combining our conceptions in an original manner.

Fancy—the same power viewed in reference to individual peculiarities, or in reference to its entertaining power.

Hate—an active feeling of dislike from personal considerations.

Detest—intense hatred, based on moral disapproval, vehemently expressed.

Abhor—strong dislike, prompting to avoid its object as injurious.

CHIEF—the principal person in action.
HEAD—The principal person in station or rank.
COMMANDER—a military chief.
LEADER—a chief, whether military or not, but implying that he is a pattern.

EXERCISE.

There is a natural and necessary repugnance between the good and the bad.

The sailors, having asked leave of the captain, were admitted to go ashore.

Can you compute the consequences of the measure that you propose?

The head of the detachment declared his antipathy against such a waste of men.

His imagination will not be governed by rules; consequently, his fancies are crude, ill-proportioned, and grotesque.

He permits that the queen, though the chief of the Anglican Church, has not the power to depose a bishop.

I hate such meanness in a man who holds himself up for an instance to his fellow-men.

Will you allow my first proposition to be true?

For twenty years he stood the acknowledged commander of the Whig party.

I never rise from a barber's chair without an increased detestation of the fashion of shaving.

I have an unaccountable repugnance against that man; yea, I abhor him; but I know nothing against his moral character.

The teacher is recommended to dictate sentences similar to the foregoing, containing not only synonyms inaccurately applied, but also violations of purity and propriety and simplicity, promiscuously intermingled. The fresh and original exercises prescribed by a teacher are more interesting than any that could be given in a book.

MISCELLANEOUS EXERCISES.

The above exercises are not enough by a jugful. So you have got to do some more. I allow to give you quantum sat. before I let you off. The fact is, my ambition is riled, and I calculate to give you particular fits. You have n't been overly much of an applicant for better than a fortnight, and I sort o' guess you 've got awful lazy. So set down, and go to work on these here exercises, and le' 's see what you can do when you try.

He has a remarkably strong fancy, and would make a fine artisan.

Yon speaker that cavorts so assumptiously remembers me of a fice in high oats. My fingers itch to take the chap a peg or two lower.

What a rippet you fellows are making! The first thing you know, you 'll make my *critter* break her bridle and run away; and then won't I be difficulted to get home?

I love these peaceable shades, but I can not long feel contented without sociable intercourse.

Then quoth Reuben, the companible Reuben, "Wilt thou plight thy word to me, sweet flower on the bush of humanity, that no other wight shall be admitted to the privilege which thou dost so cruelly refuse to me?"

But for all his affectuous appeal, she would make no promise, and the melancholious swain retired in wonderment that such charms as hissen should be uneffectual.

It was by many denied that the poems of Ossian are authentic; Macpherson, it was said, composed them, and passed them off for the products of the ancient Celtic muse. The causes for such an opinion never satiated my mind.

There is no connexity in the gent's remarks; he is gassy, and mystifies every point that he takes in hand.

But now this ci-devant literateur is devoted to the culture of cotton. His customs are all those of the planter. He has turned off the man who overseed for him last year, in order that he might have the direct management of the plantation himself.

Ah, mon cher élève, I beseech you, when you exchange school-life for the beau monde, do not become a mere follower of pleasure, going from fête to fête, and wasting your energies on bagatelles.

Do you find such marks of deity in the character or deliverances of any other teacher?

I have entered your mercantile colleague mainly for the purpose of becoming a finished scribbler.

Bacon is an example of great talents unfortified by lofty principles.

Was it my wife's health that you asked for? Oh, she is as well as any gentlewoman could be, that had been stripped from all home comforts.

Has all this argufying produced in you a settled faith of the proposal?

"Tomatoes," said she, "are very healthy; they give force to the liver."

QUESTIONS FOR REVIEW AND EXAMINATION.

What two arts are combined in the Art of Composition? What does each one of these arts teach? How should they be studied, and why so?

What is derivation? What is the difference between a derivative and a primitive word? What is meant by the radical of a derivative? What is a prefix, and what a suffix? What are the two kinds of derivation by suffixes? Which are the inflectional suffixes? When is each of these suffixes used?

When is the diction of a writer said to be pure? What are barbarisms? What are the four kinds of barbarism? Where is the English language used? What is the standard of pure English? What are provincialisms? What are slang words?

What are the three directions required by simplicity? How is the termination of every complete sentence indicated? How many and which are the full stops? What is the use of each of them? Repeat the rules for the use of capitals.

When is the suffix *s* changed into *es*? When is the final consonant of a radical to be doubled? What are the exceptions to this rule?

When does the final consonant of a radical remain single in the derivative? When is the final *e* of a radical dropped from the derivative? What exceptions to this rule?

What does propriety of diction require? Under what two heads may propriety be considered? How is lexical propriety violated? Under what three subordinate heads is it considered? What are paronyms? What is the general rule for a preposition following a Latin or Greek derivative? Why are there so many exceptions to this rule? In what does precision consist? What are redundancies? What is a pleonasm? What is tautology? What is meant by a group of synonyms? To what extent are the members of each group of synonyms alike in meaning? What is the finest test of skill in the use of language?

What is a quotation? Describe the difference between a formal, an informal, and an indirect quotation. How are formal and informal quotations indicated? How is an indirect quotation indicated?

What is style? What are the essential qualities of good style? To what two things do the essential qualities of good style have reference? What is the distinction between diction and structure? What are the four essential qualities of good diction?

What are synonyms? Why is the English language so rich in synonyms? When is the final *y* of a radical changed into *i* in the derivative? When is the final *y* of a radical retained in the derivative? When is the termination *ie* changed into *y* in the derivative? How are the suffixes *ed* and *est* both added to the same radical?

What are obsolete words? Where may they be still used? Why do obsolete words abound in the Sacred Scriptures? Give six examples of obsolete words, with their meanings. What is meant by *coining* a word? When is it allowable to coin a word? When are foreign words considered barbarisms? What are Gallicisms?

What does decorous propriety require? What are colloquialisms and vulgarisms? What are the three kinds of vulgarisms? How are numbers to be written?

BOOK SECOND.

PART FIRST.

INVENTION—RESUMED.

CHAPTER X.

DESCRIPTION.

To the Teacher.—In resuming the subject of invention, a word or two of explanation may be necessary.

It is not desirable that these exercises should be crowded together into any definite and brief portion of the pupil's course, but rather that they should be interspersed throughout a very considerable period, as occasional digressions from the regular routine. Once in two weeks is perhaps as often as the exercises in Invention should be required. In the intervals between them, daily tasks may be assigned in the various chapters that treat of the art of Expression. Coming thus as occasional exercises, if five be required in Description, five in Narration, five or more in Letters, and about the same in Historical or Biographical Sketching, these four chapters will cover about forty weeks, which is generally as much as is comprised in the scholastic year. During this time, the pupil will have been carried by daily tasks and exercises over the chapters on Structure, Punctuation, Variety of Expression, and the Translation of Poetry into Prose. But it is not intended to assign with any definiteness the proportion of time allotted to these two correlated branches, the art of Expression and the art of Invention. On the contrary, the teacher is purposely left free in this matter. Various circumstances may introduce a want of uniformity in the rate at which different classes progress through the exercises prescribed. The teacher may, for instance, find one class apt to learn the principles of punctuation, but slower in translating poetry into prose. Another class may possess the contrary aptitude. A third may be dull and slow in both chapters. He may judge it best to make the class go over some chapter a second or third time before quitting it. It is intended that he shall be free to do so; and yet the progress of the class in Invention need not be delayed in this. Advancement in one branch does not depend upon any particular degree of forwardness in the other. It is sufficient that there be a general keeping-pace in the two branches, as the pupil passes through the Manual; and this remark will apply to the whole arrangement of the work.

In the preceding exercises in Invention (Chapters II. and III.) the pupil was helped to the production of ideas by questions, lectures, etc. Now he is to be thrown more fully upon his own resources.

I. PRESENT OBJECTS.

First, the pupil must be trained to express the ideas afforded to him by direct observation. He should be required to write a description of some particular object actually in his view. For instance:

1. His desk;
2. The blackboard;
3. The stove;
4. The closet;
5. A house in sight;
6. An adjacent garden or field;
7. A tree or grove, in view;
8. The spring or the well;
9. A bank of clouds;
10. A horse, or any animal at hand.

No part of a teacher's labor is more abundantly rewarded than that employed in teaching his pupils how to see. The proper cultivation of the perceptive faculties necessarily includes the cultivation of the *thinking* powers. The young pupil does not know how or what to observe. He should therefore be taught carefully to examine what is presented to him by his senses, and to combine the impressions thus received so as to make a full, clear, and comprehensive conception of each object.

In order to this, particular attention should be given to the *order* or *method* in which he observes things. It would be well for the teacher, while the object is before the pupil, to guide him by a few questions, no matter how simple or meaningless they might, for other purposes, seem to be. Such questions are suggestive; their order is suggestive. They call up to the mind much more than their mere answers. After a very few examinations of objects thus conducted, the pupil's mind, by virtue of its own inductive tendency, will form a rule or method for itself, and will follow that method not merely in observing, but in writing out the results of such observation. Thus guided, he will soon learn to notice, first, the general appearance of an object, and then its particular parts, with their size, color, causes, uses, and resemblances. Every object will present some leading feature, around which the other parts will group themselves. To different persons, different objects may present themselves as the principal features; and this peculiarity of each mind should be respected, and allowed its legitimate play. But the taste that makes a bad selection should be kindly corrected. Not many such corrections will have been made before the pupil will have passed beyond all danger of making those sudden and grotesque transitions which offend sensible people. He will not, for instance, in describing a house, begin with the attic, or jump from the foundation to the upper apartments, and thence back to the walls. He will not describe the inside before the outside, nor the inferior apartments before the principal ones.

After some little practice has initiated the pupil into the art of observing and recording what the senses give, he should be encouraged to turn the mind's eye inward, and observe the effect of this upon his own feelings and sentiments. Almost every object that would be selected for an exercise in description will be found to possess a character, a language, and to impress some sentiment on the thoughtful mind. To detect this character, to understand this language or trace this impression, requires no great genius, not even perfect maturity of mind; but it requires attention, concentration, a calm, steady holding of the mind to the object, an effort to appreciate it, and a yielding to the influence of the scene. The greatest obstacles to this in the case of young persons are their giddiness, and a certain false shame of acknowledging their own feelings. Let these be overcome, and the results, even in the case of those that seem to be dull in other respects, will be surprising and gratifying. In a very short time the young composer will begin to produce descriptions that will be, not only accurate and vivid, but possessed somewhat of poetic grace.

II. ABSENT OBJECTS.

After a few exercises of the kind prescribed in the foregoing section, the pupil may be required to describe some object that he has seen, but which is not present at the time of writing.

1. In this exercise, let him state *the place where*, and *the time when*, or *the occasion upon which* he witnessed the object.

2. After describing its *form*, *parts*, and *uses*, let him be encouraged—

3. To express the *ideas* or *reflections* suggested by it, either when he saw it or now, as he recalls it to mind.

Here the laws of association come into play; and these the teacher may, if he see proper, explain to the pupil, who in this way will learn in what directions he may look for thoughts connected with the subject before his mind.

In performances of this kind, besides mere awkwardness of arrangement, before alluded to, most young persons will betray a tendency to depart from the matter in hand; in other words, to neglect unity. This fault must be approached with great tenderness and indirectness. As the very object of the exercise is to develop fertility of thought, not a single check should be put upon it, except in those cases where the exuberance becomes offensive or ridiculous. As before explained, *order* will be found greatly to assist the pupil in eliciting thought. The proper order should be pointed out. In many cases the teacher must, for a long period, invite and encourage fullness of utterance, at the expense of unity and the strictest good taste. After practice has opened the fountain freely, then the teacher may point out the superior beauty of those descriptions that leave one strong and vivid impression upon the reader's mind, unto the formation of which every sentence contributes its part. Thus indirectly may the pupil be incited to attempt this excellence.

It is impossible to make out a list of the subjects for description which it would be proper to assign to pupils, for the reason that each one has had his own experience, passed through certain scenes, visited and examined certain objects, and no one else can say what these may have been. The teacher must find out what objects the pupil has seen and observed with sufficient attention to write a description of them. There is in every neighborhood some interesting object or place which all that reside near it have seen; such an object or locality would make a very good subject for description. *A church* or other public building, *a mill*, *a dam*, *a factory*, or other large combination of machinery, *a fine landscape*, *a remarkable natural object*—any such object as these would answer the purpose. It is always a good plan to select for description any object or event which, at the time, may have excited peculiar interest.

CHAPTER XI.

NARRATION.

After a sufficient number of exercises has been performed in description, the pupil may proceed to narration.

§ 92. *Narration*, in its purest form, is simply a relation of events in the order of their occurrence. But in this nude form it is hardly ever used in those compositions that are intended for entertainment. Narration becomes attractive and interesting by being combined with other forms of composition, and chiefly with description. Whenever the course of events ushers upon the view any remarkable object or personage, it is always in good taste to give some description of the appearance or character of it. In this combined form of narration and description very easy exercises can be assigned, and such as will be more of a recreation than a task to the pupil. At the same time, so extensive is this field that it has afforded ample scope to the most brilliant geniuses, and contains some of the most perfect specimens of style.

In order to secure originality, it will be well at first to confine the pupil to the narration of such occurrences as he has actually witnessed or taken a part in. The following list will furnish specimens.

SUBJECTS FOR ORIGINAL NARRATIVE.

1. The history of yesterday, or of any particular day.
2. The history of a holiday.
3. A school-festival or celebration.

4. Any public celebration.
5. A particular* visit to a Sunday-school.
6. A particular* attendance at church.
7. A visit to a friend in the city or country.
8. A ride in the country.
9. An excursion to some interesting place, such as a waterfall, a cave, a mountain, etc.
10. A picnic party.
11. A fishing or sailing excursion.
12. A hunt, either by night or day.
13. A nut-gathering party.
14. Any of the ordinary pleasure-seeking occasions of the neighborhood.
15. A ride through a plantation or a visit to a manufactory, etc.
16. A trip for pleasure or other object to some more distant place.

There have occurred in the life, even of the youngest pupil that uses this book, several such occasions as those enumerated above; the teacher may select any of them as the subject of this exercise.

CHAPTER XII.

LETTERS.

Narratives and descriptions may be happily embodied in the form of *letters* to some real or imaginary friend. The freedom and naturalness appropriate to a letter make it a favorite form of composition with young people. At the same time, its practical character strongly recommends it as a field for abundant and long-continued exercise for pupils. This place is selected as the most appropriate to lay down the rules and principles of epistolary writing, leaving it to the teacher to prescribe whatever amount of exercises in it he may judge proper. Let it be borne in mind, however, that it will always be in order to require an exercise in the form of a letter,

* The pupil will observe that the subject is not the visiting of church or Sunday-school, or what such visits generally are, but *some particular visit.*

whether the *matter* of the exercise be narrative, discussion, or any other kind of composition.

§ 93. In treating of letters we shall consider: 1. The *form;* 2. The *kinds;* 3. The *style.*

§ 94. I. THE FORM OF A LETTER.

LONGWOOD ACADEMY, NEAR COLUMBUS, GA.

My dear Charley:

I propose to give you, in this form, some plain directions as to the manner of arranging the matter of a letter, illustrating my directions by the very letter which I write.

The four parts of a letter are, first, the *date;* second, the *address;* third, the *body* of the letter; and fourth, the *subscription.* I have already passed the date and the address, and am now writing the body of this letter. As you see above, the date should come at the head of the first page of the letter, toward the right-hand side of the page. It may occupy one line, or two or three, according to the number of words that may be necessary to show where and when the letter is written. One thing that you must invariably insert in the date of a letter that is sent by mail, is the name of the nearest post-office. No matter what fanciful name may be given to the house or locality in which the letter is written, the post-office name must not be omitted.

As to the style of the address, that depends upon the relation that exists between the correspondents. To a near relative, or a very intimate friend, it is allowable to use such a familiar address as I have used in this letter. But to others, the address should consist of two parts; first, the name and title of the person, in full; and second, on the next line, the complimentary address, such as *Sir*, *Madam*, etc. To an utter stranger we would write *Sir* or *Madam;* to one with whom we have had some previous acquaintance, *Dear Madam*, or *My dear Sir*. If the letter is addressed to a firm, or any collection of persons, the complimentary address should be *Gentlemen* or *Ladies*.

Some persons prefer to write the name and title of the party addressed at the foot of the letter, toward the left-hand side of the page. This is a matter of taste, but it is not proper to insert the name and title in both places.

In writing the body of the letter, be careful to leave a margin of about an inch on the left-hand side, and not to write too close to the right-hand edge. In commencing a new paragraph, let the first word be placed at a distance of *two* inches from the margin.

The style of the subscription should correspond with the relation between the parties. To a relative, it is always proper to subscribe one's self, *Your affectionate son, daughter, brother, cousin*, etc., as the case may be. To a dear friend, one may write, *Your sincere friend*, or *Truly yours*, etc. To a person whose age or social standing demands a more elaborate expression of respect, some such form as the following would be in good taste:

I have the honor to be
Your most obedient servant.

Allow me to subscribe myself
Your obliged and obt. servant.

Most respectfully and truly,
Yours, &c.

With the best wishes for your welfare,
I am, truly yours, &c.

Hoping that you will find these directions adequate to all the exigencies of your present correspondence,

I beg to be remembered as
Your affectionate teacher,
JAMES FERNLEY.

To Master Charles Thornton.

II. KINDS OF LETTERS.

§ 95. The following syllabus will show at a glance the various kinds of letters, and how they are related. The distinctions among them are given below.

Letters are
- Veritable
  - Of friendship.
  - Of business
    - Private
      - Regular.
      - Occasional.
    - Public.
- Simulated
  - Of news, or information for the public.
  - Of various literary character.

§ 96. In its very nature, a letter proper is a personal communication. In its primary intention, it is for the eye of the person addressed: whether others are to read it or not, is altogether a secondary consideration. But writers do frequently avail themselves of the epistolary form in order to publish their sentiments to the world. This gives rise to the distinction between *veritable* letters, those that are primarily intended to be personal, and *simulated*, those that assume the form of letters, with some other object in view.

§ 97. The distinction by which veritable letters are divided into letters of friendship and letters of business is obvious; so also that which separates letters on private business from those on public business. The latter are more frequently styled *official* letters. They are such as pass between persons occupying some public offices, either as the representatives of nationalities, or as those charged with the execution of the laws.

§ 98. Even among letters on private business, a distinction may be made between the regular letters of business men concerning the affairs of their business, and some occasional matters which any man is liable to be interested in, on his own account, or that of others.

§ 99. Simulated letters are divided into two classes; first the contributions of newspaper correspondents, sometimes called *news-letters*, and those in which the epistolary form is assumed as the most convenient to embody some matter of various literary character.

§ 100. All newspapers of any pretension rely upon their correspondents in distant places for supplying a very large part of the attractive matter of their columns. Such contributions generally contain an account of such recent matters of public interest as may have transpired in the locality from which the correspondent writes. Yet he is by no means confined to recent events. His communication may be a narrative of his own peregrinations, and the scenes of interest through which he passes. Or he may bring in discussions concerning politics, economy, fine arts, history, morals, or religion. There are positively no limits to his field, except those which protect the private character of individuals.

III. THE STYLE OF LETTERS.

§ 101. Beginning with the last mentioned, the style of the newspaper correspondent must have at least one characteristic, i. e., *vivacity*. With so large a scope for his pen, the public will tolerate almost any thing but *dullness*. Truthfulness, of course, is demanded of all. His judgment must be acute, his taste delicate, his mind well stored, his perceptions quick and searching. With all these mental qualifications, his style must have point and pungency.

§ 102. All letters of business should be characterized by the utmost politeness, and by a strict adherence to the matter in hand. This should always be set forth in the clearest manner consistent with brevity. As to official letters, they have hitherto been characterized by rather an excess of courtesy. But as the young student will certainly have no occasion for such a letter until his judgment and taste are sufficiently mature to enable him to decide for himself how far he shall conform to the usage, nothing more need here be said upon the subject.

§ 103. As to letters of friendship, the very best rule is for the writer to imagine that he is allowed the privilege of a short interview with his friend, and then to insert in his letter those matters that would naturally be mentioned in such an interview. The style should be clear, simple, and conversational; sprightly or humorous, perhaps, but never flippant or silly. Whatever freedom or familiarity be used, no error in spelling, grammar, or style, no slovenliness in penmanship, should be tolerated in a letter. Egotism should be avoided, and yet one must not forget that the principal interest that friends have in their correspondence consists in the fact that it is the only means by which they are to be informed each of the other's fortunes and feelings. Backbiting, the repeating of evil rumors about mutual acquaintances, or the revealing of what has been mentioned in confidence, are all as wicked and as mean in letters as in conversation. With these limitations, let the heart dictate the matter. Be *yourself* unto your friend. Pour out your soul unto him, and invite similar openness from him, and your letters will glow with interest and beauty.

If any specimens or models of letters were to be given in this Manual, this would be the place to insert them. But the compiler does not think that such things are of sufficient value to compensate for the space that they occupy. If there are persons so singularly educated, or miseducated, as to receive benefit from models of letters, they are not likely to be using this book. Moreover, the benefit which even such a person would receive from this source would be mixed with evil. They invite servile imitation, instead of that reliance on one's own judgment and good taste which it is the object of this treatise to inspire. In its very nature, a letter must reflect the mental features of the writer. Usages must be complied with to a certain extent, and in such communications as cards of invitation, etc., even formalities may be submitted to. But beyond this limited sphere, freedom and originality are desired. It would be as sensible to write out forms of conversation, like those in the French phrase-books, as to lay down models for letters. Any person that has been taught to put his words on paper, can write a letter. A very little practice is sufficient to show him the ruts of usage, into which he will naturally drop.

In place, then, of giving models to be followed, it is recommended that the pupil be required to imagine himself in various situations in life, and write letters such as would be demanded by the supposed emergencies.

PART SECOND.

EXPRESSION—RESUMED.

CHAPTER XIII.

THE STRUCTURE OF SENTENCES.

I. TERMS—PHRASES.

§ 104. Words, either singly or in groups, are the signs of ideas, and of the relations of ideas. Those that are the signs of ideas are called *terms;* those that are the signs of the *relations* of ideas are called *connectives.*

§ 105. A term may be a single word, or a group of words related: if a single word, it is called a simple term; as, *man—industrious—works—faithfully.*

§ 106. A term composed of a group of words, one of which is the principal, the rest being joined to it to modify its extension or application, is a *complex* term. Complex terms are by many grammarians called phrases. The principal word is called the *basis* of the complex term or phrase, and the other words are called the *modifiers* or *adjuncts* of the basis. Thus,

"A beautiful spring day,"

is a phrase, of which *day* is the basis, and *a, beautiful,* and *spring* are the modifiers of it.

§ 107. Modifying terms as to their function are divided into two classes; those that modify substantives, and those that modify terms other than substantives. The former are called *adjective* modifiers, the latter *adverbial* modifiers.

Thus, in the phrase, "*singing sweetly,*" *sweetly* is an adverbial modifier, because it modifies *singing,* which is not a substantive. But in the phrase, "*pretty birds,*" *pretty* is an adjective modifier, because it modifies the substantive, *birds.*

Now, we may join both phrases together, thus making the complex phrase, "pretty birds singing sweetly," of which the term *birds* is the basis; and it has two modifiers, which are both adjective modifiers, because *birds*, the basis, is a substantive. These two modifiers are the adjective word *pretty*, and the phrase *singing sweetly*. This will illustrate the manner in which complex terms and phrases are composed.

§ 108. A phrase receives its name from the part of speech which forms its basis. Thus, in the foregoing examples, *singing sweetly* is a *participial* phrase, because its basis is a participle. *Pretty birds* is a *substantive* phrase, because its basis is the substantive *birds*. The whole phrase, *pretty birds singing sweetly*, is also a substantive phrase, for the same reason. The following additional examples will illustrate all this:

Substantive phrase—A wise *man*.
Substantive phrase—*Work* to be done.
Adjective phrase—Exceedingly *beautiful*.
Adjective phrase—Most *powerful* of all.
Participial phrase—*Sowing* seed in the field.
Infinitive phrase—*To read* the book through.
Adverbial phrase—Very *abundantly*.

§ 109. Care must be taken to distinguish between the *constitution* of a phrase and its *office* or *function*. The constitution has reference to the parts of speech that compose it. It is the constitution that determines the name. But the office or function refers to the relation which it bears to the other words of the sentence. This relation may be that of a substantive, an adjective, or an adverb. Thus, in the expression, "a desire to read the book through," *to read the book through* is a phrase composed of an infinitive, its object, and an adverb. The infinitive is the basis; therefore it is called *an infinitive phrase*. But its function is that of an adjective, because it qualifies the noun *desire*.

EXERCISES.

1. Compose phrases having for their bases the following words:

Table.	Hope.	Industrious.	Bright.
Gold.	Medicine.	Industry.	Brightly.
Mountain.	Idea.	Mixing.	To esteem.
Green.	Affection.	To purify.	To render.
Handsomely.	Gay.	Socially.	Tormented.
Often.	Riding.	Height.	Asking.
To survey.	Working.	Mass.	Ruined.
To elect.	To slide.	Brightness.	Printed.
Mariner.	Ocean.	Hearing.	Wealth.

2. Combine them in complex phrases, thus:

The *idea* of a *table* moving.

To *render* my *tormented* nerves easy again.

3. Point out the office of each phrase used in these complex phrases to modify a basis.

II. CONNECTIVES—ADJUNCTS.

§ 110. Connectives are of two kinds, *subordinate* and *co-ordinate.*

§ 111. *Subordinate* connectives are those which join modifiers to their bases. With reference to the connective, the basis is sometimes called the *antecedent*, and the modifier is called the *subsequent* of the connective.

§ 112. The only kind of subordinate connectives used in phrases is the preposition. As substantives, when used as modifiers, are generally under the government of prepositions, the name *adjunct* is generally understood to mean a combination consisting of a preposition and its subsequent or governed term.

EXAMPLES OF ADJUNCTS.

In kind—With difficulty—On wheels—To bed—By digging—After eating—In contradiction.

§ 113. As the subsequent of a preposition may be not only a simple substantive term, but also a substantive phrase, we may have what are called *adjunct phrases.*

EXAMPLES OF ADJUNCT PHRASES.

In this very kind—With extreme difficulty—On four iron wheels—By digging down the hill—After eating supper—In flat contradiction.

EXERCISE.

Compose simple adjuncts and adjunct phrases embracing the following words as bases:

Ink.	Water.	Forests.
Coldness.	Fertility	Commerce.
Sailing.	Sailors.	Hunting.
Defying.	Shelter.	Respect.
Establishment.	Idea.	Walk.
Building.	Courage.	Hope.
Punishment.	Sense.	Weight.

III. COMPOUND TERMS.

§ 114. *Co-ordinate* connectives are those that unite terms or propositions that have the same relation to the other words of the sentence in which they occur.

§ 115. The only co-ordinate connectives that are used to connect terms are the conjunctions *and*, *or*, *nor*, *but*, and *but also;* sometimes with and sometimes without the help of their corresponding words, *both*, *either*, *neither*, and *not only*.

§ 116. When terms or phrases are thus connected together as co-ordinates, they make a *compound term*, and the connected terms are called its *components*.

EXAMPLES.

Comp. substantive term — Land — and — water.
comp. connec. comp.

Comp. adjective term — Either — hot — or — cold.
connec. comp. connec. comp.

Comp. adverbial term — Neither — now — nor — then.
connec. comp. connec. comp.

Comp. substantive phrase — Not only an indifferent *father*, but a dishonest *man*.

Comp. participial phrase — Both *plowing* the ground, and *casting* in the seed.

Comp. infinitive phrase—Either *to buy* the article, or *let* it alone.

EXERCISE.

Unite the following pairs of words in compound phrases.

Boys—girls.	Ice—snow.
Circle—square.	Windows—doors.
Honesty—frugality.	Truth—falsehood.
Wet—dry.	Bitter—sweet.
Brass—iron.	Dreary—forlorn.
Seldom—never.	To see—to hear.
To see—to know.	Hoisting—lowering.
Dawning—brightening.	Hill—dale.
Error—truth.	To err—to forgive.
Strict—severe.	Books—papers.
Proper—pure.	Glossy—dull.
To sing—to play.	To walk—to run.

IV. SENTENCES—PROPOSITIONS.

§ 117. A *sentence* is a collection of words so arranged and connected as to express a thought.

§ 118. In some sentences, one or more of the words have no connection with the rest of the sentence. These are said to be *independent* or *absolute.*

§ 119. All the rest of the sentence is said to be *structural.*

EXAMPLE.

Independent.	Structural.
Adam, . . .	where art thou?
Heavens! . .	what a tempest!
Why, . . .	I thought you had gone.
No; . . .	I was too late for the cars.

§ 120. The structural part of every sentence consists of one or more *propositions.*

§ 121. Propositions are of four kinds; *declarative, interrogative, exclamatory,* and *imperative.*

§ 122. A *declarative* proposition is one that expresses something to be believed.

§ 123. An *interrogative* proposition is one that seeks for information.

§ 124. An *exclamatory* proposition is one that expresses what is wonderful, or hard to be believed.

§ 125. An *imperative* proposition is one that proposes, either in the way of command or request, something to be done.

EXAMPLES.

Declarative—James reads well.
Interrogative—Can James read Latin?
Exclamatory—How well James reads!
Imperative—Read a little louder.

EXERCISE.

Compose propositions of the kind indicated after each of the following words used independently.

Father, (declarative.)
Eliza, (interrogative.)
Alas! (exclamatory.)
John, (imperative.)
Yes; (declarative.)
True, (declarative.)
Sir, (interrogative.)
Oh! (exclamatory.)
Peter, (interrogative.)
Nonsense! (declarative.)
Caitiff! (imperative.)
O Father, (imperative.)
Thou venerable chronicler of the past, (imperative.)
Whew! (exclamatory.)
Now, (interrogative.)

V. ELEMENTS—SUBJECT.

§ 126. The words or groups of words that are united together to form a proposition are called its *elements.*

§ 127. There are two kinds of elements that make up compounds of any sort, *immediate* and *remote.*

Thus flour, water, salt, and yeast are the immediate elements of bread. But the elements *of these elements*, as for instance the oxygen and hydrogen of water, the chlorine and sodium of the salt, etc., are the remote elements of bread. But when we speak of the elements of a proposition, unless we specify *remote* elements, we always mean the *immediate* elements; those that directly make up the proposition.

§ 128. The elements of propositions are of two kinds: *essential* and *accidental;* the former are those which every proposition must have,* and the latter those which a proposition may or may not have.

§ 129. The essential elements are two: the *subject* and the *predicate.*

These are best defined by reference to their use in declarative propositions. After having learned to distinguish them in that connection, the pupil can easily accommodate the definitions to the other kinds.

§ 130. In a declarative proposition, the *subject* is the term (either simple, complex, or compound) that shows what it is concerning which the declaration is made.

§ 131. The *predicate* is that part of the proposition which shows what is declared of the subject.

EXAMPLES.

Subjects.	Predicates.
Fire	burns.
The trees	are growing.
Five bushels	have been sold.
The most lamentable results . .	will follow.

§ 132. The usual order is for the subject to precede the predicate; but the contrary may sometimes take place. Thus:

Predicate.	Subject.
Now fades	the glimmering landscape.
Well said	the prophet Esaias.
There were in olden time . .	giants and long-lived men

§ 133. If the subject is a complex term or phrase, the basis of the phrase is called the *grammatical* subject, to distinguish it from the entire phrase, which is called the *entire* or *logical* subject.

* Either expressed or understood.

§ 134. The grammatical subject of every proposition must either be a substantive, or some term used as a substantive.

EXAMPLES.

Logical Subjects.	Predicates.
The fine old *mansion** of the governor . .	was entirely destroyed.
Such a terrible *commingling* of the elements .	was never heard.
To avoid temptation	is always wise.
Socrates the philosopher	did not write books.

EXERCISES.

Supply subjects to the following predicates; first, grammatical subjects consisting of simple terms only; secondly, subjects enlarged by modifiers so as to make them complex terms.

—— did not attend school.
—— was a very fine writer.
—— lay frozen all the winter.
—— used his energies well.
—— cuts the cloth in pieces.
—— softens the hardships of poverty.
—— was petulant and exacting.
—— shall be repeated.
—— stains the linen.
—— is bounded by mountains and the sea.
—— kissed him a thousand times over.
—— shines like a star.

MODEL.

George did not attend school.
The farmer's oldest boy did not attend school.

VI. THE PREDICATE.

§ 135. The essential part of the predicate of a prop osition is the finite verb that it contains. Indeed a predicate may consist of a finite verb and nothing more. Thus:

Fishes *swim;*
The stars *shone;*
William *will be rewarded.*

* The grammatical subjects are in italic.

§ 136. This finite verb that constitutes the essential part of a predicate is called the *grammatical* predicate. If there are any accidental elements joined to this verb, then the whole group of words is called the *logical* predicate. For example:

> Fishes *swim in the sea;*
> The stars *shone brightly;*
> William *will be handsomely rewarded for his generosity.*

EXERCISES.

I. Point out the logical and the grammatical predicates of the following propositions:

Nations have perished. The world is round. The honored sage has died. Love waxed cold. Bards have told of other times. The memory of the good shall grow greener with passing years. Wrinkled purses make wrinkled faces. Hard study is the price of learning. A merry heart maketh a cheerful countenance. A thing of beauty is a joy forever. Want of punctuality is a species of falsehood. No man can serve two masters. God gives every bird its food. A miser grows rich by seeming poor. A Christian is the highest style of man We must all appear before the judgment-seat.

II. Put predicates to the following subjects:

We ——. The horses ——. Edward ——. Time ——. Rainbow hues ——. Useful books ——. The present age ——. A good sewing-machine ——. Empty boxes ——. The human mind ——. Magnificent rivers ——. The smallest stream ——. A goodly person ——. Beauty ——. His uncombed hair ——. A true Christian ——. That crazy woman ——. Laborious effort ——. The poor man's cottage ——. A dull ax ——. Hills covered with verdure ——. Many a grain of sand ——. Indifference to public opinion ——. Our own consciousness ——. Extremely white paper ——. The cost of an article ——.

VII. ELEMENTS OF INTERROGATIVE, EXCLAMATORY, AND IMPERATIVE PROPOSITIONS.

§ 137. It will be seen that every proposition must contain a finite verb, whose office it is to predicate somewhat of a subject. This predication, in declarative propositions, is in the form of an assertion to be believed. But it may also be involved in the exclamation of something more or less astonishing, or in a question. Thus, whether we say, *Jane is beautiful,—How beautiful Jane is!*—or *is Jane beautiful?*—in either case we predicate *beauty* of *Jane.*

Any pupil that has learned to point out the subject and predicate in declarative propositions will have no difficulty with exclamatory and interrogative ones. To alter the definitions before given to suit these kinds would be to make difficult a very easy matter.

§ 138. With regard to imperative propositions, the case is still easier. In these, the subject is always the pronoun representing the person addressed. Hence the subject of an imperative proposition can be nothing else than the pronoun *thou*, *ye*, or *you*. But it is rarely expressed at all, the whole proposition forming the predicate.

EXAMPLES.

	GRAMMATICAL.	
	Subjects	Predicates.
Loweth the ox over his fodder?	ox.	loweth.
Will the meek be forever oppressed?	meek.	will be oppressed.
Can the doctor save him?	doctor.	can save.
How rapidly the cars run!	cars.	run.
Come to the old oak tree.	(ye.)	come.
Fling away ambition.	(thou.)	fling.
Do these men know their rights?	men.	do know.
Seest thou a man wise in his own conceit?	thou.	seest.
Give us this day our daily bread.	(thou.)	give.
How often would I have gathered them!	I.	would have gathered.
Are the fixed stars suns?	stars.	are.
How beautiful is the snow!	snow.	is.
What a world of trouble he is in!	he.	is.
Be ye therefore perfect.	ye.	be.
Be not hasty in thy speech.	(thou.)	be.

EXERCISES.

Compose sentences as follows:

1. An interrogative with *gold* as the subject.
2. An exclamatory with *iron* as the subject.

3. A declarative with *truth* as the subject.
4. A declarative with *lying* as the subject.
5. An interrogative with *hang* as the predicate verb.
6. A declarative with *struck* as the predicate verb.
7. An exclamatory with *hits* as the predicate verb.
8. An imperative with *come* as the predicate verb.
9. An imperative with *forgive* as the predicate verb.
10. An imperative with *be* as the predicate verb.
11. A declarative with *look* as the predicate verb.
13. An interrogative with *be* as the predicate verb.

VIII. ACCIDENTAL ELEMENTS—MODIFIERS.

§ 139. The accidental elements of propositions are of three kinds, *modifying*, *complementary*, and *supplementary*. Modifying elements may belong either to the subject or predicate; complementary and supplementary to the predicate alone.

§ 140. Modifying elements are those terms, whether simple, complex, or compound, that directly qualify either the grammatical subject or the grammatical predicate. Thus in the proposition,

"Fraudulent dealers seldom succeed,"

fraudulent and *seldom* are the modifying elements, because the one qualifies the subject *dealers*, and the other qualifies the predicate verb *succeed*.

§ 141. Modifying elements are of two kinds, *adjective* and *adverbial;* the former modifying substantives, or words regarded as substantives, and the latter qualifying verbs, participles, adjectives, adverbs, or prepositions.

§ 142. *Adjective modifiers* embrace not merely adjective words, limiting and qualifying, but also possessives and appositives, or nouns in apposition.

§ 143. Adjuncts are regarded either as adjective or adverbial, according as they qualify a substantive or a verb, participle, adjective, or adverb.

EXAMPLES OF ADJECTIVE MODIFIERS.

This dog is well trained.
Large rivers intersect the country.
The witness's testimony was clear.
Napoleon, *the French commander*, was again victorious.
Ships *in distress* often put into this port.

§ 144. In case the subject of a proposition is an infinitive or a participle, it may be modified by adverbial modifiers; sometimes a participle is modified both by an adjective and an adverbial modifier.

EXAMPLES.

To speak *fluently* is the gift of nature to some.
Talking *aloud* is strictly forbidden.
Your chiding him so *severely* offended him.

§ 145. *Adverbial modifying elements* are those that modify the predicate verb. They include not merely adverbs proper, but also nouns, infinitives, and adjuncts, used as adverbs. Any of these will be a *remote adverbial element* when attached, not to the predicate verb, but to any other word of the kinds usually modified by adverbs.

EXAMPLES OF ADVERBIAL MODIFIERS.

A hungry lion leaped *suddenly upon him.*
He will return *to-morrow.*
They *eagerly* seized the opportunity.
He was *incessantly* smoking.
The family resided *many years in Lexington.*
We will go *home to-morrow.*

EXERCISE.

Modify the nouns in the following propositions by adjective and the verbs by adverbial modifiers:

Lion—roars. Pen—writes. Man—lives. Flowers—bloom. Books—endure. To sleep—is sweet. Baskets—were filled. Honors—were bestowed. Blessings—were appreciated. Lamps—were burning. Commerce—was promoted. Legends—have been told. Ideas—suggest. Beauty—delights. Conscience—may condemn.

IX. COMPLEMENTARY ELEMENTS.

§ 146. The complementary element of a proposition is that term which, in some cases, is added to the predicate verb, when intransitive, to fill out its otherwise imperfect meaning.

The complementary term has a very close relation to the subject, as will be seen in the following examples:

Grass is *green.*
Horses are *quadrupeds.*
The girl looks *sick.*
Alexander was *a conqueror.*
This is *the ripest apple of all.*
Franklin has been called a *philosopher.*
Who are you?

§ 147. Because the complementary element seems to fill out or complete the predicate, the noun, adjective, or pronoun that constitutes it is often called the *predicate-noun*, *predicate-adjective*, etc.

Some grammarians call this element the *attribute* of the predicate verb. Each of these names, *the complementary element*, *the attribute*, *the predicate noun*, *adjective*, etc., has its significance, and to each there are some objections. In the present unsettled state of the grammatical nomenclature, we have no right to fix upon one to the exclusion of the others.

§ 148. Whether the complementary element be a substantive or an adjective, it may be either a simple, or a complex, or a compound term. If complex, it will have such modifiers as appropriately belong to it; that is, it will have adjective modifiers, if it is a substantive; otherwise, its modifiers will be adverbial. The following are examples of complementary elements, some of which are compound, others very complex:

Milton's poetry is always *healthful*, *bright*, and *vigorous.*
The seducers of the heart are *honor*, *affluence*, and *pleasure.*
It is *time for thee to work.*
This is *the pursuit of knowledge under difficulties.*
The chief object of education is not *to store the mind with knowledge.*

EXERCISES.

I. Point out the complementary elements in the following propositions:

Socrates was wise. The honest will be accounted worthy. The railroad is a convenience. Lions are not courageous. His old age was devoid of comfort. Large was his bounty. I am the chief of Ulva's isle. The roaring torrent is deep and wide. Are these the rewards of virtue? Be true to nature. You may be sure of it. This is the first and great commandment. The reasons given by the gentleman for his extraordinary conduct are these.

II. Supply complementary elements to the following imperfect propositions:

Learning is ——. Novel reading is ——. The Bible may be considered ——. The life of a missionary may be ——. The region beyond the grave is not ——. To calculate shrewdly is ——. The states of Greece were ——. Every teacher should be ——. Would you be ——? Death has been called ——. Art thou ——? Physical science may be ——. Time must not be ——. Washington was made ——. These beautiful pictures are ——. Can such a pirate be ——? Was the medicine ——?

X. SUPPLEMENTARY OR OBJECTIVE ELEMENTS.

§ 149. If a predicate verb is modified by several adverbial terms or adjuncts, they all bear the same relation to the verb they modify. But that is not the case with supplementary or objective elements. If a verb has more than one object, they are of different kinds and receive different names.

This remark does not apply to compound objects, that is, compound terms used as objects, the components of which will, of course, all bear the same relation to the verb.

§ 150. The object of a transitive verb is that word that expresses the thing on which the action is exerted. Thus in the proposition,

"Thomas drank wine,"

wine is the word expressing that on which the action of drinking was exerted.

§ 151. Some verbs that really imply no action, take objects; that is, they are followed by substantives that manifestly sustain the same relation to them that is sustained by objects to truly active verbs. Thus:

"Charles owned a *horse*."
"I would have *courage*."

§ 152. Some transitive verbs are followed by two substantives, the one expressing that on which the action is exerted, the other the effect or result of that action on the first object. Thus in the proposition,

"Who made Thomson president,"

the two objects are *Thomson* and *president;* the former shows on whom the action was exerted, and the latter shows the result of that action. To distinguish these, the former is called the *primary* object, the latter the *secondary* or *attributive* object.

§ 153. Moreover, sometimes the person *to* or *for* whom any thing is done is expressed by a substantive following the verb. This may likewise be expressed by an adjunct following the object, with the preposition *to* or *for* as the connective. But it is just as frequently expressed by a substantive without a preposition, preceding the true object of the verb. Thus:

"He made *me* a knife."

To distinguish this kind of object from the true object of the verb, it is called the *indirect* or *dative* object, while the true object is called the *direct* object.

§ 153. We have thus three kinds of objects, any two of which may follow a transitive verb:

1. The primary, or direct object;
2. The secondary, or attributive object;
3. The indirect, or dative object.

But whenever it is not necessary to distinguish the first of these from either of the others, as when a verb has only one object, it is sufficient to call it *the object*.

§ 155. There are a few verbs (viz., those signifying to *ask*, to *teach*, etc.) that are followed by two objects which it seems hard to designate, whether as direct and indirect objects, or as two direct objects. Thus in the proposition,

"He taught me grammar,"

it is difficult to say whether this means *he taught grammar to me*, or whether *me* is an object on which the act of teaching was exerted.

EXAMPLES.

Single object, simple.

Who made man?
They would have elected Jefferson.
I have not read Rasselas.

Single object, compound.

Who created the heavens and the earth?
They would have elected Jefferson and Burr.

Primary and secondary objects.

Who made thee a ruler?
They would have elected Jefferson president.

Direct and indirect objects.

I will sing you a song.
Would you grant him such a request?

EXERCISES.

Compose sentences containing either of the four kinds of propositions (see § 121–125), and containing the words enumerated below, in the relations as specified by the following numbers:

1. As grammatical subject.
2. As complementary element.
3. As direct or primary object.
4. As secondary object.
5. As indirect object.
6. As adjunct modifying the subject.
7. As adjunct modifying the predicate verb.
8. As adjunct modifying the complement.
9. As independent.

Hero, ...	1	2	3	4	5	6	7	8	9
Assistant, . .	1	2	3	4	5	6	7	8	9
Modesty, ...	1	2	3	4	5	6	7	8	9
Peter, ...	1	2	3	4	5	6	7	8	9
Kentucky, . . .	1	2	3	4	5	6	7	8	9
Workman, . .	1	2	3	4	5	6	7	8	9
To kill, ...	1		3	4		6		8	
Singing, . . .	1	2	3			6	7	8	

MODEL.

1. The conquering *hero* comes.
2. Jackson was the *hero* of New Orleans.
3. We will honor the true *hero*.
4. I call the self-governed man a *hero*.
5. Give the *hero* his just reward.
6. The praises of the *hero* fill every mouth.
7. He was compared to a *hero*.
8. This sword is a gift to the *hero* of Champlain.
9. *Hero*, thy name shall be our watchword.

XI. COMPLEX SENTENCES.

§ 156. A *simple* sentence is one that contains only one proposition.

§ 157. But a proposition may constitute one of the elements (either essential or accidental) of another proposition, the two thus constituting a *complex* sentence. In such cases, the proposition that is embraced in the other as part of it, is said to be *subordinate* to it.

§ 158. One proposition may be subordinate to another in two ways; either as *incorporated in* it, or *dependent upon* it. In the former case, no connective is used; in the latter, there is a connecting word, either expressed or understood, and the clause sustains to it the relation of a subsequent.

EXAMPLES.

Incorporated. Repeat the words, "*How doth the little busy bee.*"
Dependent. You may go, ***when you can say it.***

§ 159. A subordinate proposition may be either *substantive*, *adjective* (adnominal), or *adverbial*.

§ 160. If it performs in a sentence any of the functions of a substantive, standing as the subject or object of a verb, or in the predicate after an intransitive verb, or in apposition with some substantive word, it is called a *substantive* clause.

EXAMPLES.

Incorporated clause as the subject. How can it be done? is the question that puzzles me.

Dependent clause as subject. *That* he will lie, is known to every body.

Incorporated clause as object. The governor said, "What evil hath he done?"

Dependent clause as object. I would remind you *that* you have made a promise.

Incorporated clause as predicate substantive. His answer was, "I care not."

Dependent clause as predicate substantive. The difficulty has been *that* it would not stay there.

Incorporated clause as substantive in apposition. The question, What shall we eat? is a serious one.

Dependent clause as substantive in apposition. The doctrine that the sun is the center was taught by Pythagoras.

§ 161. If a subordinate proposition is used to limit some substantive in the sentence, it is called an *adjective* (or adnominal) *clause*.

§ 162. An adjective (adnominal) clause is never an incorporated clause: it is always introduced by a connective; and that connective must either be a relative pronoun, or one of the conjunctive adverbs used in the place of a relative governed by a preposition. Of course the antecedent of this connective is the word modified by the clause.

§ 163. If the modified word is a verb, participle, adjective, or adverb, then the dependent clause is said to be *adverbial*.

EXAMPLES.

1. Dependent clause as adjective element:
The book—*that I am reading*—is interesting.
He—*that endureth to the end*—shall be saved.
Study nature—*whose laws are all interesting.*
These were small states—*in which every man felt himself important.*
I will revisit the spot—*where I was born.*

2. Dependent clause as adverbial element:
The wicked flee—*when no man pursueth.*
Wheresoever the carcass is—the eagles will be gathered together.
If thine enemy thirst—give him drink.
He will never be rich—*because he is wasteful.*
He is as strong—*as Samson* (*was strong*).
Write to me every week, so—*that I may know your whereabouts.**

EXERCISE.

Insert in each of the following sentences two dependent clauses; one adjective, and the other adverbial:

The man walked. Herod killed James. He will lose his friend. Be thou obeyed. Can an evil tree bring forth good fruit? Go to Rome. Life is a great poem. Beginners need the best teachers. The day ended well. The piano is made of rosewood.

XII. RESTRICTIVE AND CIRCUMSTANTIAL CLAUSES.

§ 164. Adjective (adnominal) clauses may be distin guished into two different kinds: *restrictive* and *circumstantial.*

§ 165. A *restrictive* clause is one that is essential to the meaning of its antecedent or modified word, in the particular connection in which it occurs. A *circumstantial* clause is not absolutely essential to the meaning or truth of the proposition.

EXAMPLES.

The man (Restrictive clause. who is my friend) would not speak so

This man, (Circumstantial clause. who is my friend,) assures me of the fact.

---

* Whereabouts is a colloquial word, allowable only in conversation and familiar letters.

Restrictive clause.
The man (that hath done this thing) shall surely die.

Circumstantial clause.
This man, (who had been a galley slave among the Spaniards,) burned with a desire to avenge his wrongs.

Restrictive clause.
The river (which separates Maryland and Virginia) is 550 miles long.

Circumstantial clause.
The river Potomac, (which separates Maryland and Virginia,) is 550 miles long.

Restrictive clause.
The times (when guests were always welcome) have passed away

Adverbial clause.
They went up to Jerusalem (when he was twelve years old.)

The last two examples will show that the connective of a restrictive clause is not in every case a relative pronoun, but may be a conjunctive adverb, used in the sense of a relative governed by a preposition.

EXERCISE.

I. Compose sentences using the following clauses both as restrictive and circumstantial, limiting either the subject, the attribute, or the object of the entire proposition, changing the relative pronoun into *who*, *which*, or *that*, as the antecedent may demand.

Which bloom in spring.
Which stood on the hill.
That I saw in Charleston.
Which assist us in difficulty.
That would regard omens.
Whom we have known for many years.
Whose laws are worthy of attentive study.
That can not perish.
In which every man had a voice.
In which I take no delight.
Whom none can love.
That darkened the horizon.

MODEL.

The flowers which bloom in spring are the most regarded.
I love violets, which bloom in spring.

II. Modify the substantives in the following propositions by adjective clauses, either restrictive or circumstantial:

The river is swollen.
The picture is a master-piece.
The hunter shot the deer.
The maiden has read the book.
Impulses lead to action.
The journey was a tedious affair.
The island abounds in fruit.
Ink will stain the skin.

XIII. ADVERBIAL CLAUSES.

§ 166. Adverbial clauses are divided into four sorts; those expressive of

1. Place;
2. Time;
3. Manner;
4. Relations apprehended by the judgment.

§ 167. Adverbial clauses of place are those which have for their connective some one of the conjunctive adverbs, *where*, *whither*, *whence*, *wherever*, *whithersoever*, etc.

EXAMPLES.

I stand where Chatham stood.
I am going whence I shall not return.
He leadeth him whithersoever he will.

§ 168. Adverbial clauses of time are those which have for their connective some one of the conjunctive adverbs, *when*, *while*, *whilst*, *as*, *before*, *after*, *ere*, *till*, *until*, *since*, *whenever*, etc.

EXAMPLES.

When you have nothing to say, say nothing.

I have not seen him since he was married.

While the steam was escaping, we could hear nothing.

Shall we see you again before you leave the city?

We are apt to listen to the song of that siren until she transforms us into beasts.

As we entered the cabin, deep groans saluted our ears.

§ 169. Adverbial clauses of manner are subdivided into

1. Clauses of correspondence;
2. Clauses of proportion;
3. Clauses of consequence;
4. Clauses of equality;
5. Clauses of inequality.

§ 170. Clauses of correspondence are those whose connective is the conjunction *as*, either alone or preceded by *so*, *such*, or *same*, or followed by *if* or *though*.

EXAMPLES.

Do as you are bid.
I will bring such apples as I find.
I will act as if you were present.

§ 171. Clauses of *proportion* are connected by *the—the* used before two comparatives, as

"The more I ate, the more I wanted to eat."

§ 172. Clauses of consequence are those whose connective is the conjunction *that*, preceded by *so* or *such*.

EXAMPLES.

The old lady was so feeble that she could not stand the journey.

We will raise such a tempest of indignation that they will be obliged to yield.

§ 173. Clauses of equality are those whose connective is the conjunction *as*, preceded by *as* when equality is affirmed, by *so* when it is denied.

EXAMPLES.

These cherries are as sour as vinegar.*
That paper is not so white as this.*

§ 174. Clauses of inequality are those whose connective is the conjunction *than*, preceded by some adjective or adverb in the comparative degree.

---

* These clauses are elliptical, as will be explained hereafter.

10

EXAMPLES.

The private was braver than the captain.
The chimney is less injured than the roof.

EXERCISES.

Modify the verbs, participles, or adjectives in the following propositions by adverbial clauses of the several kinds described in the foregoing nine sections:

We dwell. Charles has gone. Light has dawned. A man was killed. A beautiful fountain rose. The oil was burning. Honor comes. The walls are crumbling. Their swords will flash. The lily is white. Snow is whiter. Henry is more candid. Was this inordinate ambition? Can a man be blameless? I ask the question plainly. Sunny hours are passing. Will man live again? You are well known in the city. Let us hear thy voice.

XIV. CLAUSES EXPRESSING RELATIONS APPREHENDED BY THE JUDGMENT.

§ 175. Clauses that express relations apprehended by the judgment are of four kinds:

1. Causal;
2. Conditional;
3. Final;
4. Adversative.

§ 176. *Causal* clauses are those that give the reason for the statement contained in the leading clause. They use the connectives *because*, *for*, *as*, *whereas*, *since*, and *inasmuch as*.

EXAMPLES.

He took medicine because he was sick.
Whereas this law is unjust, it ought to be repealed.

§ 177. *Conditional* clauses are those that express some event, the happening or not happening of which will more or less affect the truth of the leading proposition. They use the conjunctions *if*, *unless*, *though*, *lest*, *except*, *provided that*, etc.

EXAMPLES.

If you enjoy health, you should be thankful.
Unless you see miracles, you will not believe.

§ 178. *Final* clauses are those that express the purpose or motive for which the action expressed by the leading clause is performed. They use the conjunctions *that* and *lest*. *That* is sometimes strengthened by the adjunct *in order*.

EXAMPLES.

I will stay at home, in order that you may attend the lecture.
You should wear your shawl, lest you might take cold.

§ 179. *Adversative* clauses are those which concede some thing opposed to the statement of the leading clause. They use the conjunctions *though*, *although*, *notwithstanding*, *however*, etc.

EXAMPLES.

Though he is poor, he is respected.
However careless he may seem, he really is deeply concerned about it.

EXERCISE.

Compose leading clauses, to which the following subordinate clauses are to be joined, either preceding or succeeding them, as the usages of the language may seem to require:

Because I do not know him.
If you will only read the book.
That he might regain his health.
Though he was rich.
Since it is now too late to retreat.
Unless my friend objects.
In order that I might examine the case.
Although he was extremely feeble.
Whereas no one has yet been injured.
Lest you lose the golden opportunity.
That I might not be insulted by him.
As honesty is the best policy.
For no one else will trust him.

MODEL.

I can not trust him, because I do not know him.

XV. COMPOUND SENTENCES.

§ 180. Compound sentences are those that are composed of simple or complex propositions connected by co-ordinate conjunctions, expressed or understood.

§ 181. The propositions composing a compound sentence are called its members.

§ 182. If each member is complete in itself, requiring no other member to make out the sense, the sentence is said to be a full compound sentence; otherwise it is a partial compound sentence.

EXAMPLES.

FULL COMPOUNDS.

Life is short and art is long.

Either the rain must come, or the plant will die.

The vigor of Omar began to fail; the curls of beauty fell from his head, strength departed from his hands, and his feet lost their agility.

PARTIAL COMPOUNDS.

Time and tide wait for no man.

They sing and dance the livelong day.

Life is short and very uncertain.

The soil produces wheat and oats.

The altitude, not the latitude, makes the climate salubrious.

§ 183. Although it is generally by co-ordinate connectives that the members of compound sentences are connected, yet there is one variety that constitutes an exception to this rule. In this variety, the last member of the sentence has for its connective a relative pronoun, or conjunctive adverb, the antecedent of which is not any single word in the foregoing member, but the fact or circumstance therein asserted. These may be called *appended* members.

EXAMPLES.

He will not take the remedy; which makes his case hopeless.

The townsmen mutinied, and sent to Essex; whereupon he came thither.

§ 184. The conjunctions *nor* and *neither*, when not used as correlatives, but as equivalent to *and* combined with some negative, serve to connect appended members to the other parts of compound sentences, especially in poetry.

EXAMPLES.

His memory has not yet perished; nor shall it, while freedom lives.

Thou shalt be hid from the scourge of the tongue; neither shalt thou be afraid of destruction.

They never spied his welcome step again;
Nor knew the dreadful death he died
Far down that narrow glen.

XVI. PARTIAL COMPOUNDS.

§ 185. Each partial compound sentence may be considered as the resultant of contracting a full compound sentence. This contraction is what gives rise to compound terms.

EXAMPLES.

James will go to the fair,
John will go to the fair,
William will go to the fair.
Contracted.—James, John, and William will go to the fair.

This animal will eat flesh,
This animal will eat vegetables.
Contracted.—This animal will eat both flesh and vegetables.

Philosophy makes us wiser men;
Christianity makes us better men.
Contracted.—Philosophy makes us wiser, Christianity makes us better, men.

Measure your life by acts of goodness; measure not your life by years.
Contracted.—Measure your life by acts of goodness, not by years.

§ 186. In most cases a sentence that contains one or more compound terms may be resolved into as many simple propositions as there are components in all its compound terms.

EXERCISE.

Let the pupil be required to separate the parts of the following compound sentences, and to analyze each into its elements:

Intrinsic worth, and not riches, ought to procure esteem.

Milton burned with a deep yet calm love of moral grandeur.

Washington was the head of a nation, and not of a party.

Zeal without knowledge, courage without prudence, and peacefulness without principle, are dangerous qualities.

God's love to us is not a technical dogma, but a living and practical truth.

Beauty haunts the depths of the earth and sea, and gleams out in the hues of the shell, and the precious stone.

On the rich and the eloquent, on nobles and priests, the Puritans looked down with contempt.

I soon perceived that I had the power of losing and recovering these sensations, and that I could, at pleasure, destroy and renew this beautiful part of my existence.

Come when the heart beats high and warm with banquet-song and dance and wine, and thou art terrible.

XVII. CONTRACTION OF COMPLEX SENTENCES.

§ 187. Complex sentences are capable of contraction, as well as those that are compound; but in this case there is no compound term or compound element formed. The contraction of a complex sentence is effected in one of two ways: *ellipsis* and *abridgment*.

§ 188. *Ellipsis* consists in leaving out of a sentence some word or words necessary to its grammàtical construction, but not essential to its meaning. As performed upon complex sentences, it generally consists in omitting from one clause some words that can be supplied from the other.

EXAMPLES.

He can read better than I (can read).

If you accept not this opportunity, he will (accept this opportunity).

The peasant's cabin contains as much content as the sovereign's palace (contains content).

Bryant wrote good poetry while (he was) yet a youth.

Your patrons, if (they are) not already dissatisfied, will soon become so.

Though (I am) not a prophet, I can easily foretell this man's fate.

If you are not fond of wine, it may sometimes be beneficial; if you are (fond of wine), it will always be hurtful.

§ 189. A complex sentence may also be contracted by the *abridgment* of its dependent clause.

§ 190. A dependent clause is said to be abridged when it is converted into an infinitive or participial phrase, the finite verb becomes the infinitive or participle that constitutes the basis of the phrase, and the connective of the clause is omitted. Of course the infinitive or participle into which the finite verb is reduced may have modifying, complementary, or supplementary accompaniments, just as the verb has before its change.

EXAMPLES.

Dependent clauses.	Abridged phrases.
When no man pursueth	No man pursuing.
Because he is wasteful	He being wasteful.
As the birds were* sweetly singing .	The birds sweetly singing
That you would speak distinctly . . .	You to speak distinctly.

§ 191. It is a general rule, governing all abridgments, that if the subject of the dependent clause refers to the same person or thing as the subject of the leading clause, the dependent subject is dropped, being absorbed, as it were, in the leading subject.

EXAMPLES.

Full form.	Abridged.
I desire that I may read Tennyson.	I desire to read Tennyson.
I intend that I shall go to college.	I intend to go to college.
Do you know how you can solve an equation?	Do you know how to solve an equation?

§ 192. But if the subject of the dependent clause is different from that of the leading clause, it is generally

* In the abridgment this verb becomes absorbed in the participle.

retained, but changed in case. In the construction that is generally called the nominative absolute, however, the case is not changed, but the relation is.

EXAMPLES.

Full form.	Abridged.
I desire that you should read Tennyson.	I desire you to read Tennyson
I hear that he has gone to college.	I hear *of** his having gone to college.
As the steamboat has arrived, we will walk down to the landing.	The steamboat having arrived, we will walk down to the landing.

§ 193. There are three cases or sorts of abridgment:

1. A substantive clause abridged to a participial substantive phrase;

2. An objective substantive clause abridged to an objective infinitive phrase;

3. An adverbial clause abridged to a participial phrase, or to a so-called *absolute* substantive phrase.

§ 194. I. A substantive clause, whose connective is the conjunction *that*, may be abridged by changing the verb into a participle corresponding in voice and tense, dropping the connective, and either omitting the subject, according to the foregoing rule, or else reducing it to the possessive case. Thus:

Full form.	Abridged.
That he is homely, is nothing.	His being homely is nothing.
That Henry was sick, was known to us all.	Henry's being sick was known to us all.
We knew that Henry was sick.	We knew *of* Henry's being sick.
I boasted that I was a printer.	I boasted *of* being a printer.
She confessed that she had aided the rebels.	She confessed (to) having aided the rebels.

§ 195. II. An objective substantive clause may be abridged by changing the verb into an infinitive, cor-

* *Of* is inserted because the verb *hear* is not used in its transitive sense.

responding in voice and tense, dropping the connective, and either omitting the dependent subject, or changing it into the objective, as the primary object of the verb Thus:

Full form.	Abridged.
I desired that he would go to his room.	I desired him to go to his room
We believe that thou art the Christ.	We believe thee to be the Christ.
I remember that he was an old man then.	I remember him to have been an old man then.
I wished a hundred times that I might die.	I wished a hundred times to die.
The Congress resolved that they would enforce terms still more severe.	The Congress resolved to enforce terms still more severe.

§ 196. III. An adverbial clause that states the occasion whereupon, the manner how, or the reason why, any event took place, may be abridged by changing its predicate verb into a corresponding participle, omitting the connective, and conforming to the general rule as to the retaining or dropping of the subject.

§ 197. If the subject is dropped, then the participle of the abridgment limits the subject of the leading verb.

§ 198. But if the subject is retained, it is apparently* separated from all syntactical connection with the leading clause, only limited by its own participle, and whatever modifier may accompany it. Thus:

Full form.	Abridged.
When I had made a fire, I warmed myself.	Having made a fire, I warmed myself.
As I looked over the paper, I saw this advertisement.	Looking over the paper, I saw this advertisement.
As we were exceedingly tossed, we lightened the ship.	Being exceedingly tossed, we lightened the ship.

* This is generally called the nominative absolute, but it is only apparently absolute.

When shame is lost, all virtue is lost.	Shame being lost, all virtue is lost.
If we have secured peace of mind, we may smile at misfortune.	Having secured peace of mind, we may smile at misfortune.
If peace of mind has been secured, we may smile, etc.	Peace of mind being secured, we may smile, etc.
After the doors were shut, he came and stood in the midst.	The doors being shut, he came and stood in the midst.

EXERCISE.

Abridge the following complex sentences in any of the three modes that will suit:

They met daily that they might concert plans of opposition.

His favorite project was that he might make Scotland a republic.

These sycophants well know that they deserve punishment.

Some persons may think that Burt was a man of vulgar and prosaical mind.

While they had a constant apprehension of danger, how could they enjoy the fine scenery?

The English then considered that the Highland Scotch were mere savages.

If this point is admitted, we proceed to the next argument.

Since the conquest of Spain was their object, they left no means untried that they might effect a landing on the Peninsula.

When the summing up on both sides was completed, the judge proceeded to charge the jury.

As we were passing through the straits, we were detained by a dense fog.

Because some truths are difficult of comprehension, the weak reject them.

Johnson declared that wit consists in finding out resemblances.

If my reputation is utterly gone, what a wretch am I!

When this scheme was disclosed to the Helvetii, they compelled Orgetorix that he should plead his cause in chains.

As you were present, he would not tell all that he knew.

I believe that you are an impostor.

CHAPTER XIV.

PUNCTUATION.*

§ 199. Punctuation is the art of dividing written or printed discourse into certain larger or smaller portions by means of points or marks, in order that the relations of the words and clauses may be clearly seen, and their meaning readily understood.

§ 200. It is a common impression that points are intended as guides to the voice in oral reading. It is true that they serve this purpose incidentally: but their primary use has reference to the syntactical arrangement of the sentence, and the dependence of its component parts. The pupil must bear in mind that good enunciation or delivery requires many a pause where syntax does not recognize any break in the discourse; and sometimes a point is required where no pause should be made by the voice.

§ 201. Another general direction which the pupil must observe is the following: *Never insert a point unless there is some rule requiring it, or unless it is necessary to prevent a misunderstanding of the sentence. Be guided by the rules, no matter how few or how many points they may require.*

§ 202. The art of Punctuation may be conveniently discussed under four general divisions, viz.:

1. *Terminal Punctuation*, which has reference to the end of sentences;
2. *Interclausal Punctuation*, which has reference to the separation of the clauses and members of sentences;
3. *Interstitial Punctuation*, which has reference to the more minute divisions of sentences;
4. *Quotation Pointing*.

---

* The teacher is cautioned against hurrying the pupils in this chapter.

I. TERMINAL PUNCTUATION.

The general rules for Terminal Punctuation have been given in the Preliminary Exercises in the first part of this Manual. Nothing remains to be added here, except to give the rules for the *dash*, when used as a terminal point.

THE TERMINAL DASH.

§ 203. The dash (—) is used at the end of a sentence that is broken off or left unfinished.

§ 204. The dash is also added to a full stop, to indicate a greater pause or separation between the sentences than the full stop alone would require.

§ 205. On this principle, the dash is used in the narration of conversations, to indicate the change in the speaker.

EXAMPLES.

But, my good lord,—203

I pause for a reply.—204 None? then, etc.

"What!" exclaimed I, from the depths of my starvation, "nothing else? Have n't you any eggs?"—205 "No."—205 "Any cutlets?"—205 "No."—205 "Any potatoes?"—205 Ever the same reply, "No."

EXERCISE.

Supply periods, dashes, exclamation and interrogation points where they are needed in the following extracts:

1. In front of our inn, a man held in his arms a fine, well-dressed little boy, and cried in a high, loud, measured, monotonous drawl, continuously over and over "His mother died in Carlisle we have traveled twenty-seven miles to-day I have no money she left this boy yesterday he walked eighteen miles this is no deception I have seen better days friends his feet are lacerated I am in search of work I am young and strong he can not walk his mother died in Carlisle help me in my lamentations I have but sixpence for myself and boy I am compelled to beg I am young and strong his mother died in Carlisle I am in search of work his feet are lacerated" and so on we watched from the windows perhaps two minutes and saw seven persons drop coppers into his hat.

2. Thereupon I told the coachman this story:

At the Bull-ring, the other day, one woman accused another of cheating, and in return was called a liar just as I was passing, they came to blows, and hammered each other very severely, a crowd collected, and formed a ring about them in a moment it was my impulse, with perhaps two or three other persons, to rush in and part them; but "Hands off fair play" was the cry raised by the crowd so that we were in danger of being roughly handled ourselves they fought like tigers, till the blood ran freely at length the hair of one of them fell over her eyes "tut tut" said the coachman and as she tossed her head backward, and tried to draw it off with one hand she got a facer; and then, one two three down she went "fair play" shouted the crowd, as they pulled off the victor, and bore her away the fallen woman was picked up, and men and women crowded around her, to express their sympathy for her ill-luck one brought a comb, another a mug of water, and another a black bottle in a minute, she had her face washed, her hair drawn up and knotted, tobacco crowded up her nose to staunch the blood, and she had taken a good pull at the bottle and the last I saw of her, she was standing before the butcher's shop (I had forgotten to say that the victorious woman had been taken into a butcher's shop) standing before the butcher's shop with her sleeves rolled up sparring with her clenched fists, and screaming, "Come on come on Oh I 'll fight you only give me fair play, and I 'll fight you" "it must have been a nuisance," said the coachman; "where were the police" "in America every man in sight would have been a policeman, if necessary, to have parted them" "do n't you like fair fighting, then, you Americans" asked the coachman.

II. INTERCLAUSAL PUNCTUATION.

§ 206. The pupil should impress upon his mind the general principle that a simple sentence, of plain, natural structure, without ellipsis, transposition, or any other occasion for the suspension of the meaning, requires no point in it from beginning to end. It is only when the natural connections of the words are in some way interrupted, or when the simplicity of the structure is superseded by a complexity of some kind, that it becomes necessary to indicate the grouping of the words by points.

§ 207. The points used to separate the clauses of a complex, or the members of a compound sentence, are of four kinds, as follows:

The colon, (:)
The semicolon, (;)
The comma, (,)
The dash, (—)

§ 208. Of these, the colon marks the larger and more obvious divisions of a sentence; the semicolon, those not so great; and the comma, the least of all.

THE DASH INTERRUPTIVE.

§ 209. I. The dash is variable in this respect. When used alone, it denotes some interruption or sudden turn of thought, some incoherency or want of unity in a sentence.

§ 210. II. The figure of syntax called *anacoluthon* is always indicated by a dash.

§ 211. III. The dash is also used when some word or phrase of the foregoing clause is repeated for the purpose of explanation or comment.

§ 212. The pupil must be cautioned against the very objectionable practice of using the dash where a comma or some other point is properly due; a practice which results from carelessness or ignorance, and which is almost as culpable as bad spelling.

EXAMPLES.

Politicians are brilliant, versatile, profound, far-seeing—209 every thing but honest.

And bid her (you mark me!) on next Wednesday—209 but stop! what day is this?

He had no malice in his mind—209
No ruffles on his shirt.

Newton was a Christian;—211 Newton! whose mind burst forth from the fetters cast by nature on our finite conceptions.

Yes, the poor boy, the friendless Sam, with whom our story began, had become the famous Doctor Samuel Johnson!—[211] Johnson! universally acknowledged as the wisest man and the greatest writer in England.

Leonidas, Cato, Phocion, Tell,—[210] one peculiarity marks them all: they dared and suffered for their native land.

"Grindstone,—[209] cheese,—[209] cheese,—[209] grindstone!" muttered Bunker, now evidently puzzled and doubtful.

Exercises to be provided as before recommended.

Compound Sentences.

§ 213. The members of a full compound sentence are separated either by a colon, a semicolon, or a comma:

§ 214. I. A colon, if the members are long, and no connective is expressed;

§ 215. II. A semicolon, if the members are short, and there is no connective, or long, *with* a connective;

§ 216. III. A comma, if the members are short, and the connective is expressed.

§ 217. The parts or members of a contracted sentence are separated by commas;

§ 218—Unless the members are long, and subdivided by interstitial commas; in that case they are separated by a semicolon.

§ 219. An appended member (see § 184) must be separated from the preceding member by a comma or semicolon, according to the closeness of the connection.

EXAMPLES.

Satire should not be like a saw, but a sword: [214] it should cut and not mangle.

Do not think yourself perfect; [215] it is human to err.

Harbor no malice in thy heart; [215] it will be a viper in thy bosom.

It is unworthy of one great people to think falsely of another: [214] it is unjust,[216] and therefore it is unworthy.

Religion must be the spirit of every hour; [215] but it can not be the meditation of every hour.

He is a freeman whom the truth makes free,[216] and all are slaves beside.

The Jews ruin themselves at their Passovei ;[215] the Moors, at their marriages;[215] and the Christians, in their law-suits.

Scott built a castle,[216] but he broke his heart.

I have promised to pay it,[216] and I will pay it.

For I am a man under authority, having soldiers under me;[215] and I say to this man, "Go,"[216] and he goeth;[215] and to another, "Come,"[216] and he cometh;[215] and to my servant, "Do this,"[216] and he doeth it.

Beauty flows in the waves of light,[217] radiates from the human face divine,[217] and sparkles in the pathway of every child.

Prosperity is naturally,[217] though not necessarily,[217] attached to virtue and merit;[215] adversity,[217] to vice and folly.

He will not take the prescribed remedies,[219] which makes his case hopeless.

They obstinately refused to give bail;[219] whereupon the judge remanded them to prison.

They desired that we should remember the poor;[219] the same which I also was forward to do.

He has consented to insert the word in the bill,[219] which is all that I asked.

The very best method of furnishing exercises in Punctuation is as follows:

Let the teacher select some piece of composition, containing illustrations of the rules that the pupil has as yet learned, and first, run his eye over the piece to mark every point in it which is not an instance of the application of those rules. Then let him dictate the selection to the pupil, phrase by phrase, mentioning, as they occur, all the marked points, but not the others. Finally, let the pupil be required to supply all the omitted points, marking each one with the number of the section containing the rule for its insertion.

As a model, the following extract from *Kinglake's Eothen* is given, just as it should be dictated by the teacher to a pupil at this stage of his progress:

EXTRACT.

Whilst I remained at Cairo, I thought it worth while to see something of the Magicians, who may be considered as it were the lineal descendants of those that contended so stoutly against the superior power of Aaron I therefore sent for an old man who was held to be the chief of the Magicians, and desired him to show me the wonders of his art the old man looked and dressed his character exceedingly well the vast turban, the flowing beard, and the ample robes, were all that one could wish in the way of appearance the first experiment (a very stale one) which he attempted to perform for me was that of attempting to show the forms and faces of my absent friends, not to me, but to a boy brought in from the streets for the purpose, and said to be chosen at random a pan of burning charcoal was brought into my room, and the Magician bending over it, sprinkled upon the fire some sweet substances which must have consisted partly of spices, or sweetly burning woods; for immediately a fragrant smoke arose, which curled around the bending form of the wizard, while he pronounced his first incantations when these were over, the boy was made to sit down and a common green shade was bound over his brow then the wizard took ink and, still continuing his incantations, wrote certain mysterious figures upon the boy's palm and directed him to rivet his attention to these marks, without looking aside for an instant again the incantations proceeded and, after a while, the boy, being seemingly a little agitated, was asked whether he saw any thing on the palm of his hand he declared that he saw a kind of military procession with flags and banners which he described rather minutely I was then called upon to name the absent person whose form was to be made visible I named Keate you were not at Eton and I must tell you, therefore, what manner of man it was that I named; though I think you must have some idea of him already, for wherever from utmost Canada to Bundelcund wherever there was the whitewashed wall of an officer's room, or any other apartment in which English gentlemen are forced to kick their heels, there likely enough (in the days of his reign), the head of Keate would be seen scratched or drawn with those various degrees of skill which one observes in the representations of saints any body, without the least notion of drawing, could still draw a speaking, nay, scolding likeness of Keate if you had no pencil, you could draw him well enough with a poker, or the leg of a chair, or the smoke of a candle he was little more (if more at all) than five feet in height, and was not very great in girth but in this space was concentrated the pluck of ten battalions he had a really noble voice, which he could modulate with great skill but he had also the power of quacking like an angry duck and he almost always adopted this mode of communication in order to inspire respect he was a capital scholar but his ingenious learning had *not* "softened his manners," and *had* "permitted them to be fierce" tremendously fierce he had the most complete command over his temper I mean over his good temper, which he scarcely ever allowed to appear you could not put him out of humor that is, out of the *ill*-humor which he thought to be fitting for a head-master his red shaggy eyebrows were so prominent that he habitually used them as arms and hands, for the purpose of pointing out any object toward which he wished to direct attention the rest of his features were equally striking in their way, and were all and all his own he wore a fancy dress, partly resembling the costume of Napoleon, and partly that of a widow woman I could not by any possibility have named any body more decidedly differing in appearance from the rest of the human race "whom do you name" "I name John Keate" Now, what do you see" said the wizard to the boy "I see," answered the boy, I see a fair girl with golden hair, blue eyes, pallid face, rosy lips" there was a shot I shouted out my laughter, to the horror of the wizard, who, perceiving the grossness of his failure, declared that the boy must have known sin (for none but the innocent can see truth), and accordingly kicked him down stairs one or two other boys were tried but none could "see truth" they all made sadly "bad shots" notwithstanding the failure of these experiments, I wished to see what sort of mummery my magician would practice, if called upon to show me some performances of a higher order than those which had been attempted I therefore entered into a treaty with him, in virtue of which he was to descend with me into the tombs near the Pyramids, and there evoke the Devil the negotiation lasted some time, for Dthemetri*, as in duty bound, tried to beat down the wizard as much as he could and the wizard, on his part, manfully stuck up for his price, declaring that to raise the Devil was really no joke, and insinuating that to do so was an awesome crime I let Dthemetri have his way in the negotiation but I felt in reality very indifferent about the sum to be paid, and for this reason, namely, that the payment (except a very small present, which I might make, or not, as I chose) was to be *contingent on success* at length the bargain was made and it was arranged that after a few days to be allowed for preparation, the wizard should raise the Devil for two pounds ten, play or pay no Devil, no piastres the wizard failed to keep his appointment I sent to know why the deuce he had not come to raise the Devil the truth was that my Mahomet had gone to the mountain the plague had seized him he was dead.

Complex Sentences.

§ 220. Every subordinate clause of a complex sentence must be separated from its leading clause by a comma, *except in the following cases:*

§ 221. I. When either the leading clause or the subordinate is very short, and the latter comes directly after the former;

* This was my Greek servant, or valet.

§ 222. II. When the subordinate is a *dependent substantive* clause, and comes *after* the leading verb;

§ 223. III. When the subordinate is a *restrictive adjective* clause, closely following the substantive which it limits;

§ 224. IV. When the subordinate is adverbial, and closely connected to the word which it modifies by a conjunctive adverb;

§ 225. V. When the subordinate is adverbial, and is introduced by one of the conjunctions *that*, *as*, or *than*, referring to a corresponding word in the leading clause. The corresponding words or antecedents preceding these conjunctions that do not allow a comma to separate them, are:

Such, *So* } before *that;*
As, *Not so* } before *as;*
Other, *Else*, or any comparative } before *than.*

Caution.—*It must be observed, however, that the foregoing exceptions are overruled, and do not apply in the following cases;*

§ 226. I. When the subordinate precedes the leading clause (by § 241);

§ 227. II. When the subordinate clause is considerably removed from the word which it modifies, by other words intervening;

§ 228. III. When the term modified by the subordinate clause is compound;

§ 229. IV. When there are several subordinate clauses modifying the same term.

EXAMPLES.

Wealth is of no real use,[220] unless it be well employed.

Decide not by authoritative rules,[220] when they are inconsistent with reason.

We obey the laws of society,[220] because they are the laws of virtue.

If their lungs receive our air,[220] that moment they are free.

We should be ashamed of many of our actions,[220] were the world acquainted with our motives.

Tell me[221] when you expect your brother to arrive.

Socrates said[222] that he believed in the immortality of the soul.

I will go[224] whither thou goest.

He went away[221] when I came.

Go[221] where glory waits thee.

When beggars die,[226] there are no comets seen.

Socrates announced to his companions,[220] as they stood weeping around him,[227] that he believed in the immortality of the soul.

He will capture all the horses, mules, and cattle,[228] that he may meet in his march.

Come,[229] when you please,[229] as you please,[229] with whom you please.

What is more wonderful than the human eye,[220] that sees all around?

Remember whose eye it is[223] that sees you.

He was so much agitated[225] that he could not speak.

It is better to trust in the Lord[225] than to put confidence in man.

Hear the words[223] that I speak to thee.

So shall my word be,[220] that goeth out of my mouth.

Honor thy father and thy mother,[220] that thy days may be long in the land.

I will now retire,[220] as I am no longer wanted.

I will now retire[224] as I entered.

Exercises as before.

§ 230. When either of the clauses of a complex sentence, or if the members of a compound sentence, is broken into fragments by interstitial or subordinate interclausal points, the greater interclausal point should be elevated, if a comma, into a semicolon; if a semicolon, into a colon; in order to mark out clearly the construction of the entire sentence.

EXAMPLES.

Melissa, like the bee, gathers honey from every weed;[230] while Arachne, like the spider, sucks poison from the fairest flowers.

As we perceive the shadow to have moved along the dial,[217] but did not see it moving;[230] and it appears that the grass has grown,[220] though nobody ever saw it grow:[230] so the advances we make in knowledge,[220] as they consist of such minute steps,[220] are perceivable only by the distance.

§ 231—*Note.* Whenever the observance of this rule would defeat the very object of it, that is, render the sentence more obscure, it must not be insisted on.

Contracted Sentences.

§ 232. When a complex or compound sentence is contracted by ellipsis, a comma is generally used to mark the place where the omitted words belong.

§ 233. But the comma indicating an ellipsis may be omitted when the members are very short, and where the style is lively and rapid, provided there is not the least danger of obscurity.

EXAMPLES.

The wise man considers what he wants; the fool,[232] what he abounds in.

Life is precious, and death[233] certain.

§ 234. The contraction of a sentence by abridgment does affect its punctuation;

§ 235—Except in the case in which a substantive clause, *before* the leading verb, and separated from it by a comma, is abridged into a participial *phrase;* this demands the removal of the comma. Thus:

That he is homely,[226] is nothing.
Abridged. His being homely[235] is nothing.

§ 236. When a sentence is contracted by combination, so that the resulting partial compound contains a compound term, it must be punctuated by the rules for Interstitial Punctuation (§ 245–268.)

THE COINCIDING OF POINTS.

§ 237. Whenever two rules coincide in requiring a point at one place, if not the same, the greater point supersedes the less. But if one of them is a dash, or the period indicating an abbreviation, both points should be used. Nevertheless, with the single exception of the exclamation point, it is not allowed to double any point.

EXAMPLES.

The question,[220] What is beauty?[237] will puzzle any one to answer.

If he desires the degree of A. M.,[237] let him see that he deserves it.

I take—[209] eh!—[237] as much exercise—[209] eh!—[237] as I can, Madam Gout.

INDEPENDENTS AND CONTEXTUALS.

§ 238. All words and phrases that are either independent (absolute) or contextual, or in any manner disconnected with the structural part of the sentence, must be separated from it by one comma, or two if necessary.

Contextual words are those that indicate the connection of the sentence, as a whole, with the paragraph, or the body of the discourse.

To the foregoing rule there are two exceptions:

§ 239—1. Interjections, exclamations, and some vocative words and phrases are followed by the exclamation point.

§ 240—2. The responsive words, *yes*, *yea*, *no*, *nay*, are sometimes separated from the rest of the sentence by a colon.

EXAMPLES.

Secondly,[238] this conduct is forbidden in the Bible, in express terms.

Unquestionably,[238] Napoleon was a genius.

Why,[238] this is rank injustice.

Well,[238] do as you please.

Generally speaking,[238] the slaves were contented.

In the last place,[238] my hearers,[238] this is a word of comfort.

Boy,[238] bring me my horse.

Come,[238] Anthony,[238] and young Octavius,[238] come,[238] revenge yourselves alone on Cassius.

To return to my subject,[238] I would remark that these principles are acknowledged by all who have discussed the question.

This said,[238] he formed thee,[238] Adam,[238]—thee,[238] O man!

Merciful Heaven![239] how can we save him?

Alas![239] my noble boy![239] that thou shouldst die!

Soldiers and fellow-citizens![239] I congratulate you on this victory.

No:[240] you never think of me now.

Has he left you?—Yes:[240] but I care not.

Transpositions.

§ 241. When there is a transposition of the elements of a proposition, so that an adverbial, or complementary, or objective element comes *before* the verb, or if there is any other departure from the natural order, a comma or two must be introduced to mark the transposition.

But to this rule, there are the following exceptions:

§ 242—I. When the sentence is not very long, and the inversion is so complete as to throw the subject last, no comma is required.

§ 243—II. When the inversion is made by placing some adjunct at the beginning of the sentence, the comma may be omitted, if its omission will not cause obscurity.

§ 244—III. Transpositions are so frequent and natural in poetry that it is not necessary to use the same strictness in marking them as in prose.

Examples.

To those who labor,[241] sleep is doubly pleasant.

Of all the passions,[241] pride is the most unsocial.

All the appearances of nature,[241] I was careful to study.

Whether such a person as Homer ever existed,[241] we can not say.

Whom he loveth,[241] he chasteneth.

Silver and gold have[242] I none.

Down from this towering peak[243] poured a roaring torrent.

Through her rags[243] do the winds of winter blow bleak.

In infancy[243] the mind is peculiarly ductile.

To thee[244] I pour my prayer.
Remote from towns[244] he ran his godly race.

III. INTERSTITIAL PUNCTUATION.

§ 245. The only point that is used to indicate the subdivisions of a clause or member of a sentence is the comma; and the pupil needs again to be cautioned to use it *only* where the rules strictly require it.

Compound Terms.

§ 246. The interstitial punctuation of a compound term depends upon the simplicity of its components, and the presence or absence of the connecting conjunction. If the components are simple terms, or terms almost simple (such as a noun accompanied by a single modifier, or a verb with its adverb), united by a conjunction expressed, a separating point is not necessary.

§ 247. But if the components are decidedly complex, or if the conjunctions are not expressed before every component but the first, separating commas are demanded.

§ 248. If the components are arranged in pairs, commas are placed between the pairs.

EXAMPLES.

Liberty[246] and eloquence have been united in all ages.

We often see rank[246] or riches preferred to merit[246] or talent.

The good[246] and the evil grow together in this world.

Industry[246] and honesty[246] and temperance are all essential to happiness.

Alfred the Great was a brave,[247] pious,[247] and patriotic prince.

The mountains rise like vast supernatural intelligences, taking a material shape,[247] and drawing around themselves a drapery of awful grandeur.

It is wonderful what genius[246] and perseverance will do.

Sink or swim,[248] live or die,[248] survive or perish,[248] I give my hand[246] and my heart to this vote.

§ 249. An apparent compound term is sometimes formed by introducing an explanatory or equivalent word or phrase after the word it explains, with the conjunction *or*. Whenever there is the least danger of obscurity, the added phrase must be preceded by a comma.

EXAMPLES.

The happiest bird of our spring is the Bob-o'-Lincoln,[249] or Bobolink,[220] as he is commonly called.

He bought a book called "City Scenes,[249] or a Peep into London."

§ 250. When the compound term is a modifying element, and comes immediately before the word that it modifies; or when it is a series of verbs in immediate connection with their common subject going before them, or their common object coming after; or when it is an adverbial, complementary, or supplementary element coming directly after the verb; then no comma should intervene to separate the compound term from its proper syntactical connection.

EXAMPLES.

White,[247] red,[247] and yellow[250] roses were growing on intertwined bushes.

Alfred the Great was a brave,[247] wise,[247] and patriotic[250] prince.

The discourse was beautifully,[247] elegantly,[247] and forcibly[250] delivered.

The child[250] can creep,[247] skip,[247] walk,[247] and run.

The arts[250] prolong,[247] comfort,[247] and cheer[250] human life.

True politeness is[250] modest,[247] unpretending,[247] and generous.

Learn[250] patience,[247] calmness,[247] self-command,[247] disinterestedness,[247] love.

ADJUNCTS.

§ 251. When a preposition is removed some way from from its antecedent by the intervention of several words, a comma is often placed before it to prevent obscurity.

§ 252. This rule also applies to the word *to* used as the sign of the infinitive.

§ 253. If the preposition is immediately preceded by some adverb qualifying it, the comma must of course precede the adverb.

EXAMPLES.

The moonbeams dance to and fro with the breeze and the waves,[251] through the livelong night.

Methinks this suit needs not be long pending,[217] but may be decided without any more ado,[251] with a great deal of equity.

From their sides spout cataracts of flame,[251] amidst the pealing thunder of a fatal artillery.

As I was stepping down from the fence,[220] I saw a large snake coiled up,[253] just under my outstretched foot.

Tyrants,[220] when reason and argument make against them,[220] have recourse to violence,[252] to silence their opponents.

Subject Pointing.

§ 254. When the grammatical subject of a proposition is directly followed by its verb, or is separated only a little way from it by the intervention of a few words, no comma should be allowed to precede the verb, so as to divide it from the subject.

§ 255. But when the entire or logical subject is very long, so as to throw the grammatical subject some distance from the verb, or if the logical subject, though quite short, contains a verb, then a comma is generally necessary to separate the subject and predicate of the proposition.

EXAMPLES.

Grand,[247] gloomy,[247] and peculiar,[241] he[254] sat upon his throne a sceptered hermit.

He that takes up the opinions of any church without examining them,[255] has neither truly searched after truth,[217] nor found it.

He who teaches,[255] often learns himself.

The idea of what ought to be,[255] rises from the bosom of what is.

Appositives.

§ 256. Two or more nouns, or nouns and adjectives, grouped together so as to form one complex name, such as *Paul the Apostle*, *Peter the Great*, *the river Indus*, *the Rocky Mountains*, etc., must not be separated by a comma.

§ 257. But if the latter word of such a group is a noun clearly in apposition with the former, or if it is an adjective or participle accompanied by several modifying words, a comma should be placed before it.

EXAMPLES.

The Caucasus[256] Mountains and the Ural[256] Mountains form the boundary between Europe and Asia.

John C. Calhoun,[257] the greatest of American statesmen,[255] was never president of the United States.

Worship thy creator,[257] God.

The cotton was bought by Jones[256] Brothers and Co.

Roll on,[238] thou[256] dark and deep blue ocean,[238] roll!

Thou,[238] Father,[238] mark'st the tears I shed.

The majestic main,[257] a secret world of wonders in itself,[255] sounds His eternal praise.

James,[257] awkward in his person,[255] was not qualified to command respect.

PARENTHETICALS AND INTERPOSITIONS.

§ 258. Any word, phrase, or clause, that is inserted in a sentence to explain the leading proposition, or introduce an incidental remark, is called a *parenthesis*, and must be designated as such by being inclosed in the curve marks (such as those which inclose this clause).

EXAMPLES.

Matilda ([258] such was the lady's name)[258] smiled sweetly at this address.

Are you still ([258] I fear from the tone of your letter you must be)[258] troubled with these apprehensions?

For I know that in me ([258] that is, in my flesh)[258] dwelleth no good thing.

§ 259. Some recent writers use, instead of parenthetic curves, two dashes, to inclose a parenthesis; but the practice, though it may be tolerated, is hardly to be encouraged.

§ 260. Sometimes a word, phrase, or clause, though properly belonging to the sentence, is introduced in such a manner as to interrupt the regular connection of the other words of the sentence, somewhat in the manner of a parenthesis. This is called an *interposed* word or phrase, and it must always be separated by points from the rest of the sentence.

§ 261. If the interposed phrase is short and simple, so as to require no commas within it, a comma before and after it is proper.

§ 262. But if it contains a comma in itself, then it must be preceded and followed by a dash.

EXAMPLES.

The passions of mankind,[260] however,[260] frequently blind them.

Nothing on earth,[261] I tell you,[261] could induce me to reveal it.

Nations,[261] as well as men,[261] fail in nothing that they boldly and resolutely attempt.

Every passion,[261] however base or unworthy,[261] is eloquent.

I would stamp God's name,[261] and not Satan's,[261] upon every innocent pleasure.

Milton was,[261] like Dante,[261] a statesman and a lover.

In the heathen world,—[262] where man had no divine revelation,[217] but followed the impulse of nature alone,—[262] religion was the basis of civil government.

§ 263. This rule may be interpreted to cover those forms of quotation in which the specification of the author is succinctly given near the beginning of the quotation.

EXAMPLES.

"I am glad,"[263] said the priest,[263] "that you are come."

"With all thy getting,"[263] says Solomon,[263] "get understanding.

REPETITIONS AND ENUMERATIONS.

§ 264. Words or phrases repeated for the sake of emphasis must be separated by commas.

§ 265. But if the repetition is abrupt, or proceeds from hesitation, or is used for the sake of introducing a new thought, a dash is more properly used.

EXAMPLES.

Verily,[264] verily,[264] I say unto you, etc.

Quit, [264] oh! quit this mortal frame.

It is—[255] it is—[265] the cannon's opening roar.

He is gone—[265] gone to return no more.

§ 266. When there is an enumeration of items, or examples, or particulars, if it is formally introduced by such words as *thus*, *following*, *as follows*, *this*, *these*, etc., the whole enumeration must be preceded by a colon, and the several items separated by semicolons or commas, according to their length.

§ 267. But if no such formal introductory word is used, and if the enumeration comes at the end of a sentence, a semicolon must precede it, and commas must separate the items.

§ 268. Sometimes it is thought desirable to denote the enumeration in the form of a column or vertical list, still retaining its sentential connection with the foregoing matter. In that case a dash must precede the enumeration.

§ 269. If an enumeration is introduced into the very body of a sentence, whether preceded by the connective *as* or not, it is to be accompanied and separated by commas throughout.

EXAMPLES.

The human family is composed of five races, as follows:[266] the Caucasian,[266] the Mongolian,[266] the American,[266] the Maylayan,[266] and the African.

There are four genders;[267] the masculine,[267] the feminine,[267] the common,[267] and the neuter.

I will put you these articles at the following prices, viz.—[268]

Sugar @ 18 cents;
Coffee @ 32 "
Rice @ 15 "

Articles for which *we* are dependent on foreign commerce,—[262] as coffee,[269] tea,[269] pepper,[269] cinnamon,[269] and spice,—[262] are,[261] after all,[262] not among the necessaries of life.

V. QUOTATION POINTING.

In addition to the rules for the marking of quotations given in the Preliminary Exercises toward the beginning of this Manual, the following are needed to complete this branch of the subject:

§ 270. If one quotation is included within another, the interior one is marked by a *single* inverted comma at the beginning and a single apostrophe at the end. If the interior quotation contains still another, the marks are doubled again.

§ 271. When the quotation extends through several paragraphs of prose, or stanzas of poetry, the double inverted commas stand at the beginning of each paragraph or stanza, and the double apostrophes at the end of the last only.

§ 272. If the quoted poetry is not broken into stanzas, a single inverted comma stands at the beginning of each line.

§ 273. If the quotation is introduced by some such words as *thus*, *following*, *as follows*, *these words*, etc., it should be preceded by a colon.

§ 274. If the quotation is preceded by such words as those mentioned in the foregoing rule, and is broken from the preceding part of the discourse so as to begin a new paragraph, it should also be preceded by a dash after the colon.

EXAMPLES.

A minister of some experience remarks,[220] [12]"I have heard more than one sufferer say,[220] [270]'I am thankful;[215] God is good to me;'[215,270] and,[220] when I heard that,[220] I said,[220] [270]'It is good to be afflicted.'"[270,12]

I was struck with this sentence:[273—274] [12]"Channing,[257] the friend of humanity in every condition and under every garb,[255] says,[220] [270]'When I consider the greater simplicity of their lives,[247] and their greater openness to the spirit of Christianity,[220] I am not sure but that the [270]"golden age"[270] of manners is to begin among those who are now despaired of for their want of refinement.'"[270,12]

What a wonderful mixture of humor and pathos there is in these verses of Oliver Wendell Holmes'![5—274]

[271]"But now he walks the streets,[216]
And he looks at all he meets
So forlorn;[215]

And he shakes his feeble head,[232]
That it seems as if he said,[220]
[270]'They are gone!'[5, 270]

[271]"The mossy marbles rest
On the lips that he has press'd
In their bloom;[215]
And the names he lov'd to hear
Have been carved for many a year
On the tomb.[2]

[271]"My grandmama has said—[259]
Poor old lady![5] *she* is dead
Long ago—[259]
That he had a Roman nose,[216]
And his cheek was like a rose
In the snow.[2]

[271]"But now his nose is thin,[216]
And it rests upon his chin
Like a staff;[215]
And a crook is in his back,[216]
And a melancholy crack
In his laugh.[2]

[271]"I know it is a sin
For me to sit and grin
At him here;[215]
But the old three-corner'd hat,[247]
And the breeches,[247] and all that,[255]
Are so queer![5]

[271]"And if I should live to be
The last leaf upon the tree
In the spring,[220]
Let them smile as I do now,[251]
At the old forsaken bough
Where I cling."[2, 271]

[272]'O thou great Movement of the Universe,[247]
'Or Change,[247] or Flight of Time,—[220, 259] for ye are one!—[5, 259]
'That bearest silently this visible scene
'Into night's shadow and the streaming rays
'Of starlight,[238] whither art thou bearing me?[4]

'I feel the mighty current bear me on,[217]
'Yet know not whither.[2] Man foretells afar
'The courses of the stars;[215] the very hour
'He knows,[227] when they shall darken or grow bright;[215]
'Yet doth the eclipse of Sorrow and of Death
'Come unforewarn'd.[2] Who next of those I love,[255]
'Shall pass from life,[217] or,[261] sadder yet,[261] shall fall
'From virtue?[4] Strife with foes,[247] or bitterer strife
'With friends,[247] or shame and general scorn of men—[259]
'Which who can bear?—[4, 259] or the fierce rack of pain,[255]
'Lie they within my path?[4] Or shall the years
'Push me,[261] with soft and inoffensive pace,[261]
'Into the stilly twilight of my age?[4]
'Or do the portals of another life
'E'en now,[220] while I am glorying in my strength,[220]
'Impend around me?[4] Oh![5] beyond that bourne,[241]
'In the vast cycle of being which begins
'At that broad threshold,[241] with what fairer forms
'Shall the great law of change and progress clothe
'Its workings?[4] Gently—[259] so have good men taught—[259]
'Gently,[247] and without grief,[241] the old shall glide
'Into the new;[215] the eternal flow of things,[261]
'Like a bright river of the fields of heaven,[261]
'Shall journey onward in perpetual peace."[2, 271]

BRYANT.

Let the pupil be drilled by abundant exercise in dictation and the insertion of omitted points, until perfectly familiar with the foregoing rules. Such practice is valuable, not merely for the skill in punctuation which it imparts, but for the insight into sentential structure which it demands, and eventually induces.

CHAPTER XV.

VARIETY OF EXPRESSION.

§ 275. One of the acquirements most important to the young composer is the ability to express a sentiment in different ways. This is called Varying the Expression of a thought. It may be effected in several methods, all reducible to two general heads: 1. Changing the structure of the sentence; 2. Recasting the thought in a sentence entirely different.

I. CHANGE OF SENTENTIAL STRUCTURE.

§ 276. This is further reducible to three classes of operations, as follows:

1. The Use of Equivalent Elements;
2. Change of the Form of Predication;
3. Transposition of Elements.

1. THE USE OF EQUIVALENT ELEMENTS

§ 277. The three classes of sentential elements which may be said to have equivalents belonging to the several forms of Terms, Phrases, and Clauses, are—

1. Adjective Elements;
2. Substantive Elements;
3. Adverbial Elements.

§ 278. To change an element of any one of these three kinds into an element of the same function, but having a different form, is called Converting an Element.

1. THE CONVERSION OF ADJECTIVE ELEMENTS.

§ 279. An element of a sentence having the function of an adjective may be—

1. An adjective term, whether simple, complex, or compound;
2. A possessive term;
3. A noun in apposition;
4. A participial or infinitive phrase;
5. An adjunct;
6. A relative clause.

The following sentences contain examples of these according to the numbers:

1. A *frugal* man will save much.
2. *This man's* farm has made him rich.
3. Milton, *the author of Paradise Lost*, died poor.

4. The eagle, *watching his chance*, pounced upon him.
5. The heir *of great expectations* has lost all.
6. The mechanic *who is industrious* will succeed.

It is very evident that in many cases one of these forms of adjective elements is convertible into several, if not all, of the others, without any considerable alteration of the meaning. Thus in the following sentences, the adjective elements indicated by the italics are of a different form in each instance.

1. A *prudent* man will observe his associates.
4. A man *having prudence* will observe, etc.
5. A man *of prudence* will observe, etc.
6. A man *who is prudent* will observe, etc.

Again:

2. *Washington's* grave is on the bank of the Potomac.
4. The grave *containing the remains of Washington*, is on the bank, etc.
5. The grave *of Washington* is on the bank, etc.
6. The grave *that holds the remains of Washington* is on the bank, etc.

Again:

3. Columbus, *the discoverer of America*, was born in Genoa.
6. Columbus, *by whom America was discovered*, was born in Genoa

EXERCISE.

Let the pupil vary the expression in the following sentences by changing any of the adjective elements indicated by italics, into some other form.

He was a visionary of a *successful* kind.

He assumed a *ridiculous* gravity.

We pronounced him an *unskillful* workman

Their *undisciplined* bravery was *unavailable*.

The questions became *perplexing*, even *annoying*.

Thoughts, *which will never die*, are now being published to the world.

The sum of *human* happiness remains nearly the same.

My days *of pleasure* are nearly at an end.

The Baron de Hazenbury, an *experienced* warrior, feared the determination of the Swiss.

Ye *whose hearts are fresh and simple*, who have faith in God and nature, who believe that in all ages every *human* heart is human;

that in even *savage* bosoms, there are longings, yearnings, strivings, for the good (*which*) *they comprehend not;* that the *feeble* hands and *helpless*, *groping* blindly in the darkness, touch His right hand in the darkness, and are lifted up and strengthened,—listen to this *simple* story, to this song of Hiawatha!

The path *of success* in business is invariably the path of *common sense.*

This was one of the dreams *of his youth.*

He thought that he had opened a *new* way to the *opulent* East.

His *earnest* words left on my *susceptible* mind an impression *never to be effaced.*

He was *averse to mixing with society.*

His desires were *boundless.*

The nature of the Deity is *incomprehensible.*

The woman that was drowning, and the man who rescued her, are engaged to be married.

2. The Conversion of Substantive Elements.

§ 280. The different forms which a substantive element may bear in a sentence, are the following:

1. A noun or pronoun;
2. An infinitive or participle;
3. A nominal phrase, that is a noun accompanied by modifiers;
4. An infinitive or participial phrase;
5. A substantive clause.

EXAMPLES.

1. *Theft* is wrong.
2. *Stealing* is wrong.
2. It is wrong to steal.
3. *The secret appropriation of the property of another* is wrong.
4. *To take without leave what belongs to another* is wrong.
4. *Secretly taking the property of another* is wrong.
5. *That one should take what belongs to another* is wrong.

1. He never relished calculation.
2. He never loved to calculate.
2. He was never fond of calculating.
3. He never relished the process of computing numbers.

3. He was never fond of arithmetical processes.
4. He never relished computing numbers.
4. It was never agreeable to him to compute numbers.
5. It was never agreeable to him that he should compute numbers.

EXERCISE.

Convert the substantive elements italicized in the following sentences into some other form.

Attention, *application*, *accuracy*, *method*, *punctuality*, and *dispatch*, are the principal qualities required for the efficient *conduct* of business of any sort.

Repealing this or that act of parliament can not restore America to our bosom.

Forced *concessions* are not to be relied upon.

To select the best period for the action was the difficulty.

A craving for rest was to him a sure sign of impaired vigor.

Intense *earnestness* was his characteristic trait.

His scheme was *to call forth* the utmost abilities of all.

Happiness is the fruit of *doing work well.*

That you have wronged me doth appear in this.

Man's *inhumanity* to man makes countless thousands mourn.

3. CIRCUMLOCUTION.

§ 281. The conversion of any simple term into an equivalent complex term is called *circumlocution*. This name is also given to any process by which we use many words to express what might be expressed in few. The circumlocution by which we substitute a nominal phrase for a single substantive is a matter of sufficient impor tance to demand a separate exercise.

EXERCISE.

Convert the following substantives into equivalent nominal phrases:

Women—water—fire—the sun—the moon—the planets—a tyrant—a hunter—a soldier—a ruler—a lawyer—birds—a railroad—gold—iron—glass—books—friends—a school—schoolmasters—physicians—merchants—ships—music—painting—printing—poetry—history—America—Paris—Holland—St.Helena—Napoleon—Alfred—Moses—Judas.

MODEL.

Women—the fair sex—the daughters of Eve—the help-meet of man—the weaker vessel—the angels of the household, etc.

4. The Conversion of Adverbial Elements.

§ 282. Under this head we will consider:

1. The equivalents of simple adverbs;
2. The equivalents of adverbial clauses.

§ 283. I. The Equivalents of Simple Adverbs. Simple adverbs are the equivalents of adjuncts (nouns with prepositions) and can be converted into them with great facility.

EXAMPLES.

The consul resides *here—in this place.*
He met the foe *courageously—with courage.*
He will come *promptly—in due time.*
This expresses the thought *precisely—with precision.*

§ 284. II. The Equivalents of Adverbial Clauses. Adverbial clauses are susceptible of various kinds of conversion into equivalents, the principal of which are the following:

§ 285. (1.) An adverbial clause that expresses the occasion whereupon, the manner how, the reason why, or the end for which, a thing is done, or an event takes place, may be abridged in some one or more of the modes described in § § 190–198.

EXAMPLES.

When I found that I had missed the road, I retraced my steps.
Abridged. Finding that I had missed the road, I retraced my steps.
Because they have met with no disasters, they are vainly confident.
Abridged. Having met with no disasters, they are vainly confident.

§ 286. (2.) Sometimes a compound sentence is susceptible of reduction to the abridged form. This is the case when one of the members, like the subordinate clause of a complex sentence, expresses the occasion, manner, or reason, of the fact stated in the other member.

EXAMPLES.

At last the bridge was completed, and the army passed over.

Abridged. The bridge being at last completed, the army passed over.

I was exceedingly exhausted, and soon fell asleep.

Abridged. Being exceedingly exhausted, I soon fell asleep.

§ 287. (3.) A complex proposition containing a causal clause is convertible into a compound proposition with an illative member.

§ 288. An illative member is one introduced by one of the conjunctions, *therefore*, *hence*, *then*, *consequently*, *wherefore*, and *whence*. It expresses the logical conclusion or inference authorized by the foregoing member.

EXAMPLES.

Complex sentence with causal clause. The moon is eclipsed, because the earth intervenes between her and the sun.

Compound sentence with illative member. The earth intervenes between the moon and the sun; therefore the moon is eclipsed.

Complex sentence with causal clause. We dislike some persons because we do not know them well.

Compound sentence with illative member. We do not know some persons well, consequently we dislike them.

Complex sentence with causal clause. Since you are now well, you may cease taking the medicine.

Compound sentence with illative member. You are now well; hence you may cease taking the medicine.

§ 289. (4.) A conditional clause is capable of being expressed into two ways; one with the conditional conjunction expressed, the other with it understood. In the latter form, the subject is put after the verb or its first auxiliary, as in interrogative sentences.

EXAMPLES.

If the cause were good, he would not be so fearful of defeat.

Without the conjunction. Were the cause good, he would not be so fearful of defeat.

If I had an ax, I would cut down this tree.

With conjunction understood. Had I an ax, I would cut down this tree.

§ 290. (5.) A sentence containing a conditional clause may be converted into a compound sentence, with either an imperative or interrogative proposition for one of its members.

EXAMPLES.

If the cause were good, he would not be so fearful of defeat.

Conditional clause converted into an imperative member. Let the cause be good, and he will* not be so fearful of defeat.

Conditional clause converted into interrogative member. Is the cause good? He will* not be so fearful of defeat.

EXAMPLE OF A CONDITIONAL IN FOUR FORMS.

1. If you would read my story, you could judge for yourself.
2. Would you read my story, you could judge for yourself.
3. Read my story, and you can judge for yourself.
4. Will you read my story? then you can judge for yourself.

§ 291. (6.) Adversative clauses of different shades of meaning are convertible into three different forms.

§ 292 (*a.*) In one, the clause remains adversative, but the arrangement and the connective are changed.

EXAMPLE.

Though he was so rich, yet no man called him haughty.—Rich as he was, yet no man called him haughty.

§ 293. (*b.*) In a second kind the adversative clause is convertible into an adjunct with the preposition *with*, *without*, *notwithstanding*, *despite of*, etc.

EXAMPLES.

Although he has faults, I love him;—Despite of his faults, I love him.

Though he was so feeble, he devoted the whole day to study;—With all his feebleness, he devoted the whole day to study.

§ 294. (*c.*) In a third kind, the adversative connective

* Observe the change in the tense.

is changed into the modifier *however*, *whatever*, etc., limiting some word in the adversative clause.

EXAMPLE.

Though he is poor, he is respected;—However poor he is, he is respected.

Though storms come, I shall be safe;—Whatever storms come, I shall be safe.

EXAMPLES OF ADVERSATIVE CLAUSES IN THE DIFFERENT FORMS.

Though all others forsake him, I shall not:—Whoever forsakes him, I shall not.

Although it was so hot, we worked on through the day:—Hot as it was, we worked on through the day:—Despite the heat, we worked on through the day.

EXERCISE.

Convert the following sentences into their equivalents by any of the above-described methods that will apply.

The good which men do is not lost, though it is often disregarded

As they are crowded in filth, the poor cease to respect each other.

It were no virtue to bear calamities, if we did not feel them.

If you make men intelligent, they will become inventive.

Though a civilization may die, it leaves imperishable memorials.

People are rude and impolite, because they are ignorant.

We obey the laws of society, because they are the laws of virtue

While the bridegroom tarried, they all slumbered and slept.

Dare to be good, though evil may surround you.

If their lungs receive our air, that moment they are free.

2. Change of the Form of Predication.

§ 295. Of this mode of varying expression there are four kinds, each applicable to a limited number of sentences.

§ 296. I. An affirmative can often be converted into an equivalent negative, or a negative into an equivalent affirmative, by the use of a word of opposite meaning in the predicate.

EXAMPLES.

Henry is diligent.—Henry is not indolent.

The tree is not dead.—The tree is alive.

§ 297. II. A proposition in which the active voice of a transitive verb is used, can be converted so as to use the passive voice, and *vice versa.*

EXAMPLES.

Galileo invented the telescope.—The telescope was invented by Galileo.

The exercises will be conducted by one of the vice-presidents.—One of the vice-presidents will conduct the exercises.

§ 298. III. When the subject of a proposition is an infinitive coming before the verb, it can be changed in form by using the pronoun *it* as a substitute for the infinitive, and throwing the infinitive (together with its modifiers) after the predicate.

EXAMPLES.

To buy an unnecessary article merely because it is cheap, is not economical.

Changed. It is not economical to buy an unnecessary article, merely because it is cheap.

To excite false hopes is wrong.

Changed. It is wrong to excite false hopes.

§ 299. IV. A proposition containing an intransitive verb in the predicate may be changed by using the adverb *there* as a substitute for the subject, and throwing the entire or logical subject after the predicate.

This idiomatic arrangement is preferable when a verb that is commonly copulative is used attributively, or when the predicate verb is without modifiers, and the logical subject is very long.

EXAMPLES.

Silence was in heaven.—There was silence in heaven.

In Antioch, a man celebrated for his wisdom and piety lived.—In Antioch, there lived a man celebrated for his wisdom and piety.

A poor exile of Erin came to the beach.—There came to the beach a poor exile of Erin.

EXERCISE.

Let the teacher select any piece, say one in the reading-book used by the class, or taken from any book within the comprehension of the pupils, and require them to vary as many of the sentences as can be, by the conversion of their elements or the change of their predicates, by any of the modes described in this chapter. It must be remembered that the object is not to improve the style, but simply to familiarize the pupils with the various modes of expressing a thought; the selection of the best mode being reserved for a future chapter.

3. Transposition of Elements.

§ 300. There is a certain order in which the elements of a sentence are said to come *naturally;* an order which results mainly from the fact that, according to the genius of the English language, the grammatical relations between the words are indicated, to a very large extent, by their relative position. The rules for this arrangement are given in some grammars. It is not necessary to rehearse them here. It may be stated, however, that in the arrangement of adjuncts, clauses, and members, a very great freedom is allowed, and to some extent, also, in the arrangement of the essential and accidental elements of a proposition. The following examples will best illustrate this:

(1.) The verb placed before the subject.

Ebbs the crimson life-tide fast.
Fell the snow o'er all the landscape.

(2.) Attribute and subject transposed.

Great is Diana of the Ephesians.
The gist of the matter is this.

(3.) Object and verb transposed.

The withering tree its blossoms shed.
The depths of the ocean its presence confessed.

(4.) Subject and object transposed.

Eyes have they, but they see not.
Sweet strains of music hear we then.

Note. This form of transposition, as well as the preceding, can rarely be made without endangering the sense, unless either the subject or the object is a pronoun.

(5.) Object placed before the subject.

Lands he could measure; times and tides presage.

Yet a few days, and thee the all-beholding sun shall see no more in all his course.

(6.) Adverbial adjunct thrown to the beginning.

In power and wealth, exult no more.

Into that glorious world, he constantly beckons us to follow him.

To public opinion, all states must, in a measure, bow.

(7.) Adverbial adjuncts interchanged in position.

(1.) The throat of the animal was closed at last, as if by a vice, by the gladiator's hands.

(2.) The throat of the animal was closed as if by a vice, at last, by the gladiator's hands.

(3.) The throat of the animal was closed by the gladiator's hands at last, as if by a vice.

(1.) Seizing the monstrous carcass, he threw it, with an oath, far from him, as a trophy, beneath the imperial box.

(2.) Seizing the monstrous carcass, he threw it far from him, as a trophy, with an oath, beneath the imperial box.

(3.) Seizing the monstrous carcass, he threw it beneath the imperial box, far from him, as a trophy, with an oath.

(4.) Seizing the monstrous carcass, he threw it as a trophy, with an oath, far from him, beneath the imperial box.

(8.) Subordinate clause and leading clause transposed.

Whom ye ignorantly worship, him declare I unto you.

What is the right path, few take the trouble of inquiring.

All you hear believe not.

When a nation determines on war, it is wisdom to intrust their chief with plenary powers.

If there is danger that he turn out to be a Cromwell or a Napoleon, that should make them weigh well the necessity for the war.

He is a freeman, whom the truth makes free.

Because the night was dark, they could not proceed.

The foregoing embrace those forms of transposition that ordinarily occur. Let the pupil now be trained to a free use of all of them, in the transposition of the sentences in the following:

EXERCISE I.

He did not read that valuable history which you lent him.

Virgil has justly contested the praise of judgment with Homer.

A little rivulet flowed at the bottom of the garden.

There is a calm fountain of sober thought underneath our happiest mirth.

Sensible men have a strong antipathy to egotists and pedants.

We show ourselves superior to injuries by forgetfulness of them.

We approach one another in approaching the summit of a mountain.

Idleness is the most incorrigible of all evil habits.

The evening star has lighted her crystal lamp.

Books can not be profitably read without much thought.

Distinct articulation is an essential requisite of good delivery.

Try to find a reason for not being angry, before giving way to anger.

Man catches a glimpse of the vast significance of the unseen and the eternal through the dim veil of the visible and perishing.

The Muse of History, too often blind to true glory, has handed down to posterity many a destroyer of thousands of his fellow-men; she has left us in ignorance of the name of this real hero, of Haarlem.

A man can not take the full measure of his knowledge before he is hurried out of life's school; hence we are forced to regard this as only the lowest form of our existence.

EXERCISE II.

Let the teacher select some piece, and require the pupils to vary all the sentences it contains by one or more of the foregoing methods, and also by the use of synonyms.

MODEL.

1. But in all his disputations, it was an invariable maxim with him never to interrupt the most tedious or confused opponents; though, from his pithy questions, he made it evident that, from the first, he anticipated the train and consequences of their reasonings.

2. But in all his debates, his invariable rule was never to interrupt the most irksome or confused antagonists; though he proved by his pithy interrogatories that, from the first, he foresaw whither their reasonings tended, and where they would end.

3. But it was a rule from which he never swerved in all his disputations, never to break in upon the remarks of his opponents, however tedious and confused they might be; though his significant questions made it evident that he anticipated, from the first, the drift and consequence of their arguments.

4. But in all his discussions, though from his pithy questions it was made evident that he anticipated the train and consequences of his opponents' reasonings from the first; yet he made it an invariable rule never to interrupt them, no matter how irksome and prolix they might be.

5. But though he made it evident, by his pithy questions, that he foresaw from the first the train and consequences of the reasonings of his opponents in all his disputations, yet it was his invariable maxim never to check them, however tedious or confused they might be.

6. But though he anticipated from the first, the drift and conclusions of his opponents' arguments, as was made evident by his pithy questions, yet it was a maxim from which he never swerved in any disputation, not to interrupt even the most tedious and confused of them.

7. But to interrupt opponents, however tedious or confused in their remarks, was what he never allowed himself to do in any of his disputations; though it was made evident by his pithy questions that, from the first, the train and consequences of their reasonings were anticipated by him.

II. RECASTING THE SENTENCE.

§ 301. The mode of varying the expression, which is called "recasting the thought in a different sentence," is one that is not subjected to any fixed rule or described by definite terms. It is the imitation of just such differences as constitute the peculiarities of individual styles. What words a writer may select to express a thought depends on an incalculable combination of accidents, and the variety of possible expressions for any thought it is impossible to designate. All the exercises under this head must be purely the result of the pupil's own ingenuity. The following model will show what is intended:

It is required to recast in different sentences the expression, *All men must die.*

1. We must all die.
2. All mankind must die.
3. Death is the fate of all men.
4. It is fated that all men shall die.
5. Death is the inevitable lot of all.
6. The dissolution of our existence is fated.
7. It is a law of nature that human life shall have its termination.
8. Human life is limited.

9. There is nothing more certain than death.
10. Death is the fate that awaits all men.
11. Death is the unavoidable destiny of all that live.
12. Nothing is more certain than that we all must die.
13. Man is mortal.
14. Mortality is a necessary condition of human nature.
15. All the paths of life lead unto the grave.
16. Every man must pay the debt of nature.
17. We must all return to the dust.
18. Every man must surrender his hold on life.

Let the teacher dictate short and easy sentences to be thus varied by recasting, to the extent of the pupil's abilities.

CHAPTER XVI.

THE TRANSLATION OF POETRY INTO PROSE.

§ 302. Before applying the principles of the preceding chapter to the rendering of English poetry into English prose, such as will not transgress any of the rules of style yet delivered, it is necessary to explain and enumerate what are called *poetic licenses.* These are forms of expression, more or less opposed to what the rules of prose style require, which the poets are allowed to use, partly to compensate for the restrictions laid upon them by the demands of meter and rhyme, and partly because the very irregularity thus allowed them imparts an indefinable charm to their phraseology. Yet these irregularities must not be looked upon as innovations. On the contrary, nearly all are ancient forms that were in common use when the language was in the freedom of its youth. What the poets demand is that they shall not be forced by the usages of modern prose to lay aside these ancient forms, now invested with the peculiar charm of antiquity. Those poetic licenses which can not be thus accounted for as relics of the antique, will be found to be the imitations of classical idioms, whose claim to allowance is of the same nature. The very spirit and genius of poetry is fantastic: its dress may well correspond. But far other are the aims of prose, and hence, for prose there are no licenses. Even the poet is not allowed every liberty. Though he may draw upon the vocabulary and the syntax of the entire language, past as well as present, and even imitate the peculiarities of the classic tongues, yet beyond this he can not go. He must have precedent, Saxon, Norman, or classic, for every departure he makes from prose usage. Thus it comes to pass that all the poetic licenses may be specified and generalized. We reduce them, first, to three general heads:

1. Peculiarities of diction;
2. Syntactical violences;
3. Strong figures.

I. PECULIARITIES OF POETIC DICTION.

§ 303. These may be conveniently considered under these three heads:

1. Words rarely found elsewhere than in poetry;
2. Peculiar forms of words;
3. Compounds peculiar to the poets.

§ 304. I. Of the words rarely found elsewhere than in poetry, there are:

(*a.*) *Nouns*, such as benison, emprise, fane, guerdon, ken, welkin, sheen;

(*b.*) *Adjectives*, such as darkling, darksome, globous, agape;

(*c.*) *Verbs*, such as ween, trow, espy.

(*d.*) *Prepositions* or *adverbs*, such as neath, besouth, thorough, sans, etc.

§ 305. II. Of the peculiar forms of words, there are:

(*a.*) Primitives, used as if they had no derivative of the part of speech required. Such as

amaze for amazement	lone for lonely
adorn for adorned	scant for scanty
acclaim for acclamation	slope for sloping
consult for consultation	submiss for submission
even for evening	yon for yonder
fount for fountain	list for listen
helm for helmet	ope for open
lament for lamentation	hark for hearken
morn for morning	dark for darken
plaint for complaint	threat for threaten
weal for wealth	sharp for sharpen
disturb for disturbance	wilder for bewilder
fail for failure	lure for allure
dread for dreadful	reave for bereave
drear for dreary	vail for avail
hoar for hoary.	bide for abide

(*b.*) Abbreviated forms of words; such as

targe for target	corse for corpse
ebon for ebony	eve for even
vermil for vermilion	

(*c.*) Words enlarged by paragoge; such as

paly for pale	steepy for steep
stilly for still	vasty for vast

(*d.*) Adjectives formed by the suffix *y*, and adverbs by *ly*, such as are not common in prose; such as

dimply	sheety	writhy
gleamy	spiry	haply
heapy	steely	inly
moony	towery	felly

(*e.*) Verbs formed by the prefix *be*, and adverbs by the prefix *a*, used where the primitive form, or some other derivative form, would have been used in prose; such as

bedim	begird	beweep
bespread	bespray	(*part.* besprent)
bedeck	(*part.* bedight)	adown
anear	aneath	atween
atwixt	aright	aleft

These adverbs are often used as prepositions.

§ 306. III. Compounds peculiar to the poets.

world-rejoicing
dewy-skirted
hollow-whispering
sky-woven
strange-voiced
ill-omened
hell-doomed
all-bearing
famine-struck

II. SYNTACTICAL VIOLENCES.

§ 307. These may be arranged under the five following heads:

1. Violent ellipsis;
2. Pleonasm;
3. Hyperbaton;
4. Enallage;
5. Foreign idioms.

§ 308. I. Violent ellipsis.

(*a.*) Of the article.

What dreadful pleasure! there to stand sublime,
Like shipwreck'd mariner on desert coast.—BEATTIE.
Brought death into our world, and all our woe,
With loss of Eden.—MILTON.

(*b.*) Of the relative.

For is there aught in sleep can charm the wise?—THOMSON.

(*c.*) Of the antecedent.

Who steals my purse, steals trash.—SHAKESPEARE.
Sleeping found by whom they dread.—MILTON.

(*d.*) Of the principal verb.

Who does the best his circumstance allows,
Does well, acts nobly; angels could no more.—YOUNG
To whom thus Eve, yet sinless.—MILTON.
What would this man?—POPE.

(*e.*) Of a preposition, thus making an intransitive verb take an object, apparently:

Gazing the inverted landscape, half afraid
To meditate the blue profound below.—THOMSON.

§ 309. II. Pleonasm.

It curled not the Tweed alone, that breeze.—Scott.
And the moon, it was under my feet.—Wesley.

§ 310. III. Hyperbaton, or the transposition of words from their natural syntactical place.

No hive hast thou of hoarded sweets.—Allen.
Straight knew him all the bands
Of angels under watch.—Milton.
Parts the fine locks, her graceful head that deck.—Darwin.
To slowly trace the forest's shady scene.—Byron.
When first thy sire to send on earth
Virtue, his darling child, design'd.—Gray.
And rage he may, but he shall rage in vain.—Pope.
Peeping from forth their alleys green.—Collins.
Robs me of that which not enriches him.—Shakespeare.
When beauty, Eden's bowers within,
First stretched the arm to deeds of sin.—Hogg.

§ 311. IV. Enallage, the use of one part of speech or of one modification of a word for another.

(*a.*) The most common enallage among the poets is the use of the adjective for the adverb.

They fall successive and successive rise.—Pope.
Thither continual pilgrims crowded still.—Thomson.
His praise, ye winds, that from four quarters blow,
Breathe soft or loud.—Milton.

(*b.*) The possessive form of a noun limiting the word *self* instead of the compound personal pronoun.

Affection's self deplores thy youthful doom.—Byron.
Thoughtless of beauty, she was beauty's self.—Thomson.

(*c.*) Adjectives for nouns, to express qualities that could not properly be so expressed in prose.

Earth's meanest son, all trembling, prostrate falls,
And on the boundless of thy goodness calls.—Young.
To thy large heart give utterance due; thy heart
Contains of good, wise, just, the perfect shape.—Milton.

§ 312. V. Foreign idioms, mostly imitations of classical constructions; a tendency that may account for several of the preceding irregularities.

(*a.*) Giving to the imperative mood a first or third person.

Turn we a moment fancy's rapid flight.—THOMSON.
And what is reason? Be she thus defin'd:
Reason is upright stature in the soul.—YOUNG.

(*b.*) Using the infinitive substantively with a greater freedom than is proper in prose.

He knew
Himself to sing, and build the lofty rhyme.—MILTON.
For not to have been dip'd in Lethe lake
Could save the son of Thetis from to die.—SPENSER.

(*c.*) Using participles after the manner of the Latin.

He came, and, standing in the midst, explain'd
The peace rejected, but the truce obtained.—POPE.

(*d.*) Using *or* and *nor* for *either* and *neither*, corresponding with a following *or* or *nor*.

Or by the lazy Scheldt or wandering Po.—GOLDSMITH.
Wealth heap'd on wealth, nor truth, nor safety buys.—JOHNSON.

III. STRONG FIGURES.

§ 313. It is of course to be expected that the style of poetry should be more abundant in what are called figures of speech than ordinary prose. But in translating poetry into prose, there is no necessity to change any of the figures, unless it be the stronger forms of *metonymy* that occur. Metonymy consists in the transfer of some name or epithet from its proper object to another to which it sustains some relation. The following examples will illustrate this kind of figures.

The plowman homeward plods his *weary* way.—GRAY.
And *drowsy* tinklings lull the distant folds —GRAY.
Imbitter'd more and more from *peevish* day to day.—THOMSON.

All thin and naked to the *numb cold* night.—SHAKESPEARE.
The *warbling* hill, the *lowing* vale.—MALLET.
In the *happy* garden placed.—MILTON.

Of course some of these metonymies can only be reduced by circumlocutions; others by a simple transfer of the words.

"The weary plowman plods his way homeward"—is so near the meaning of the original that it may be allowed to stand for the prose rendering. In the second example, "tinklings that make one feel drowsy," is surely prosaic enough. Perhaps it is not necessary in every case to reduce the metonymy to its literal meaning, as figures of this class are certainly allowable in prose.

The careful study of the foregoing peculiarities of poetic diction will enable the pupil to perform the very improving exercise of turning poetry into good prose. The models will show what is intended.

"Now fades the glimm'ring landscape on the sight,
And all the air a solemn stillness holds,
Save where the beetle wheels his droning flight,
And drowsy tinklings lull the distant folds:

"Save, that from yonder ivy-mantled tower,
The moping owl does to the moon complain
Of such as, wand'ring near her secret bower,
Molest her ancient, solitary reign.

"Beneath those rugged elms, that yew-tree's shade,
Where heaves the turf in many a mold'ring heap,
Each in his narrow cell forever laid,
The rude forefathers of the hamlet sleep."

THE SAME TRANSLATED INTO PROSE.

The glimmering landscape now fades upon the sight, and a solemn stillness holds all the air, except where the beetle wheels his droning flight, and drowsy tinklings lull the distant folds; (and) except that the moping owl, from yonder tower mantled with ivy, complains to the moon of such as wander near her secret bower, and molest her ancient solitary reign. The rude forefathers of the hamlet, each laid forever in his narrow cell, sleep beneath those rugged elms, (and) in the shade of that yew-tree, where the turf heaves in many a moldering heap.

'Haste hither, Eve, and, worth thy sight, behold
Eastward among those trees, what glorious shape
'Comes this way moving; seems another morn
'Risen on mid-noon; some great behest from Heaven
'To us perhaps he brings, and will vouchsafe
'This day to be our guest. But go with speed,
'And what thy stores contain bring forth, and pour
'Abundance, fit to honor and receive
'Our heavenly stranger: well we may afford
'Our givers their own gifts, and large bestow
'From large bestow'd, where Nature multiplies
'Her fertile growth, and by disburd'ning grows
'More fruitful; which instructs us not to spare."

THE SAME TRANSLATED.

Eve, hasten hither, and behold eastward among those trees, what glorious shape, worth thy sight, comes moving this way. Another morn seems (to be) risen on mid-noon. Perhaps he brings some great command from Heaven to us, and will vouchsafe to be our guest this day. But go speedily, and bring forth what thy stores contain, and receive our heavenly stranger. We may well afford (to) our givers their own gifts, and largely bestow from what was largely bestowed, (living as we do) where Nature multiplies her fertile growth, and grows more fruitful by disburdening; which instructs us not to spare.

Yet a few days, and thee
The all-beholding sun shall see no more
In all his course; nor yet in the cold ground,
Where thy pale form was laid, with many tears,
Nor in the embrace of ocean, shall exist
Thy image. Earth, that nourished thee, shall claim
Thy growth, to be restored to earth again.
And, lost each human trace, surrendering up
Thine individual being, shalt thou go
To mix forever with the elements,
To be a brother to the insensible rock,
And to the sluggish clod, which the rude swain
Turns with his share, and treads upon.

TRANSLATED INTO PROSE.

After a few days, the sun that beholds all things shall see thee no more in all his course; and thy image shall exist neither in the cold ground, where thy pale form shall have been laid, nor in the embrace of the ocean. The earth that nourished thee, shall claim thy growth, to be resolved to earth again. And thou, having lost each trace of humanity, surrendering up thine individual being, shalt go to mix forever with the elements, to be a brother to the insensible rock, and to the sluggish clod, which the rude swain turns with his share, and which he treads upon.

QUESTIONS FOR REVIEW AND EXAMINATION,

PROMISCUOUSLY ARRANGED.

What kind of style is required in the contributions of newspaper correspondents? What is the distinction between the constitution of a phrase and its office? Which are the accidental elements of a proposition? What is a simple sentence? What connectives are used to join clauses of time to their antecedents? What is an adversative clause, and by what connectives is it joined to its antecedent? What is the rule for the case of the subject of a dependent clause when it is expressed in the abridgment? What points are used as interclausal, and what are their comparative separating powers? When different rules require different points at the same place, how are the conflicting requirements adjusted? What is the rule for the pointing of a parenthesis? What is circumlocution? Are poetic licenses generally innovations or antiquated forms? What is metonymy? What is narration?

By what should all business letters be characterized? What is the distinction between subordinate and co-ordinate connectives? What are the four kinds of propositions, and how are they distinguished? What is the distinction between adjective and adverbial modifiers? What is a complex sentence? Which are the five kinds of clauses of manner? What are compound sentences? How many cases of abridgment are there, and which are they? What point is used to indicate some change or interruption in the proper course of the sentence? What are the rules for pointing interposed phrases? Of what are most adverbs equivalents?

What is the character of those poetic licenses that are not antiquated forms? What are the four parts of a letter? What rule is given to guide the young writer in letters of friendship? What is meant by the antecedent, and what by the subsequent of a subordinate connective? What are the elements of a proposition? Which parts of speech may be used as adjective modifiers? What is a subordinate clause? In what way are clauses of correspondence connected to their antecedents? What are the components of a compound sentence called? In what two ways may a substantive clause be abridged? What are the rules for pointing between the members of a compound sentence? How are independent and contextual words and phrases pointed? What are the two exceptions to these rules? What is the rule for the pointing of an interposition near the beginning of a quotation, indicating the author of it? What kinds of adverbial clauses are capable of abridgment?

Why are there no licenses for prose? Where should the date of a letter be placed? What common errors should be avoided in familiar letters? What kind of subordinate connectives are used in phrases? Explain the distinction between immediate and remote elements? When are adjuncts adjective, and when adverbial? What is the distinction between a dependent and an incorporated clause? In what way are clauses of proportion connected to their antecedents? What is the distinction between a full and a partial compound? In what two ways may an adverbial clause be abridged? What are the rules for pointing the separation between the parts of partial compound sentences? What are the rules for the pointing of transpositions? What three exceptions to them? What are the rules for the pointing of repetitions?

What kind of compound sentence is capable of being changed into the form of an abridgment? What limit or restriction must even a poet observe in his licenses? If a letter is intended for any other than a relative or very intimate friend, of what two parts should the address consist? What are terms? What are adjuncts? What is the distinction between the essential and the accidental elements of a proposition? Which parts of speech may be used as adverbial modifiers? When is a subordinate clause substantive? In what way are clauses of consequence connected to their antecedents? What are appended members, and what connectives do they use? What is punctuation? What is the punctuation for appended members? What point is used to indicate divisions in sentences less than clauses? What are the rules for pointing an enumeration of particulars? What is the equivalent of a complex sentence containing a causal clause? To what three general heads may poetic licenses be reduced? Give some forms of subscription of a letter intended for a person who is not a relative or an intimate friend. What are connectives? What are adjunct phrases? Which are the essential elements of a proposition? What is the complementary element of a proposition? When is a subordinate clause adjective? In what way are clauses of equality joined to their antecedents?

Of what is each partial compound sentence the resultant? What is the true intention in using points? What is the general rule for separating a subordinate clause from the rest of the sentence? What are the five exceptions to this general rule? In what four cases do these exceptions not hold, the case being governed by the general rule? Into what three forms is a complex sentence containing a conditional clause reducible? What five forms of words are peculiar to poetry? How are letters (epistles) classified? What is the distinction between a simple, a complex, and a compound term?

Which are the co-ordinate connectives used to connect the components of compound terms? What is the subject of a declarative proposition? By what other names is the complementary element of a proposition known? What is always the connective of an adjective clause? In what way are clauses of inequality connected to their antecedents? Into how many simple propositions may every compound proposition be resolved? What is the general caution concerning the use of points? What is the rule for the punctuation of an alternative introduced by the conjunction *or*? Under what two heads may all modes of varying the expression be reduced?

To what three heads may all peculiarities of poetic diction be reduced? What is the distinction between veritable and simulated letters? What is a phrase? What are components? What is the predicate of a declarative proposition? What is the object of a transitive verb? When is a dependent clause adverbial? What four kinds of clauses express adverbial relations? In what two ways may complex sentences be contracted? Under what four general divisions may Punctuation be discussed? What are official letters? What are news-letters? What kinds of topics may be treated in news-letters? What is the basis of a phrase? What are modifiers? Into what two classes are modifiers divided? How are phrases named? What is a sentence? What is the distinction between independent and structural terms? What is the distinction between the grammatical and the logical subject? What is the distinction between the grammatical and the logical predicate? What is always the subject of an imperative proposition? What is the distinction between the primary and the secondary object? What is the distinction between the direct and the indirect object? What kinds of verbs have two direct or primary objects? What is the distinction between a restrictive and a circumstantial clause? Into what four sorts are adverbial clauses divided? What connectives are used by adverbial clauses of place? What are causal clauses, and how are they connected to their antecedents? What are conditional clauses, and how are they connected? What are final clauses, and how connected? In what does ellipsis consist? When is a dependent clause said to be abridged? What is the rule for the suppression or the retaining of a subject in an abridgment? What are the three rules for the use of the dash as a terminal point? What kind of sentence requires no point except at the end? What features of sentential structure require points? What is the rule for raising the power of a point from a less to a greater? What is the rule for the punctuation of an ellipsis? In what case does abridgment affect punctuation? What is the rule for the punctuation of a compound term? What is the rule for the punctuation required between a compound term and the rest of the sentence? What are the rules for the punctuation of displaced adjuncts? What is the rule for the pointing required between subject and predicate? What are the rules for the pointing of appositives? What are the three modes of varying the expression by changing the sentential structure?

What three classes of elements have equivalent forms into which they are convertible? What are the six forms of an adjective element? What are the five forms of a substantive element? What is an illative member? In what three ways is a complex sentence containing an adversative clause convertible? In what four ways may the form of predication be changed? Which are the eight most common forms of transposition? What five kinds of syntactical violences are allowed in poetry? What is hyperbaton? What is enallage?

BOOK THIRD.

PART FIRST.

INVENTION—RESUMED.

CHAPTER XVII.

HISTORICAL AND BIOGRAPHICAL SKETCHING.

HITHERTO the descriptions and narrations required of the pupil have been those pertaining to his own experience, or such as might have been his. He is now to be led into a different field, the field of history. He must learn to give a comprehensive view of facts beyond his own actual observation, and to describe objects, scenes, and events, more or less known to all acquainted with literature.

The great danger in this exercise is the actual surrender of all originality. As the exercise necessarily compels the pupil to look into books for his facts, and even for their relations and characterization, he will be tempted to copy, either by the eye or the memory, the very thoughts and phraseology of his authorities. To prevent this, the following plan, approved by long trial, is recommended.

Let the subject be selected, and a sufficient time allowed for the pupils that compose the class to inform themselves concerning it. By a certain day each is required to present a number of questions, calling for any facts or opinions in connection with the subject. These questions are collated by the teacher, the duplicates cast out, and all the rest distributed, without reference to their authorship, among the pupils. Each will thus receive a certain number of questions, the answers to which he must prepare by an appointed day. On that day the class is convened for the hearing of these answers, and for the interchange of views which the questions and answers may elicit. By this means the subject receives a pretty thorough discussion; the knowledge concerning it is made common stock; the ideas and views which each one entertains are loosened from the text of the authorities, and begin to assume the freedom and vigor of *digested* knowledge.

Immediately upon the close of this discussion, or it may be at some other appointed hour, the class, in the presence of the teacher, proceed to write out their views on the subject, giving any form to the composition, either narrative, essay, or letter, as he may choose to require. These compositions are then to be subjected to the processes of criticism, correction, re-writing, etc., as heretofore prescribed.

As good subjects for such exercises the following list is given, which might be extended indefinitely. The character of—

Abraham,	Regulus,	Peter the Great,
Joseph,	Hannibal,	Cromwell,
Jacob,	Cleopatra,	Voltaire,
Moses,	Cæsar,	Newton,
Samson,	Mahomet,	Galileo,
Saul,	Zenobia,	Cowper,
David,	Alfred,	Josephine,
Peter,	Madame Roland,	Richard Cœur de Lion,
Paul,	William Tell,	Capt. John Smith,
Aristides,	Isabella of Castile,	Franklin,
Themistocles	Columbus,	Jackson,
Pericles,	Luther,	Humphrey Davy,
Socrates,	Wesley,	Elizabeth of England,
Demosthenes,	Shakespeare,	Judson,
Alexander,	Bacon,	Mrs. Judson,
Cincinnatus,	Milton,	Sister Rosalie.

The Crusades.
The Discovery of America.
Venice.
The Conquest of England by the Normans.
Jerusalem.
Florence.
The Exodus of the Israelites from Egypt.
The Ancient Grecian Games.
The Battle of Waterloo.
The Destruction of Carthage.
Pompeii.
The Settlement of Virginia.
The First American Revolution.
The Siege of Troy.
The Expulsion of the Kings from Rome.
The Founding of Rome.

CHAPTER XVIII.

THE DRAWING OF PARALLELS.

It will greatly add to the interest and disciplinary power of such an exercise as the foregoing, to embrace in one discussion and composition two characters or historical passages that have some points of resemblance. The bringing out into prominence the points of similarity and of dissimilarity is called *drawing a parallel* between the two.

The following list will afford examples of pairs of subjects to be thus treated:

Geography and History.
Spring and Autumn.
The East and the West Indies.
The Valley of the Danube and of the Ohio.
The Alps and the Andes.
The Ganges and the Mississippi.
The Bedouin Arabs and the American Indians.
The Irish and the Scotch.
The Dutch and the Ancient Greeks.
The English and the French.
Moses and Romulus.
Samson and Hercules.
David and Alfred.
Zenobia and Mary, Queen of Scots.
Charlemagne and Peter the Great.
Julius Cæsar and Louis Napoleon.
Addison and Johnson.
Goldsmith and Irving.
Macaulay and Gibbon.
Webster and Calhoun.
The Growth of Popular Freedom in Rome and in England.
The Spanish Conquests in America and the British in India
The Reformation in Germany and in England.
Christianity and Mohammedanism.
Ancient and Modern Warfare.
Grecian and Gothic Architecture.
The Poet and the Orator.
The Preacher and the Editor.

PART SECOND.

EXPRESSION—RESUMED.

CHAPTER XIX.

STRUCTŪRE—UNITY.

§ 314. The essential properties of good style that refer to the structure of sentences are five:

1. Unity;
2. Purity;
3. Clearness;
4. Strength;
5. Harmony or Euphony.

The first of these has reference to the quantity of a continuous discourse which may properly be embraced in one sentence; the second relates to the demands of grammar on style; the other three all refer to the mode of arranging the words.

I. SENTENTIAL UNITY.

§ 315. This property of good style requires that no more should be embraced in one sentence than the mind can easily apprehend at once.

Strict unity would demand that each sentence should have one leading subject, and present only one scene before the mind. And this is what is required in every simple, complex, and partial compound sentence. With regard to such, it is rare that any practical difficulty occurs. But with regard to loose compound sentences, usage does sanction the grouping together of events and assertions that have not a very close connection or interdependence. Here it is that the judgment and taste of the writer must be trained, so as to avoid, on one hand, a dangling and wearisome succession of clauses, or, on the other, the chopping of a discourse into a series of detached propositions. Rules alone are insufficient for this training. The teacher should, in the presence of his pupils, criticise some extract either of good or faulty style, taking up sentence after sentence, and examining each, to test its merits in respect to unity. The pupil should be encouraged to do likewise with his own compositions. This, together with the abundant and careful reading of good authors, and the occasional memorizing of remarkably fine passages, will most infallibly inculcate a nice discrimination as to the structure of sentences.

§ 316. The following are given as special rules for the application of the foregoing principle.

§ 317. I. It is not proper to bring into one sentence, different events, scenes, or assertions, unless they have an obvious connection.

§ 318. II. The common object or idea that forms the bond of union between different assertions, must occupy such a position in the sentence as that all the clauses may naturally group themselves around it.

§ 319. III. It is seldom agreeable to put together into one sentence, assertions that tend to awaken different tones of feeling.

§ 320. IV. Long parentheses, or interposed clauses that lead away the mind from the main assertion, are always destructive of unity.

§ 321. V. The unity of a sentence requires that it should be brought to a full and perfect close, and that no after-thought be added, beyond the point where the structure of the sentence would lead us to expect a pause.

These rules may be illustrated by the following ex amples.

"At last the coach stopped, and the driver, opening the door, told us to get out; which we did, and found ourselves in front of a large tavern, whose bright and ruddy windows told of the blazing fires within; which, together with the kind welcome of the hostess, and the bounteous supper that smoked upon the board, soon made us forget the hardships of the long, cold ride."

In this sentence, different events and scenes are grouped together, whose only thread of connection is the feelings of the passengers. And yet those feelings are not all of the same character, nor are they put in such a position in the sentence as to contribute to its unity. It should be divided into three sentences, at least.

Plutarch, speaking of the Greeks under Alexander, says:

"Their march was through an uncultivated country, whose savage inhabitants fared hardly, having no other riches than a breed of lean sheep, whose flesh was rank and unsavory, by reason of their continual feeding upon sea-fish."

In this sentence there is no element of unity, but a medley of ideas, quite as distasteful as the fishy mutton.

"All the precautions of prudence, moderation, and condescension, which Eumenes employed, were incapable of mollifying the hearts of those barbarians, and of extinguishing their jealousy; and he must have renounced his merit and the virtue which occasioned it, to have been capable of appeasing them."

Here the point of connection is the *jealousy of the barbarians.* In the first member, this is made the object of a participle used as an adjunct, modifying the attribute (predicate adjective) of the verb. In the second member, it is the object of the verb in a relative clause, used to modify the object of the verb. This violates the second of the foregoing rules.

"Tillotson died in this year; he was exceedingly beloved both by King William and Queen Mary, who nominated Dr. Tennison, Bishop of Lincoln, to succeed him."

Here the mention of the good prelate's death, and the bereavement of the reigning sovereigns, appeal to quite a different feeling from that which is appropriate to the mention of a successor.

"The quicksilver mines of Idria, in Austria, (which were discovered in 1797, by a peasant, who, catching some water from a spring, found the tub so heavy that he could not move it, and the bottom covered with a shining substance which turned out to be mercury,) yield, every year, over three hundred thousand pounds, of that valuable metal." Comment is unnecessary.

"Every man has his work allotted, his talent committed to him; by the due improvement of which, he may, in one way or other, serve God, promote virtue, and be useful to the world; for which he shall surely receive his reward." This last clause is a palpable violation of Rule V (above).

EXERCISE I.

Let the pupil criticise the following sentences, showing how in each case unity is violated, and how the sentence is to be correctly divided.

The lion is a noble animal, and has been known to live fifty years in a state of confinement.

London, which is a very dirty city, has a population of two millions and a quarter.

The notions of Lord Sunderland were always good; but he was a man of great expense.

The Chinese women are for the most part industrious; and use as embellishments of their beauty, paint, false hair, oils, and pork fat.

At Coleridge's table we were introduced to Count Frioli, a foreigner of engaging manners and fine conversational powers, who was killed the following day by a steamboat explosion.

A short time after this injury, he came to himself; and the next day, they put him on board a ship, which conveyed him first to Corinth, and thence to the island of Ægina.

The Britons, daily harassed by cruel inroads from the Picts, were forced to call in the Saxons for their defense; who consequently reduced the greater part of the island to their own power; drove the Britons into the most remote and mountainous parts; and the rest of the country, in customs, religion, and language, became wholly Saxon.

By eagerness of temper and precipitancy of indulgence, men forfeit all the advantages which patience would have procured; and, by this means, the opposite evils are incurred to their full extent.

This prostitution of praise does not only affect the gross of mankind, who take their notion of characters from the learned; but also the better sort must, by this means, lose some part at least of their desire of fame, when they find it promiscuously bestowed on the meritorious and undeserving.

We left Italy with a fine wind, which continued three days; when a violent storm drove us to the coast of Sardinia, which is free from all kinds of poisonous herbs, except one; which resembles parsley, and which, they say, causes those who eat it to die of laughing.

We next took the cars, which were filled to overflowing, and brought us to a landing, where a boat was in waiting that looked as if it were a century old; but which, while we were examining its worm-eaten sides, put off at a rate which soon showed us that its sailing qualities were by no means contemptible, and taught us the practical lesson that it is unsafe to judge of the merits of a thing by its external appearance.

The famous poisoned valley of Java (which, as Mr. Loudon, a recent traveler in that region, informs us, is twenty miles in length and is filled with skeletons of men and birds; and into which it is said the neighboring tribes are in the habit of driving criminals, as a convenient mode of executing capital punishment) has proved to be the crater of an extinct volcano, in which carbonic acid is generated in great quantities, as in the Grotto del Cane at Naples.

The usual acceptation takes profit and pleasure for two different things, and not only calls the followers or votaries of them by the several names of busy and idle men, but distinguishes the faculties of the mind, that are conversant about them; calling the operations of the first, wisdom; and of the other, wit;—which is a Saxon word, used to express what the Spaniards and Italians call *ingenuo*, and the French, *esprit*, both from the Latin: though I think wit more particularly signifies that of poetry, as may occur in my remarks on the Runic language.

To this succeeded that licentiousness which entered with the Restoration, and from infecting our religion and morals fell to corrupting our language; which last was not likely to be much improved by those who made up the court of King Charles the Second; either such as had followed him in his banishment, or who had been altogether conversant in the dialect of these fanatic times; or young men who had been educated in the same country; so that the court, which used to be the standard of correctness and propriety of speech, was then, and I think has ever since continued, the worst school in England for that accomplishment; and so will remain, till better care be taken in the education of our nobility, that they may set out in the world with some foundation of literature, in order to qualify them for patterns of politeness.

In this uneasy state, both of his public and private life, Cicero was oppressed by a new and deep affliction, the death of his beloved daughter Tullia; which happened soon after her divorce from Dolabella; whose manners and humors were entirely disagreeable to her.

The sun approaching melts the snow, and breaks the icy fetters of the main, where vast sea-monsters pierce through floating islands, with arms which can withstand the crystal rock; whilst others, that of themselves seem great as islands, are by their bulk alone armed against all but man, whose superiority over creatures of such stupendous size and force, should make him mindful of his privilege of reason, and force him humbly to adore the great Composer of these wondrous frames, and the Author of his own superior wisdom.

EXERCISE II.

As an additional exercise in Unity, let the teacher assign to each pupil in the class, some extract, the sentences of which he must divide as far as possible without destroying their meaning, into short and isolated propositions. When this has been done, let the results be exchanged amongst them, so that each may have the dismembered sentences of an extract, the original of which he has not seen. Then let each be required to re-combine, according to his own judgment, the sentences given to him, and let these results be compared with the originals.

The following is given as a model of this process of subdivision and recomposition. The original is

HUME'S ACCOUNT OF THE LAST DAYS OF QUEEN ELIZABETH.

The Earl of Essex, after his return from the fortunate expedition against Cadiz, observing the increase of the queen's fond attachment toward him, took occasion to regret that the necessity of her service required him often to be absent from her person, and exposed him to all those ill offices, which his enemies, more assiduous in their attendance, could employ against him. She was moved with this tender jealousy, and making him the present of a ring, desired him to keep that pledge of her affection, and assured him, that, into whatever disgrace he might fall, whatever prejudices she might be induced to entertain against him, yet, if he sent her that ring, she would immediately, upon sight of it, recall her former tenderness; would afford him a patient hearing, and would lend a favorable ear to his apology.

Essex, notwithstanding all his misfortunes, reserved this precious gift to the last extremity; but after his trial and condemnation, he resolved to try the experiment, and he committed the ring to the Countess of Nottingham, whom he desired to deliver it to the queen. The countess was prevailed on by her husband, the mortal enemy of Essex, not to execute the commission; and Elizabeth, who still expected that her favorite would make this last appeal to her tenderness, and who ascribed the neglect of it to his invincible obstinacy, was, after much delay and many internal combats, pushed by resentment and policy to sign the warrant for his execution.

The Countess of Nottingham falling into sickness, and affected with the near approach of death, was seized with remorse for her conduct; and having obtained a visit from the queen, she craved her pardon, and revealed the fatal secret. The queen, astonished with this incident, burst into a furious passion. She shook the dying countess in her bed; and crying to her that *God might pardon her, but she never could*, she broke from her, and thenceforth resigned herself over to the deepest and most incurable melancholy. She resisted all consolation; she even refused food and sustenance; and, throwing herself on the floor, she remained sullen and immovable, feeding her thoughts on her afflictions, and declaring life and existence an intolerable burden to her. Few words she uttered; and they were all expressive of some inward grief which she cared not to reveal; but sighs and groans were the chief vent which she gave to her despondency, and which, though they discovered her sorrows, were never able to ease or assuage them.

Ten days and nights she lay upon the carpet, leaning on cushions which her maids brought her; and her physicians could not persuade her to allow herself to be put to bed, much less to make trial of any remedies which they prescribed to her. Her anxious mind, at last, had so long preyed upon her frail body, that her end was visibly approaching; and the council, being assembled, sent the keeper, admiral, and secretary, to know her will with regard to her successor. She answered, with a faint voice, that, as she had held a regal scepter, she desired no other than a royal successor. Cecil requesting her to explain herself more particularly, she subjoined, that she would have a king to succeed her; and who should that be, but her nearest kinsman, the King of Scots?

Being then advised by the Archbishop of Canterbury to fix her thoughts upon God, she replied, that she did so, nor did her mind, in the least, wander from Him. Her voice, soon after, left her; her senses failed; she fell into a lethargic slumber, which continued some hours; and she expired gently, without further struggle or convulsion, in the seventieth year of her age, and forty-fifth of her reign. So dark a cloud overcast the evening of that day, which had shone out with a mighty luster, in the eyes of all Europe!

THE SAME WITH THE SENTENCES DIVIDED.

The Earl of Essex, after his return from the fortunate expedition against Cadiz, observed the increase of the queen's fond attachment toward him. He took occasion to regret that the necessity of her service required him often to be absent from her person. This absence exposed him to all those ill offices which his enemies, more assiduous in their attendance, could employ against him. She was moved with this tender jealousy. She made him the present of a ring. She desired him to keep that pledge of her affection. She assured him that, into whatsoever disgrace he might fall, whatsoever prejudices she might be induced to entertain against him, yet, if he sent her that ring, she would immediately, on sight of it, recall her former tenderness. She would afford him a patient hearing. She would lend a favorable ear to his apology.

Essex, notwithstanding all his misfortunes, reserved this precious gift to the last extremity. But after his trial and condemnation, he resolved to try the experiment. He committed the ring to the Countess of Nottingham. He desired her to deliver it to the queen. The husband of the countess was the mortal enemy of Essex. He prevailed upon his wife not to execute the commission. Elizabeth still expected that her favorite would make this last appeal to her tenderness. She ascribed the neglect of it to his invincible obstinacy. She was, after much delay, and many internal combats, pushed by resentment and policy to sign the warrant of his execution.

The Countess of Nottingham fell into sickness. She was affected with the near approach of death. She was seized with remorse for her conduct. She obtained a visit from the queen. She craved her pardon and revealed the fatal secret. The queen was astonished with this incident. She burst into a furious passion. She shook the dying countess in her bed. She cried to her that *God might pardon her, but she never could.* She broke from her. She thenceforth resigned herself over to the deepest and most incurable melancholy. She resisted all consolation. She even refused food and sustenance. She threw herself on the floor. She remained sullen and immovable, feeding her thoughts on her afflictions, and declaring life and existence an intolerable burden to her. Few words she uttered. They were all expressive of some inward grief which she cared not to reveal. Sighs and groans were the chief vent which she gave to her despondency These, though they discovered her sorrows, were never able to ease or assuage them.

Ten days and nights she lay upon the carpet. She leaned on the cushions which her maids brought her. Her physicians could not persuade her to allow herself to be put to bed. Much less (could they persuade her) to make trial of any remedies which they prescribed to her. Her anxious mind, at last, had so preyed upon her frail body that her end was visibly approaching. The council were assembled. They sent the keeper, admiral, and secretary, to know her will with regard to her successor. She answered, with a faint voice, that, as she had held a regal scepter, she desired no other than a royal successor. Cecil requested her to explain herself more particularly. She sub joined that she would have a king to succeed her; and who should that be, but her nearest kinsman, the King of Scots?

She was then advised by the Archbishop of Canterbury to fix her thoughts upon God. She replied that she did so, nor did her mind, in the least, wander from Him. Her voice soon after left her. Her senses failed. She fell into a lethargic slumber, which continued some hours. She expired gently, without further struggle or convulsion, in the seventieth year of her age, and forty-fifth of her reign. So dark a cloud overcast the evening of that day, which had shone out with a mighty luster, in the eyes of all Europe.

CHAPTER XX.

PURITY OF STRUCTURE.

§ 322. As purity of *diction* consists in the avoiding of all words and phrases that do not belong to the language, so purity of *structure* demands that the sentences of a discourse shall be constructed as the laws of the language allow. These rules are embraced in what are generally known as the Rules of Syntax, and are to be found in every good grammar. The violation of them is called *solecism.* These rules have reference to the use or omission of words, their arrangement, and their form.

It is presumed that the pupil who has progressed thus far in this Manual, will have mastered the rules and observations contained in his grammar, and will have been to some extent drilled in the correction of solecisms. But as this is an exercise of such importance as to justify frequent review in the education of every young person, the following collection of solecisms, miscellaneously introduced, will be found not without value at this stage of progress. Let the teacher require the pupil to tell in each case, (1) precisely what word is wrong, (2) in what respect or why it is wrong, (3) what rule or principle it violates, and (4) how the sentence would read when corrected.

A compendium of the rules of syntax that are susceptible of violation is inserted in Appendix No. I., in order to convenience of reference in the correction of compositions.

EXERCISES.—SOLECISMS TO BE CORRECTED.

The quarrels of lovers is the renewal of love.

Rebecca took goodly raiment and put them upon Jacob.

He was married to a most beautiful Jew.

Each man, woman, and child know the hour when the mighty blow is to be struck.

Him and me are of the same age.

The governor is a very clever man; but the governess is a perfect tiger. I wonder that he was ever married to her.

It is him that has made us, and not we ourselves.

I found him mending of his shoe.

Charles hat is not so large as Moses.

The corpse of the Mexicans were left to the wolf and the vulture.

These sort of conveyances are now altogether out of use.

Take a little wine for thine often infirmities.

This work embraces all the minutia of the science.

When you hear the bell to ring, then bid the servant to come to me quick.

We have, and will be, your friends.

If the twelve apples actually costed six pence, then two apples should cost one pence.

The committee was divided in its opinions on the question.

Let every one answer for themselves.

Of his oxens, one was much littler than the other.

Solomon and me, we taken our guns and stood waiting for them to come.

The vermins were so numerous that we could raise no fowl.

Hill and dale doth boast thy blessing.

Charity to the poor, when governed by knowledge and prudence, there are no persons who will not admit to be a virtue.

I knew it to be he all the time.

He never took two shot at one deer, but often killed two deers with one shot.

If thy heart be as mine, give to me thy hand.

The object of his ambition was the king's of England crown.

The heathen are them people that worship idols.

I heard of John catching five or six fine trout in that same hole.

He looks faintly after his excessive exertion.

What a quantity of radiuses you have gotten in your circle.

I have not read the book, and I do not intend to.

Fifty sail was seen approaching the coast.

The queen of night has hid its face behind the clouds.

He has four brethren, and they are all poetic genii, as well as himself.

The fault that I pointed out to him, and which he himself confessed to me, have not yet been corrected.

I and William and you will all go to-night.

By accident, I throwed one of the dies out of the backgammon-box.

He is very unwell, and therefore should remain at home.

I find Mr. Wilson, he that you saw with me yesterday, to be an interesting man.

How can he help hisself?

They spent the whole day in the hearing the witnesses.

I can not say whether Webster or Worcester's Dictionary is the best.

If that is yourn, take it and go along; but you will not have ourn, no matter how much you may want it.

Let each esteem other better than themselves.

What do you think of me going into the army?

Was it your brother's remain that you were watching, or somebody else's?

Nothing is left us but to quietly accept the proposition.

I was conscious that I had neither ate nor drank any thing.

If General Wolfe clomb only one hill, he should properly be said to have climbed the Height of Abraham.

None but thou, O mighty prince, canst avert the blow.

Wisdom, and not wealth, procure esteem.

Each boy and girl must keep their own seat.

I have a bad cold now, but I will have a worser one, if I might go out in this rain.

Neither William nor you nor I has any money to spare.

Which asset should you prefer to deposit with me?

I shall be read a lecture when I get home.

I know thou to be an upright man.

Come and spend the evening with my wife and I.

I have had my horse shoed at last.

They ridiculed the rebel's, as they called him, loyalty to his state.

On learning of his mistake, he offered an apology.

I drawed a black line around all that he writ; and I think the printer mought have done it right.

Me being present, he could say nothing against it.

He had went away long before I arrived.

Good order in our affairs, and not mean savings, produce great profits.

My orders were that every officer would remain at his own head-quarter.

Before you left Sicily, you was reconciled to Verres.

The horse is already engaged with the enemy, and it will soon be re-enforced by the foot.

The drowning man cried out, "I will be drowned! nobody shall help me!"

Congress have adjourned for three months.

A great number of spectators were present, and every one of them were delighted.

I had much rather do it myself.

The wicked are suffered to flourish till the sum of his iniquities be full.

His English partialities swerved him from the path of neutrality.

Be that as it will, I shall not despair yet.

Who should I meet the other day but my old friend Jones?

If the description is general and barren of circumstances, it will lack of interest.

You had better have left those wasps alone.

Richard the Lion-hearted's, as he is called in history, glorious career made him the idol of his subjects.

I never have, and never will, consent to such an arrangement.

The next time I will try and keep further to the right.

Every body, even down to the servants, are kind to her.

The army was badly cut up, but made good their retreat.

The earth is my mother; I will recline on its bosom.

A well-furnished mind is more preferable than wealth.

"'Squire," says I, "circumstances alters cases."

He is not so hospitable as her.

Generation after generation pass away.

They choosed, as they thought, the lesser evil of the three.

Whom do men say that I am?

The peasantry goes barefoot, but the middle class makes use of wooden shoes.

I approve, and will give hearty support to, the measures proposed.

On the next day of the Lord, the Rev. Mr. Smith shall preach in this house.

Every precaution were in vain: when the jailer opened the door, the prisoner was done gone.

I intended to have planted the seeds as soon as it rains.

Slates are stone, and used to cover the roofs of houses.

I would be obliged to you, if you will lend to me that book.

Whence comes all the powers and prerogatives of rational beings?

The club has long since dispersed and gone to its homes.

There are many faults in spelling which neither analogy nor pronunciation offer any excuse for.

The public is invited to attend the burial.

Six hundred head is ready to be butchered.

Such opinions as that is leading our youth astray.

The ecclesiastical and secular powers concurred.

Competition is excellent, and the vital principle of trade.

Sure enough, I did go, and answered my accusers triumphant.

He based his argument on the truth that God was always merciful.

No one ought to injure, or wound the feelings of, his neighbor.

I could have saw them easy.

Submit to the will of thy Father which art in heaven.

This people draweth near to me with their lips, but its heart are far from me.

He was a man of taste and possessing an elevated mind.

Either the author or his publishers, one, is to blame.

I know not whom else are expected to be present.

The inventor displayed a gold and silver medal that had been; on two separate occasions, presented him.

Every passenger must hold their own tickets.

I charge him with a forsaking his duty.

All the horses and men which were killed, laid unburied on the field.

I would go, if I was him.

Twenty sail has already passed the bar, and twelve more is in the offing.

Are neither of those men worthy of public confidence?

I am happy in the friend which I have long proved.

Put up those gloves for Clara and I.

She was much older than him.

In avoiding of one error, guard against its opposite.

Between the old and the new mansion is a fine grove of trees.

This is the only bargain that had or could be made.

Even if he bids you to come, you need not to go.

He was anxious to have read Cowper.

The boys mother, as well as his father, deserve great praise.

Every person in the community, whatever may be their condition, should contribute to the common weal.

This prodigy of learning, this scholar, critic, and antiquarian, were destitute of civility.

A great majority of our authors are defective in style.

I have come for to see you, because I knew that you was my old master's friend.

The Bible is divided into the Old and New Testament.

There were no one in the house save we two.

As soon as I seen the track, I knowed he had mistook the road.

The preacher contended that the Bible was the source of the highest benefits.

That man is prudent which speak little.

He can not be persuaded to take the prescribed remedies; which make his case hopeless.

The child whom we have just seen is the darling of its parents.

If any officer or member neglect to perform their duty, they shall forfeit their place.

The crowd was so great that the judges with difficulty made their way through them.

I beseech ye that ye sorrow not as them that have no hope.

Neither of those men are aware that their opinions are false.

When we arrived at the orchard, we found that the peaches had all fell off, and were devouring by the hogs.

He mistaken the road, and had like to have froze to death.

Moses was the meekest man of whom we read in the Old Testament.

I propose that you and I eat your dinner together, and then proceed to your different tasks.

The men and the things which he has studied, has not improved his morals.

In the judgment, no action, no word, no thought can escape, whether they are good or evil.

He invited my brother and I to examine his library.

Mr. Drake overseed for my father six years, and then sat up for hisself.

I found him better than I expected to have found him.

He hath suffered and died
To redeem such a rebel as me.

A miserable pedant and bigot were then wielding the scepter of Great Britain.

May Anna and me go to church this evening?

Man is not such a machine as a clock or a watch which move merely as they are moved.

If he will not hear his best friend, whom will be sent to admonish him?

I shall premise with a few general observations, foreshadowing of the scope of my subsequent remarks.

'The nations not so bless'd as thee
'Must in their turn to tyrants fall!'

It was observed in the preceding chapter that the conjunction *or* had a double sense.

On this trial, the judge and jury's sentiments were at variance.

He and you may go, but I and she will remain.

The cares of this world, the deceitfulness of riches, they often choke the growth of piety.

Was any person besides the merchant present? Yes: both him and his clerk witnessed the whole affair.

Two substantives, when they come together, and do not signify the same thing, the former must be in the genitive case.

From the character of those who you associate with, your own will be estimated.

Those who accuse us of denying of it, belie us.

The governor's veto was writing, while the final vote was taking in the senate.

Society themselves are injured by these sort of actions.

The commander of the detachment, he was killed, and the soldiers, they all fled.

To be moderate in our views, and proceeding temperately in the pursuit of them, are the best way to insure success.

You would not accept it, if you was me.

Yesterday I seen your cousin; she that lives in Columbus.

Let Anna and I go to the dressmaker's, if you please.

The damsel asked for John's the Baptist's head.

Coleridge, the poet and philosopher, have many admirers.

The senator gained nothing further by his speech, but to be commended for his eloquence.

He is more bold and active, but not so wise and studious, as his companions.

No person was ever so perplexed, or sustained the mortifications, as he has to-day.

These arts have and will enlighten every person who shall attentively study them.

How a seed grows up into a tree, and the way the mind acts upon the body, are mysteries we can not fathom.

By intercourse with the world, we may improve, and rub off the rust of, a retired education.

Those savage people seemed to have no other standard on which to form themselves, except what chances to be fashionable and popular.

Novelty produces in the mind a vivid and an agreeable emotion.

He received his commission from the then secretary of war.

The time for William making the experiment now arrived.

The reward has already, or will hereafter, be given him.

Poetry has a natural alliance with, and often strongly excites, our noblest emotions.

On these causes depend all the happiness or misery which exist among men.

We adore the Divine Being, he who is from eternity to eternity.

Thou, Lord, who hath permitted affliction to come upon us, shall, in due time, deliver us from it.

Not only in this place were there security, but an abundance of provisions.

Not one in fifty of those that call themselves deists understand the nature of the religion they reject.

Virtue and mutual confidence is the soul of friendship. Where these are wanting, disgust or hatred often follow little differences.

Time and chance happeneth to all men; every person do not consider who govern those powerful causes.

Habits must be acquired as early in life as possible, of temperance and self-denial, that we may be able to resist pleasure, and to endure pain, when either of these interfere with our duty.

The error of resting wholly on faith or on works, is one of those seductions which most easily misleads men.

The enemies who we have most to fear are those of our own hearts.

Themistocles concealed the enterprises of Pausanias, either thinking it base to betray the secrets trusted to his confidence, or imagined it impossible for such ill-concerted schemes to take effect.

Christ applauded the liberality of the poor widow, who he had seen casting of her two mites into the treasury.

This is one of the duties which requires peculiar circumspection.

He that has ears to hear, let him hear.

The grand temple consisted of one great and several smaller edifices.

The girls school was better conducted formerly than the boys; but now it is hard saying which is the more orderly.

You must be sensible that there is no other person but me who could give the information desired.

Year after year steals something from us; till the decaying fabric totters of itself, and crumbles at length into dust.

It is amazing his propensity to this vice, against every principle of interest and honor.

He acted agreeable to the dictates of prudence, though he were in a situation exceeding delicate.

They admired the countryman's, as they called him, candor and uprightness.

No persons feel the distresses of others so much as them that have experienced distress themselves.

Cæsar wrote in the same manner that he fought.

I could not buy it nor borrow it.

There was no place so hidden nor remote as the plague did not find it.

No problem is so difficult which he can not solve.

This pen does not write good.

Every man can not afford to keep a watch.

You have been fooling with that bellows for this two hours.

The four first benches are reserved for the pupils, so that they will be in nobody else's way.

Allow me to respectfully present you with a gold watch.

The performance was approved of by all who saw it.

He is not rich and incompetent for business.

The victory seemed like a resurrection from the dead, to the Eastern States.

The supplying an army of contractors, General Jackson had objected to, as highly objectionable.

It is an acknowledged fact by some of our most experienced teachers, that but few persons can write a full page without the transgressing in some way the rules of style.

That fellow's being a poet, I never heard mentioned before.

Then did the officer lay hold of him and executed him immediately.

Whom is that person whom I saw you introduce, and present him to the president?

I offer observations that a long and checkered pilgrimage have enabled me to make on man.

Propriety of pronunciation is the giving to every word the sound which the most polite usage of the language appropriates to it.

The book is printed very neat, and on fine wove paper.

The fields look so greenly that I am tempted to roam over them.

He is a new created knight, and his dignity sets awkward on him.

A too great variety of studies dissipate and weaken the mind.

James was resolved to not indulge himself in such a cruel amusement.

Calumny and detraction are sparks, which if you do not blow, they will go out of themselves.

They that honor me I will honor; and them that despise me shall be lightly esteemed.

I have not nor shall not consent to a proposal so unjust.

This treaty was made at Earl Moreton the governor's castle.

The business was no sooner opened, but it was cordially acquiesced in.

As to his general conduct, he deserves punishment as much, or more, than his companion.

He acted independent of foreign assistance.

They understand the practical part better than him; but he is much better acquainted with the theory than them.

The people's happiness is the statesmans honor.

Be solicitous to aid such deserving persons who appear destitute of friends.

Ignorance, or the want of light, produce sensuality, covetousness, and those violent contests about trifles, which occasions so much misery and crimes in the world.

No human happiness is so complete as does not contain some imperfection.

This is the person who we are so much obliged to, and we expected to have seen, when the favor was conferred.

What can be the reason of the committee having delayed the business?

I know not if Charles was the author, but I understood it to be he.

When we see bad men to be honored and prosperous in the world, it is some discouragement to virtue.

The furniture was all purchased at Wentworth's, the cabinet-maker's.

It is right said that though faith justify us, yet works must justify our faith.

PART THIRD.

INVENTION—RESUMED.

CHAPTER XXI.

EXEMPLIFICATION, OR ILLUSTRATIVE FICTION.

In preceding chapters the pupil has been exercised in narration, simply as such. It is now proper that he should be directed to those forms of narration that have some other end in view than the mere recounting of events.

§ 323. There is not a more effective method of enforcing important truth, or of teaching lessons of high value, than the exemplification of them in pleasing narrative. It is an old adage that "example is better than precept," and even when the example is a fictitious one, yet, if it be conceived in a life-like and natural manner, it carries with it a force far superior to mere dry argument or injunction. Hence it becomes important to be able in this pleasing way to commend to others the dictates of good sense and of virtue.

It may be thought by some to have been better to prescribe the illustration of moral truth by veritable examples, before proceeding to the invention of fictitious ones. But there are some reasons for the contrary course. The events of real life are very complex, both in their causes and their results. It is difficult to find a pure illustration of any moral truth. To select from the tangled meshes of actual events, the single thread of results that are fairly referable to one cause, is beyond the powers of the generality of young persons. It requires experience; experience in two ways: first, to furnish facts; secondly, to impart the wisdom to trace the connections of facts to their causes. Moreover, the acquaintance of young people does not reach far beyond the circle of their friends; and it would be a very improper thing to require a pupil to narrate cases, drawn from the community around, such as he might conceive to be illustrations of the evil effects of some foible or vice. His fictitious cases will generally bear a sufficient resemblance to actual ones, to answer all the demands of a stickler for fact.

Fiction, then, is the preferable field. It obviates all difficult and delicate matters connected with personal character. The imagination of the young is vigorous, and calls for exercise. Let the exercise be supplied; let it be guided unto useful ends. The task of writing compositions becomes no task, but a pleasure, when it is made a means of indulging the forward fancy.

§ 324. First, let the pupil be instructed as to the different kinds of fiction. These, in prose, are *Novels*, *Romances*, and *Tales*. The last differs from the two preceding only in the matter of length, being shorter than they. Novels and romances differ from each other in the degree to which they follow nature and probability. The novel aims to reflect real life; the romance does not hesitate to introduce the marvelous and the supernatural. It is obvious that a tale, be it ever so short, will be characterized by a likeness to one or the other of these two classes of more extended fictions.

It is, then, that form of tale which resembles the novel, *the tale that reflects real life*, that the pupil should first attempt. Not because it is easier to *excel* in this style of fiction, but because it is easier to do any thing at all at it. As there is nothing like an example to make things clear, the following example is introduced to give some idea of the kind of production here required.

LOUISA SIMONS; OR APPLICATION.

Louisa Simons was a bright, intelligent girl of fourteen, amiable and ambitious, the joy of her parents, the pride of her teachers, and far advanced in all her studies, except arithmetic.

"Oh, mother!" she exclaimed frequently, "this is the day for the blackboard; and a *black day* to me! I hate arithmetic! I wish the multiplication table had never been invented! There is not such an expressive verse in the world as the old one,—

'Multiplication is vexation,
 Division is as bad;
The Rule of Three does puzzle me,
 And Practice drives me mad.'"

Mrs. Simons sometimes reproved her for her vehemence; sometimes soothed, and sometimes encouraged her; but finding her more and more excited, she addressed her one day, gravely and anxiously, thus:—

"My daughter, you make me unhappy by these expressions I am aware that many minds are so constituted as to learn numbers slowly; but that close attention and perseverance can conquer even natural defects, has been often proved. If you pass over a rule carelessly, and *say* you comprehend it, when really from a want of energy you have failed to grasp it, you will never learn; and your *black days*, when you become a woman, and have responsibilities, will increase. I speak feelingly on this subject, for I had the same natural aversion to arithmetic as yourself. Unfortunately for me, a schoolmate, quick at figures, shared my desk. We had no blackboards then, and she was kind or unkind enough to work out my sums for me. The consequence is that I have suffered repeatedly in my purse and in my feelings, from my ignorance. Even now I am obliged to apply to your father in the most trifling calculations, and you must sometimes have noticed my mortification under such circumstances."

"I look to you for assistance," continued she, affectionately, to Louisa. "You have every advantage; your mind is active, and in other respects disciplined, and I am sure your good heart will prompt you in aiding me."

Louisa's eyes looked a good resolution; she kissed her mother, and commenced her lesson with the right feelings. Instead of being angry with her teacher and herself because every thing was not plain, she tried to clear her brow, and attend to the subject calmly.

Success crowned her efforts, while, added to the pleasure of acquisition, she began to experience the higher joy of self-conquest and her mother's approbation. She gave herself up to diligent study, and conquered at length the higher branches of arithmetic.

Louisa, the eldest of three children, had been born to the luxuries of wealth, and scarcely an ungratified want had shaded her sunny brow. Mr. Simons was a merchant of respectable connections; but in the height of his prosperity, one of those failures took place which occur in commerce, and his affairs became suddenly involved in the shock which is often felt so far in the mercantile chain. A nervous temperament and delicate system were soon sadly wrought upon by this misfortune, and his mind, perplexed and harassed, seemed to lose its clearness in calculation, and its happy view of life. Louisa was at this period seventeen years of age; her understanding clear and vigorous, her passions disciplined, and her faculties resting, like a young fawn, for a sudden bound.

It was a cold autumn evening; the children were beguiling themselves with wild gambols about the parlor; Mr. Simons sat leaning his head upon his hand, gazing upon an accumulated pile of ledgers and papers; Mrs. Simons was busily sewing, and Louisa, with her fingers between the leaves of a closed book, sat anxiously regarding her father.

"Those children distract me," said Mr. Simons, peevishly.

"Hush, Robert! Come here, Margaret!" said Mrs. Simons, gently; and taking one on her lap, and another by her side, whispered a little story, and then put them to bed.

When Mrs. Simons left the room, Louisa laid aside her book, and stood by her father.

"Don't disturb me, child," said he, roughly. Then recollecting himself, he waved his hand gently for her to retire, and continued. "Do not feel hurt, dear, with my abruptness. I am perplexed with these complicated accounts."

"Father," said Louisa, hesitatingly, and blushing, "I think I could assist you, if you would permit me."

"You, my love?" exclaimed he, laughing, "these papers would puzzle a deeper head than yours."

"I do not wish to boast, dear father," said Louisa, modestly, "but when Mr. Random gave me my last lesson, he said—"

"What did he say?" asked Mr. Simons, encouragingly.

"He said," answered Louisa, blushing more deeply, "that I was a better accountant than most merchants. And I do believe, father," continued she, earnestly, "that if you would allow me, I could assist you."

Mr. Simons smiled sadly; but to encourage her desire of usefulness, opened his accounts. Insensibly he found his daughter following him in the labyrinth of numbers.

Louisa, with a fixed look and clear eye, her cheek kindling with interest, and her pencil in her hand, listened to him. Mrs. Simons entered on tiptoe, and seated herself softly at her sewing. The accounts became more and more complicated. Mr. Simons, with his practiced habits, and Louisa, with her quick intellect and ready will, followed them up with fidelity. The unexpected sympathy of his daughter gave him new life. Time flew unheeded, and the clock struck twelve.

"Wife," said he, suddenly, "matters are not as desperate as I feared; if this girl gives me a few more hours like these, I shall be in a new world."

"My beloved child!" said Mrs. Simons, pressing Louisa's glowing cheek to hers.

Louisa retired, recommended herself to God, and slept profoundly. The next morning, after again seeking His blessing, she repaired to her father; and again, with untiring patience, went through the details of his books, copied the accounts in a fair hand, nor left him until his brow was smoothed, and the phantom of bankruptcy had disappeared.

A day passed by, and Louisa looked contemplative and absorbed. At length she said:

"Father, you complain that you can not afford another clerk at present. You have tried me, and find me worth something; I will keep your books until your affairs are regulated, and you may give me a little salary to furnish shells for my cabinet."

Mr. Simons accepted her offer with a caress and a smile. Louisa's cabinet increased in value; and the beautiful female handwriting in her father's books was a subject of interest and curiosity to his mercantile friends.

And from whence, as, year after year, wealth poured in its thousand luxuries, and Louisa Simons stood dispensing pleasures to the gay, and comforts to the poor, did she trace her happiness? *To early self-conquest.* MRS. CAROLINE GILMAN.

As this class of compositions has of late years become so extensive and powerful an agency, somewhat for evil, but vastly more for good, it becomes desirable that the talent and taste of young persons should be carefully trained in this field of literature. The following hints will not, therefore, be out of place.

§ 325. "The chain of incidents on which a fiction is founded is called its *plot.* A plot should not be glaringly improbable; it should be moral, consistent in all its parts, and so managed as to keep alive the reader's interest throughout. This is often insured by reserving some important denouement for the last."

§ 326. By saying that the plot should be moral, it is meant that its tendency or influence should be in favor of morality. If vicious personages are introduced, or vicious actions described, the perpetrators should never be represented as gaining, in the long run, by their iniquity. But in accordance with the teachings of the Bible and the moral sentiments of mankind, wickedness should always be made to work misery, and virtue find its reward either in some form of worldly prosperity, or in a happy, hopeful death.

The direction to "keep up the interest of the reader throughout by reserving some important denouement to the last," is one that applies more justly to the novel than to the tale. The brevity of the latter allows its plot to be much simpler than that of the novel. And yet, in every fiction, the skillful use of mystery, provided all be made plain at the last, adds to the entertainment afforded by the work.

§ 327. "Next to a good plot nothing is so necessary to success in fictitious composition as a striking and life-like portraiture of character. The peculiarities of the individual personages introduced into the story must be maintained throughout. Whatever each says or does must harmonize with the character assigned to him by the writer."

The following list of "morals," or lessons proper for illustration, is given for the convenience of the pupil.

1. The practical advantages of a knowledge of mathematics.
2. The advantage of a knowledge of chemistry.
3. The benefit of newspapers.
4. The pleasures of a hunter's life.
5. The perils of a seaman's life.
6. The hardships and moral dangers of a soldier's life.
7. The art of making others happy.
8. Make the best of every thing.
9. True and false politeness.
10. The danger of contracting a fondness for games.
11. The evils of being a slave to fashion.
12. The evils of being over-worked.

13. The evils of extravagant living.
14. The danger of a talent for ridicule.
15. Patience and perseverance will overcome mountains.
16. A goodly apple is often rotten at the core.
17. Lying is a bad trade.
18. Knowledge is power.
19. The advantages of system.
20. Resist the beginnings of evil.
21. Necessity is the mother of invention.
22. A wounded reputation is hard to cure.
23. A good cause makes a stout heart.
24. A soft answer turneth away wrath.
25. The fruits of labor are sweeter than the gifts of fortune.
26. A rolling stone gathers no moss.
27. Prosperity is a severer test of virtue than adversity.
28. The folly of striving to please every one.
29. The folly of not governing the tongue.
30. The folly of contracting a passion for novel-reading.
31. The lasting effects of early impressions.
32. The advantage of a love for one's trade.
33. The evils of emulation.
34. The advantage of having a sincere friend.
35. The evils of flattery.
36. The nobleness of a life devoted to doing good.
37. What good a little child can do.
38. How to govern the temper.

CHAPTER XXII.

DIALOGUE.

After some practice in the exercises of the foregoing chapter, it will occur to the pupil that much of the life-like interest of a tale results from the ingenious introduction of *conversation* between the personages of his story. This suggests a new field for the exercise of his powers; a field to which he may with profit confine his energies for a time: *the invention of Dialogue.*

§ 328. First, the Dialogue, like the illustrative tale, must have an object. The composer must aim to set forth some truth, or to display some character, or to discuss some question. This aim must be before him all the time.

§ 329. Secondly, he must invent his characters, and the circumstances under which they come together. For a beginner, it is best to take characters such as he has seen and heard. By and by, he may trust himself to bring in personages, beyond the sphere of his own observation, and he may even venture to lay his scene in the remote past.

§ 330. But withal, let him remember that it is a capital quality of a dialogue to have each of the personages (technically called *dramatis personæ*) strongly marked in character; each must be strikingly distinguished from all the others by his occupation, sentiments, diction, manners, disposition, every thing about him. Other things being equal, the more striking the contrasts of character, the easier it is to write the dialogue.

§ 331. Thirdly, he must take especial pains to make each personage speak and act consistently with the character attributed to it. Every utterance must, if possible, be such as to betray that character; such as would, from the mouth of any other, be a plain incongruity. Hence, it is not advisable to have too many personages; and it must be confessed that the finest passages in dialogue-writing are colloquies between two only.

§ 332. Fourthly, neither the entire dialogue, nor any single speech in it, must be long. Quick repartee is the life of dialogue.

As a good specimen of the kind of composition above recommended, the following is taken from AIKEN:

ALEXANDER AND THE ROBBER.

ALEXANDER. What! art thou the Thracian robber, of whose exploits I have heard so much?

ROBBER. I am a Thracian, and a soldier.

ALEXANDER. A soldier? a thief, a plunderer, an assassin! the pest of the country! I could honor thy courage; but I must detest and punish thy crimes.

ROBBER. What have I done of which you can complain?

ALEXANDER. Hast thou not set at defiance my authority; violated the public peace, and passed thy life in injuring the persons and properties of thy fellow-subjects?

ROBBER. Alexander, I am your captive; I must hear what you please to say, and endure what you please to inflict. But my soul is unconquered; and if I reply at all to your reproaches, I will reply like a free man.

ALEXANDER. Speak freely. Far be it from me to take the advantage of my power, to silence those with whom I deign to converse!

ROBBER. I must, then, answer your question by another. How have you passed your life?

ALEXANDER. Like a hero. Ask Fame, and she will tell you. Among the brave, I have been the bravest; among sovereigns, the noblest; among conquerors, the mightiest.

ROBBER. And does not Fame speak of me, too? Was there ever a bolder captain of a more valiant band? Was there ever—but I scorn to boast. You yourself know that I have not been easily subdued.

ALEXANDER. Still, what are you but a robber, a base, dishonest robber?

ROBBER. And what is a conqueror? Have not you, too, gone about the earth like an evil genius, blasting the fair fruits of peace and industry; plundering, ravaging, killing without law, without justice, merely to gratify an insatiable lust for dominion? All that I have done to a single district, with a hundred followers, you have done to whole nations, with a hundred thousand. If I have stripped individuals, you have ruined kings and princes. If I have burned a few hamlets, you have desolated the most flourishing kingdoms and cities of the earth. What is then the difference, but that as you were born a king, and I a private man, you have been able to become a mightier robber than I?

ALEXANDER. But if I have taken like a king, I have given like a king. If I have subverted empires, I have founded greater. I have cherished arts, commerce, and philosophy.

ROBBER. I, too, have freely given to the poor, what I took from the rich. I have established order and discipline among the most ferocious of mankind, and have stretched out my protecting arm over the oppressed. I know, indeed, little of the philosophy you talk of; but I believe neither you nor I shall ever atone to the world for the mischief we have done it.

ALEXANDER. Leave me. Take off his chains and use him well. Are we, then, so much alike? *Alexander like a robber?* Let me reflect!

This branch of composition has, of course, a natural connection with the regular drama; but it would be premature for the pupil to attempt the latter with all its intricacy of plot, its artistic arrangement of scenes and acts, and its allotment of award in the catastrophe, in his present state of advancement. And yet, so far as particular scenes in dramas illustrate the requirements and excellences of dialogue, they may be profitably studied as models. Several such may be found in every good reading-book or speech-book, and the teacher may furnish others as far as may be required.

PART FOURTH.

EXPRESSION—RESUMED.

CHAPTER XXIII.

CLEARNESS OR PERSPICUITY.

§ 333. This property of style consists in so arranging the words and clauses of a sentence as to indicate the meaning promptly, and in rejecting all expressions that would bring in the least obscurity or doubt as to the author's meaning. This property of style has been indirectly discussed in all the preceding chapters on *Expression;* inasmuch as a sentence whose diction is pure, proper, simple, and precise, whose structure is deformed by no solecism or want of unity, is not in much danger of being charged with a want of clearness. And yet there are certain requirements of perspicuity that are not covered by any of the foregoing rules. The perfection of style demands that he who reads or hears a discourse shall never for one moment be delayed by any doubt or puzzle as to the intended meaning, or have any other suggested by the collocation of the words.

§ 334. The faults opposed to Clearness may be arranged under two general heads, *Obscurity* and *Ambiguity.*

I. OBSCURITY.

§ 335. A sentence is obscure when the reader or hearer is in the least puzzled to gather any coherent meaning from it, or to comprehend at a glance all the conditions or qualifications of the assertion that the author intended to express.

§ 336. The sources of obscurity, aside from the violations of all preceding rules, are the following:

1. Misexpression;
2. Improper ellipsis;
3. Superabundance of words;
4. The complicated structure of the sentence.

§ 337. I. *Misexpression* consists in using such phraseology as, strictly interpreted, conveys a different meaning from that intended. This fault in Structure corresponds to Imprecision in Diction. It is a fault against which many of the rules of Syntax are leveled, but there are some instances of it which escape all of them. Such are these:

"He plays a good fiddle."

"I liked to have gotten one or two broken heads."

"A luxuriant growth of flower-gardens and shrubbery surrounded the house."

"The curved line is made square instead of round, for the reason before mentioned."

"Prepositions are derived from the two Latin words, *præ* and *pono*, which signify *before* and *place*."

§ 338. II. *Improper Ellipsis* is the most frequent source of obscurity. Ellipsis of words that are not necessary to the prompt understanding of a sentence is far from being a fault of style. But conciseness is not to be sought at the expense of clearness. The following are examples of this error:

"They saw, and worshiped the God that made them."

"Intrinsic and relative beauty must be handled separately."

"They crowded around the door so as to prevent others going out."

"Under this head, I shall consider every thing necessary to a good delivery."

§ 339. III. *Superabundance of words.* As obscurity may be caused by using too few, so likewise may it result from using too many words. This is not exactly the same error that has been referred to in the chapter on Precision. There the superfluous words were simply unnecessary; here they are positively injurious to the sense, tending to convert it into nonsense. The following are examples:

"He brought about a reformation as complete as it was possible for so corrupt a world to be reformed."

"Have they ascertained the person who gave the information?"

"Socrates was born at Athens, 470 B. C.; and though there were no demonstrations of joy for the event made at his birth, yet this one, then and thus unnoticed, was destined for a great purpose to be accomplished by him."

§ 340. IV. *A complicated structure.* The rules of syntax will, if followed, prevent nearly all the cases of obscurity that might arise from this cause. The only three cases that need here to be mentioned are the following.

§ 341. (*a.*) A series of words of the same part of speech, some of which have different syntactical relations from the others.

EXAMPLE.

But unto them that are contentious, and do not obey the truth, but obey unrighteousness, indignation, and wrath; tribulation and anguish, upon every soul that doeth evil; to the Jew first, and also to the Gentile.

§ 342. (*b.*) An awkward arrangement of modifiers, particularly modifying adjuncts, by which the basis of one seems to be the antecedent of another, or the connective is liable to be referred to the wrong antecedent.

EXAMPLES.

Habits must be acquired of temperance and self-denial.

Claudius was canonized among the gods, who scarcely deserved the name of a man.

§ 343. (*c.*) Words, phrases, or clauses that are co-ordinately connected may be so arranged that it is not at once obvious which the connected parts are; this produces obscurity.

EXAMPLES.

He is not rich and incompetent for business.

The bed-clothes, pile carefully on the floor, and the crockery, throw out of the window.

He not only owns a house, but also a large farm.

Sir William Davenant was born in 1605 at Oxford, where his father kept an inn, and was educated at that university.

II. AMBIGUITY.

§ 344. Ambiguity is the fault of a sentence that is capable of two meanings, making it necessary for the hearer or reader to turn aside from the current of thought long enough to decide which meaning is intended.

§ 345. Ambiguity may be produced in three ways:

1. By the use of equivocal terms in such a connection as not to make the intended meaning clear;

2. By making a representative word stand for two different words in the same sentence;

3. By an unhappy arrangement of modifiers or connectives.

§ 346. I. Equivocal terms are those which have more than one meaning. By this are meant, not the mere shades of meaning which a word naturally comes to have by figurative application, but those independent, irrelative significations which some words possess. Perspicuity requires that when such a word is used, it should be in such a connection as shall promptly and unmistakably indicate the meaning intended.

Thus, when I say "That man was imprisoned for forging," no one would understand me to use the word *forging* in any other sense than that of *counterfeiting*. Its other signification, *forming by the hammer*, would scarcely be thought of in such a connection. But when I say, "A man who has lost his eye-sight has in one *sense* less consciousness than he had before," the word *sense*, being used after the mention of eye-sight, might very naturally be supposed to refer to one of our five senses, which is not the case.

§ 347. The most effectual remedy for equivocal language, supposing that for some reason it is important to retain the equivocal word, is to mention the term to which it is opposed, or else to employ a synonymous word along with it; a species of tautology which is permissible in such cases. Thus, the word *moral* is sometimes relieved of ambiguity by such a phrase as "the moral as opposed to the physical," or "the moral as opposed to the intellectual," or "the moral as opposed to the immoral," according to the intended signification in the passage. This method is cumbrous, but clearness is so important a quality that every thing else must be sacrificed unto it, if necessary.

§ 348. The following are some of the words most liable to be used equivocally.

Of. This preposition, when used after a noun expressive of action, is ambiguous. Sometimes its subsequent is the *agent* of the action, sometimes the *object.*

Thus, the phrase *the love of parents* may mean either the affection entertained by parents for their offspring, or that entertained by their children toward them.

§ 349. *Or.* This conjunction always connects alternatives; but sometimes alternatives of *things*, sometimes of *names* for the same thing.

In the sentence, "He was more ancient than Zoroaster, or Zerdusht," a person ignorant of the fact that these were two names for the same person, would be at a loss to understand the assertion.

§ 350. *More.* This word is sometimes an adjective in the comparative degree, sometimes an adverb qualifying an adjective, and putting it in the comparative. It should not be used in both relations in the same phrase.

Thus, "He uses more and more convincing arguments than his adversary," contains a violation of this rule. The first *more* means *in greater number;* the second *more* qualifies *convincing.* But the sentence might be misunderstood to assert that the arguments were increasingly convincing beyond those of the adversary.

§ 351. *Do* is sometimes a representative verb, and in other situations has a meaning of its own.

In the sentence, "I have long since learned to like nothing but what you do," one is at a loss to know whether the last phrase means "nothing but what you like," or "nothing but what you perform."

§ 352. II. Ambiguity may be occasioned by making a representative word, such as a pronoun, for example, stand for two different words in the same sentence. Important as it is to avoid this fault, it must be confessed to be one of the most difficult achievements of good writing. The pupil will often find that it requires all his skill in varying the expression to avoid using the same pronoun to represent objects in the same sentence; and some instances will occur in which it can not without great awkwardness be avoided.

EXAMPLES.

He told his father that he (the son) had insured his (the father's) life; so that in no event could his (the son's) estate be damaged by his (the father's) death.

One may have an air which proceeds from a knowledge of the matter before him, which (knowledge) may naturally produce some motions of his head and body, which (motions) might become the bench better than the bar.

In such sentences as the first of the foregoing, if there be no other way of relieving the difficulty, the use of the direct quotation will banish all ambiguity. "He said to his father, 'I have insured your life, so that in no event can my estate be damaged by your death.'"

The latter of the foregoing examples may be divested of all that is objectionable by recasting the entire sentence, thus: "A knowledge of the matter before him might give one such an air and produce such motions of the head and body as would suit the bench better than the bar."

§ 353. III. An unhappy arrangement of modifiers or connectives may cause ambiguity, as will be seen from the following examples.

EXAMPLES.

For sale: the latest style of white men's hats.

Theism can only be opposed to atheism or polytheism.

The Romans understood liberty, at least, as well as we.

The following lines were written by one who, for more than ten years, had been confined in the penitentiary, for his own diversion.

EXERCISES.

I. *Obscure and Ambiguous Sentences to be Corrected.**

While the band was playing, the air was so still that we could distinguish every air that was played, even at that distance.

He was inspired with a true sense of that function.

They were persons of moderate intellects even before they were impaired by their passions.

In the proper position of adverbs the ear carefully requires to be consulted, as well as the sense.

The bark Ferdinand is soon expected to sail.

And so this is the base lie that lies at the bottom of all this disturbance.

The more I see of his conduct, I like him better.

He advanced against the fierce old man, imitating his address, his pace, and career, as well as the vigor of his horse and his own skill would allow.

They seemed to be nearly dressed alike.

I wished some one would hang me a hundred times.

There sat the lady sewing, with a Roman nose.

Even if he should become a scholar, will his manners ever become a professor's chair?

There are so many advantages of speaking one's own language well, and being master of it, that, let a man's calling be what it will, it can not but be worth our taking some pains in it.

He determined to invite back to the island the king, and to call together his friends.

I saw two men digging a ditch with soldiers' caps and striped pantaloons.

I charge this officer with having abandoned his charge at the critical moment when we were expecting the enemy's charge upon us.

* The teacher would do well to require the pupils to write out a full criticism of each sentence, either on paper or on the blackboard, explaining every fault, and specifying the rule violated.

The people of this country possess a healthy country and fertile soil.

The clerk told his employer that whatever he did, he could not please him.

By greatness I not only mean the bulk of any single object, but the distinctness of the whole view at a single glance.

My Christian and surname begin and end with the same letters.

Let us consider by what social arrangements virtue and goodness may have the most and the most powerful motives.

In the circumstances I was at that time, my troubles heavily pressed on me.

You will not hardly say that clergymen have the least right to your protection.

He only read one book.

Charlemagne patronized not only learned men, but also established several educational institutions.

A taste for useful knowledge will provide us with a great and noble entertainment when others leave us.

He talks all the way upstairs to a visit.

Men look with an evil eye upon the good that is in others, and think that their reputation obscures them, and their commendable qualities stand in their light; and therefore they do what they can to cast a cloud over them, that the bright shining of their virtues may not obscure them.

She felt persuaded that the relation of master and slave was filled with duties that would require strict Christian piety, watchfulness, and prayer, to enable one to bear with patience, gentleness, and forbearance the many vexations that would inevitably come, and to prosecute with wisdom, skill, and persevering labor, all that would be required of one to perform.

Mr. Jones tells, when he is in one of his jovial moods, a good story, and takes off a character finely.

In the distribution of the negroes, care was taken to place them in complete families.

In these vagaries, her mind was sure almost to wander off home, and dwell upon its loved scenes.

He was willing to buy or sell, either way.

Either give me your note, or pay me cash, one.

It is all one to me; I had as lief do one as either.

Mrs. H. was not like a majority of boarding-house keepers.

He aimed at nothing less than the crown.

Sixtus the Fourth was, if I mistake not, a great collector of books, at least.

He chiefly spoke of virtue.

Without firmness, nothing that is great can be undertaken, or difficult can be accomplished.

Pharaoh-nechoh went up against the King of Assyria, and Josiah went out against him, and he slew him at Megiddo, when he had seen him.

Some productions of nature rise in value according as they more or less resemble art.

Scholars should be taught to scrutinize the sentiments carefully advanced in all the books they read.

I beg of you never let the glory of our nation, who made France tremble, and yet has the gentleness to be unable to bear opposition from the meanness of his own countrymen, be calumniated for partisan purposes.

Stuff a cold and starve a fever.

And, seeing dreams are caused by the distemper of the inward parts of the body, there can be no reason to interpret them as inward revelations from a superior being.

What can be more extraordinary than that a person of mean birth, no fortune, no eminent qualities of body, which have sometimes, or of mind, which have often, raised men to the highest dignities, should have the courage to attempt, and the happiness to succeed in, so improbable a design as the destruction of one of the most ancient and most solidly founded monarchies upon the earth?

(The foregoing has faults of more than one kind. Point them all out. So likewise is the following, faulty in many ways.)

William Hazlitt, so his father hoped, would embrace the ministerial career, and was educated with this view,—among other things, taught music; but he never got beyond a performance of "God save the King" on the harpsichord; and though it is clear he appreciated pulpit oratory,—see his description of the noble sermon which he heard Coleridge preach at Shrewsbury,—he was no more fit for the pulpit than was Coleridge, the ex-dragoon Cumberbatch, the future author of "Kubla Khan," and later, the oracular guest of the Greens at Highgate, to whose feet, as to those of a Gamaliel, persons decided or undecided in their philosophies thronged to listen for the great song of incoherent, yet deep and lofty thoughts, delivered in the noblest language and the most impressive style, which the Seer poured out, by way of relief to himself and of comfort for those who repaired to his shrine, and bowed before the mystical speech of its Oracle.

II. *Correct all the Errors and supply the vmitted Points in the following extract.*

After subtracting from the general mass of the current literature of the day that which possesses an infidel tendency decidedly and a very superficial discrimination would show that it constitutes no small portion of the whole still that which remains is composed in so large a measure of that which is corrupting by its tendency to minister to the base passions or secularizing by the steadiness with which all Christian reference is ignored and repudiated that in respect of the effects and consequences upon the Christian interests of society its influence is hardly less positively injurious it is a curious fact that the largest portion of the most elegant literature of the day and especially of that which is denominated light literature and which from the nature of its topics and the attractiveness of its style constitutes the staple of the reading of the public of this country though the product of minds not disposed to doubt the authority of the Bible is for the most part destitute of all Christian reference and both in its spirit and substance is as if Christianity had no existence among men but in addition we have but to frequent the various book marts of the country to see the vast amount of impure corrupting literature without even the merit of literary excellence to redeem it which in a cheap form is retailed out to the people and which now constitutes a large portion of the reading matter of the masses it is this conduct of the literature of the world with such steadied repudiation of all Christian spirit and aim in other words it is this divorcement of literature from the spirit of Christianity which has created that aversion of literary men to evangelical Christianity about which the celebrated John Foster has written so profoundly which has tended to make the profession of literature unfavorable to right Christian experience which creating the impression that the Christian empire is not co-extensive with the mind but that there are regions of mental range unembraced in the dominion of Christianity has fostered an infidel spirit that has made literature itself an agency of secularization and for the alienation of the mind from the spirit and objects of right Christianity

PART FIFTH.

INVENTION—RESUMED.

CHAPTER XXIV.

ORIGINAL QUESTIONS FOR A PLAN.

In Chapter III. the teacher was recommended to elicit thoughts on assigned subjects by asking questions, the answers to which were to be furnished by the pupils, and properly framed into a connected composition. It is now proper to require the pupil himself to furnish the questions appropriate to a given subject; and the subject given need not be so simple as those contemplated in Chapter III. The course proper to be pursued will be very similar to those recommended for previous exercises in Invention. First, the pupils are required to make a first draught of questions on the given subject. This must be done in the presence of the teacher. Then these first draughts are exchanged among the pupils for criticism. Among other points, the order of the questions becomes matter of criticism. When alterations are suggested, reasons should be given for the arrangement proposed. In this way, without the necessity for any local rules, the judgment and taste of the pupils will be practically trained to a rational and pleasing *method* of producing their thoughts.

After the first draughts have thus been amended by mutual criticism, and the second draughts made, the teacher should revise these carefully, and perfect the arrangment of the questions. Lastly, from these questions, the compositions are to be written in the same general manner as prescribed in Chapter III.

The following specimen of a scheme of questions, with the criticisms made upon it, and the final arrangement of it, will show what is meant.

BIOGRAPHY.

Questions of the First Draught.

1. What is biography?
2. What examples of biography can you cite?

3. Which is the best?
4. What is the use of biography?
5. What makes biography so interesting?
6. Are the biographies of great men interesting to young persons?
7. Are those of women to boys? Why?
8. How does biography differ from history?
9. What is autobiography?
10. Have we any autobiographies in the Bible? JOHN SMITH.

Criticism on the foregoing.

I think that a very important question has been left out, that ought to come in as No. 2, namely: What are the different kinds of biography?

Question 4 should be altered so as to read *uses* for *use;* for there must be more than one use of biography.

I think the 8th question ought to come nearer to the first, because it is closely connected with the definition of biography.

I am inclined to think that the 2d and 3d questions ought to have been put last of all.

I would suggest an additional question or two: Is not biography more useful to the generality of mankind than history? Why?

I do not think that question 7th has sufficient connection with this subject. WILLIAM JONES

Second Draught. Amended after the Criticism.

1. What is biography?
2. What are the different kinds of biography?
3. How does biography differ from history, as to its nature?
4. What are the uses of biography?
5. Why is biography more useful to the generality of people than history?
6. What makes biography so interesting?
7. Are all kinds of biography interesting to all classes of readers? If not, specify which for which.
8. What is autobiography?
9. How does it compare with other kinds as to credibility and interest?
10. Are there any biographies in the Bible?
11. Which is the best biography in the English language?

JOHN SMITH.

CHAPTER XXV.

THE CONSTRUCTION OF ABSTRACTS.

Alternately with the exercises prescribed in the previous chapter, it is recommended that the pupil be required to draw up abstracts of any pieces of good composition, selected by the teacher. He is to be taught to indicate, sometimes by short sentences, but mostly by comprehensive phrases or titles, the several topics introduced in any given discourse. In thus tracing the course of thought which gifted minds have taken, the pupil will unconsciously catch their style of arrangement. He will see how skillfully and naturally they pass from point to point, and in what manner they elaborate each point in succession. He will also learn how they subordinate one thought to another, and set forth the various subdivisions of one part of their subject, before passing to another; thus securing clearness and vigor in their handling of the subject.

As an illustration of the exercise above prescribed, we give the following abstract of Patrick Henry's *great speech in favor of resisting the aggressions of Great Britain.*

1. The folly of a reluctance to be convinced of an unpleasant truth.
2. Judging by the past, the intention of the British ministry is to enslave America.
3. No other reason for their sending fleets and armies to America.
4. All peaceable resources on the part of Americans exhausted.
5. *The only remaining resource is war.*
6. The replies to the objection based on the weakness of the Americans.
    (1.) We shall not grow stronger by postponing resistance.
    (2.) A proper use of our resources will prove our strength.
    (3.) God will help us.
    (4.) No chance left now, for the war is begun.
    (5.) No retreat now but in slavish submission, which is worse than death.

As this exercise is a very important one, another example is given: the abstract of Irving's *celebrated piece entitled* "The Broken Heart."

1. Contrast between the nature of man and the nature of woman, as to the passion of love.

2. Contrast of the effects of disappointed love on the two sexes.
   (1.) Woman broods in secret over her unhappy lot.
   (2.) The interest and relish of life is gone.
   (3.) Her untimely end.
   (4.) Comparison to a tree killed by a secret worm.

3. Out of the many instances known to the author, he selects one pre-eminent for pathetic interest; the daughter of Curran, betrothed to Emmet.
   (1.) Sketch of the character and fate of Emmet.
   (2.) The love of Miss Curran.
   (3.) Her grief for his death intensified by the manner of it.
   (4.) The effect of the want of sympathy.
   (5.) Her appearance at scenes of festivity.
   (6). The suit of a young officer.
   (7.) His success in gaining her hand, but his failure to make her forget her first love.
   (8.) Her melancholy end.

As specimens of good pieces of composition to be thus analyzed, or condensed into an abstract, the following list is given.

Addison's Reflections on the Attributes of God as seen in Creation: No. 565 of the Spectator.

Addison on the use of the Fan: No. 102 of the Spectator.

Addison's Reflections in Westminster Abbey.

Blair's Lecture on the History of Eloquence.

Blair's Lecture on the Eloquence of Popular Assemblies.

Hume's Delineation of the Character of Queen Elizabeth.

Macaulay's Delineation of the Character of Louis XIV.

Macaulay's Essay on Milton.

Macaulay's Essay on the Philosophy of Bacon.

Johnson's Criticism of Shakespeare in his "Preface to Shakespeare."

Johnson's Essay on the Writings and Genius of Pope.

Johnson's "Voyage of Life."

Prescott's Delineation of Queen Isabella.

Prescott's Description of Montezuma's Way of Life.

Everett's Remarks on the Landing of the Pilgrims.

Everett's Panegyric of England.

Lady Mary Wortley Montague's Letters on Female Education.

Blackstone's Chapter on the Rights of Persons.

Blackstone's Chapter on the Rights of Property

Channing's Lecture on Self Culture.

Channing's Lecture on the Elevation of the Laboring Classes.
Channing's Lecture on the Present Age.
Robertson's Introduction to the History of Charles V.
Any of the speeches of Webster, Calhoun, Clay, Seward, etc.

Of all forms of composition to be subjected to this process, sermons are the easiest; and if this book is used by any young ministers seeking to improve their style, copious exercises in the analyzing of good sermons are recommended in this place.

CHAPTER XXVI.

FORMING OF ORIGINAL PLAN.

The pupil will now be sufficiently advanced to enter upon the invention of schemes, analyses, or abstracts, for his own compositions. He will have learned something of the way in which trained minds put forth their thoughts; and without having any fixed rule or model to guide him, which could only apply to a few subjects, he must be required to furnish as good a scheme as he can on any assigned subject. The following are specimens.

GARDENING.

1. What it is—how distinguished from farming.
2. What separate processes are involved in it—each described.
3. Character of the whole employment—comparison with other employments.
4. Different kinds of gardening—the purposes for which they are pursued, and the different personages, localities, etc., appropriate to each.
5. Its antiquity—the character of ancient gardening.
6. Its improvements in modern times.
7. The usefulness of even pleasure gardening.
8. The simple and elevating kinds of pleasure derived from a garden.
9. What eminent men have said on this subject.

DREAMS.

1. What they are?
2. Different points of contrast between dreams and waking thoughts
3. Various causes.
4. Instances of them as thus caused.

5. Superstitious views of them, with instances.
6. Remarkable fulfillments of dreams.
7. The question considered whether prophetic dreams are still granted to men.

After the manner of the foregoing let the pupil be required to draw up schemes on several of the following subjects, and, after criticism, to write essays from them.

Farming.	Hunting.	Government.
Writing.	Dairy-work.	Traveling.
Books.	Newspapers.	Poetry.
Painting.	Slavery.	Dress.
Amusements.	Missionary Life.	Intemperance.
Schools.	Arms.	Hope.
Churches.	The Sabbath.	Inventions.
War.	The Steam-engine.	Cooking.
Music.	Paper.	Preaching.
Arithmetic.	History.	Pictures.
Geography.	Fashion.	Gunpowder.
Chemistry.	Commerce.	Letter-writing.
Gambling.	Botany.	House-keeping.
Mountains.	Friendship.	Early Rising.
Bathing.	Courage.	Conscience.
Fishing.	Honesty.	Sunday-schools.
Beasts of Burden.	Patriotism.	The Sewing-machine.
Teaching.	Weaving.	Cotton.

PART SIXTH.

EXPRESSION—RESUMED.

CHAPTER XXVII.

STRENGTH.

§ 354. This is that property of style which imparts to it the power of arresting attention and forcibly influencing the mind.

Of course the amount of influence which uttered thought will have will depend on several things. If spoken, the tones and gestures of the speaker will greatly determine its effectiveness. Whether spoken or written, its impressiveness will be very largely dependent on the character of the thought itself. Still, much is due to the style. Many a train of thought possessed of intrinsic worth has failed to produce its due effect by being expressed in a weak style; and many a common-place idea has awakened attention and admiration because happily expressed.

Strength of style has reference to two things, *General or Prevailing Vivacity*, and *the Production of Emphasis*.

I. GENERAL VIVACITY.

§ 355. The requirements of this quality of style may be conveniently considered under the four following heads:

1. The quantity and kind of words used;
2. Their arrangement in sentences;
3. The arrangement of sentences in paragraphs;
4. The use of connectives.

§ 356. I. *The quantity and kind of words used.* This is strictly an element of Diction rather than of Structure, and the rules that bear on it are very nearly the same as those of Precision. Indeed Precision is a very considerable source of Strength. In most cases the strength of a writer is in proportion to his conciseness. Verbosity enfeebles. Mere epithets, expletives, and the mentioning of unnecessary circumstances, are to be avoided.

Young writers are apt to encumber their style by the use of descriptive adjectives, expressive of some quality that has no particular bearing upon the leading thought of the sentence. This feature of style which is rather a beauty than a blemish in poetry, has in prose quite a contrary effect. From want of a disciplined taste, this is imitated by the young composer. The habit is contracted of qualifying nearly every noun with some adjective, and as these are necessarily repeated from time to time, they become trite and disgusting. Open the pages of any third or fourth rate novel or magazine, and such phrases as these crowd upon the vision: "beautiful flowers," "bright sun," "twinkling stars," "green earth," "wide world," "cold world," "bounding sea," "rolling sea," "briny deep," "golden harvests," etc. Hence the rule, *Never in prose use an adjective, unless its meaning tends to elucidate or enforce the main thought of the sentence.*

§ 357. One of the forms of *Tautology* is a violation of Strength. This consists in reiterating an idea, with but a trifling variation, if any, in a following clause or member. The following are

EXAMPLFS.

"He was so old and palsied that his limbs shook continually, *and his hands and knees trembled all the time.*"

They agreed to the terms proposed, *and accepted the conditions.*

§ 358. Here also can be traced a resemblance to what, in some languages at least, constitutes a poetic beauty. By consulting the style of the Psalms of David, one will soon be convinced that it must have been considered, in the original Hebrew, a great beauty for the latter member of a sentence to resemble the former in its structure.

This has been shown by Dr. Lowth to constitute the distinctive feature of the Hebrew verse; and it was effected very often at the cost of simple reiteration of the thought. As an instance, observe the structure of the following verses, taken from the 24th Psalm.

The earth is the Lord's . and the fullness thereof;
The world . . . . . . and they that dwell therein.

For he hath founded it . upon the seas,
And established it . . . upon the floods.

Who shall ascend . . . into the hill of the Lord?
Or who shall stand . . . in his holy place?

§ 359. Strength is not in every case effected by reducing the number of words to the lowest amount compatible with Clearness. It is sometimes sought by the very opposite course, to wit, by the repetition of words which, by the operation of the rules of Syntax, would be omitted. Of this form of Strength, the style of Macaulay affords abundant examples. Indeed, it may be doubted whether he does not sometimes repeat a word or phrase without thereby adding to the strength. In the most of cases, however, it is, in his hands, a very effective expedient.

EXAMPLES.

"The spirit of religion and the spirit of chivalry concurred to exalt his dignity."

"But the king's military means and military talents were unequal to the task."

"The extreme section of one class consists of bigoted dotards; the extreme section of the other class consists of shallow and reckless empirics."

"It was painful for him to call upon them to make sacrifices; but from sacrifices which were necessary to the safety of the English nation and of the Protestant religion, no good Englishman and no good Protestant would shrink."

§ 360. *Alliteration* is one of the devices by which writers sometimes seek Strength. This consists in using words that begin with or abound in some one letter or sound, either in very close connection, or in similar constructions in adjacent members. If carried too far, it becomes a source of weakness rather than of Strength; but if used sparingly and with no appearance of premeditation, has a decided tendency to vivacity or impressiveness.

EXAMPLES.

"A fellow-feeling makes us wondrous kind."

"Who shall decide when doctors disagree?"

"The mighty hopes that make us men."

"Had not my steward ran away without making up his accounts, I had still been immersed in sin and sea-coal."

The new feud of Protestant and Papist inflamed the old feud of Saxon and Celt.

Many of the rules of Simplicity have also a bearing on Strength, especially that which instructs us to prefer concrete to abstract terms, and specific to general descriptions. But it is unnecessary to reiterate them in this connection.

§ 361. II. *The arrangement of words in sentences.* On this point the requirements of Strength so nearly coincide with those of Clearness, that it is difficult to give any directions applicable to the former and not the latter. And yet Clearness and Strength are very distinguishable qualities. Clearness very seldom requires any transposition of the elements of a sentence; whereas such transpositions are frequently demanded in order to impart vivacity and Strength.

Nothing could be clearer than the sentence "Diana of the Ephesians is great." But how much more vigorous is the form "Great is Diana of the Ephesians!"

Again, compare these two. "The wonderful invention of Homer is what principally strikes us, on whatever side we contemplate him." "On whatever side we contemplate Homer, what principally strikes us is his wonderful invention."

Is it not manifest that the latter is the stronger form of expression? Plain as it is, however, that Strength depends very largely on arrangement, it is exceedingly difficult to reduce the matter to any consistent rules. As a general thing, the pupil must be left to his own judgment, trained by abundant reading of good authors, and by the critical suggestions of his teacher, made as occasion calls for them.

On two especial points, however, the standard authors in Rhetoric have prescribed rules, which may be allowed to have some force, but which are restricted by so many exceptions as to be of very partial value.

§ 362. One of these recommends what is called the *climactic* arrangement of terms, clauses, and members. *Climactic* means ascending like the steps of a ladder; and to understand the meaning of the rule, it must be understood that long words and cumbrous combinations of them in phrases and clauses are, in some sense, *higher* than shorter and simpler expressions. The rule, thus interpreted, amounts to a direction to put the shorter term clause, or member, before the larger. And in cases of expressions of different intensity of meaning, the weaker should precede the stronger.

EXAMPLES.

Idleness is the parent of every vice; but well-directed activity is the source of every laudable pursuit and worldly attainment.

Endless existence is a great truth; but an immortality of pure and holy affections is far greater.

Cultivate a kind, generous, and sympathizing temper.

In heaven live the friends, benefactors, deliverers, and ornaments of our race.

§ 363. The other of the two rules above referred to, is that no sentence should be terminated with an adverb, preposition, or other inconsiderable word, unless the rules of emphasis demand it.

Such complex verbs as *bring about*, *lay hold of*, *come over to*, *clear up*, etc., do not usually make so energetic a termination to a sentence as a simple verb. The pronoun *it*, especially when preceded by a preposition, makes a very feeble ending. How weak and ungainly is the sentence—"He is one whom good men are glad to be acquainted with"! How much better to say, "He is one with whom good men are glad to be acquainted"!

"Such things were not allowed formerly," is weak. The preferable arrangement is, "Formerly such things were not allowed."

§ 364. And yet this rule must not be too rigidly applied to the style of conversations, letters, and popular oratory. There is often a homely vigor in a relative clause ending with a preposition; and whatever may be the effect upon the elegance or euphony of a sentence, it certainly does sometimes add to its vivacity and avoids stiffness to let a short sentence end with one of the adverbial appendages above mentioned. There is a pleasing naturalness and force in the expressions, "the book you were speaking of,"—"the man he was talking to,"—"the freedom we fought for," etc.

§ 365. III. *The arrangement of sentences in a paragraph.** In every extended paragraph the bearing of every sentence upon what precedes should be explicit and unmistakable.

This is principally effected by the use of conjunctions and contextual phrases, the rules for which will be given in the next division of the chapter.

§ 366. When several consecutive sentences develop or illustrate the same idea, they should, as far as possible, be formed alike. This is called the rule of Parallel Construction.

§ 367. The opening sentence of a paragraph, unless obviously preparatory, should indicate with some prominence the topic of the paragraph.

§ 368. In the course of the paragraph there should occur no *dislocations*, that is, sudden turns of thought, such as would create confusion. But the entire paragraph should possess unity, having a definite purpose, and avoiding all digressions and irrelevant matter.

* The remarks under this head are condensed from Alexander Bain.

§ 369. Every paragraph should possess such a degree of unity as to be capable of being indicated by a caption or running title.

§ 370. Due proportion should obtain between principal and subordinate statements.

§ 371. IV. *The use of connectives.* The words of connection and transition between clauses, members, and sentences, may be made, according to the skill or the awkwardness of the writer, sources of strength or of weakness.

It is always a source of weakness for *two prepositions, having different antecedents, to be co-ordinated in connection with a common subsequent.*

This mode of expression has been called "the splitting of particles;" a name not very applicable to it as it occurs in English construction. The proper name for it is the one implied in the italicized words above. The following is an example.

"Though personally unknown to, I have always been an admirer of, Mr. Calhoun."

The way to correct it is to complete the first clause, and let the last, if either, be elliptic; thus:

"Though personally unknown to Mr. Calhoun, I have always admired him," or "been an admirer of him."

It is proper to remark that the very construction here condemned, enjoys a kind of toleration in *legal* and *formal* documents. The object in such compositions is not strength but clearness. Perhaps a good deal may be conceded to the usages of a profession proverbial for its attachment to what is old and of long standing; but in all compositions that have any pretension to literary merit, this construction must be disallowed.

§ 372. The most enfeebling of all practices in writing is the constant repetition of the conjunction *and*, whether as a contextual or a member-joining particle. It is a fault into which young persons are peculiarly apt to fall. Sometimes in writing a narrative, when their minds are eagerly carrying on the thread of the story, they will indite a series of sentences, each commencing with the formula "and then," or "and so;" altogether unaware of the slovenly manner in which they are using language. To avoid this, let the pupil avail himself of all the expedients in his power for varying the expression, and avoid the necessity of using this one conjunction so often.

§ 373. With regard to the use of co-ordinating conjunctions in a series of terms or short clauses, there are two different figures of syntax, directly the opposite of each other, each of which may be so used as to contribute to Strength. They are called *Asyndeton* and *Polysyndeton.* In the one, the connecting conjunction is entirely omitted from a series of co-ordinates; in the other it is carefully repeated, either before every member of the series, or else between each pair. In the former, the object is to present a succession of spirited images; in the latter, the writer desires to make the mind of the reader dwell upon each successive thought, not passing from it until its full force is felt. But they both possess what is called the *cumulative* power; heaping up before the mind a combination of thoughts that are intended powerfully to affect it. Witness the following examples, in which these figures are combined with the *balanced* construction, showing that St. Paul evidently delighted in such rhetorical devices.

"There is one body and one spirit, even as ye are called in one hope of your calling; one Lord, one faith, one baptism, one God and Father of all, who is above all and through all and in you all." (Observe how the asyndeton and the polysyndeton are combined in the foregoing extract.)

"Charity vaunteth not itself, is not puffed up, doth not behave itself unseemly, seeketh not her own, is not easily provoked, thinketh no evil, rejoiceth not in iniquity, but rejoiceth in the truth; beareth all things, believeth all things, hopeth all things, endureth all things." (See § 359.)

"It is sown in corruption, it is raised in incorruption: it is sown in weakness, it is raised in power: it is sown a natural body, it is raised a spiritual body."

"Who shall separate us from the love of Christ? shall tribulation, or distress, or persecution, or famine, or nakedness, or peril, or sword?'

"For all things are yours; whether Paul or Apollos or Cephas; or the world or life or death; or things present, or things to come;—all are yours, and ye are Christ's, and Christ is God's."

§ 374. No single feature of style more plainly marks the mature mind, conversant with literature, than the judicious use of contextual connectives. These include not merely the conjunctions, but all those adverbs and adverbial phrases that indicate the relation of the sentences which they severally introduce, to the preceding context. All of them, including the conjunctions, have been subjected to a searching classification, which, however, is of no great practical value. To base upon such a classification a system of rules, would be to invest with difficulty a matter which would be more economically learned from extensive and varied reading.

II. THE PRODUCTION OF EMPHASIS.

§ 375. Emphasis is a matter properly belonging to elocution; nevertheless it is in the power of a writer so to arrange his sentence as to show at a glance which is the right word to be stressed, and indeed almost to compel a reader to enunciate it with approximate correctness.

The structure of sentences is too diversified to admit of any rules determining what precise place the emphatic word should occupy. But this general principle may be laid down: *any departure from the ordinary and grammatical consecution of the words or elements of a sentence calls attention to the words that are thus thrown out of their natural place, and invites emphasis upon them.*

§ 376. There is an idiomatic mode of emphasizing the subject of certain propositions. This consists in introducing the sentence with the expletive *there* or *it*, and then bringing in the subject *after* the predicate.

Thus, to say—"It is he that hath made us, and not we ourselves,"—puts a much stronger emphasis on the word *he* than to say—"He made us, and not we ourselves."

And the sentence,—"There is gold in these hills,"—makes the word *gold* much more emphatic than when expressed thus,—"Gold is in these hills."

§ 377. Repetition is often used for the purpose of producing contrast. It is of two kinds; *exact* and *modified* repetition: *exact*, when the very word or words are repeated; *modified*, when they are reiterated with some change.

EXAMPLES.

"Come back! *come back!*" he cried in grief. (Exact.)

Down, *down* they sunk, and the quick returning waters smoothed out every ripple, and left the sea as if they had not been. (Exact.)

Remember March, the ides of March remember! (Modified.)

Oh, nothing; a little thing;
A very little thing; I only shoot
At my child. (Modified.)

Add to your faith, virtue; and to virtue, knowledge; and to knowledge, temperance; and to temperance, patience; and to patience, godliness; and to godliness, brotherly kindness; and to brotherly kindness, charity.*

§ 378. Caution. *Never repeat a word unless clearness or emphasis requires it.*

§ 379. Contrast involves a kind of emphasis, or is the frequent occasion of it. Generally when two things are compared, not only their points of resemblance, but of difference, are set forth. The rules of Strength require that whenever such an opposition is expressed, there should be some resemblance in the diction and structure of the sentence, or parts of sentence, which express it. Sometimes the antithesis is conveyed by two co-ordinated words or phrases in the same sentence; sometimes by similar members or clauses. Such regularity should not be kept up

* This series is rather too long for the emphasis to be sustained.

with rigid exactness during too many clauses, for then the very monotony of the cadences become a source of weakness. The following celebrated example of finely drawn antithesis is taken from Pope, whose style is remarkable for its tendency to the balanced structure:

"Homer was the greater genius; Virgil, the better artist: in the one we most admire the man; in the other, the work. Homer hurries us with a commanding impetuosity; Virgil leads us with an attractive majesty. Homer scatters with a generous profusion; Virgil bestows with a careful magnificence. Homer, like the Nile, pours out his riches with a sudden overflow. Virgil, like a river in its banks, with a constant stream. And when we look upon their machines, Homer seems like his own Jupiter in his terrors, shaking Olympus, scathing the lightnings, and firing the heavens; Virgil, like the same power, in his benevolence, counseling with the gods, laying plans for empires, and ordering his whole creation."

EXERCISES.

Correct all the violations of the rules of Strength that occur in the following sentences; also, any other faults that may occur in them:

You should rise at the time when the lark rises, and also retire to bed when the lark does.

Those who are weak struggle to obtain freedom; those who are strong struggle to obtain power.

The present question is whether I shall continue to exist, or bring my existence to a termination.

It is sown in corruption; it is raised an incorruptible body.

I rather choose to wrong him who is dead, to perpetrate injustice on your humble speaker and you, the gracious listeners, than do what is injurious to those who are such honorable men.

A principle of our religion is that we should not revenge ourselves on our enemies, or take vengeance on our foes.

For us to behold the divine works of God with coldness or indifference, or to survey the beauties of creation without an inward satisfaction and complacency, is impossible.

He has talents which are unfolding into life and vigor rapidly, and indomitable energies.

The faith he professed, and which he became an apostle of, was not his invention.

Higher examples of noble daring, dreadful suffering, and heroic endurance, were never exhibited in the history of the world than, during the revolution, by the Whigs of North Carolina. The whole state was overrun by an overwhelming force of the enemy, from the mountains to the sea. Driven into the gloomy and impenetrable swamps almost, from their homes, the spirit of liberty survived even there; and South Carolina proved that the spirit of her people was invincible, by her conduct, though her soil might be overrun.

Poverty induces and cherishes dependence; and corruption is increased and strengthened by dependence.

I look upon this thing as my bounden duty, so far as I am enabled to do it, and so long as I keep within the bounds of truth, the limits of equity, and the confines of decency.

Thought, and language, which is the expression of thought, act and react upon each other mutually.

I am not disposed to travel into regions of conjecture, but to relate a narrative of facts that have actually taken place.

I went full of a great many serious reflections home.

Sensualists who habitually afford to their appetites inordinate gratifications, by their gross excesses and frequent indulgences, debase their mental intellects, enfeeble their corporeal bodies, and wear out their spirits.

His crimes and his wicked, wicked deeds had brought him into extreme distress which could not have been more violent without endangering life, and involved him in extreme perplexity.

Generosity is a showy virtue, which many persons are very fond of.

May the happy message be applied to us, in all the virtue, strength, and comfort of it!

Though the efforts of Alfred were insufficient entirely to banish the darkness of the age he lived in, yet he greatly improved the condition of the men of his country, and was the means of doing much good to them.

Ingratitude is not a crime that I am chargeable with, whatever other faults I may be guilty of.

This bird had a great antipathy to, but was not in the least afraid of, dogs and cats. Sometimes he had battles with, but always came off victorious over, them. At one time, to try his courage, four strong cats were brought near to, in order to fight with, him. A piece of raw meat was thrown down amongst them; but the bird beat them all, and took the meat to himself.

Though virtue borrows no assistance from, yet it may often be accompanied by, the advantages of fortune.

As the strength of our cause does not depend upon, so neither is it to be decided by, any critical points of history or chronology or language.

Shakespeare was a man of profound genius, and whose bold and striking thoughts must be admired in every age by men.

While the earth remaineth, seed-time, harvest, cold, heat, summer, winter, day, night, shall not cease.

The body of this animal was strong and proportionable and beautiful.

There is nothing which more than steady application, and a habit of observation, promotes knowledge.

The knowledge he has acquired, and the habits of application he possesses, will render him probably very useful.

Their idleness and their luxury and their pleasures and their criminal deeds and their immoderate passions and their timidity and their baseness of mind, have dejected them to such a degree as to make them weary of life.

In one individual the development of Christian knowledge was prepared for by his previous stand-point.

He was killed in the first battle he was in after his return to the army.

It is absurd to judge poets by precepts which they did not attend to.

When the affairs of the good man have required business, and his business was a matter of discipline, and his discipline was to pass upon a sinning person, or had a design of charity, his duty met the infirmities of a man, and anger was its instrument, and the instrument became stronger than the prime agent, and raised a tempest, and overruled the man; and then his prayer was broken, and his thoughts were troubled, and his words went up toward the cloud, and his thoughts pulled them back again, and made them without intention, and the good man sighs for his infirmity, but must be content to lose the prayer, and he must recover it when his anger is removed, and his spirit is becalmed; and then it ascends to heaven upon the wings of the holy dove, and dwells with God, till it returns, like the useful bee, laden with a blessing and the dew of heaven.

Men of the best sense have been touched, more or less, with these groundless horrors and presages of futurity, upon surveying the most indifferent works of nature.

He that cometh in the name of the Lord, is blessed.

Every one that puts on the appearance of goodness, is not good.

And Elias with Moses appeared to them.

Where are your fathers? and do the prophets live forever?

We came to our journey's end at last with no small difficulty, after much fatigue, through deep roads and bad weather.

Virgil has justly contested with Homer the praise of judgment, but his invention remains yet unrivaled.

Let us employ our criticism on ourselves, instead of being critics on others.

Let us implore superior assistance, for enabling us to act well our own part, leaving others to be judged by Him who searcheth the heart.

The vehemence of passion, after it has exercised its tyrannical sway for a while, may subside by degrees.

This fallacious art debars us from enjoying life instead of lengthening it.

Indulging ourselves in imaginary enjoyments, often deprives us of real ones.

How will that nobleman be able to conduct himself, when reduced to poverty, who was educated only to magnificence and pleasure?

Charity breathes long suffering to enemies, courtesy to strangers, habitual kindness toward friends.

Gentleness ought to diffuse itself over our whole behavior, to form our address, and regulate our speech.

The propensity to look forward into life is too often grossly abused, and immoderately indulged.

The regular tenor of a virtuous and pious life, will prove the best preparation for immortality, for old age, and death.

These rules are intended to teach young persons to write with propriety, elegance, and perspicuity.

Sinful pleasures blast the opening prospects of human felicity, and degrade human honor.

In this state of mind, every employment of life becomes an oppressive burden, and every object appears gloomy.

They will acquire different views, applying to the honorable discharge of the functions of their station, and entering on a virtuous course of action.

Every emotion of envy dies in me, when I look upon the tombs of the great; when I read the epitaphs of the beautiful, every inordinate desire goes out; my heart melts with compassion, when upon a tombstone I meet with the grief of parents; I consider the vanity of grieving for those whom we must quickly follow, when the tomb of the parents themselves I see.

In order to present her early compliments to her lord, dressed in the robe of innocency, fearless of danger, long before the trees have ventured to unfold their leaves, even while the icicles are pendant on our houses, the snowdrop, foremost of the lovely train, breaks her way through the frozen soil, and steps forth.

The ornaments of a building lose most of their attractions, unless they conduce to some useful end either in appearance or reality, however fine they may be.

Next unto her sanctity and holiness of life, it is meet that our English housewife be a woman of great modesty and temperance, as well inwardly as outwardly;—inwardly, as in her behavior and carriage toward her husband; wherein she shall shun all violence of rage, passion, and humor; coveting less to direct than to be directed; appearing ever unto him pleasant, amiable, and delightful; and though occasion of mishaps or the misgovernment of his will may induce her to contrary thoughts, yet virtuously to suppress them, and with a mild sufferance, rather to call him home from his error than with the strength of anger to abate the least spark of his evil; calling into her mind that evil and uncomely language is deformed, though uttered even to servants; but most monstrous and ugly, when it appears before the presence of a husband;—outwardly as in her apparel and diet, both which she shall proportion according to the competency of her husband's estate and calling, making her circle rather straight than large; for it is a rule, if we extend to the uttermost, we take away increase; if we go a hair's breadth beyond, we enter into consumption; but if we preserve any part, we build strong forts against the adversaries of fortune, provided that such preservation be honest and conscionable.

QUESTIONS FOR REVIEW AND EXAMINATION.

Which are the five essential properties of good style that refer to the structure of sentences? In what respects do they differ? What does sentential unity require? Which kind of sentences allows some departure from the strictest unity? What is the best method of inculcating a good judgment with respect to unity?

Which are the five special rules for unity of sentences?

What does purity of structure demand? Where are the rules of purity of structure to be found? What is solecism?

Why is it better to practice young persons in the illustration of moral truth by fictitious than by real examples? How are novels, romances, and tales distinguished from one another? What are the four requirements with regard to dialogue? What are *dramatis personæ?*

In what does clearness consist? What are the two faults opposed to clearness? How are they distinguished? When is a sentence obscure? Which are the four sources of obscurity? What is misexpression? When is ellipsis improper? What are the three kinds of complicated structure that are not met by the rules of Syntax?

What is ambiguity? In what three ways may it be produced? What are equivocal terms? What is the requirement of perspicuity with regard to equivocal terms? What is the most effectual safeguard against ambiguity, when an equivocal word is necessarily used in questionable connection? How is *of* ambiguous? How is *or* ambiguous? How is *more* ambiguous? How is *do* ambiguous?

What is strength? To what two things does strength have reference? To what four things does general vivacity refer?

What relation has precision to strength? What does strength require with regard to expletive adjectives? What are the requirements of strength with regard to tautology? What is the distinctive feature of Hebrew verse? How is strength affected by repetition?

What is alliteration, and how does it affect strength? How do clearness and strength differ as to arrangement? What is a climactic arrangement?

What does strength require with regard to terminal words? Are short words never to be allowed at the end of a sentence? What are the rules of strength with regard to paragraphs?

How does the co-ordination of prepositions having different antecedents affect strength? In what compositions is this tolerated? What are the requirements of strength with regard to the word *and*? What is asyndeton? What is polysyndeton? When is each advantageous to strength?

What has strength to do with emphasis? Which are the two kinds of repetition, and how distinguished? When is repetition allowable? How does strength require that contrast shall be expressed? How does a protracted antithesis expressed in balanced sentences affect strength?

What is style? What is the distinction between diction and structure? Which are the four essential qualities of good diction? How are they distinguished? What is the distinction between barbarism and solecism? Which are the four kinds of barbarism? How distinguished? Which are the two kinds of unauthorized words? What is the distinction between lexical propriety and decorous propriety? What is the difference between a paronym and a synonym?

BOOK FOURTH.

PART FIRST.

INVENTION—ARGUMENTATION.

CHAPTER XXVIII.

PRELIMINARY EXERCISES IN REASONING.

A great deal of the matter of discourse consists in giving reasons for opinions or assertions. The young composer should be extensively exercised in this department of the art. A few cautions are necessary.

§ 380. I. He should be careful that what he alleges as a reason for an assertion is not the same truth merely expressed in different words. For instance, if the object were to prove that lettuce is an opiate, and the proof adduced should be—because it produces sleep,—it is very evident that the latter proposition is only a variation of the former, and constitutes no reason for it. This is what logicians call the fallacy of *begging the question.*

But it is well to observe that the assertion that lettuce produces sleep, if admitted to be true, does prove something: what does it prove? It proves that we are justified in applying the name *opiate* to lettuce, or, which is the same thing, in referring lettuce to the class of opiates.

When, therefore, an assertion is given to be proved, we must consider whether it is required to prove the fact or truth involved in the assertion, or only to justify the application of a term. If the former, no mere variation in the form of expression will answer as a reason or proof.

§ 381. II. One argument must not be included in another. This error is very similar to the one just mentioned. It consists in expressing one reason for an assertion in two or more different modes, and adducing them as if they were different and independent proofs. It is well enough in the setting forth of a reason, to present it in various lights, so that every one may rightly apprehend it. This is done for the sake of clearness and strength; but it is dishonest and damaging to a cause to pass off for a number of arguments what only amounts to one.

If it were required to prove that *plagiarism should be avoided*, and a writer should adduce the two following propositions as reasons, viz.: 1. Because it injures the mind; 2. Because it ruins the intellectual faculties;—would not the sophistry be manifest? What are the *intellectual faculties* but the *mind?* And how is it possible to *ruin* a thing without *injuring* it? To be sure, *ruin* is a stronger expression than *injure*, but the meaning in these two sentences is practically the same. Whether plagiarism in any given instance would *ruin* the mind or only *injure* it, depends upon the extent to which it is practiced. These two pretended reasons, therefore, are only one, and in order to exert their proper influence on the judgment, should be offered as only one.

§ 382. III. Sometimes a reason alleged does not directly prove the given proposition, but requires, in order to show its bearing upon the latter, a train of arguments, one depending on another, like the links of a chain. Now if any two of these links or connected arguments be set forth as *independent* arguments, it will constitute a fallacy.

For instance, let the assertion to be proved be—There can be no enjoyment of property where there is no government; if the reasons adduced be—

(1.) Because there can be no enjoyment of property without the enforcement of laws;

(2.) Because there can be no enjoyment of property where every man may do as he pleases;

—A little reflection will show that these two reasons are only different links of the one chain that connects the existence of government with the enjoyment of property. That chain would be something like the following:

1. There can be no enjoyment of property where every man may do as he pleases.

2. Every man may do as he pleases if there is no law enforced.

3. No law will be enforced until it is enacted by adequate authority.

4. There can neither be authority adequate to enact laws, nor power to enforce them, without government.

5. Therefore there can be no enjoyment of property where there is no government.

With these hints to guide him, let the pupil be required to produce arguments in support of given propositions.

§ 383. When a proposition is thus formally set forth to be sustained by proofs, it is called a *thesis*.

The following models will show the kind of exercise that is recommended.

Thesis. Music should be cultivated.

ARGUMENTS OR REASONS.

1. Because it is an innocent entertainment.
2. Because it refines the feelings.

Thesis. Pride should be repressed.

ARGUMENTS OR REASONS.

1. Because it injures the character.
2. Because it deprives one of happiness.

Thesis. A classical is superior to a mere English education.

ARGUMENTS OR REASONS.

1. Because it requires a higher degree of patience and diligence to accomplish it;

2. Because it exercises more abundantly the faculties of attention, memory, judgment, and taste;

3. Because it qualifies one for the enjoyment of literature and the society of literary men.

Let the teacher prescribe to the pupil theses for proof, easy at first, and advance to more difficult ones by degrees, subjecting all to criticism and emendation as before directed.

COMPLEX ARGUMENTS.

Sometimes an argument advanced in support of a thesis is not so obvious or ascertained but that it requires to be proved, as if it were itself a thesis. This will produce a complex argument. Take for example the second of the theses whose proof is given as a model in the foregoing division of the chapter, and observe how each of its proofs is susceptible of subordinate proof.

Thesis. Pride should be repressed.

1. Because it injures the character.

(1.) For it is, in itself, the most odious of all qualities in the estimation of the good. Which fact is not only the sign of its being evil, but the cause of evil, in that it deprives one of all sympathizing association with those who can do us good.

(2.) Because it prevents self-improvement, without which, character deteriorates.

2. (Pride should be repressed) because it deprives one of happiness.

(1.) By making one discontented;

(2.) By bringing one into collision with his fellow-men, who will not always accord to him what he thinks to be his due;

(3.) Because it eventually alienates all one's friends.

Let the pupil be thus required to give reasons in support of reasons for a given thesis, making the argument as complex as the particular subject seems to demand, carefully observing the cautions above given.

ARGUMENTATIVE ESSAY.

As a further exercise, after the complex argument has been, by criticism and emendation, made as near perfect as may be, let it be taken as the plan for a composition, and the several heads or proofs amplified, making it a full and complete essay. This course may be pursued with profit for some time before the exercises of the next chapter are taken up.

CHAPTER XXIX.

THE SOURCES OF ARGUMENT.

From even his limited experience in argumentation as afforded by the exercises prescribed in the preceding chapter, the pupil will be prepared to appreciate such help as may be afforded by the classification of the sources of argument, and the inculcation of principles to guide him in the selection of arguments appropriate to the different kinds of theses.

§ 384. The sources of argument may be conveniently arranged under six general heads.

1. Proofs from Explication or Analysis;
2. Proofs from Antecedent Probability;
3. Proofs from Signs or Consequences;
4. Proofs from Instances or Examples;
5. Proofs from Analogy;
6. Proofs from Testimony or Authority.

I. PROOFS FROM EXPLICATION OR ANALYSIS.

§ 385. Sometimes a proposition is sufficiently proved by simply explaining the terms. This explanation may be effected in one of five different modes:

1. Definition;
2. Enumeration;
3. Distinction;
4. Limitation;
5. Interpretation.

1. Definition.

§ 386. A true definition is made up of two parts, the genus and the differentia.

These are technical terms of Logic, but they are not difficult to understand.

§ 387. The word *genus* means *class* or *kind*. When a term is defined, the first thing is to refer it to its proper class.

Thus *geography* would be called a *science;* a *dog* is a *quadruped;* a *pear* is a *fruit; paper* is a *substance;* a *sword* is a *weapon; sorrow* is an *emotion; printing* is a *process*, etc.

Care must be taken that the genus to which any object is referred be not too remote from the object. It is the *proximate* or nearest genus that is wanted in a definition. Thus to refer *dog* to the class *creature* would be too indefinite; *animal* would not be much better; *quadruped* is perhaps the best that could be used without going into scientific terms.

§ 388. The *differentia* is that quality or those qualities which distinguish the object or kind of objects in question from all the others embraced in the genus.

Thus the differentia of geography would be *of the earth.* The entire definition,—Geography is the science of the earth.

When we define *paper* as a substance made of rags reduced to a pulp, and generally used for writing or printing, the differentia is composed of the circumstances, *made of rags reduced to a pulp*, and *generally used for writing or printing.*

When *printing* is defined as a process of stamping characters or pictures on a surface, all that follows the word *process* is the differentia by which printing is distinguished from other processes.

§ 389. The differentia must be *positive*, as opposed to negative; it must be *intelligible;* it must not contain a synonym or paronym of the word defined; and it must be expressed with the utmost precision.

Let the teacher dictate a number of words to be defined by the pupils, from his own understanding of them, without access to a dictionary; and then let these be subjected to mutual criticism by the members of the class. Let the exercise be repeated at the teacher's discretion.

2. Enumeration.

§ 390. Sometimes a term can be explained by enumerating all that it includes or comprehends. This is the only way to make plain such terms as the following: *the uses of iron; the domestic animals; the points of the compass; the five oceans; the five senses; the forms of government*, etc.

Let the pupil explain by enumeration the following terms:

The advantages of the Sabbath.

The points of man's physical inferiority to other animals.

The subjects for reflection suggested by the recurrence of New-year's day.

The virtues of King Alfred.

The discoveries of Sir Isaac Newton.

The wonders of animal instinct.

The lovely traits in the character of Joseph.

The elements of domestic happiness.

The advantages of machinery.

The benefits conferred by railroads.

The peculiarities of the Irish character.

The marks of design in the structure of the eye.

The benefits of printing.

The varieties of literature.

The varieties of manufacture concerned in the making and furnishing of a carriage.

The advantages of steam power over other motive powers.

The applications of the screw.

The nervous stimulants used by men.

The points of superiority of Christian over Mohammedan morality.

The advantages of marriage over polygamy.

The superior adaptedness of mercury for thermometers..

3. Distinction.

§ 391. A third method of explication is by pointing out the difference or differences between the given term or topic and some other with which it might be confounded.

Thus *character* is by many confounded with *reputation;* but it is very distinct from the latter, and may be actually different. Character is the present state of a man's soul, as the product of nature, circumstances, and his own actions. Reputation is what he is thought to be by the most of those who know him.

In this manner let the pupil point out the following distinctions:

Commerce and Navigation.	Knowledge and Wisdom.
Accent and Emphasis.	Decision and Obstinacy.
Anger and Hatred.	Bravery and Heroism.
Enthusiasm and Fanaticism.	Happiness and Pleasure.
Credulity and Superstition.	Modesty and Shame.

Geography and Topography.
Art and Science.
Conscience and Reason.
Genius and Talent.
Education and Instruction.
Crime and Sin.

4. Limitation.

§ 392. It is very often the case that a proposition is true when understood in a certain sense, and not true in another. Hence, it becomes a very important matter, in all cases in which there is the least danger of being misunderstood, to prepare the way for argument by *explaining in what sense it is to be taken.* In many cases, this will supersede any further argument. A proposition that might be disputed by some, would be universally conceded, if carefully explained in what respect it is to be understood.

For instance, the maxim, Familiarity breeds contempt, is limited in its application to the intercourse of faulty beings. For the only reason that could be assigned for the maxim is that familiarity reveals the existence of faults, a knowledge of which is incompatible with respect. Of course this reason would not hold good in the case of those characters that are free from such faults. If it should be replied that there are no such characters, *that* opens a different question. But the ideal possibility of characters devoid of those faults which induce contempt deprives the maxim of its claim as a universal truth, and makes it highly proper to lay down the foregoing limitation.

Let the pupil be required to explain in what respect, or to what extent, the following propositions are true:

Water boils at 212° Fahrenheit.
Mercury is the best substance for thermometers.
Every creature of God is good.
Swear not at all.*
The face is an index of the mind.
It is never right to deceive a man.
Lay not up for yourselves treasures upon earth.
A little learning is a dangerous thing.
Woman's mind is equal to man's.

* In the case of imperative propositions, the pupil must show to what extent they are binding.

A classical is superior to a mere English education.

Knowledge is power.

A man is known by his companions.

It is cruelty to the innocent to spare the guilty.

Take no thought for the morrow.

It is not lawful to do evil that good may come.

Necessity knows no law.

Love thy neighbor as thyself.

Opportunity makes the thief.

Train up a child in the way he should go, and when he is old he will not depart from it.

Men are responsible for their opinions.

Society has no right to control the pursuits of individuals.

Internal improvements should be left to private enterprise.

Aristocracy is a social evil.

Rebellion is a crime.

5. Interpretation.

§ 393. A proposition is often expressed in such language, figurative or enigmatical, as requires to be *interpreted* before it can be made the subject of argument. Of this nature are the generality of proverbs, which contain the results of human experience expressed in some quaint or striking manner, so as to be easily remembered, and quickly quoted when the occasion demands. Whenever the truth which they contain becomes the subject of discussion, or is itself adduced as an argument, it becomes necessary to fix with the utmost accuracy the meaning they convey.

Thus the maxim, "Draw not the bow before the arrow is fixed," is a figurative maxim borrowed from archery. The lesson it teaches may be expressed in plain language,—Never commence a decisive course of action until fully prepared for it. By a "decisive course of action" is meant one that will compel a speedy issue, either in success or disaster.

Let the pupil interpret in this manner the following apothegms:

Rome was not built in a day.

A goodly apple is often rotten at the core.

Make hay while the sun shines.
A little straw may show which way the wind blows.
Necessity is the mother of invention.
Contentment is the true philosopher's stone.
The love of money is the root of all evil.
Ye (who?) are the salt of the earth.
A rolling stone gathers no moss.
It is hard for an empty bag to stand upright.
Science is the handmaid of religion.
Every man is the architect of his own fortune.
Cut your coat according to your cloth.
Where there 's a will there 's a way.
Every grain hath its bran.
Between two stools one comes to the ground.
It is good fishing in troubled waters.
Every body's business is nobody's business.
Little strokes fell great oaks.
No cross, no crown.
More things spring in the garden than the gardener sowed.
A stone that is fit for the wall is not to be left in the way.
One ounce of discretion is worth two pounds of wit.
A thing of beauty is a joy forever.
Better bend the neck than bruise the forehead.
A bad workman quarrels with his tools.
The more schools, the fewer jails.
We live in deeds, not years.
The pen is mightier than the sword.

II. PROOFS FROM ANTECEDENT PROBABILITY.

§ 394. This mode of reasoning consists in showing that, *from the very nature of a thing*, it may be expected to operate in a certain way. This is reasoning from causes to effects, from antecedents to consequents.

Thus if the given thesis were, A republic can not long exist without parties; and if one should attempt to show this from the natural tendency of men to differ on practical measures, coupled with the fact that in republics the opinions of the people have to give direction to public measures, that would be a fair case of reasoning from antecedent probability.

Or, if the thesis were, An experienced military commander is more likely to make a good governor than a literary recluse;

—And the reason adduced should be, Because his occupation has habituated him to the management of men, and to the sense of public responsibility;

—That would be an argument of the kind now under consideration.

The following is a list of theses in proof of which arguments from antecedent probability would be appropriate:

Books alone can never teach the use of books.
Power discovers the real disposition of a man.
In anger we are apt to form erroneous conclusions.
A new version of the Bible would not be generally received.
Judges ought not to be elected by the people.
Climate has some influence upon national character.
The pulpit affords a finer field of eloquence than the bar.
The reading of history preserves the mind from bigotry.
Education in seclusion fosters prejudice.
Great Britain will never meet the fate of Rome.
The study of nature has a beneficial influence on character.
The offering of rewards does not produce a healthy activity.
The observance of the Sabbath reduces popular ignorance.
Direct taxation is the best mode of supporting government.
The profession of lawyers should not be abolished.
The study of a language improves the mind.
The prohibition of the sale of ardent spirits by law is not expedient.
Boys and girls should attend school together.
Perfection is not to be expected in man.
Employment is the best preservative of innocence.
Prosperity has greater trials than adversity.
Self-knowledge is the best of all kinds of knowledge.
The employment influences the character.
The occupation of the farmer is essential to society.

III. PROOFS FROM SIGNS OR CONSEQUENCES.

§ 395. This is the principal kind of proof adduced in establishing facts. It consists in the pointing out of those circumstances which can be accounted for only by the supposition that the supposed fact did take place.

For instance, if the thesis were, The commerce of Solomon extended to the East Indies; by adducing the fact that *apes* and *peacocks* are mentioned among the articles of his cargoes, one would be reasoning from signs.

Or, if one should endeavor to show that the taste of the ancient Greeks was highly cultivated, by pointing out the remains of their buildings, statuary, carvings, painting, and literature, he would be giving proofs from signs.

The following is a list of theses to be proved by signs:

Abraham was strong in faith.

Moses was not ambitious.

King Saul was fickle.

David was a hero.

Solomon's reign was one of splendor.

Socrates was superior to his countrymen.

Alexander was selfish.

Cicero was vain.

The Saracens were once a learned people.

The Romans occupied Palestine.

The art of printing has advanced civilization.

Commerce made Venice the center of intelligence.

Christianity is of Divine origin.

Grecian mythology developed the taste.

The exclusive direction of the attention to accomplishments has weakened this woman's mind. (Imaginary case.)

The pen is mightier than the sword.

The Crusades benefited Europe.

The human race have descended from one pair.

Commerce has contributed to the advancement of civilization.

The Bible has conferred great blessings on mankind.

America was once peopled by a race more civilized than the Indians.

"Robinson Crusoe" is not wholly a true story.

The English people must have sprung from the same race as the German.

Human nature was the same in the days of Abraham, Isaac, and Jacob that it is now.

IV. PROOF FROM INSTANCES OR EXAMPLES.

§ 396. Of all methods of proof this is at once the easiest and the most entertaining. The sources of it are personal observation, the testimony of our associates or others, the current periodical literature of the day, history, biography, etc. When cited to establish an argument, the instances must be *real*, not fictitious, and they must be cases included under the general statement they are adduced to substantiate. Their value in all cases is in proportion to the degree to which they represent the whole class. Any opposing instance or example is sufficient to destroy the universality of the thesis, and require that it be limited as described in § 392, or expressed only in general terms.

Suppose the thesis were, Fashionable living spoils the heart; and the person required to prove this should know some three or four clear instances of it, say Mrs. D, Mrs. H, Mrs. S, and Miss W, his course would then be to describe these cases, showing that the moral deterioration in each case could be rationally traced to her fashionable life.

Or, if it should be required to prove that True prayer is likely to be answered, and the instances of Abraham, Jacob, Moses, Joshua, Gideon, Samuel, David, Elijah, etc., were adduced, that would be a process of proof of this description.

Let the following theses be proved by examples or instances:

Dogs are affectionate and faithful.

Rats are cunning.

Pictures are instructive.

Conquerors are generally cruel, or indifferent to suffering in others.

Intemperance produces wretchedness.

Hurricanes are destructive.

Dishonesty is bad policy.

Heretics used to be tortured.

Missionary life is full of danger.

It is dangerous for boys to use guns.

Tobacco is injurious to health.

Republics have been ungrateful.

Extravagance leads to poverty.

Commerce makes nations rich.

All is not gold that glitters. (Interpret.)

Christianity has originated benevolent institutions.

Climate influences the occupations of a people.

A careless watch invites a vigilant foe.

Necessity is the mother of invention.

Luxury has ruined nations.

In the progress of civilization, the arts precede science.

Early associations have a lasting effect.

The best progress is often slow.

A love for one's profession is a great help to excellence in it.

Some of the most gifted men have been unhappy in their domestic life.

V. PROOFS FROM ANALOGY.

§ 397. Analogy is a kind of similarity. Two things may be similar in several respects, in form, size, color, composition, nature. But they are analogous only when they have similar relations to some other thing, or when they produce like effects.

Thus *morphine* is in its appearance similar to *quinine*, but in its effect as a medicine analogous to *laudanum*, which it does not at all resemble.

§ 398. Proof by analogy consists in arguing from similarity in certain respects which are known, to certain other respects which are not known. It never can amount to any more than a moderate degree of probability, and is more useful in confirming other forms of proof, or in leading to them, than as an independent argument.

It is arguing from analogy to urge that the aurora borealis must have an electrical origin, because appearances very similar are produced by passing an electrical current through the vacuum of an air-pump receiver.

A beautiful instance of the argument from analogy forms the basis of the parable of the Prodigal Son.* If an earthly father would receive with forgiveness and joy a returning prodigal, after all his career of profligacy and licentiousness, so will God, who is at least as tender-hearted as men, receive with forgiveness and joy a penitent sinner.

Let the following theses be proved by analogy:

The moon is a sphere.

The planets are inhabited.

---

* As indeed it is the basis of nearly all the parables.

The future state will be one of rewards and punishments.

Traveling in Switzerland is delightful.

Early piety is the most effectual.

The invisible world is a social state.

The world is not governed by chance.

Men are unequal in natural talent.

There are truths in Scripture yet undiscovered.

Taste can be improved by association.

Rich men have their trials.

Legends change by transmission.

College life induces prejudices.

An increase of wealth in the nation would increase vice.

The establishment of a national church would injure the morals of the American people.

Public lectures promote popular intelligence.

Early habits are hard to change.

This continent was once under the ocean.

The English language will be spoken all over North America.

The Chinese Empire will be dismembered.

The theater will (or will never) be regenerated.

Phrenology will (or will never) command general acceptance.

Continuous exertion is necessary to attain eminence.

Fear is the mark of a mean spirit.

VI. PROOFS FROM TESTIMONY OR AUTHORITY.

§ 399. This is by no means an unimportant or inefficient source of proof; but the extent to which it can be used must depend upon the amount of the author's reading and the accuracy of his memory. We are always pleased to know what great minds have thought on any subject. But there is such a thing as going too far with it. In matters of mere opinion, or in inference from facts, we are generally most inclined to argue the question, or have it argued, out before us. And with proper restrictions, this is the proper spirit. But it is always allowable for a writer to strengthen either his premises or his conclusion by quotations from men of recognized eminence. These quotations should never be long.

Let the pupil adduce quotations from such sources as are within his reach confirming the following theses:

Nothing is beneath the care of Providence.
Jesus Christ arose from the dead.
There will be a final day of retribution.
God is long-suffering.
Freedom is dear to man.
Modesty is one of the finest ornaments of the female character.
No earthly state yields pure happiness.
War is a dreadful evil.
The study of languages improves the mind.
Disappointment is the common experience of men.
Pride is difficult to eradicate.
Life in the country is preferable to life in town.
Man can be influenced by love more than by any other principle.
The nature of man is one of dignity.
A life of pleasure is unsatisfactory.
The loveliest season is spring.
The American Indians possess some good traits.
The study of nature is peculiarly delightful.
Books are a copious source of enjoyment.
Fashionable people are heartless and selfish.
Christian hope sustains the soul in death.
Life without health is a burden.
The loss of children wrings the heart with grief.
Temperance in enjoyment yields the most durable of all sensual pleasures.
A guilty conscience is a dreadful torment.
Suspicion haunts the guilty mind.

VII. PROOFS OF DIFFERENT KINDS COMBINED.

§ 400. There are many theses that admit of proofs drawn from several of the sources that have now been enumerated and described. It will now be the task of the pupil to write several forms of argument in support of one thesis. In doing this he must be informed that the order in which these sources of proof have been here introduced is not that which is best in a varied or combined argument. Explication should always come first; but of the others, he may bring in each in the position that may seem to him best.

The following directions for argumentation in general will be found judicious.

§ 401. Never undertake to prove a self-evident proposition.

The attempt can not fail to be damaging to the author. Either it creates the suspicion of ignorance on his part, or it insinuates a want of capacity in those whom he addresses.

§ 402. Begin with a clear statement of your subject, or with an introduction which will naturally lead to that. If an introduction is used, it should be striking, appropriate, and proportionate.

§ 403. Observe a regular sequence in your arguments, that each one may naturally lead to the other.

§ 404. Let your chief arguments be few and cogent; and make them bear as directly on the point to be proven as possible.

Superfluous arguments efface stronger ones, exhaust patience, and encourage the idea that where weak arguments are used, the point is weak. If the few are strong, they will be effectual.

§ 405. Express your arguments in as few words as possible, consistent with perspicuity.

§ 406. Illustrations should be so intermingled with arguments as to relieve and please the mind, and thus produce variety without confusion.

§ 407. Arguments should be arranged in the inverse order of their importance; the least important first, the strongest leading up the rear. They should form a climax.

§ 408. Opposing arguments should be considered in the introduction or exordium; suasive ones in the conclusion.

§ 409. Do not state the different arguments too formally, so as to give the composition an air of stiffness and pedantry. But learn to pass gracefully from argument to argument, as if one naturally suggested another. At the same time, the precise bearing of each one upon the question should be made clear, so that the force of none be lost.

With these hints let the pupil prove the following theses in as many modes as he can.

Sectarianism has hindered the progress of true religion.

Scholastic emulation is disastrous to the finest elements of character.

Public opinion is the strongest restraint on human passion.

Commerce makes a nation intelligent and rich.

Mankind are more indebted to the Jews than to the ancient Greeks and Romans.

A free press will, sooner or later, overthrow every form of oppression.

Erroneous opinions can not be suppressed by force.

The passion for dress is the great obstacle in the elevation of woman.

Occasional excitements are essential to progress.

Literary fame is the most permanent.

He that ruleth his own spirit is better than he that taketh a city.

Fanaticism is a kind of insanity.

Astronomy proves an intelligent Creator.

Old age can be made a happier season than youth.

Ambition is incompatible with true philanthropy.

Pride is never proper nor beneficial.

Extravagance leads to poverty.

The fruits of labor are sweeter than the gifts of fortune.

Enjoyment consists in action rather than in possession.

Virtue is strengthened by habit.

We owe much to the Saracens.

The art of printing has advanced civilization.

PART SECOND.

EXPRESSION—RESUMED.

CHAPTER XXX.

EUPHONY AND HARMONY.

§ 410. The fifth and last essential property of style so far as Structure is concerned is Harmony. Together with this, it is proposed to consider that quality of diction which is called Euphony. Harmony and Euphony both refer to that power which good style has to afford a pleasure to the listener, similar to that produced by music. This has been called "pleasing the ear." Euphony denotes this quality as possessed by individual words; Harmony the same quality as produced by the combination of words in sentences, and by a certain indefinable correspondence between the sound of the sentence and the meaning which it conveys.

This last-mentioned variety of Harmony belongs more especially to poetry, and is sometimes designated as the rhetorical figure, *onomatopœia.* On this account it needs no further treatment here. The rules that are now to be given are those of Euphony and of that variety of Harmony which consists in the happy combination of words in sentences and sentences in paragraphs.

§ 411. The first general rule is—

I. *Avoid all combinations of sounds that are harsh, grating, or unmelodious.* This includes the following special rules.

§ 412. (1.) The iteration of the same sound or the same combination of sounds, either in a single word, or in words that come near together, is unpleasant to the ear.

This fault is called *Tautophony.* It is exemplified in such words as *probably*, *identity*, *lowlily*, *farriery*, *ratiocination;* and in such combinations as *been in intimacy*, *an antidote*, *to two tunes*, great*er error*, ins*tead* of a *steady*, uni*form form*ality, etc. The following sentences are intolerable: "I confess with hum*ility*, the ster*ility* of my fancy, and the deb*ility* of my judgment." "The public*ation* of this alleg*ation*, though at the instig*ation* of the entire deleg*ation*, was a viol*ation* of his promise."

§ 413. It may be regarded as a kind of exception to this rule that alliteration, skillfully introduced, conduces to strength: see § 360. The pupil will observe the following distinctions between the two cases. (1.) In the alliteration that conduces to strength, the iterated sound is never at the termination of the words, so as to make a kind of rhyme. (2.) The iterated sounds occur in a kind of balanced or rhythmical structure.

For example, "*fe*llow *fee*ling;" in *sin* and *sea*-coal; Protestant and Papist; Saxon and Celt.

The first of these examples, *fellow feeling*, is not so good as either of the others, for the reason that the words *fellow* and *feeling* are not in co-ordination. It is similarity of initial sound in similar parts of speech, sparingly used in similar constructions, that constitutes the impressive alliteration. All other iterations of sound are offensive.

It must be borne in mind, however, that a writer sometimes of *set purpose*, introduces a displeasing combination of sounds, deliberately sacrificing euphony to strength.

§ 414. (2.) A crowding together either of consonants or vowels has a bad effect: they should be well alternated.

This condemns such words as *pledg'd*, *prob'd'st*, fifthly, burden'st, logarithms, etc., and such combinations as great*est str*ain, shar*p br*ier, id*ea of*, etc. These are to be avoided, if any other words or arrangement will express the meaning as well, but if not, then they must be tolerated.

§ 415. (3.) Several short unaccented syllables coming together are offensive to the ear, especially when they constitute the latter part of a long word whose accent is on or near the first syllable.

EXAMPLES.

Derogatorily, unprecedentedness, introductorily, *in an un*enviable manner, mer*cenary*, *illibe*rality, peremptorily, etc.

§ 416. (4.) A succession of long syllables is extremely unpleasant, whether the words are monosyllabic or diversified.

EXAMPLES.

Learn this hard task well. Load twelve broad-horns brimful. Our grandsires ate oat-meal cakes, as we now eat corn-bread.

§ 417. (5.) A succession of long and short syllables regularly alternated becomes displeasing, if continued so as to sound like metrical composition.

Even in verse, harmony requires an occasional interruption to the regularity of the accent; and, of course, prose will admit of unvaried measured movement less than verse.

EXAMPLES.

Oh, what joy it is to dwell among the fadeless glories there, and drink the rapture of that holy bliss!

Homer's sparkling rills of nectar, streaming from celestial fountains, tempt our thirsty throats no longer.

Anguish protracted through numberless centuries surely would finally render destruction a blessing.

§ 418. II. *The clauses or members of a sentence should be arranged so as to produce an agreeable impression on the ear.* Under this are the following special directions.

§ 419. (1.) The members should not be so long as to exhaust the breath.

It is, of course, possible to take breath anywhere in a sentence; but there are certain connections between words which would render a pause long enough to take breath exceedingly improper. This rule forbids that these connections should be preserved continuously for so great a space as to offend a cultivated ear. The following from Tillotson is an instance of the violation of this rule.

"This discourse concerning the easiness of God's commands does, all along, suppose and acknowledge the difficulties of the first entrance upon a religious course, except only in those persons who have had the happiness to be trained up to religion by the easy and insensible degrees of a pious and virtuous education."

§ 420. (2.) The sentence should not, by transposition or the insertion of modifiers, be broken up into short fragments, requiring a frequent arrest of the flow of the voice.

EXAMPLE.

"It is likewise urged, that there are, by computation, in this kingdom, above ten thousand persons, whose revenues, added to those of my Lords the Bishops, would suffice to maintain, at their present rate of living, half a million, if not more, poor men."

§ 421. (3.) Long parentheses are always unpleasant to the ear, as well as weakening to the mental impression produced by the sentence.

§ 422. (4.) All the requirements of Strength bearing on the arrangement of words in sentences (see §§ 361–364) are likewise important to Harmony. Especially do the climactic arrangement and the sonorous terminal word tend to give a pleasing sound to a sentence. To acquire an ear for these, it is necessary to read extensively the productions of good authors.

EXERCISE.

Correct the violations of Euphony and Harmony found in the following sentences.

He was mortifyingly reprimanded for the mischievousness of his behavior.

A mild child is more liked than a wild child.

It is he that has committed the deed, at least accessorily.

This is distinctly stated in an encyclical letter of that age.

Proselytism prevails principally in the exclusive sects.

Though religion will acknowledgedly bring us under some restraints, they are very tolerable; and not only so, but desirable on the whole.

Ambition creates seditions, wars, discords, hatred, and shyness.

No mortal author, in the ordinary fate and vicissitude of things, knows to what use his works, whatever they are, may, some time or other, be applied.

Study to unite with firmness, gentle, pleasing manners.

There are no persons, or assuredly if there are any, they are very few in number, who have not, at some time of life, either directly or indirectly, with or without consciousness on their part, been of service to their fellow-creatures, or at least a portion of them.

Thou rushedst into the midst of the hottest contest, and swervedst not.

The slow horse that keeps on his course may beat the fast one that stops to eat or sleep by the way.

Sober-mindedness and shame-facedness are by some considered as evidences of virtuousness of principle.

Generally speaking, a prudent general will avoid a general engagement unless his forces are equal, or nearly so, to those of the opposing general.

Energy, industry, temperance, and handiness are excellent recommendations of mechanics.

Hydrophobia (which is derived from two Greek words signifying *fear of water*, and is so called from the aversion to that element which it produces in human patients suffering from its attack, though it seldom causes a similar aversion in the animal from whose bite it originates) sometimes does not display itself for months after the poison has been received into the system.

Should liberty continue to be abused as it has been for some time past (and, though demagogues may not admit it, yet sensible and deserving men will not deny it), the people will seek relief in despotism or in emigration.

Hence the importance of compliance with precedents.

His disposition is not toward erudition, but to superficial acquisition of knowledge.

It was not a proper occasion for the use of moral suasion.

The epicure excessively indulges his appetite with delicacies.

He affected the statesman, and ostentatiously expatiated on the measures of "the coalition party," as he called it.

The habitual use of the written ritual rendered his performances formal.

Providence delivered them up to themselves, and they tormented themselves.

PART THIRD.

INVENTION—RESUMED.

CHAPTER XXXI.

THE ORATION.

§ 423. All prose compositions are divisible into two kinds, *spoken* and *written* discourse. The former is *primarily* intended to reach the mind through the ear; the latter, through the eye. Yet a spoken discourse may be committed to writing, and through that means reach more minds than those to whom it was originally delivered. And obviously, a discourse may be written with the intention to deliver it orally on a particular occasion. But even when thus reduced to writing, it is still classed as a *spoken* discourse. All its phraseology indicates its design, and the circumstance of its past or future delivery.

§ 424. This distinction is of importance, as it affects the application of some of the rules of composition to the discourse. In a written essay, we expect a strict adherence to all the rules of style. In a spoken discourse, we allow much freedom, and connive at many a transgression of rule. In a spoken discourse, we expect the style to be characterized by diffuseness, animation, abundance of ornament, etc.

The proper field of oratory is the popular assembly, and its proper object is persuasion or excitation to action. Hence it flourishes only where the people possess some form or degree of liberty. The ancient republics of Greece and Rome furnished fine examples of it, and it was there studied as a distinct and complete art, having its exact rules and forms. Their rhetoricians or professors of oratory have handed down to us the several divisions of a regular oration, with minute specifications of the manner in which each part should be composed according to the nature of the occasion. But such an artificial manner as would be produced by very strict adherence to any prescribed form would, to us, be very offensive. Our ideal of the orator is that he is one inspired by the occasion and for the occasion; that his manner should have all the self-forgetfulness, the heroic fearlessness, the irresistible ardor of one carried away by a strongly excited passion for truth, justice, and humanity. Though we know that this is not to be expected in every case, yet we can not brook any thing directly repugnant to it. Hence any sign by which the speaker betrays the fact that his words are previously selected and arranged, insensibly spoils the charm. He who succeeds in persuasive oratory must either be the man really inspired, and owing all his power to his enthusiasm, or he must be an artist so perfectly accomplished as to conceal his art. But genuine inspiration may overtake the trained as well as the untrained orator; and when the two are combined, when the speaker, drilled by assiduous practice, finds an occasion that lifts him above himself, then the result is wonderful, defying all description, all calculation. Such was the case with Demosthenes. In him we find the well-drilled orator; for him arose the unwonted occasion; and the world still rings with his renown.

Let not, then, the young aspirant trust to the mere inspiration of an occasion, the nature and influence of which he can not foresee. But let him qualify himself by assiduous practice to stand with self-possession before an audience, to think coherently when all eyes are upon him, and to speak in good style, made natural by habit, and thus hold himself ready for the afflatus which an occasion may produce. And as, after all, the scheme of the oration as taught by the old rhetoricians was not an unnatural one, but the very course dictated by the laws of the human mind, it is well that the modern orator should be familiar with its manner of procedure, and in all his training exercises follow it, so far as each particular theme will permit, until it becomes habitual with him.

§ 425. The six formal divisions of a regular oration are—

1. The Exordium, or Introduction;
2. The Division, or Arrangement;

3. The Statement;
4. The Reasoning, or Arguments;
5. The Appeal to the Feelings;
6. The Peroration, or Conclusion.

I. THE EXORDIUM, OR INTRODUCTION.

§ 426. The object of this is to render the hearers well disposed, attentive, and open to persuasion.

To accomplish the first of these ends, he must exhibit modesty, candor, and sympathy with the audience.

To secure the second, that is, to awaken attention, he may hint at the importance, novelty, or dignity of the subject.

To render his hearers open to conviction, he may endeavor to remove any prejudices they may have formed against the position that he intends to take.

As it is very important to have a good introduction, the following special rules are given.

§ 427. I. An exordium must be easy and natural. It must appear, as Cicero says, "to have sprung up from its own accord from the matter under consideration."

§ 428. II. Modesty is essential. The speaker must not promise too much, nor raise expectations which perhaps he may not fulfill. He should never boast of what he is going to prove or disprove.

§ 429. III. His style at the beginning should be particularly free from faults. The interest of his audience in his theme is not yet so great as to prevent their criticising him, and his faults will not then be pardoned.

§ 430. IV. An exordium is not the place for vehemence or passion. If the occasion is one that calls for intense feeling, and all the audience are known to be in sympathy with the speaker, and if there is no arguing needed, and the speaker is conscious of power to sustain himself to the end, then an impassioned burst at the beginning may be allowed; but all these conditions are rarely fulfilled in any one case.

§ 431. V. A speaker should not, in his exordium, anticipate any material division of his subject. Particularly should he guard against letting an argument peep out in the introduction that he intends to produce in all its power in the fourth general head.

§ 432. VI. The exordium should be, both in length and character, suited to the subject, and the discourse that is to follow.

II. THE DIVISION, OR ARRANGEMENT.

§ 433. This is that part of a discourse in which the speaker makes known what plan he intends to pursue. Of course it always supposes more or less of preparation for the occasion. It is quite frequently the case that a discourse would be injured by introducing a *division* in it. If the plan of it is extremely simple, if the arguments are only one or two in number, or if, for any reason, the speaker does not wish to show beforehand what direction his remarks will take, it would be better to have no formal division.

When the division is employed, the following rules for it should be observed.

§ 434. I. The several parts into which the subject is divided should be really distinct; no one should include another.

§ 435. II. The heads taken should be those into which the subject naturally divides itself.

§ 436. III. The several heads should exhaust the subject.

§ 437. IV. There should be no unnecessary multiplication of heads, to distract and weary the hearer.

§ 438. V. A natural order should be followed; the simplest parts should be first discussed, and afterward the more difficult ones that are founded on them.

§ 439. VI. The terms in which the division is expressed should be as concise as possible; there should be no redundancy, or circumlocution, or figurative expression.

III. THE STATEMENT.

§ 440. In this division the facts connected with the subject are set forth. This forms a very important part of legal or forensic speeches. In stating the facts, the orator must present them in simple and forcible style; he must keep strictly within the bounds of truth, and yet in the light most favorable to his cause; bringing forth into prominence every circumstance that bears to his advantage, and explaining away, as far as possible, every thing that makes against him.

IV. THE REASONING, OR ARGUMENTATION.

As this has been made the subject of a previous chapter, nothing further need be said about it.

V. THE APPEAL TO THE FEELINGS.

This is sometimes called the *Pathetic* part. The following rules apply to it.

§ 441. I. Consider whether the subject properly admits it; if it does, whether it is better to postpone it until after the Reasoning, or blend it with the several arguments. Different orators pursue different plans in this regard, and both with equal success. The young orator should be guided by his own taste, and the nature of the subject and of the arguments.

§ 442. II. Never *formally* set apart one head of a discourse for the pathetic, or give warning of your intention to the hearers. Bear in mind that the proper way to excite any particular feeling is to present the appropriate object of it or occasion for it vividly before the mind: not to belabor the audience with an exhortation to their *duty* to feel thus or so.

§ 433. III. Be careful to use language appropriate to passion; not high-sounding declamation, but unaffected and simple diction. All digressions and formal comparisons should be avoided.

§ 444. IV. The Appeal to the Feelings should not be too long or too elaborate.

VI. THE CONCLUSION.

§ 445. In many cases no additional part is necessary, the Appeal to the Feelings constituting the best conclusion that the oration could have. At other times, a resume or recapitulation of the whole argument is good. The close should not be abrupt; neither should it be protracted beyond the time when the speaker, by his manner or other indications, has led his audience to expect a conclusion. The last sentence should be dignified, graceful, without affectation.

It was the custom in the ancient schools of rhetoric to require the pupils to compose and deliver orations adapted to supposed occasions, such as fictitious trials for grave offenses, and important state measures for hypothetical emergencies. It is left with the teacher to decide whether he shall pursue that course with the pupils using this book. If he adopt it, he must, of course, invent for his pupils the hypothetical cases in which they shall exercise their powers.

It is always a good plan, when there happen to be practical questions before the public mind, either of the particular section, or of the country at large, to propose these as proper themes for orations by the pupils. The issues of a political canvass in which measures and not men are pending, important trials awaiting adjudication, railroad projects, or any scheme of public improvement, benevolent enterprises, and mooted questions of social reform, are all favorable occasions for rhetorical effort, which no teacher having pupils sufficiently advanced should allow to pass unimproved.

Should it be objected to the use of political canvasses as above recommended, that it would give the pupils a taste for the immoral and degrading practices of politicians, it is replied that the measure here recommended is one of the very means for the correction of those immoralities. Our country being republican, the people must be interested in politics. Our young men should be prepared, while yet in school, to take their part in this field, intelligently, and in accordance with good morals. They must be trained to discuss measures on their own merits; they must be early inspired with an honorable loathing toward all vituperation, calumny, sophistry, and the like, which so largely disgrace the world of American politics. They must be taught to use, without abusing, the great privileges of free discussion and the elective franchise. Unto this end, no better means can be suggested than the writing and, after revision by the teacher, the delivery of orations on the political issues of the day.

PART FOURTH.

EXPRESSION—RESUMED.

CHAPTER XXXII.

THE ORNAMENTATION OF STYLE.

§ 446. All the preceding chapters that have treated of Expression, have been occupied with the Essential Qualities of Style; the successful cultivation of which will exonerate a writer from all blame. But this is not enough. High and rare as is the excellence which the rules of Purity, Propriety, Precision, Clearness, etc., demand, the imagination and the heart call for more; Style must be ornamented.

§ 447. The ornaments of Style imparted by the imagination and the passions are generally called Figures. They have been defined as deviations from the plain and ordinary mode of discourse, in order to give it greater effect. They are thus seen to be more closely allied to Strength and Harmony than any of the other essential qualities of Style.

Though Figures are defined to be departures from the simple and plain modes of expression, it must not be concluded that they are rare or difficult. On the contrary, they are used equally by all classes, and in all stages of society. If there be any difference in this respect, it is the barbarian, the child, and the plebeian that are figurative in their language, rather than the enlightened, the mature, and the cultivated. It will be found on examination that the great bulk of our words, especially nouns, adjectives, and verbs, are not only capable of being used in a figurative sense, but are actually so used; in some cases, more frequently as figures than literally.

Take for example the word *hard*. For every instance of its literal use, as in the phrases *hard wood*, *hard stone*, etc., other passages can be found in which it is used figuratively, as in the phrases *hard heart*, *hard head*, *hard task*, *hard times*, *hard master*, *hard winter*, etc.

The first exercise, then, that should be required of the pupil in this direction, should be the use of given words, first in their literal sense, then in their figurative senses.

MODEL.

MOVE.—1. In endeavoring to *move* the lumber, the man fell and broke his arm.

2. The prospect of danger or of death can not *move* me from my purpose.

EXERCISE.

Use the following words in sentences in both their literal and figurative senses.

roll	cap	leap	free
carpet	volume	march	current
dress	bed	oblique	movement
wing	tongue	steady	gale
foot	turn	wavering	step
base	rise	gentle	impulse
heart	full	agitated	freedom
arm	fly	progressive	course

§ 448. The figures in common use are the following:

1. Simile;
2. Metaphor;
3. Allegory;
4. Metonymy;
5. Synecdoche;
6. Antithesis;
7. Paradox;
8. Hyperbole;
9. Personification;
10. Vision;
11. Irony;
12. Apostrophe;
13. Interrogation;
14. Innuendo;
15. Meiosis;
16. Onomatopœia;
17. Climax.

SIMILE, METAPHOR, AND ALLEGORY.

§ 449. These three figures are all founded on the relation of *resemblance;* hence, they are in many respects subjected to the same rules. They are thus distinguished.

§ 450. A *simile* is the express assertion of resemblance between things *different in kind.* It is generally (but not in every case) indicated by the word *like*, *as*, *so*, or *thus*. When it is extended or elaborate, it is generally called a *comparison.*

It is not every comparison, however, that is a simile. When objects are compared in respect of quantity or degree, or to see how they differ, there is no simile; it is only when the object of the comparison is to trace likeness that a comparison becomes a figure of similitude.

§ 451. A *metaphor* is the direct application of a name, epithet, attribute, or predicate, properly belonging to one object, to another that resembles it in the respect implied. It is distinguished from the simile by the circumstance that it does not *assert*, but only *implies*, resemblance.

§ 452. An *allegory* is a narrative representing objects and events that are intended to be symbolical of other objects and events having a moral or spiritual character. Fables and parables are generally, but not universally, allegorical. An allegory has been represented as a metaphor carried out, or a succession of harmonious metaphors bearing upon one subject.

These distinctions will be illustrated by the following examples.

SIMILES.

A merry heart doeth good *like* a medicine.
The king's favor is *as* dew upon the grass.
As the door turneth upon his hinges, *so* doth the slothful upon his bed.
Up rose the sun, and up rose Emilie.
(Word of similitude omitted.)

COMPARISON.

Trade, *like* a restive horse, is not easily managed: where one is carried to the end of a successful journey, many are thrown off by the way.

METAPHORS.

The *sun* of *liberty* is set; we must light the *candles* of industry and economy.

To Thee my thoughts continual *climb*.

Father, thy hand
Hath reared these venerable *columns;* thou
Didst *weave* this verdant *roof.*

Bright o'er the wasted scene thou *hoverest* still,
Angel of comfort to the failing soul.

ALLEGORY.

A child is born. Now take the germ, and make it
A bud of moral beauty. Let the dews
Of knowledge, and the light of virtue, wake it
In richest fragrance, and in purest hues.
When passion's gust, and sorrow's tempest shake it,
The shelter of affection ne'er refuse;
For soon the gathering hand of death will break it
From its weak stem of life, and it shall lose
All power to charm. But if that lonely flower
Hath swell'd one pleasure, or subdued one pain,
Oh, who shall say that it has lived in vain,
However fugitive its breathing hour?
For virtue leaves its sweets wherever tasted,
And scatter'd truth is never, never wasted.

EXERCISES.

I. Let the pupil expand the following suggested analogies into similes, comparisons, or allegories, as may suit his taste.

Life—a journey.
Youth—morning.
Knowledge—a hill.
Earth—a mother.
The world—a car.
The world—a stage.
Genius—marble.
Talent—a field.
Charity—the sun.
Learning—reaping.
Pestilence—wild beast.
Calumny—clouds.
Temptation—passing a dangerous place.
A child's death—the blighting of a flower.

II. Select some material objects to which the following subjects bear some analogy, and point the resemblance by simile, allegory, or metaphor, as in the preceding exercise.

Death.
War.
Justice.
A man of integrity.
Sin.
Peace.
Memory.
A missionary.

A college.	College friends.
False friends.	Hope.
The hope of renown.	The mother of a family
A distracted state.	A tyrant.
Unexpected prosperity.	Lingering decline.
A miser.	A liberal man of wealth.

III. Compose sentences or paragraphs in which the following words shall be as metaphors.

Light	Mountain	Swamp	Rock
Dregs	Desert	Diamond	Ruby
Corn	Strata	Crystal	Rough
Orbit	Iron	Root	Fruit
Wave	Seed	Lily	Fungus
Flower	Ripe	Bone	Tongue
Cloak	Health	Fox	Parrot
Attraction	Breath	Bee	Butterfly
Storm	Viper	Plow	Thrash
Tide	Shepherd	Palace	Steer
Stream	Cement	Defeat	Capital
Yoke	Wreck	Spin	Weave
Star	Forge	Harbor	Blister
Thunder	Wed		

RULES FOR FIGURES OF RESEMBLANCE.

§ 453. The rules that apply to figures of resemblance depend upon the object or purpose for which the figure in the particular case is used. This purpose may be one of the three following, or two, or all combined, viz.:

1. To make the subject more clear and intelligible;
2. To afford pleasure to the hearer or reader;
3. To excite or heighten feeling.

§ 454. I. When the first of these is the object, then the following rules apply.

§ 455. (1.) The resemblance should turn on the circumstance or quality relevant to the matter in hand.

This was violated by the clergyman who prayed that God would be "a rock to them afar off upon the sea." Now a rock on land is desirable for a foundation; a tall rock, for its shadow in a hot sunny plain; or in a river ford, as making a good firm bottom. But out upon the sea, a rock is the mariner's greatest danger. Hence the inappropriateness of the metaphor.

§ 456. (2.) It is not proper to base a similitude on what is not generally known, or less intelligible and obvious to the senses than the object itself.

Cowley violates this rule in the following line:

"The Holy Book like the eighth sphere doth shine."

§ 457. (3.) Figures of similitude must not be based on resemblances so faint as to be difficult to be traced.

The following quotation from Shakespeare contains a simile that violates this rule.

"Here, Cousin, seize the crown:
'Here on this side, my hand; on that side, thine.
'Now is this golden crown like a deep well,
'That owes two buckets, filling one another;
'The emptier ever dancing in the air,
'The other down unseen and full of water;
'That bucket down and full of tears, am I,
'Drinking my griefs, while you mount up on high."

Here, with all the effort of the poet to explain his simile, it is exceedingly hard to see the resemblance between the crown and the well with two buckets, or between the immersed bucket and the speaker, still less between the dangling empty bucket and the person addressed. It may be set down as a good rule that when a figure of resemblance is so obscure as to need explanation, it would better be discarded.

§ 458. (4.) If a figure is intended to elucidate a subject, no irrelevant circumstances should be introduced.

The following is an instance in point:

"My kindred have fallen from me like dead leaves from a tree in autumn, *which strips it of its loveliest appendages.*"

Poets are exceedingly apt to violate this rule, by lugging in some unnecessary circumstance to fill out the meter or afford a rhyme. The following stanza contains a simile of uncommon beauty; but the phrase "many a wave-beat shore" seems to be inserted for the foregoing reason.

"Man's the rugged lofty pine
That frowns o'er many a wave-beat shore;
Woman's the slender, graceful vine,
Whose curling tendrils round it twine,
And deck its rough bark sweetly o'er."

§ 459. (5.) It is always a source of obscurity and an occasion of disgust to combine in one sentence two inconsistent metaphors on the same subject. This is technically called *mixing* metaphors.

The following is a stereotype example from Addison:

"I *bridle* in my struggling muse with pain,
That longs to *launch* into a bolder strain."

Here he first makes his muse a steed to be bridled in, then a ship to be launched.

Another: "This institution had its *foundation* in the feudal system; but its *fruits* are now enjoyed by all civilized nations." That which has a foundation can not have fruits.

§ 460. II. The rules that apply to those figures that proceed from a desire to please are the following.

§ 461. (6.) There should be no unpleasant discord between the things compared, such as results from the comparing of an object to what greatly transcends it in dignity or elevation; or the illustration of some principle in spiritual life by some process or custom in the sporting world.

This rule was shockingly violated by the preacher who said,—"Charity, my brethren, is the trump card in the game for eternal life."

The following couplet is likewise a violation of this rule.

"Loud as a bull makes hill and valley ring
So roared the lock when it released the spring."

§ 462. (7.) Care should be taken not to introduce any distasteful circumstance or accompaniment in the similitude.

The following from Lucretius is an instance.

"Sweet it is, when the winds are agitating the waters on a wide sea, to witness from the land the spectacle of another's distress; not because it is agreeable to us that any should suffer, but because it is pleasant to behold the ills ourselves are free from. Sweet also is it to look upon the mighty encounters of war spread over the plains, without sharing the danger. But nothing is sweeter than to occupy the well-girt, serene temple raised by the learning of the wise, whence we may look down upon others, and see them straying and wandering, rivals in intellect, and in the pride of birth, striving night and day by surpassing labor to rise to wealth and to win dominion."

Here the feeling of security from woes that are afflicting others is presented under two comparisons; that of witnessing from the land one struggling in a stormy sea, and that of beholding the havoc of war from some safe retreat. But the beauty of the similitudes is sadly marred by the suggestion of situations in which any good person would be tortured with sympathy, instead of chuckling with selfish delight.

§ 463. (8.) *Ceteris paribus*, similitudes always please in proportion to their novelty and originality. In a spoken discourse, the freshness of a metaphor may atone for its faultiness in other respects. But stale and trite similitudes always tend to disgust. If not brought out very prominently, they may be tolerated; but if the least stress is laid upon them, if they occupy any considerable space in the sentence, or constitute any thing more than a mere appellation or allusion, they are offensive.

§ 464. (9.) It is never in good taste to blend plain language with metaphorical; or at least, after the metaphorical word has once been uttered, to represent the object in the same sentence without figure.

Pope violates this rule, when, in addressing the king, he says,

"To thee the world its present homage pays;
The harvest early, but mature the praise."

The demand of rhyme led him to return to the literal word *praise*, when the figure would have required *crop*.

The student should know that all words expressive of operations of the mind or the relations of abstract or metaphysical truth, were originally metaphors. The poverty of language and the early dependence of the mind on the senses for knowledge, led to this. But a metaphor that is constantly used to represent a certain psychical or metaphysical idea rapidly loses its figurative character, and comes to be the precise and literal expression of that idea. When such is the case, it becomes a matter of extreme delicacy to decide whether, if such a word is used with one that is confessedly a metaphor, there is a mingling of plain with figurative language or not. Each case must be judged on its own merits.

§ 465. (10.) In order to be pleasing, a metaphor should not be carried too far. In this respect metaphors differ from comparisons, and still more from allegories. A comparison somewhat extended is not unpleasing, and in an avowed allegory, the more numerous the points of analogy suggested, the better. But when a writer, starting with only a metaphor, runs it out until it begins to grow into an allegory, he infallibly disgusts his readers.

Young, speaking of old age, says it should

> "Walk thoughtful on the silent, solemn shore
> Of that vast ocean it must sail so soon;"—

Thus far the metaphor is very beautiful; but he goes on to say,

> "And put good works on board; and wait the wind
> That shortly blows us into worlds unknown,"—

He thus spoils the figure.

§ 466. III. When a figure founded on resemblance is introduced for the purpose of exciting or intensifying feeling, the following rules apply.

§ 467. (11.) Formal comparisons must not be put into the mouths of those who are at the time in great bodily distress, or under passionate excitement, such as fear, remorse, anger, despair, etc. A comparison implies a certain composure of the mind. It may be made by one describing a case of suffering or passion, but never by the individual affected.

Shakespeare violates this rule when, in Henry VI., he makes the dying Warwick compare himself to a felled cedar.

§ 468. (12.) The similitude should be elevating or degrading to correspond with the feeling which is sought to be awakened. If it be admiration of the subject, or sympathy with it, the thing to which it is compared, or whose name is given to it, should be attractive, noble, or inspiring; *and yet not too far removed in elevation from the subject.* On the contrary, if antipathy or contempt is the aim of the writer, he will naturally draw his similes and metaphors from those things that are repulsive or degrading.

It follows from this that when a writer, not intending to throw contempt or repulsiveness upon his subject, uses comparisons or metaphors that have this tendency, he commits a palpable error. Thus Homer is liable to censure for comparing the Grecian host rushing from their tents into the battle, to a swarm of wasps provoked by children.

As similitudes may be improperly degrading, so they can be enormously elevated or grand for the subject, and produce a feeling opposite to the one intended. For instance, "His massy forehead rose above his eyebrows like some beetling crag overhanging the shaded valley below."

"The sentences of wisdom issued from his mouth like trains of richly-laden cars from a railway tunnel."

It hardly constitutes an exception to this rule that fables and parables admit of descent to the very humblest forms and modes of existence, to illustrate any moral truth or principle, however sublime. It is the principal aim of the parable and the fable to arrest the attention, and elucidate truth, not to arouse emotion directly.

EXERCISE.

Let the pupil be required to write a criticism of each of the following examples of the violation of the foregoing rules, explaining what in each case is the error or errors, and which rules are transgressed.

Rosaline had budded into a magnificent creature.

Thousands of women (writers) have toiled over books that proved millstones, and drowned them in the sea of letters.

All these debts and mortgages had been conquered.

Emma and Henry were bright little jewels, of the ages of eight and ten respectively.

No; there are silent chambers in her heart, whose niches cry for daily food.

The breath of the wind as it ushers in the icy fetters of a long, cruel winter.

We are often the creatures of circumstances.

> Half round the globe, the tears pump'd up by death,
> Are spent in watering vanities of life.

No human happiness is so serene as not to contain any alloy.

> Now from my kind embrace by tempests torn,
> Our other column of the state is borne,
> Nor took a kind adieu, nor sought consent.

Trothal went forth with the stream of his people, but they met a rock; for Fingal stood unmoved. Broken, they rolled back from his side. Nor did they roll in safety; the spear of the king pursued their flight.

There is a time when factions, by the vehemence of their own fermentations, stun and disable one another.

I intend to make use of these words in the thread of my speculations.

Hope, the balm of life, darts a ray of light through the thickest gloom.

The scheme was highly expensive to him, and proved the Charybdis of his estate.

He was so much skilled in the empire of the oar, that few could equal him.

The death of Cato has rendered the senate an orphan.

Let us be attentive to keep our mouths as with a bridle; and to steer our vessel aright, that we may avoid the rocks and shoals, which lie every-where around us.

> At length Erasmus, that great injur'd name
> (The glory of the priesthood and the shame),
> Curb'd the wild torrent of a barb'rous age,
> And drove those holy Vandals off the stage.

> In this our day of proof, our land of hope;
> The good man has his clouds that intervene;
> Clouds that may dim his sublunary day,
> But can not conquer; even the best must own
> Patience and resignation are the columns
> Of human peace on earth.

Dryden, describing the Supreme Being as extinguishing the great fire in London by an opportune rain sent in answer to the prayers of His people, says:

"A hollow crystal pyramid he takes,
In firmamental waters dipped above;
Of this a broad extinguisher he makes,
And hoods the flames that to their quarry strove."

"The Alps,
The palaces of nature, whose vast walls
Have pinnacled in clouds their snowy scalps."

Those whose minds are dull and heavy do not easily penetrate into the folds and intricacies of an affair, and therefore can only scum off what they find at the top.

"The sun, in figures such as these,
Joys with the moon to play:
To the sweet strains they advance,
Which do result from their own spheres;
As this nymph's dance
Moves with the numbers which she hears."

In Shakespeare's Richard II., a gardener gives these directions to his servants:

"Go, bind you up yon dangling apricots,
Which, like unruly children, make their sire
Stoop with oppression of their prodigal weight;
Give some supportance to the bending twigs.
Go thou; and, like an executioner,
Cut off the heads of too fast-growing sprays,
That look too lofty in our commonwealth;
All must be even in our government."

"The tackle of my heart is cracked and burnt;
And all the shrouds wherewith my life should sail
Are turned to one thread, one little hair:
My heart hath one poor string to stay it by,
Which holds but till thy news be uttered."

He can not buckle his distemper'd cause
Within the belt of rule.

My bleeding bosom sickens at the sound.

In Addison's Cato, Portius, bidding his beloved Lucia an eternal farewell, uses the following language:

"Thus o'er the dying lamp the unsteady flame
Hangs quivering on a point, leaps off by fits,
And falls again, as loth to quit its hold.

——— Thou must not go; my soul still hovers o'er thee,
And can't get loose."

"Nor could the Greeks repel the Lycian powers,
Nor the bold Lycians force the Grecian towers.
As, on the confines of adjoining grounds,
Two stubborn swains with blows dispute their bounds,
They tug, they sweat; but neither gain nor yield,
One foot, one inch, of the contended field."

Speaking of the fallen angels, searching for mines of gold, Milton says:

"A numerous brigade hastened: as when bands
Of pioneers, with spade and pick-ax armed,
Forerun the royal camp to trench a field
Or cast a rampart."

On the wide sea of letters, 't was thy boast
To crowd each sail, and touch at ev'ry coast;
From that rich mine how often hast thou brought
The pure and precious pearls of splendid thought!
How didst thou triumph on that subject tide,
Till vanity's wild gust, and stormy pride,
Drove thy strong mind, in evil hour, to split
Upon the fatal rock of impious wit!

Since the time that reason began to bud, and put forth her shoots, thought, during our waking hours, has been active in every breast, without a moment's suspension or pause. The current of ideas has been always moving. The wheels of the spiritual engine have exerted themselves with perpetual motion.

The man who has no rule over his own spirit, possesses no antidote against poisons of any sort. He lies open to every insurrection of ill-humor, and every gale of distress. Whereas he who is employed in regulating his mind, is making provision against all the accidents of life. He is erecting a fortress into which, in the day of sorrow, he can retreat with satisfaction.

Tamerlane the Great writes to Bajazet, emperor of the Ottomans, in the following terms: "Where is the monarch who dares resist us? Where is the potentate who does not glory in being numbered among our attendants? As for thee, descended from a Turcoman sailor, since the vessel of thy unbounded ambition has been wrecked in the gulf of thy self-love, it would be proper that thou shouldst take in the sails of thy temerity, and cast the anchor of repentance in the port of sincerity and justice, which is the port of safety; lest the tempest of our vengeance make thee perish in the sea of the punishment thou deservest."

There is not a single view of human nature that is not sufficient to extinguish the seeds of pride.

My tears are the sooner dried up when they run on my friend's cheeks in the furrows of compassion.

METONYMY AND SYNECDOCHE.

§ 469. These two figures are supposed to have some resemblance the one to the other. They both consist in the transfer of a name or epithet to an object that bears some relation to its proper object, other than the relation of resemblance or contrast. The relations that are embraced in the figure of *Motonymy* are

1. The sign to the thing signified;
2. The instrument to the agent;
3. The container to the content;
4. The effect to the cause;
5. The cause to the effect, including
   (*a*.) The author to his works;
   (*b*.) The progenitor to his posterity;
6. The abstract attribute to the object or substance possessing it;
7. The concrete person or substance to the attribute characterizing it.

The relations embraced in the *Synecdoche* are

1. The part to the whole;
2. The whole to a part:
3. The material to the thing made of it;
4. The circumstance or characteristic to the person to whom it belongs;
5. The definite for the indefinite of the same kind.

All of these will be illustrated by examples.

1. *Metonymy of the Sign for the Thing Signified.* He aims at the crown. Am I a soldier of the cross?

2. *Metonymy of the Instrument for the Agent.* The pen is mightier than the sword. The wilderness has receded before the ax and the plow.

3. *Metonymy of the Container for the Content.* Ye devour widows' houses. The bottle has been his ruin. He that steals my purse, steals trash. Boston is more literary than Quebec. He keeps a good table.

4. *Metonymy of the Effect for the Cause.* Gray hairs should be respected.

5. *Metonymy of the Cause for the Effect.* This nation's strength is in its schools. This painting is a Reubens. Ye are my glory and my joy. It is my chief *delight* to read the Word of God. Adorned with gay religions.

(*a.*) *Metonymy of the Author for his Works.* Have you read Shakespeare? We study Euclid.

(*b.*) *Metonymy of the Progenitor for his Posterity.* Israel shall be saved. The burden of Moab.

6. *Metonymy of the Abstract Attribute for the Object or Substance possessing it.* Youth and beauty meet to chase the hours, etc. Verdure clothes the hills. Folly laughs where Wisdom weeps.

7. *Metonymy of the Concrete for the Abstract.* Wisely keeps the fool within. The father yearns in the true prince's breast.

§ 470. There is a variety of figure that by some authors is classed with Metonymy, but by others made a distinct figure under the name of the *Transferred Epithet.* It consists in applying an *adjective* to a noun that is not properly the name of the object possessing the quality, but of some object bearing to that quality some of the relations included in Metonymy.

The following are examples of it:

The plowman plods his *weary* way. Hence to his *idle* bed. With *easy* eye thou mayst behold. Thick as *autumnal* leaves. Beheld from the *safe* shore. On that *opprobious* hill. The *hospitable* door.

The following are examples of the several kinds of Synecdoche:

1. *Synecdoche of the Part for the Whole.* His arm soon cleared the field. All hands at work. They sought his blood. She rules the waves.

Included under this head is the *Synecdoche of the Species for the Genus.* They were gone to buy bread. He is a common cut-throat. Rum was his ruin.

Also, *the Synecdoche of the Individual for the Species:* this particular kind is sometimes called *Antonomasia.* Every man is not a Solomon. Some village Hampden. Some Milton, pregnant with celestial fire.

2. *The Synecdoche of the Whole for the Part.** The smiling year. The police were informed of it. Every creature adores Thee.

3. *The Synecdoche of the Material for the Thing made of it.* The marble speaks. The iron entered into his soul. Bring the parchments.

4. *The Synecdoche of the Circumstance or Characteristic for the Person to whom it belongs.* The Stagirite (for Aristotle). The Corsican (for Napoleon). The Beloved Disciple. Le Grand Monarque. The Wise Man. The Galilean.

5. *The Synecdoche of the Definite for the Indefinite of the same kind.* Ten thousand stood at his right hand. A dozen men plunged after him. Three-score years and ten. Nine tenths of every man's happiness depends on the reception he meets with in the world.

EXERCISE.

Compose sentences each of which shall contain two words of the following list, or any of their derivatives, one or both of them being used by Metonymy or Synecdoche.

Peace	Plain	Knight	Indian
Sun	Steel	Road	Sword
Head	Bier	Guilt	Ark
Dear	Peal	Scene	Lyre
Breast	Bread	Soul	Grief
Wood	Reign	Cicero	Bay
Vein	Pain	Clime	Prince
Write	Sail	Link	Eden
Fur	Course	Ring	Ararat
Tale	Foot	Crew	Bitter
Weak	Might	Throne	Aaron
Flower	Sower	Delight	Water
Dew	Tide	Whale	Blind
Prey	Herd		

* This form is rare and doubtful.

MODELS.

Guilt avoids the *sun*.

Canst thou bring life to this mute *bier*, and change that knell to *pealing* joy?

His *knightly steel* will never ring on Glory's plain again.

Let the teacher dictate additional exercises at his pleasure.

HYPERBOLE—PERSONIFICATION—VISION—IRONY.

§ 471. The common ground of these four figures is that they all contain the assertion of what is not literally true; further than that they have no particular connection.

§ 472. *Hyperbole* is an exaggeration of the literal truth. It departs from the truth in the statement of the *degree* to which any quality or effects extend.

Examples are abundant in ordinary conversation; much more so than they ought to be. Such as, *as cold as ice*, *as hot as fire*, *as sick as I can be to live*, *as dry as a bone*, *cords of money*, etc.

The proper occasion for this figure is violent passion; so violent as to distort the perceptions and the judgment. Even then it must be kept within proper bounds, or it becomes ridiculous. Though the offspring of the most violent passion, instances are not wanting of hyperboles uttered in mental composure, that are very pleasing. The following are examples of this figure:

"A lover may bestride the gossamer
That idles in the wanton summer air,
And yet not fall;—so light is vanity."

"So frowned the mighty combatants
That hell grew darker at their frown."

"And there are also many other things which Jesus did, the which, if they should be written every one, I suppose that even the world itself could not contain the books that should be written."

§ 473. *Personification* is the attribution of personal parts, qualities, or actions to what is literally impersonal. The personal qualities are intelligence and emotion, and all the acts, looks, and manners connected with these: even sex is regarded as a personal quality when attributed to a neutral object.

EXAMPLES.

"Let the field be *joyful!*"—"Nature *sings* his praise."—"This *angry* flood."

"Earth *felt* the wound; and Nature from her seat
Sighing, through all her works *gave signs of woe*,
That all was lost."

"His form
Had not yet lost all *her* original brightness."

§ 474. *Vision* is the narration of past (or future) events in the present tense, as if actually taking place before the author's eyes.

EXAMPLES.

"They rally, they bleed, for their kingdom and crown."

"First peer up the mountain tops; then the lower hills; then the whole ocean is an archipelago; then the continental mass appears, but stubbornly contested by muddy lakes and bays and lagoons; but at last, it is the green earth with the silvery brooks and the quiet rivers, and busy life swarming over it."

"Arise, shine! for thy light is come, and the glory of the Lord is risen upon thee!"

§ 475. *Irony* consists in asserting the direct reverse of the truth, when its absurdity is so manifest that the bare expression of it is sufficient to bring it into contempt, and to expose all who may have maintained it to ridicule.

Elijah used this figure to turn upon the priests of Baal, vainly striving to induce their false god to attest his power, the storm of popular wrath. "Cry aloud!" said he; "for he is a god; either he is talking, or he is pursuing, or he is in a journey, or peradventure he sleepeth, and must be awaked."

Job also uses Irony in retort upon the aggravating reasonings of his friends: "Doubtless ye are the people; and wisdom will die with you!"

EXERCISES.

I. Represent the following subjects hyperbolically.

The depth of a chasm.
The height of a mountain.
The darkness of a cloudy night.
The violence of a tempest.
The numbers in a crowd.
The speed of a racer.
The selfishness of a seeker after wealth.

The magnitude of waves in the sea.

The heat of a furnace.

The heartlessness of a belle.

The beauty of a sunset scene.

The villainy of a tempter.

II. Represent the following as in Vision.

The meeting of Adam and Eve.

The Deluge.

The Confusion of Tongues at Babel.

The Arrested Sacrifice of Isaac.

The Wrestling of Jacob with the Angel.

The Commission of Moses from the Burning Bush.

The Fall of Jericho.

The Last Meeting of David and Jonathan.

The Death of Absalom and its Sequel.

The Arrest and Conversion of St. Paul.

The Conversion of the Philippian Jailer.

The Taking of Troy.

A Gladiatorial Fight.

III. Personify the following.

The Arctic Cold	Death	The Trade Winds
Evening	Memory	France
Moon	Faith	America
Morning	Murder	The Mississippi
Sun	The Alleghanies	War
Revenge	Ignorance	Sleep
Time	Superstition	Britain
Hope	Wisdom	Commerce
Care	Greece	Freedom
Love	Italy	Gold

ANTITHESIS—PARADOX.

§ 476. These two figures are thus put together, not because they are similar, or have any considerable agreement, which they do not have, but solely that they may by the learner be accurately discriminated. Their only point of agreement is that they both involve a kind of opposition or contrast. But the contrast is different: in Antithesis it is between the things, their associations or their relations; in Paradox the contrast is between the ordinary meaning of a word and that intended in the given connection.

§ 477. *Antithesis* may be defined as the explicit and pointed statement of the difference or differences between two things that are in some way related.

§ 478. It is susceptible of division, first, into Antithesis between things (including persons and conceptions), and that between the acts, relations, or circumstances of things. Moreover, the genus of Antithesis drawn between things is capable of subdivision into two species, viz.: those drawn between correlatives, counterparts, or contradictories; and those drawn between species of the same genus, or individuals of the same species.

Antitheses between counterparts are such as those drawn between *Light* and *Darkness*, *Motion* and *Rest*, *Hot* and *Cold*, *Pleasure* and *Pain*, *Ego* and *Non-ego*, etc. Those between members of the same class are such as are drawn between *Heat* and *Light* (natural agents or forces), *Industry* and *Frugality* (thrifty virtues), *Painting* and *Sculpture* (fine arts addressed to the eye), *Perception* and *Conception* (mental faculties), etc. Those between the acts, relations, or circumstances of things are such as are drawn between *Boiling* and *Effervescence*, *Step-father* and *Foster-father*, *Taste* and *Odor*, *In summer* and *In winter*, *Sleeping* and *Awake*, etc.

§ 479. It is a rule of Antithesis that its power to please depends upon the closeness of the relation between the contrasted objects. Two members of a lower genus afford a more pleasing contrast than two of a higher class; two individuals of a species, still more pleasing. Sometimes a very striking antithesis may be drawn between the acts or states of the same individual in different circumstances.

§ 480. Another rule is that the beauty of an Antithesis depends upon the number of points of contrast that are brought out.

Hence the very finest examples of Antithesis are those drawn between two characters or individuals very much alike in many respects, but shown to be in very many points unlike. When such an Antith esis is expressed according to the rules of Style laid down in § 379, the very highest beauty of this kind is produced.

The finest fields for the display of this beauty are found in History and Higher Criticism.* In the former, Macaulay, in the latter, Pope has attained the highest eminence among English authors.

§ 481. *Paradox* consists in bringing together two expressions, one or both of which must be taken in some other than its usual sense, or as representing an object that has some other than its usual tendencies or associations.

Generally the two objects thus brought together before the mind are remotely connected by a chain of causation or association; and the figure consists in dropping all the intermediate links, and bringing into direct mental contact what, thus apprehended, produces a kind of shock to the mind. This shock is often the result, not of any incongruity in the sense which the words are seen to have in the sentence, but of the incongruity of the *other*, the *discarded* senses of the words, which are obscurely suggested by the words themselves, and seem to flit about in the background of the sentence.

The following examples will illustrate these remarks:

"Rejoicing in tribulation."—"Having nothing and yet possessing all things."—"When you have nothing to say, say it."—"The legendary age is a past, that never was present."—"By indignities men come to dignities."

"Some people are too foolish to commit follies."

"Nothing so fallacious as facts, except figures."

"Language is the art of concealing thought."

"'T is all thy business, business how to shun."

"What is writ, is writ."

"Where snow falls, there is freedom."

EXERCISE.

Let the pupil be required to compose full and extended Antithesis on the following pairs of subjects:

Spring and Autumn.	Morning and Evening.
Industry and Indolence.	Temperance and Intemperance.
Intelligence and Ignorance.	Barbarism and Civilization.
Christianity and Paganism.	Faith and Infidelity.

* The criticism of men, things, measures, etc.

Pride and Humility.
Modesty and Immodesty.
Joy and Sorrow.
Wisdom and Folly.
Peace and War.
Decision and Indecision.

Geography and History.
Anatomy and Physiology.
Conscience and Taste.
Spring and Summer.
Temperance and Asceticism.
Pastoral and Agricultural Life.
Faith and Doubt.
Learning and Wisdom.
Chemistry and Physics.
Memory and Imagination.
Joy and Cheerfulness.
Morning and Noon.
Learning and Superficiality.
Judaism and Christianity.
Pride and Vanity.
The Sublime and the Beautiful.

Abraham and Jacob.
The Ancient and the Modern Drama.
David and Alfred.
Alexander and Hannibal.
Samson and Hercules.
The Style of Addison and of Johnson.
Elijah and John the Baptist.
The Style of Gibbon and of Macaulay.
Luther and Wesley.
The Poetical Merits of Milton and Pollok.
Charles I. and Louis XVI.
Gothic and Grecian Architecture.

APOSTROPHE—INTERROGATION—INNUENDO—MEIOSIS.

§ 482. In the four figures thus grouped together, the opposition to the literal truth is oblique, and not direct. There is no assertion of what is not literally true, but there is in each case, something implied, which is at variance with the facts.

§ 483. In *Apostrophe* the figurative element consists in the address of the sentence or passage. If it occurs in a discourse addressed to a certain party, this figure involves a *turning away* from that party to address another, sometimes present, but more generally absent or dead, and for the time ideally conceived as a person present. But apostrophe does not always occur in a discourse; sometimes it constitutes the whole discourse. In such case, the figure consists in directing the address to an object that is not literally capable of receiving it.

Christ's address to Jerusalem, in Matt. xxiii., 37–39, is a well-known instance of Apostrophe. So also St. Paul's address to Death and the Grave in 1 Cor. xv., 55. Cicero's First Oration against Catiline opens with an apostrophe to Catiline himself. Also Satan's Soliloquy, found in the first part of Book Fourth of *Paradise Lost*, begins with an apostrophe to the sun; and Milton himself in the opening of Book Third makes an apostrophe to Light;—both celebrated as among the finest passages of that noble poem. The well-known piece of Halleck's called Marco Bozzaris, ends with the following apostrophe.

"Bozzaris, with the storied brave
Greece nurtured in her glory's time,
Rest thee;—there is no prouder grave
E'en in her own proud clime.
We tell thy doom without a sigh;
For thou art Freedom's now, and Fame's—
One of the few, the immortal names,
That were not born to die."

§ 484. The figure of *Interrogation* consists in asking a question (in form), not for the purpose of gaining information, but of more strongly asserting the answer which the questioner evidently expects the hearer mentally to make.

The expectation of the questioner is indicated by his use or omission of the negative adverb qualifying the verb: if an affirmative answer is expected, the negative particle is used; as,

"And does not Fame speak of me too?"

But if a negative answer is expected, then the question is without the negative adverb; as, "Hast Thou eyes of flesh? or seest Thou as man seeth?"

A kind of negative answer is likewise expected, when a figurative interrogation uses an interrogative word, such as *how*, *where*, *when*, *why*, or *what*.

EXAMPLES.

"Why stand we here idle?"—Implying there is no good reason for it.—"What is it that gentlemen wish? What would they have?"—

Implying that they can not easily tell what they wished to have.—Then follows that remarkably thrilling interrogation,—"Is life so dear, or peace so sweet, as to be purchased at the price of chains and slavery."

§ 485. *Innuendo* consists in suggesting a thought indirectly, sometimes by the assertion of what would logically lead to the unexpressed meaning, at other times, by the bare allusion of some circumstance which the author expressly declines to enlarge upon. In the former case it is called *Insinuation;* in the latter, *Apophasis.*

EXAMPLES.

Fuller said of Camden, the antiquarian,—"He had a number of coins of the Roman Emperors, and a good many more of the later English kings;"—meaning that he was rich. This is Insinuation.

"Your idleness, not to mention your impertinence and dishonesty, disqualifies you for the situation." This is Apophasis.

§ 486. *Meiosis* consists in suggesting a fact or truth by asserting what falls far short of the actual case. Thus to say—"He was not without a good opinion of his own abilities,"—is to assert by implication that he had a *high* opinion of his own abilities.

"Rome was not built in a day," implies that it took a long time to build the great city.

EXERCISE.

Compose apostrophes to the following objects, embracing in each one either an interrogation, an innuendo, or a meiosis.

Washington	The Photographic Art
Galileo	Oxygen
Columbus	Electricity
John Howard	The Human Conscience
The Hebrew People	The Bible
Athens	The Stars
Socrates	The Telescope
Venice	The Ice-king
Florence	Cotton
The Pyramids	Alcohol
Jerusalem	The Cholera

The Athenian Acropolis	The Newspaper Press
The Spirit of Liberty	Iron
Science	The American Eagle
Poetry	The Steam-engine
Painting	The Schoolmaster
The Spirit of Beauty	Gold

ONOMATOPŒIA—CLIMAX.

These are the two remaining figures, left thus to the last, because they could not without some violence be included in any of the foregoing groups of figures.

§ 487. *Onomatopœia* consists in using a word or group of words to express an object of sound or motion, the very utterance of which tends, by similarity, to suggest the object it signifies.

EXAMPLES.

hiss	roar	bow-wow	rumble
buzz	mew	pop	clatter

"Loud sounds the ax, redoubling strokes on strokes,
On all sides round the forest hurls her oaks
Headlong. Deep echoing groan the thickets brown,
Then, rustling, crackling, crashing, thunder down."

"Soft is the strain when Zephyr gently blows,
And the smooth stream in smoother numbers flows.
But, when loud surges lash the sounding shore,
The hoarse, rough verse should, like the torrent, roar."

"Next Anger rushed, his eyes on fire,
In lightnings owned his secret stings;
In one rude clash he struck the lyre,
And swept with hurried hand the strings."

"With woeful measures wan Despair—
Low sullen sounds his grief beguiled;
A solemn, strange, and mingled air,
'T was sad by fits, by starts 't was wild."

§ 488. *Climax* consists in so arranging the words of a series, or the parts of a sentence, that the least impressive shall stand first, and the successive members of the series or sentence grow in strength unto the last.

EXAMPLES.

"Sensualists, by their frequent indulgences and gross excesses, enfeeble their bodies, wear out their spirits, and debase their minds."

"It is an outrage to *bind* a Roman citizen; to *scourge* him is an atrocious crime; *to put him to death* is almost a parricide; but to CRUCIFY him—what shall I call it?"

"The cloud-capp'd towers, the gorgeous palaces,
The solemn temples, the great globe itself,
Yea, all which it inherit, shall dissolve,
And, like an insubstantial pageant faded,
Leave not a rack behind."

Having now learned the nature and form of all the principal figures used in discourse, let the pupil be required to point out the various figures that occur in his reading lessons, and also to produce instances of the different kinds of figure, searched out by himself from such books and periodicals as he may have access to.

CHAPTER XXXIII.

CRITICISM.

At this stage of the pupil's progress he will be prepared to engage in the most difficult and test-affording exercise of Criticism. It is not to be expected that the immature minds of youth can perform any very searching analysis of a literary work or extract, or form judgments upon it that would be acknowledged as authoritative. Nevertheless it is well for each one to be trained to independence of thought, to close scrutiny of language and reasoning, and to the formation of opinions, and the support of them by argument, concerning what they read. As introductory to this exercise, it is recommended that the teacher first lead the minds of the pupils by questions concerning any selected piece; requiring these questions to be answered in a critical essay on the given piece. The following model will show what is recommended.

EXTRACT FROM CARLYLE.

1. Curious is it to consider how different appearance is from reality, and under what different shape and circumstances the truly most important man of any given period might be found. Little can we

prognosticate, with any certainty, the future influences from the present aspect of an individual.

2. How many demagogues, Crœsuses, conquerors, fill their own age with joy or terror, with a tumult which promises to be perennial; and in the next age die away into insignificance and oblivion! These are the forests of gourds that overtop the infant cedars and aloe-trees, but, like the prophet's gourd, wither on the third day.

3. What was it to the Pharaohs of Egypt, in that old era, if Jethro, the Midianitish priest and grazier, accepted the Hebrew outlaw as his herdsman? Yet the Pharaohs, with all their chariots of war, are buried deep in the wrecks of time; and that Moses still lives, not among his own tribes only, but in the hearts and daily business of all civilized nations.

4. Nor is it only to those primitive ages when religions took their rise, and a man of pure and high mind appeared not only as a teacher and philosopher, but as a priest and prophet, that our observation applies. The same uncertainty in estimating present things and men holds more or less in all times.

5. When Tamerlane had finished building his pyramid of seventy thousand human skulls, and was seen standing at the gate of Damascus, glittering in steel, with his battle-ax on his shoulder, till his fierce hosts filed out to new victories and new carnage, the pale looker-on might have fancied that nature was in her death-throes; for havoc and despair had taken possession of the earth, and the sun of manhood seemed setting in seas of blood.

6. Yet it might be that on that very gala-day of Tamerlane a little boy was playing ninepins on the streets of Mentz, whose history was more important to men than that of twenty Tamerlanes.

7. The Tartar Khan, with his shaggy demons of the wilderness, passed away like a whirlwind, to be forgotten forever; and that German artisan has wrought a benefit which is yet immeasurably expanding itself, and will continue to expand itself through all countries and through all times.

8. What are the conquests and expeditions of the whole corporation of captains, from Walter the Penniless to Napoleon Bonaparte, compared with those movable types of Johannes Faust?

9. Truly it is a mortifying thing for your conqueror to reflect how perishable is the metal which he hammers with such violence; how the kind earth will soon shroud up his bloody foot-prints; and all that he achieved and skillfully piled together will be but like his own

canvas city of a camp—this evening loud with life, to-morrow all struck and vanished,—"a few earth-pits and heaps of straw!"

10. For here, as always, it continues true that the deepest force is the stillest; that, as in the fable, the mild shining of the sun shall silently accomplish what the fierce blustering of the tempest has in vain essayed. Above all it is ever to be kept in mind that not by material but by moral power are men and their actions to be governed.

11. How noiseless is thought! No rolling of drums, no tramp of squadrons, no immeasurable tumult of baggage-wagons, attends its movements. In what obscure and sequestered places may the head be meditating, which is one day to be crowned with more than imperial authority; for kings and emperors will be among its ministering servants!

12. It will rule not over but in all heads, and with its solitary combinations of ideas, as with magic formulas, bend the world to its will! The time may come when Napoleon himself will be better known for his laws than for his battles; and the victory of Waterloo prove less momentous than the opening of the first Mechanics' Institute.

QUESTIONS TO ELICIT CRITICISM ON THE FOREGOING.

What is the subject or theme of this extract? Under what more general truth is this comprehended, in the introduction? Can you trace the narrowing series of observations by which the author comes to his theme? How many illustrations of his theme does he give? Do the more ancient or more modern come first? Can you detect any reason for this in the paragraph numbered "4"?

Why, in the first sentence of the first paragraph, does he use the transposition, "curious is it"? What contrast is implied or suggested in the latter member of this sentence? Why does he qualify the adjective *most important* by *truly*? Why does he qualify the noun *period* by the participial adjective *given*?

In the second sentence, what relation have the two adverbial elements, *little* and *with any certainty*? Would it have been better to say—"With how little certainty can we prognosticate," etc.? Is Crœsuses a proper or a common noun? Why capitalized? By what figure of speech is it used thus? Is it a beauty or a defect to omit the conjunction that connects *demagogues*, *Crœsuses*, and *conquerors*? What figure in the use of the word *age*? Is it proper to apply the epithet *perennial* to tumult? Suppose a tumult is one of terror; is it proper to say it PROMISES to be perpetual or perennial? What figure in the use of the word *die*? What figure in the words *gourds*, *cedars*, and *aloe-trees*? Is the metaphor maintained as such to the end of the sentence? What figure in the expression, *the third day*?

Is the word *Pharaohs* used figuratively like *Crœsuses*? Why not? Why does the author use the demonstrative *that* in the phrase *in that old era*? Who was "the Hebrew outlaw"? By what figure is he thus represented? Why is there no danger of obscurity in using this circumlocution? Why is it preferable in this connection to the proper name of the man?

What antithesis occurs in the last sentence of the third paragraph? In what sense is it true that *Moses still lives*? What then does *Moses* stand for, and by what figure of speech? Does not this require that "*the Pharaohs*" should be taken in a like figurative sense? Why is the adjunct—"with all their chariots of war"—joined to *Pharaohs*? Is it a mixture of metaphor to say "buried in the wrecks of time"? Why not?

What reason can you give for the author's seizing upon that moment in the life of Tamerlane when he stood, as represented in the fifth paragraph, at the gate of Damascus, in order to assert what is found in the latter part of that sentence; viz., that "the pale looker-on," etc.? Why is the ideal *looker-on* described as PALE? What figure in the sentence—*For havoc and despair*, etc.? What figure in—"The sun of manhood seemed setting in seas of blood"? How would you express the thoughts of the last two clauses of this paragraph literally? Who was the little boy that might have been playing in the streets of Mentz, and for what did he afterward become celebrated? Why does the author imagine him as "playing in the streets"? By what figure is Tamerlane called *The Tartar Khan*? Who are meant by "his shaggy demons of the wilderness," and why are they so called? In what respects were Tamerlane and his army like a whirlwind?

Does the eighth paragraph contain a *figurative* comparison? Why not? Who was Walter the Penniless? Why is he spoken of as if he were the first of "the corporation of captains"? What does the author mean by "the corporation of captains"? By what figures is *captains* put for *commanders*? Is the interrogation of the eighth paragraph figurative or literal? Why? Why does the author express himself in that way, rather than literally?

In the ninth paragraph, is the use of the preposition *for* consistent with precision? Give your reasons. Why is the noun *conqueror* limited by *your*? Is this use of the second person pronoun as common in America as in England? What precise idea do the English mean to convey by it? What is meant by the "metal which he hammers"? Does the conqueror hammer metal? How? Why is the noun *earth* qualified by the epithet *kind*? Why *footprints* with *bloody*? What figures are used in these two expressions? What is the sense of the word *but* before like? How would you explain it by conversion into its opposite negative, by § 296? What is the force of the preposition *of* between *city* and *camp*? Wherein consists the beauty of the comparison drawn between the conqueror's works and his itinerant camp? What figures are involved in the phrase "loud with life"? Why is *loud* better than *noisy*?

In the first line of the tenth paragraph, what does *always* qualify? Is this a comparison? Figurative? Is *deepest* used literally? What is the figure? What would the literal expression be? Can you recite the fable alluded to in the tenth paragraph? How is this fable to be interpreted so as to confirm and illustrate the theme of the extract? What is the distinction between *material* and *moral* power?

In the eleventh paragraph, second sentence, why is the verb *attends* in the singular? Wherein consists the propriety of making these negative assertions concerning the *movements of thought*? In what sense does *thought move*, or what is meant by the *movements* of *thought*? What figure is involved in the use of the word *head*? Is it not a mixture of metaphorical and plain language to use the word *head* in two senses in consecutive clauses? Why not? What authority is alluded to as "more than imperial"? How will *kings* and *emperors* be *ministering servants* to the *philosopher*?

How do you explain the first sentence of the twelfth paragraph? What is the exact point of the comparison expressed in the clause, "as with magic formulas"?

Why is it proper to speak of *bending the world*? In what respect is this different from Shakespeare's expression—"that eye of his, whose *bend* doth awe the *world*"? Why is the noun *Napoleon* qualified by the appositive *himself*? How will the better remembrance of Napoleon's laws than of his battles illustrate the theme of the writer? Of what importance was the opening of the first Mechanics' Institute? What are Mechanics' Institutes? Do you know where and when the first one was opened? Of what importance was the victory of Waterloo?

How many and what similes are used in this piece? Enumerate all the metaphors in it. All the metonymies. All the synecdoches. All the antitheses. All the personifications. All the figurative interrogations.

After one or two exercises in Criticism, in which the aid of such questions as the foregoing has been afforded by the teacher, the pupil may be required to produce original Criticisms, on assigned pieces, without such help.

PART FIFTH.

INVENTION AND EXPRESSION COMBINED.

CHAPTER XXXIV.

EXTEMPORANEOUS COMPOSITION.

§ 489. No course of instruction and discipline in the Art of Prose Composition would be complete without a portion devoted to extemporaneous composition. By this is meant the framing of thoughts on any given subject, and the proper expression of them, either without any preparation, or with the mere pre-arrangement of the plan, leaving the language to be suggested at the time of the delivery. It was a recommendation made by no less an orator than Henry Clay to young men seeking to qualify themselves as public speakers, to spend at least fifteen minutes each day in uttering, in solitude, without any premeditation, their thoughts upon a subject selected at random. This recommendation he enforced by the assertion that to such a custom, maintained for years, he himself owed, in no small degree, whatever of success he had attained as a speaker. The student who is earnestly striving to gain excellence in the use of his own language will need no further urging to adopt such a practice. The fruits of this secret culture will not be long in making their appearance.

§ 490. As an additional method of securing the cultivation of the art of ready and correct expression, it is recommended that a pair of earnest students unite to afford mutual assistance in this exercise. Let them retire from observation, and speak by turns, in speeches of five minutes each, their thoughts on any assigned subject. It would be well for them to take some question susceptible of debate, and choosing opposite sides, discuss its merits. While one is speaking, let the other note, not merely his arguments, but his language, his method, his gestures. The arguments he will reply to in his own rejoinder; but let him reserve his criticisms on his comrade's performance for kindly mention after the exercise is over. Such private drill will admirably prepare the young performers for the more difficult arena of

DEBATING BY THE CLASS.

§ 491. If a class of youths pursuing the course prescribed by this Manual have caught the spirit appropriate to the study, they will, long before progressing thus far in the book, have perceived the propriety of turning the class into a lyceum for the discussion of questions and other literary performances. Such an expedient can not be too highly recommended. It has received the indorsement of many eminent men. Lord Mansfield, Edmund Burke, Charles James Fox, and John P. Curran, as well as the illustrious American mentioned above, all have confessed themselves greatly indebted to such associations for the skill they acquired in oratory and debate.

If, as is desirable for young men attending ordinary schools or academies, the class debate is conducted by the teacher as the presiding officer, he will of course establish such rules and arrangements as he deems best. If the debating class is a number of students in the same high-school or college, they may organize themselves into a lyceum, and adopt their own constitution and by-laws. Admirable suggestions for such an association are to be found in *McElligott's American Debater*, to which parties interested are referred.

§ 492. It must be borne in mind that, although in extemporaneous speaking considerable freedom is allowed, and, of beginners especially, no high degree of accuracy or elegance of style should be exacted, yet it is certainly one of the aims of extemporaneous debate to cultivate the art of speaking, not only forcibly as to logical power, but with as strict attention to all the rules of Style as the most fastidious ear would demand. Let every young speaker lay down the rule—*Never to allow himself in any known violation of propriety in any respect.* Let him never excuse himself for any fault pointed out to him. Let him never defend his own utterances, when usage or authority is clearly against him. Let him never cling to an embellishment that others do not relish, although they can give no reasons for it. He must aim to do in regard to style what can be done only in very few things,—*offend nobody.* Withal, he must never become discouraged with the inveteracy of habit, by the multiplicity of rules, by the infinity of chances for error, or by the mortification of failure.

The following list presents a few of the questions that afford good fields for debate.

Does wealth exert more influence than intelligence?

Should a criminal be capitally condemned on circumstantial evidence?

Are banks more beneficial than injurious?

Ought military schools to be encouraged?

Should colleges be endowed?

Did the French revolution advance the cause of liberty in Europe?

Is there any real danger of the over-population of the globe?

Is country life more favorable to the cultivation of virtue than life in a city?

Is history a more useful study than biography?

Is ambition more destructive of personal happiness than avarice?

Is it the duty of good men to discountenance the theater?

Is the Bible more essential to the spread of Christianity than the living ministry?

Does poetry demand a higher order of genius than oratory?

Does military life tend to qualify men to become good civil governors?

Has Mohammedanism produced more evil than good?

Is it ever right to deceive a rational man?

Should the chief end of civil punishment be the reformation of criminals, or the prevention of crime?

Ought the state to provide for the free education of all children within its borders?

Is it expedient to form colonies of convicts?

Would a congress of nations be practical or beneficial?

Was the field of eloquence in ancient Greece or Rome superior to that in our own country?

Are novels more injurious than beneficial?

Is it expedient to unite manual with mental labor in an educational establishment?

Which exerts the greater influence on society, the teacher or the preacher?

Which controls public opinion more extensively, the ministry or the newspaper press?

Does a natural proclivity to crime diminish the guilt of the act?

Should a member of the American House of Representatives be bound by the will of his constituents?

Do savage nations possess an exclusive right to the soil?

Should the right of suffrage be co-extensive with resident manhood?

Is a lawyer justifiable in defending a cause that he believes to be bad?

Ought the Protective Policy or the Free Trade principles to prevail?

Ought gambling to be suppressed by law?

Which is the better for the development of good character, poverty or riches?

Ought the liberty of the press to be restricted?

Ought imprisonment for debt to be abolished?

Should corporal punishment be allowed in schools?

Ought religious institutions to be supported by law?

Should infidel publications be suppressed by law?

Should atheists be eligible to office?

Has government a right to suppress Mormon or Mohammedan polygamy?

Are all mankind descended from one pair?

Is man responsible for his belief?

Can any of the moral attributes of God be proved from the light of nature?

Is a scholastic education preferable to a private one?

Are the principles of the Peace society practicable?

Should the course of study in college be the same for all pupils?

Are monastic orders favorable to the cultivation of true piety?

Are inequalities of rank in society favorable to social progress?

Was the influence of Jefferson upon his age and country beneficial?

Was Bonaparte greater in the field than in the cabinet?

Have the United States the right to forbid European interference with other American governments?

Does morality keep pace with civilization?

Which has done the greater service to the cause of truth, philosophy or poetry?

Is the cultivation of the Fine Arts conducive to virtue?

Has sectarianism done more to advance or retard the interests of Christianity?

Is a "little learning" more dangerous than ignorance?

QUESTIONS FOR REVIEW AND EXAMINATION.

What is the fallacy of *begging the question*? In what case will a mere variation of the form of expression afford a kind of proof? What is a thesis? Which are the six sources of argument? Which are the five modes of Explication?

Of what is every true definition composed? What is meant by a *genus*? What is *differentia*? What are the requirements of the differentia in a definition? What is explication by enumeration? What is explication by distinction? What is explication by limitation? What is explication by interpretation?

What is meant by proof from antecedent probability? What is meant by proof from signs or consequences? What is meant by proof from instances or examples? What value does any particular instance or example have as proof? What is *analogy*? What is proof by analogy? What is proof from testimony or authority?

Which are the nine general rules for argumentation?

What is the distinction between Euphony and Harmony? Which are the two general rules for Euphony? Which are the five special rules under the general rule forbidding all harsh, grating, unmelodious combinations of sounds? What is tautophony? How are the iterations that conduce to Strength distinguished from those that violate Euphony?

Which are the four special rules under the general rule requiring an agreeable arrangement of clauses and members?

Into what two classes are all prose compositions divisible? What are classed with spoken discourses? In what respects are spoken discourses different from written as to style? What is the proper field of oratory, and what is the proper object? How was oratory studied in ancient Greece and Rome? What bad effect would be produced by a strict adherence to the forms of the ancient rhetoricians?

What is our ideal of the orator? How do signs of elaborate preparation affect an orator's audience? To what does Demosthenes owe his fame?

What kind of preparation should the young aspirant after oratorical excellence make?

Which are the six formal divisions of a regular oration? What are the objects of the exordium, and how are they secured? Which are the six special rules for the exordium? Which are the six special rules for the division or arrangement? What is the part of an oration called the statement? In what department of oratory is the statement very important? Which are the four special rules for the appeal to the feelings? What are the general cautions concerning the conclusion of an oration?

By what means is style ornamented? What are Figures? Which are the seventeen figures in most common use?

Which three figures are founded on resemblance? What is a simile? What is a comparison? What kinds of comparisons are not similes? What is a metaphor? How distinguished from simile? What is an allegory? What relation has allegory to metaphor?

What three objects prompt to the use of figures of resemblance? Which five rules apply when the object is to elucidate a subject? Which five when the object is to please simply? Which two when the object is to arouse feeling?

How have all our words denoting mental and metaphysical ideas been obtained?

What two figures are based on other relations besides those of resemblance and contrast? What is Metonymy? What is Synecdoche? What is the figure of Transferred Epithet?

What four figures are founded on direct opposition to the literal truth? What is hyperbole? What its proper occasion? What is personification? What is vision? What is irony?

What two figures are based on contrast? How do they differ? What is antithesis? How divided and subdivided? What are the two rules, or principles, that apply to antithesis? Which are the finest fields for the use of antithesis?

What is paradox? What four figures are based on an oblique opposition to literal truth? What is apostrophe? What is figurative interrogation? What is innuendo? Into what two kinds divided? What is meiosis?

What is onomatopœia? What is climax?

What recommendation did Henry Clay make to young men seeking to attain the art of extemporaneous speaking? What modification of this is here recommended as an additional private practice? What great men have recommended debating societies? What directions are given to those who desire to use the debating society as a means of improvement?

APPENDIX I.

COMPENDIUM OF THE RULES OF SYNTAX.

ABRIDGED FROM BUTLER'S GRAMMAR.

§ 493. A noun or pronoun, annexed to another noun or pronoun, for the sake of explanation or emphasis, is put in the same case; as, "*Paul* an *apostle;*" "The *city Rome;*" "*We men* are mortals;" "These words were spoken to *us men;*" "Brutus killed *Cæsar*, *him* who had been his friend."

The annexed word is said to be in *apposition* with the other.

§ 494. It is proper to use the comparative degree when the two parties compared are represented as distinct from each other. It would not be correct to say, "Solomon was wiser than the Hebrew kings," because Solomon was one of those kings.

§ 495. It is proper to use the superlative when one of the parties is included in the other. Thus, "Solomon was the wisest of the Hebrew kings;" but it would be incorrect to say, "Solomon was the wisest of all the *other* Hebrew kings," because *other* makes the parties quite distinct.

§ 496. Double comparatives and superlatives should be avoided; as, "*more wiser*, *worser*, *most straitest*," etc.

§ 497. *This* and *that* refer to singular nouns, *these* and *those* to plural nouns; as, *that kind*, *those kinds*.

§ 498. When objects are contrasted, *that* and *those* refer to the first mentioned, *this* and *these* to the last; as, "Virtue and vice are as opposite to each other as light and darkness; *that* ennobles the mind, *this* debases it."

"Farewell my friends! farewell my foes!
My peace with *these*, my love with *those!*"—BURNS.

§ 499. Singular nouns are sometimes improperly used with numeral adjectives which denote more than one; as, "Twenty *pound*."

§ 500. Yet such expressions as twenty *head of cattle, a hundred yoke of oxen, ten sail of vessels*, are authorized.

§ 501. *Each, every, either, neither*, always refer to nouns in the *third person singular;* and verbs and pronouns referring to them should, consequently, be in the third person singular; as, "Each [person] of you *has his* faults,"—not "*have your* faults."

§ 502. But such expressions as *every three weeks* are correct, because the whole is taken as *one* portion of time.

§ 503. *Either* and *neither* can not properly be applied to more than two objects. "*Either* of the *three*," should be "*Any one* of the three;" and "*Neither* of the three," should be "*None* of the three."

§ 504. After some verbs, particularly after certain infinitive verbs, it is often difficult to decide whether adjectives or adverbs should be used. After *to be*, or *to become*, it is easy to see that the word should be an adjective, and not an adverb; but when other verbs are employed, it is more difficult to decide.

The following directions will enable us to decide correctly in most instances.

§ 505. I. The adverb should not be used, if the corresponding adjunct will not convey the intended idea.

§ 506. II. When the verb *to be* and the verb *to become* can be substituted for any other, without materially changing the sense or the construction, that other verb must be connected with an adjective, and not with an adverb.

§ 507. Pronouns agree with their antecedents in gender, number, and person; as, "This is the friend of *whom* I spoke; *he* has just arrived;" "Lying is a vice *which* I despise; *it* is disgusting."

§ 508. Pronouns referring to two or more nouns, when the objects are taken together, should be in the plural; as, "*John* and *James* attend to *their* studies."

§ 509. The nouns in such cases are generally connected by *and.* But *and* may come between nouns when the objects are not taken together; as, "John (and not James) attends to *his* studies;" "*Every* book, and *every* paper, is kept in *its* place;" "*Each* book, and *each* paper, is kept in *its* place;" "*No* book, and *no* paper, is out of *its* place."

§ 510. When the nouns express different characters of *the same* person, the pronouns should be singular; as, "*That* great statesman and general lost his life."

§ 511. When two or more nouns in the singular, are connected by *or* or *nor*, the objects are not taken together, and the pronoun must be singular; as, "Either John or James attends to *his* studies;" "Neither John nor James attends to *his* studies."

§ 512. When the objects are taken together, and the nouns or pronouns are of *different persons*, the plural pronoun referring to them must be of the *first person*, if one of the antecedents is of the first person; and of the second, if the antecedents are of the second and third persons; as, "James, and thou, and I, are attached to *our* country;" "James and I are attached to *our* country;" "James and thou are attached to *your* country."

§ 513. Collective nouns in the singular may have pronouns in the plural, when reference is made to the individuals composing the collection; as, "The *multitude* eagerly pursue pleasure as *their* chief good."

§ 514. The neuter pronoun *it* is applied to infants and to animals whose sex is unknown, or unnecessary to be regarded.

§ 515. The relative *who* is applied to persons, and *which* to things without life and to the lower animals; as, "The *man who;* the *book which;* the *horse which.*"

§ 516. When things and the lower animals are spoken of as persons, they take pronouns representing persons; as, "*Night*, sable goddess, from *her* ebon throne;" "The *lion* said to the *ass*, *who* had been hunting with *him*."

§ 517. The relative *which* is sometimes applied to young children; as, "The child *which* was sick." It was formerly applied to all persons; as, "Our father *which* art in heaven." The interrogative *which* is applied to persons and things indiscriminately; as, "*Which man* did you see?" "*Which book* did you read?"

§ 518. A collective noun, when it does not refer directly to the individuals composing the collection, should not be represented by *who*. Thus, we should not say, "He is on the committee *who* was appointed;" but *that* or *which* was appointed.

§ 519. The relative *which* sometimes stands after the proper name of a person; but in such cases it refers, not to the person, but to the *word;* as, "Herod—*which* [word] is another name for cruelty."

§ 520. *Which* sometimes stands after a common noun denoting a person, when the character and not the person is referred to; as, "He is a good writer, *which* [thing] is all that he professes to be."

That is used in preference to *who* or *which* in the following cases:

§ 521. I. After adjectives in the superlative degree; as, "Charles XII. was one of the *greatest* madmen *that* the world ever saw."

§ 522. II. After *same*, *very*, and *all;* as, "He is the *same* man that I saw before." "He is the *very* man *that* did it;" "It was *all that* he could do."

§ 523. III. After *who;* as, "*Who that* knows him would speak thus?"

§ 524. IV. When the relative refers to both persons and things; as, "The *men* and *cities that* he saw."

§ 525. *That* never admits a preposition before it, but it may be the object of a preposition following it. We can not say, "This is the man *of that* he spoke;" but we may say, "This is the man *that* he spoke *of*." *That* is sometimes used when a preposition is omitted; as, "In the day *that* thou eatest thereof;" that is, in the day *in which.*

§ 526. It is inelegant to mingle the solemn and familiar styles in addressing the same object; as, "Aleefa, *thou* art more beautiful than the moon on her fourteenth night, but *your* wickedness causes me to hate *you*."

§ 527. A change should not be made from one relative to another in the same connection; thus, it is improper to say, "The man *that* met us to-day, and *whom* you saw yesterday, is the mayor of the city."

§ 528. A relative clause which modifies the subject should not be placed after a noun in the predicate; thus, "He should not keep a horse that can not ride," should be, "He that can not ride should not keep a horse."

§ 529. The English language is deficient in not having a pronoun of the third person singular, applicable to either sex. But the deficiency does not justify the use of a plural pronoun in such cases. If necessary, the masculine pronoun will represent both genders; thus, "If any member of the church wishes to withdraw, *he* may signify it to the minister privately."

§ 530. The subject of a finite verb is put in the nominative case.

§ 531. The verb must agree with its subject in number and person.

§ 532. When an infinitive or clause is the subject, it requires a verb of the third person singular.

§ 533. When the subject consists of two or more nominatives connected by *and* expressed or understood, the verb must be plural.

§ 534. This remark applies to infinitives and clauses, when they express distinct actions or states of being; as, "To be rich, and to be happy, *are* different things." But when they describe *one* act or state, the verb is to be singular; as, "To toil all the year through, and get nothing for it, *is* very hard."

§ 535. When the connected nominatives denote but one person, the verb is singular; as, "The saint, the father, and the husband prays."

§ 536. If the singular nominatives between which *and* is placed, are not taken togther, the verb is singular; as, "John, and not James *attends;*" "John, and James also, *attends.*" In each of these sentences, *John* is the subject of *attends*, and *James* is the subject of the verb *attends* understood. Thus, "John attends, and James attends not;" "John attends, and James also attends." The verb which is expressed agrees, of course, with the nominative that belongs to it; if that nominative is plural, the verb should be plural, etc.; as, "*Friends*, not merit, *cause* his promotion."

§ 537. When two or more singular nominatives are connected by *or* or *nor*, the objects are taken separately, and the verb is singular; as, "John or James *attends;*" "Neither John nor James *attends.*"

§ 538. Collective nouns in the singular may have verbs in the plural, when the reference is to the individuals composing the collection; as, "The *multitude* eagerly *pursue* pleasure;" that is, the persons composing the multitude.

§ 539. When a collective noun denotes the collection as *one body*, the verb must be singular; as, "The *company was* large." Here we do not mean that the persons composing the company were large.

§ 540. A nominative after *many a* demands a singular verb; as, "Full *many a flower is* born."

§ 541. When the nominatives connected by *or* or *nor*, are of different persons or numbers, the verb agrees with the nominative next to it; as, "Either thou or I *am* concerned;" "I or thou *art* to blame;" "Neither you nor he *is* in fault;" "Neither poverty nor riches *were* injurious to him."

In general, it is better not to use such constructions as these. A verb is supposed to be understood with each of the nominatives, except that which is next to the verb; and it is generally better to express it, or to use some other form for conveying the idea. Thus, "Either thou art concerned, or I am;" or, "One of us is concerned;" "I am to blame, or thou art;" or, "One of us is to blame;" or, "The blame rests on me or thee;" "He was injured by neither poverty nor riches," etc.

§ 542. Every finite verb not in the imperative mood should have a subject expressed, except when the verb is connected to another.

§ 543. The adjuncts of the nominative should not affect the form of the verb; thus, "The *number* of oysters *increases*,"—not *increase;* "The ship, with all the crew, *was* lost,"—not *were.*

§ 544. A noun or pronoun in the predicate, after any but a transitive verb in the active voice, is put in the same case as the subject, when it denotes the same person or thing; as, "I *am* he;" "Stephen *died a* martyr;" "He *was called* John;" "*I took* it *to be him.*"

§ 545. The predicate nominative is sometimes placed before the verb, and the subject after the verb, particularly when the predicate is an interrogative pronoun; as, "Who is he?" "A train-band *captain* eke was he."—COWPER.

There is an error in the following sentence: "*Whom* do men say that I am?" If the subject and predicate were placed in their usual order, the sentence would be, "Do men say that *I* am *whom?*" *Whom* should be *who*, because the subject *I* is in the nominative.

§ 546. The nominative case is never used without a verb, except in the following cases:

§ 547. I. When an address is made; as, "*Plato*, thou reasonest well."

§ 548. II. In mere exclamations; as, "O, the *times!* O, the *manners!*"

§ 549. III. When the attention is directed to an object before an affirmation is made respecting it; as,

"The Pilgrim *Fathers*, where are they?"

§ 550. IV. When a noun and a participle are used instead of a dependent clause; as, "*Shame* being lost, all virtue is lost;" that is, *when shame is lost.*

§ 551. A noun or pronoun used to limit a substantive by designating the possessor of the object, should be put in the possessive case.

§ 552. When two or more nouns are used as the designation of one individual, the possessive termination is added to the last; as, "*Paul the apostle's* advice;" "*General Washington's* tent;" "*Smith the bookseller's* house;" "*The Duke of Wellington's* exploits."

Here *Wellington's* is not in the possessive, but in the objective after *of; Duke* is in the possessive, but the whole is taken as one name, and the possessive termination is placed at the end.

§ 553. When the possessive termination is placed thus, the words are so closely connected as to form but one name. If any thing more is added, the termination must be placed after it. We may say

"Charles Stuart's death," or, "The King of England's death," but not "Charles Stuart, the King of England's death."

"This fact appears from Dr. Bacon of Birmingham's experiments." Here "of Birmingham" is added to the name of the individual to designate his place of residence, and the possessive termination should not be placed after *Birmingham.*

§ 554. When two or more nouns in the possessive case are connected by *and*, the possessive termination should be added to each of them; as, "These are *John's* and *Eliza's* books."

It would be better to say, "These books belong to John and Eliza."

§ 555. But if objects are possessed in common by two or more, and the nouns are closely connected without any intervening words, the possessive termination is added to the last noun only; as, "These are John and Eliza's books."

It would be better to say, "These books belong in common to John and Eliza."

§ 556. A possessive is not properly a substantive in construction; hence it can not have a noun or pronoun in apposition with it.

Instead of, "These psalms are David's, the king, priest, and prophet of the Jewish people," we may say, "These psalms were written by David," etc. Instead of, "I left the parcel at Smith's, the bookseller and stationer," we may say, "I left the parcel at the residence (or shop) of Smith, the bookseller and stationer."

§ 557. Nothing, except some necessary modifying word, should come between the possessive case and the name of the object possessed. "She began to extol the farmer's, as she called him, excellent understanding," should be, "She began to extol the excellent understanding of the farmer, as she called him."

§ 558. A participial noun, either alone or modified by other words, may be placed after the possessive case; as, "I am opposed to John's *writing;*" "I am opposed to his *devoting himself so exclusively to one subject.*"

This is one of the most common idioms of the language; and no other case than the possessive should be used in the preceding and similar sentences. Thus, when we wish to express opposition to the performance of the action, it is incorrect to say, "I am opposed to John writing."

§ 559. The object of a transitive verb is put in the objective case; as, "*He built* a house."

§ 560. When the subject and object are nouns, the object must usually be placed after the verb, because the position in the sentence determines the case; thus, "Alexander conquered *Darius,*"—not "*Darius* conquered Alexander."

But when pronouns are used, the object may be placed before the verb; as, "*Him* followed his next mate;" "The *subject* he has examined."

As relatives and interrogatives stand as near as possible to the beginning of their clauses, they always precede the verb; as, "He *whom* I serve is eternal;" "*Whom* do you serve?"

§ 561. Some intransitive verbs are followed by an objective of kindred signification to their own; as, "He *runs* a *race;*" "They *live* a happy *life.*" Allied to this construction are such expressions as the following: "Death *grinned* horribly a ghastly *smile;*" "Her lips *blush* deeper *sweets;*" "Groves, whose rich trees *wept* odorous *gums* and *balms;*" "From that sapphire fount the crisped brooks *ran nectar.*"

§ 562. Transitive verbs are sometimes improperly used as intransitive; as, "I must premise *with* three circumstances;" "I can not allow *of* that." The preposition should be erased in each one of these sentences. *To locate* is sometimes improperly used as intransitive; as, "He has located in Cincinnati;" by which is meant that he has become a resident of Cincinnati.

§ 563. Intransitive verbs are sometimes improperly used as transitive; "He repented *him* of his design." *Him* should be erased. It is not elegant to say, "He *grows* corn;" or, "This land *grows* corn." We should should say, "He *raises* or *cultivates* corn;" "This land *produces* corn."

§ 564. Some verbs may be followed by two objectives denoting the same person or thing; as, "Romulus called the *city Rome.*"

The verbs referred to in this remark, are all those verbs that in the passive voice have a predicate nominative; such as, *to choose, to appoint, to elect, to constitute, to render, to name, to call, to esteem, to consider, to reckon.*

After some of these verbs we may suppose an ellipsis of the verb *to be;* as, "I consider him [to be] a good man."

§ 565. Some verbs are followed by two objectives, the former denoting the person *to* or *for* whom the act is performed, the latter the proper object of the action. The former is sometimes called the *dative*, or the *indirect* object. When this is made to follow the direct or proper object, it must be governed by a preposition. Thus, "James gave me a book;" "James gave a book to me." "Buy me a book;" "Buy a book for me."

§ 566. When the passive voice is used, care must be taken that no other than the proper and direct object of the action be made the subject of the verb. Thus, it is incorrect to say, "I was given a book by James;" "He was presented with a cane," etc. Such expressions as "The horse has been looked at," "A doctor will be sent for," etc., are allowable, but not elegant.

§ 567. The object of a preposition is put in the objective case.

§ 568. *Home*, and nouns denoting time, extent of space, and degree of difference, are put in the objective case without a preposition; as, "He went *home;*" "I was there five *years;*" "He rode forty *miles* that *day;*" "The pole is ten *feet* long;" "This is a great *deal* better than that."

A preposition may be supplied with some of these; as, "He went [to] home;" "I was there [during] five years;" "This is [by] a great deal better than that;" "He rode forty miles [on] that day." With others it is difficult to say what preposition may be supplied. Some say, "He rode [through] forty miles;" "The pole is long [to] ten feet."

§ 569. The objective is used without a preposition after the adjective *worth*, and sometimes after *like*, *near*, and *nigh;* as, "This hat is worth five dollars;" "He is like [to] his father."

§ 570. After the active voice of the verbs *bid*, *dare*, *feel*, *hear*, *let*, *make*, *need*, *see*, and some others, the infinitive is used without *to;* as, "He bids me *come;*" "I saw him *write;*" "We heard him *tell* the story."

To is generally expressed after the passive voice of these verbs; as, "He was seen *to write.*"

The verbs after *may*, *can*, *must*, etc., are infinitives with *to* omitted.

§ 571. The perfect infinitive is sometimes improperly used for the imperfect [present]; as, "Yesterday I hoped *to have seen you.*" The perfect infinitive represents an action as *past* at the time referred to; but this infinitive is used to express an action which, though past at the time of speaking, was not so at the time to which the finite verb refers. This sentence should be, "Yesterday I hoped to see you."

If we intend to refer the *seeing* to the time denoted by *yesterday*, and the *hoping* to some previous time, we should say, "I had hoped to see you yesterday."

§ 572. Participles are modified in the same way as their verbs are. Thus, if the verb is followed by the objective case, so is the participle; as, "He *sees* me," "*Seeing* me," "*Having seen* me."

If the verb has two objectives, the participle has also; as, "He *calls* him John," "*Calling* him John," "*Having called* him John."

If the verb takes a predicate nominative, so does the participle; as, "He *is* a judge," "*Being* a judge," "*Having been* a judge."

The same adjuncts that modify the verb, modify the participle; as, "He *speaks* of me," "*Speaking* of me," "*Having spoken* of me."

§ 573. When a noun is limited by an adjective, though it may have the form of a participle, it is simply a noun, and should be construed as such.

Thus, "By *the observing of* these rules;" "This is *a complete forsaking of* truth;" "For *the* more *easy reading of* large numbers."

Errors are sometimes committed by leaving out *of* after such nouns; as, "By the observing these rules. Both the adjective and *of* may be omitted, however, and then the word becomes a participial noun; as, "By observing these rules."

The participial noun should not be followed by *of;* as, "By *observing of* these rules." If the verb from which it is derived is followed by *of*, the participial noun is also; as, "He spoke *of* those rules," "By speaking *of* those rules."

§ 574. When the participle is changed into a noun, it can not be modified by adverbs, as the participial noun may be; thus, it is incorrect to say, "For the more *easily* reading of large numbers;" but "For reading large numbers more easily" is correct.

§ 575. The participial noun is often connected with the possessive case; as, "I have some recollection of his *father's being* a judge."

§ 576. When the auxiliary perfect participle (or the passive, which is the same in form) differs in form from the past tense of the verb, one is often incorrectly used for the other; thus, "I done" for "I did;" "I seen" for "I saw;" "I have went" for "I have gone;" "I have wrote" for "I have written." Such errors should be carefully avoided.

§ 577. Adverbs should be placed as near to the words which they modify as they can be without producing harshness.

The same remark applies to adjuncts. Any more definite rule would be liable to so many exceptions as to be nearly useless.

§ 578. Such adverbs as *only*, *merely*, *chiefly*, are frequently misplaced; thus, "I only saw John, and not James;" "I saw John only, but did not speak to him." The first sentence should be, "I saw only John," or, "I saw John only;" the second should be, "I only saw John."

In the familiar language, *here*, *there*, and *where*, are used for *hither*, *thither*, and *whither*.

§ 579. Two negatives should not be used to express a negation, because they destroy each other, or are equivalent to an affirmative;

thus, "*Nor* did they *not* deserve the condemnation," means that they *did* deserve it.

§ 580. Adjectives should not be used as adverbs, nor adverbs as adjectives; "He writes *beautiful*," should be, "He writes *beautifully*;" "The *above* lines," should be, "The *preceding* lines;" "Thine *often* infirmities," should be, "Thy *frequent* infirmities."

§ 581. After the comparative degree, and after *other* and *else*, *than* is used to introduce the term expressive of the excluded party (see § 494); this term is generally an elliptical clause, and should be in that case which would be required if all the words were supplied. Thus, "He is greater than I,"—not "*than me*," because there is an ellipsis of the predicate *am great* after *I*.

§ 582. It is an exception to this rule that *whom*, and not *who*, is used after *than*, as if it were a preposition.

§ 583. *As* frequently has the force of a preposition before nouns denoting *office*, *character*, or *respect wherein;* as, "They employed him as a clerk;" "He is not gifted as a speaker;" "I give you this advice as your friend."

This function of the word must be carefully discriminated from its use as a conjunction, connecting an elliptical clause to some foregoing word. Thus, "He was as busy as a clerk;" "I am not so gifted as he."

§ 584. Two parts of different propositions may be connected, when the remaining part of the one is the same as that of the other; as, "This always has been, and always will be, admired."

But if the remaining part of one is not the same as that of the other, the two parts should not be connected. Thus, it is incorrect to say, "This always has, and always will, be admired," because, if *be admired* is added to the first part, it will be, *has be admired.*

"He was more beloved, but not so much admired as Cynthio." This is inaccurate, because we can not say, "He was more beloved *as* Cynthio." It should be, "He was more beloved *than* Cynthio, but not so much admired"—*as Cynthio* being understood.

§ 585. After expressions denoting *doubt*, *fear*, and *denial*, *but*, *but that*, or *lest* is often improperly used instead of *that;* as, "I do not doubt *but that* he is honest;" "I am afraid *lest* he may not return."

§ 586. That tense which by most grammarians is called the *subjunctive form of the subjunctive present*, is proper when the event spoken of is both *future* and *contingent*, and is proper in no other case. Hence, it is improper to say, "Though man *be* a sinner, yet he is not beyond the reach of mercy," because the contingency or condition is not future. It is also improper to say, "If he *repents*, he will be forgiven," because the contingency or condition *is future*.

This tense has been more properly styled the *Contingent Future*.

§ 587. That tense which by most grammarians is called the *subjunctive* form of the subjunctive past, is proper when a supposition is made which is known to be contrary to the actual state of the case, and it is proper in no other connection. Hence it is improper to say, "Though he *were* poor, yet he was respected," because no supposition of an unreal case is made at all. It is also improper to say, "Even if he *was* rich, he would not be haughty," because the case is evidently a supposed one, and not actual.

This tense has been more properly styled the *Subnegative Present*.

APPENDIX II.

ENGLISH SYNONYMS.

TAKEN FROM LYND'S CLASS BOOK OF ETYMOLOGY.

ABANDON—desert, forsake; leave, give up, cast off, quit; renounce, resign, relinquish, reject, surrender, abdicate, yield, cede, concede, forego. *See* Give *up*, Leave, Cast *back*.

ABANDONED—reprobate, profligate, corrupt, depraved, vitiated, vicious, wicked; lorn, forlorn, left, forsaken; deserted, helpless, destitute, lost, desperate, hopeless; outcast, cast off. *See* Wicked, Hopeless, Loose.

ABASE—depress, cast down, debase, disgrace, lower, make low; humble, humiliate, reduce. *See* Lower, Disgrace, Humble.

ABHOR—hate, detest, abominate, loathe. *See* Disgust.

ABIDE—stay, continue, remain; endure, last. *See* Stay, Lasting.

ABILITY—capacity, capability, capableness, cleverness, competence, competency, adequacy, adequateness, sufficiency, efficiency; skill, tact, address, dexterity; genius, talent, faculty, power. *See* Power.

ABLE—capable, competent, adequate, sufficient, efficient, qualified, skillful, clever, expert, adroit, dexterous; powerful, strong, vigorous. *See* Powerful, Active, Clever, Strong, Inadequate.

ABODE—habitation, dwelling, residence, domicil, house; *for a short time*, visit, sojourn, sojourning. *See* House.

ABOUNDING—sufficient, copious, abundant, overflowing, ample, plentiful, plenteous, fertile; prevailing, prevalent; exuberant. *See* Fruitful, Enough, Generous, Excess, Large.

ABRIDGE—abbreviate, compress, contract, epitomize, condense; reduce, curtail, shorten. *See* Take.

ABRIDGMENT—compendium, compend, abstract, synopsis, epitome, summary, abbreviation; contraction, diminution, reduction. *See* Shorter.

ABRUPT—sudden, unlooked for, unexpected, unforeseen; rough, rude, coarse; uneven, rugged; steep, craggy, precipitous; unconneoted. *See* Bold, Sudden.

ABSTAIN—refrain, forbear, withhold, desist, discontinue, hold off, cease, stop. *See* Keep, Leave.

ABSTAINING—abstinent, abstemious, sober, temperate, moderate. *See* Sober.

ABUSE—scurrility, invective, vituperation, opprobrium, insult, insolence, reproach.

ABUSE—revile, reproach, vilify, vituperate, insult; scurrilize, inveigh against, declaim, upbraid, chide, scandalize; ill-use, deceive, impose on. *See* Chide, Gibe, Beguile, Misuse, Injure, Reproach, Deceive.

ABUSIVE—opprobrious, scurrilous, insulting, insolent, scandalous, reproachful, vituperative, offensive, injurious. *See* Hurtful.

ACCENT—emphasis, stress.

ACCIDENTAL—fortuitous; casual, contingent, incidental, adventitious, adscititious, appendant, annexed, non-essential. *See* Additional.

ACCOMPANYING—attending, going with, concomitant, connected, conjoined, concurrent, collateral. *See* Connected.

ACCOMPLICE—accessory, abettor, confrere, colleague, partner, associate, companion; ally, confederate, assistant. *See* Companion.

ACCOMPLISH—effect, effectuate, achieve, do, execute, perform, complete, realize, fulfill. *See* Do, Perfect, Bring *about*, Compass.

ACCOMPLISHMENT—performance, execution, achievement, effectuation, fulfillment, completion, realization; acquisition, acquirement, attainment. *See* Performance, Completion, Work.

ACCOMPLISHMENTS—refinements, embellishments, elegancies; endowments; qualifications, attainments, acquirements. *See* Qualification.

ACCORDANT—agreeing with, concordant, consonant, consistent, congruous, compatible, conformable, agreeable, suitable. *See* Agreeable, Suitable, Answerable to.

ACCOUNT—description, relation, explanation, narration, narrative, history, story, recital, detail. *See* Chronicle, Memoir.

ACCOUNTABLE—responsible, answerable, amenable, subject to, obnoxious, liable. *See* Answerable, Subject.

ACCUSE—impeach, indict, charge; arraign; impute to, attribute to. *See* Lay, Count.

ACID—*See* Sour.

ACQUAINT—apprise, communicate, inform; disclose, reveal; make familiar. *See* Make known, Tell.

ACQUAINTANCE—friend, associate, companion; familiar, intimate. *See* Companion, Intimacy, Familiarity.

ACQUIESCENCE—quiet assent, resignation. submission; endurance, patience; consent, assent, compliance; accordance, agreement. *See* Agreement, Approbation, Agree to.

ACT *between*—interpose, intercede; mediate, intermediate; meddle, intermeddle, interfere. *See* Interrupt.

ACTIVE—expert, dexterous, adroit, alert, vigorous, strenuous, agile, nimble, brisk, lively, animated, sprightly, quick, prompt, ready; industrious, diligent, assiduous, sedulous; practical, operative. *See* Lively, Quick, Ready, Diligent, Able, Effect *producing*.

ACTUAL—real, true, authentic, certain, genuine, positive; incontestible, unquestionable, irrefragable, irrefutable, undoubted, indubitable. *See* Doubted, *not to be*, Certain, Genuine, Positive.

ADDITION—something added; additament; accession, increase, augment, augmentation, accretion; appendix, appendage, supplement; annexation; addenda. *See* Increase.

ADDITIONAL—supplemental, supplementary, adventitious, adscititious, supernumerary, supervenient; added, superadded, appended, appendant, annexed, affixed, attached. *See* Accidental.

ADDUCE—cite, quote. *See* Call.

ADORN—*See* Beautify.

ADVANCEMENT — progression, progress; preferment, promotion; proficiency, improvement; forwardness. *See* Improvement.

ADVERSARY—opponent, antagonist, opposer, combatant, Satan, foe, enemy.

ADVICE—counsel, information, instruction; notice, intelligence; deliberation, consultation. *See* Caution, Knowledge.

AFFECTING—moving, touching, pathetic, tender; exciting the passions or affections; impressive; pitiable. *See* Pitiable.

AFFECTION—attachment, fondness, kindness, devotion, devotedness; regard, love. *See* Kindness, Attachment.

AFFECTIONATE—loving, kind, fond, warm, tender. *See* Warm, Kind, Loving, Hearty.

AFFRONT—insult, indignity, outrage; provocation, irritation, exasperation; ill-treatment, abuse. *See* Injury, Offend, Abuse.

AFFRONTING—insulting, provoking, irritating, exasperating, aggravating; apt to affront; petulant, hasty, irritable. *See* Impertinent, Invidious.

AFRAID—timid, timorous, fearful; pusillanimous, dastardly, cowardly. *See* Fearful, Cowardice.

AFRAID, *be*—apprehend, fear, dread. *See* Fear.

AGITATION—commotion, striving; disturbance, perturbation, excitement; emotion, trepidation, tremor; discussion. *See* Fear, Stir, Trouble, Trembling.

AGREE *to*—comply, accede, consent, assent, acquiesce, approve, accord, conform. *See* Approve.

AGREE *with*—harmonize, be consistent, acquiesce, coincide, concur.

AGREEABLE—pleasant, pleasing, gratifying, delightful, delectable; acceptable, grateful, welcome; accordant. *See* Accordant, Becoming, Suitable, Amiable, Grateful.

AGREEABLE, *not*—inconsistent, incongruous, incompatible, unsuitable, discordant, incoherent.

AGREEMENT—accordance, concurrence, union, unison, harmony; contract, covenant, convention, compact, bargain, stipulation, truce, peace, treaty. *See* Acquiescence, Concord, League, Bargain, Disagreement, Arrangement, Communion.

AID—*See* Assist.

AIM—purpose, purport, intention, design, object, end, tendency, drift, scope; wish, aspiration, desire. *See* Direction, Desire, End, Object, Meaning.

AIM—strive to hit a mark; direct, point, level; aspire to, pretend to; endeavor, seek. *See* Seek, Wish *for*.

ALL—*See* Whole.

ALLAY—calm, quiet, tranquilize, soothe, compose, appease, soften, relieve, alleviate, mitigate, abate, diminish, assuage. *See* Ease, Lessen, Soft, Still.

ALLIANCE—connection, affinity, league, confederacy, treaty, compact; combination. *See* League, Company.

ALLOW—suffer, permit, tolerate; concede, admit, grant. *See* Grant, Give, Suffer, Support, Own.

ALLURE—*See* Tempt.

ALMIGHTY—all-powerful, omnipotent. *See* All, Able, Powerful.

ALONE—*See* One, Single.

ALONE—solitary, desolate, desert, forlorn, retired, remote, sole, single, lonely, only. *See* Lonely, Desolate, Solitary.

ALWAYS—incessantly, ever, perpetually, continually, constantly; unchangeably, immutably, unalterably, irrevocably. *See* Changeable.

AMENDS—compensation, reparation, restitution, requital, atonement, satisfaction. *See* Restoring, Satisfaction, Pay.

AMENDS, *make*—compensate, recompense, remunerate, reward; repair, satisfy, requite, atone. *See* Expiate, Reward, Satisfy.

AMIABLE—lovely, sweet, gentle, kind, soft, obliging; pleasing, charming, fascinating, enchanting, accomplished, attractive, prepossessing, engaging, agreeable, delightful, admirable. *See* Obliging, Charm, Agreeable.

AMUSING—diverting, entertaining, beguiling, interesting, sportive, recreating; droll, comical, comic, ludicrous, farcical, ridiculous. *See* Laughable, Odd, Sport, Beguile.

ANCESTOR—progenitor, forefather, predecessor. *See* Old.

ANCIENT—*See* Old.

ANGER—wrath, resentment, dudgeon, ire, irritation, irritability, indignation, exasperation, excitement, displeasure, disapprobation; choler, rage, passion, spleen. *See* Displeasure, Rage, Malice.

ANGER—incense, irritate, enrage, exasperate, heat, kindle, enkindle, inflame, fire, incite, stimulate, provoke, excite. *See* Displease, Burn, Stir, Heighten.

ANGRY—irritated, incensed, exasperated, vexed, excited; irrascible, ireful, wroth, choleric, passionate, hot, hasty, impetuous; inflamed, red; raging, furious, tumultuous, provoked. *See* Hot, Fretful, Cross, Passionate, Hasty, Tumultuous.

ANIMATE—enliven, quicken, invigorate, inspire, exhilarate; instigate, incite, inspirit, embolden, encourage, impel, stimulate, urge, move, actuate. *See* Cheer, Quicken, Encourage, Move, Stir.

ANNUL *laws or rules*—do away with, make void, nullify, disannul, cancel, abrogate, abolish, repeal, revoke, recall. *See* Call *back*, Overrule.

ANSWERABLE—accountable, responsible, amenable, liable. *See* Accountable, Subject.

ANSWERABLE for, *be*—guarantee, warrant, secure, be responsible or accountable, be surety or security for, pledge, vouch for. *See* Pledge, Security.

ANTICIPATE—precede, prevent, forestall,

prepossess, foretaste, prejudge, forerun. *See* Prevent, Go.

APHORISM—maxim, axiom, apophthegm, saying, adage, proverb; saw, by-word. *See* Say, Speech.

APPEAL—refer, submit; call on, invoke. *See* Refer, Call.

APPEAR, *make*—manifest, demonstrate, evince; reveal, display, discover; seem, look. *See* Discover, Look.

APPEARANCE—phenomenon, scene, semblance, show, figure, form, seeming, likeness, resemblance, air, look, manner, aspect; mien, deportment, gait; verisimilitude, probability, likelihood; plausibility, speciousness. *See* Form, Aspect, Attitude, Likeness, Show, Ghost.

APPEASED, *not to be*—implacable, inexorable, unappeasable, relentless, unrelenting. *See* Unrelenting, Deadly.

APPLY—lay on; use, employ, adhibit, put, refer; dedicate, devote, assign, allot, apportion; suit, agree; make request, solicit, have recourse, betake. *See* Refer, Dedicate, Assign, Ask.

APPOINT—ordain, order, depute, prescribe, fix, devote, allot, constitute, institute, provide, apportion, assign, parcel. *See* Ordain, Assign, Fix.

APPROACH—approximate, draw nigh, come near, draw near. *See* Draw, Near.

APPROVE—*See* Praise.

APPROBATION—approval, consent, assent, acquiescence, concurrence. *See* Praise, Acquiescence, Leave.

ARBITER—*See* Judge.

ARBITRARY—depending on will or discretion, despotic, tyrannical, imperious, peremptory, positive; absolute, unlimited, unrestrained, unrestricted, optional, discretionary. *See* Despotic, Positive.

ARGUE—*See* Think.

ARGUE—dispute, reason, debate, contend, discuss, altercate, controvert, question; prove, evince; expostulate, remonstrate. *See* Reason.

ARGUMENT—dispute, reasoning, debate, contention, discussion, altercation, disputation, controversy, contest, reason, proof, allegation, evidence; remonstrance, expostulation. *See* Proof, Reason, Dissertation.

ARM—*See* Covering.

ARRANGEMENT—symmetry, proportion, adjustment, adaptation; harmony, agreement, accordance. *See* Order, Disposition, Agreement.

ART, *without*—artless, guileless, ingenuous, candid, open, frank; unaffected, natural. *See* Open, Fair.

ART, *made by*—artificial, factitious; feigned, fictitious. *See* Forged.

ASCEND—*See* Mount.

ASHAMED—*See* Modest.

ASHAMED, *make*—abash, shame, confound, confuse, disgrace. *See* Disgrace, Shame.

ASK—request, solicit, entreat, beg, petition, require, claim, crave, demand. *See* Invite, Beg, Apply.

ASK *questions*—question, interrogate, inquire.

ASPECT—mien, air, physiognomy, appearance. *See* Appearance, Look.

ASPERSE—accuse falsely, slander, defame, calumniate, detract, vilify, scandalize. *See* Slander, Disgrace.

ASSEMBLY—*See* Company, Council.

ASSERT—vindicate, justify, maintain, aver, affirm positively, defend. *See* Declare, Clear.

ASSIGN—allot, appoint, grant, designate, fix, specify; make over, transfer, alienate; allege, show, bring forward, advance, adduce, state; devote, apportion, appropriate, set apart. *See* Appoint, Ordain, Set *apart*.

ASSIST—aid, succor, relieve, help; conduce, contribute, minister, administer. *See* Help, Minister, Support, Oblige.

ASSUME, *falsely*—arrogate; usurp; affect, pretend.

ATONE—*See* Expiate.

ATTACHMENT—adherence, adhesion; fondness, affection, love, regard, esteem, inclination, addiction; fidelity, faith. *See* Affection, Stick.

ATTACK—fall upon, assail, assault, impugn, oppose. *See* Incursion, Onset.

ATTEMPT—effort, endeavor, trial, experiment, essay; enterprise, undertaking. *See* Essay, Try, Dare.

ATTENTION—stretching to, application, study, devotion, assiduity, diligence; civility, courtesy. *See* Diligence, Civility, Politeness.

ATTITUDE—position, figure, posture; action, gesture, gesticulation. *See* Appearance, Form.

AUDACITY—boldness, hardihood, impudence, insolence, effrontery. *See* Impudence, Bold.

AUTHOR—*See* Writer.

AUTHORIZE—give authority, empower; authenticate; instruct, direct, give a right. *See* Invest, Instruct.

AVARICE—love of money, avariciousness, covetousness, cupidity. *See* Desire.

AVERSE—backward, unwilling, loth, reluctant. *See* Unwilling.

AVOID—*See* Shun.

AWAKEN—waken, rouse, arouse; incite, excite, stir up, provoke, stimulate. *See* Stir, Move.

AWARE—conscious, apprised; watchful, vigilant, guarded, cautious, attentive, wary. *See* Wary, Watchful.

AWKWARD—clumsy, unnatural, uncouth, clownish, unpolished, untoward, unhandy, inconvenient, bungling, unready; inelegant, unpolite, ungraceful. *See* Blunt, Barbarous, Polite, Countryman.

AX—*See* Weapon.

BACKWARD—*See* Averse.

BACKWARD, *go*—retrograde, retrocede, retreat, retire, recede. *See* Go.

BAD—*See* Malicious, Wicked.

BAFFLE—balk, frustrate, thwart, foil, disappoint. *See* Put *down*, Defeat.

BAND—*See* Tie.

BAND—shackle, fetter, manacle, collar, chain, bond, tie, bandage; company, society, association, coalition, league, confederacy; gang; crew. *See* Company, League, Tie.

BANE—pest, plague; poison, ruin. *See* Hurt.

BANISH—*See* Exile.

BANISHMENT—exile, transportation, deportation, expatriation, ostracism; proscription, outlawry, expulsion. *See* Exile.

BARBAROUS—uncivilized, rude, savage, vandalic, unlettered, illiterate, untutored, ignorant, barbarian; cruel, ferocious, inhuman, inhospitable. *See* Cruel, Bloody, Ignorant, Awkward.

BARE—uncovered, naked, rude, detected; destitute, poor, indigent, empty, unfurnished, deficient, scant, scanty; plain, simple, unadorned. *See* Naked, Poor.

BARGAIN—*See* Agreement, League, Condition.

BARGAIN—negotiate, treat with; agree, stipulate, contract, covenant, capitulate. *See* Agree, League.

BARREN—sterile, effete, unfruitful, unproductive, arid. *See* Idle, Poor.

BASTARD—illegitimate, natural; spurious, not genuine, false, supposititious, adulterate. *See* Spurious, Genuine, *not*.

BATTLE—fight, conflict, combat, duel, contest, contention, encounter, struggle, engagement, action, rencounter. *See* Fight, Argument, War.

BEAM—ray, gleam, glitter. *See* Shine.

BEAR, *bring forth*—*See* Breed.

BEAR—suffer, support, endure, tolerate, sustain, undergo, be patient; carry, convey, transport; bring forth, produce, beget. *See* Suffer, Passive, Support, Beget, Produce.

BEASTLY—brutal, brutish, bestial; sensual, irrational; coarse, filthy. *See* Brutal.

BEAT—*See* Bruise.

BEAT—strike, hit, thrash; break, hammer, bruise, pulverize; defeat, conquer, vanquish, subdue, overcome, overthrow, overpower, smite, afflict. *See* Palpitate, Bruise, Overcome, Defeat.

BEAUTIFUL—beauteous, pretty, handsome, elegant, fair, graceful. fine; decorated, ornamented, embellished, adorned, ornate, decked; lovely, charming, attractive. *See* Fair, Charming, Amiable, Nice.

BEAUTIFY—adorn, decorate, embellish, deck, bedeck, enamel, array, attire, dress, grace, ornament, embroider; gild, polish, refine, smooth, furbish, burnish. *See* Dress, Invest.

BECOMING—decent, befitting, suitable, fit, meet; agreeable. graceful, comely. *See* Fit, Meet, Suitable, Polite.

BEFITTING—*See* Becoming.

BEG—supplicate, beseech, implore, entreat, crave, pray, petition. *See* Ask, Wish *for*, Entreaty.

BEGET—*See* Breed, Cause.

BEGIN—commence, take rise, originate; enter on, start, resume. *See* Found, Origin, Preface, Introduce.

BEGUILE—delude, deceive, impose on;

elude; pass pleasingly, divert, amuse, entertain. *See* Deceive, Cheat, Amusing.

BEHAVIOR—conduct, demeanor, deportment, carriage, port, manners, address. *See* Manners, Aspect, Appearance.

BEHEAD—decapitate, decollate, guillotine. *See* Kill, Head.

BEHOLD—*See* Look.

BELIEF—faith, credence, credit, trust, confidence; creed. *See* Confidence, Hope, Faithfulness, Unbelief.

BEMOAN—*See* Mourn.

BEND—*See* Incline, Crooked.

BENEFIT—profit, service, use, avail; good, advantage, blessing, favor conferred. *See* Privilege, Use, Good, Interest, Gain.

BENT—flexure, flexion, curvity; bias, inclination, disposition, tendency, drift, scope, turn, direction, propensity; prepossession, influence, sway. *See* Disposition, Direction, Humor, Course, Crooked.

BEQUEATH—*See* Will.

BETOKEN—signify, portend, augur, presage, forebode, predict, foreshow, denote. *See* Denote, Bear, Foretell, Omen.

BETTER—meliorate, ameliorate, amend, emend, improve; rectify, correct, reform; advance, support. *See* Correct, Improvement.

BEWAIL—*See* Grieve.

BEWARE—*See* Aware, Wary.

BID—call, invite, ask, summon; command, order, direct; offer, propose; denounce, threaten. *See* Call, Offer, Invite, Ask.

BIG—great, large, bulky, huge; protuberant, pregnant; full, fraught; swelled, tumid, inflated; haughty, proud. *See* Great, Large, Greatness, Full, Swell, Bombastic.

BIGNESS *of body*—corpulence, corpulency, lustiness, fleshiness, grossness; fatness, obesity, coarseness; bulk, size. *See* Size, Greatness, Fatness.

BILE—*See* Anger.

BIND—*See* Tie.

BIRTH—*See* Beget.

BITTER—*See* Sour.

BLACK—*See* Dark.

BLAME—*See* Censure, Reproach.

BLAME—censure, upbraid, reproach, condemn, reprehend, chide, reprove, disapprove. *See* Reproach, Chide, Fault, Culpable.

BLAMELESS—inculpable, unblamable, irreproachable, irreprehensible, irreprovable, innocent, guiltless; unblemished, spotless, faultless, immaculate, unspotted. *See* Stain, Blemish, Culpable.

BLAZE—glare, flare, flame; irradiate, illume, illumine, illuminate, emblaze, blazon, publish. *See* Gleam, Shine, Publish.

BLEMISH—stain, spot, flaw, tint, speck, scar; imperfection, fault, defect; stigma, reproach, disgrace, taint, deformity, turpitude. *See* Stain, Fault, Blame, Disgrace, Reproach.

BLESS—*See* Happiness.

BLOCKHEAD—stupid fellow, dolt, thick skull, clodpoll, clodpate, clodhopper, numskull, dunce, dullard, bullhead, lubbard, lubber, drone, sluggard, idler, booby, losel, scoundrel. *See* Countryman, Villain.

BLOODY—sanguinary; murderous, cruel, savage, barbarous. *See* Cruel, Barbarous, Skill.

BLOT—*See* Stain, Blemish, Expunge.

BLUNT—*See* Dull.

BLUNT—obtuse, dull, not sharp, pointless, edgeless; plain, unceremonious, uncivil, rude, unpolished, unpolite, rough, inelegant, indelicate, abrupt, coarse. *See* Awkward, Dull, Polite.

BOASTER—vaunter, braggadocio, braggart, bragger, bravo, puffer, rodomont, rodomontadist, rodomontador, blusterer, bully, swaggerer. *See* Vaunting.

BOIL—seethe, bubble, effervesce. *See* Hot.

BOLD—daring, courageous, brave, intrepid, fearless, undaunted, dauntless; confident, not timorous; audacious, insolent, contumacious, impudent, rude, forward, barefaced, shameless; licentious; steep, abrupt. *See* Determined, Foolhardy, Brave, Impertinent, Courage.

BOMBASTIC—bombast, inflated, pompous, swelled, tumid, turgid, high-sounding, hyperbolical, grandiloquent, magniloquent. *See* Big, Swell.

BONDAGE—*See* Liberty, *being deprived of.*

BORDER—*See* Brink, Edge.

BORN—*See* Beget.

BOUND—limit, restrict, qualify, restrain. confine, circumscribe; end, terminate. *See* End, Qualify, Confine, Limited.

BOUND *back*—rebound, recoil; resound, reverberate, echo. *See* Cast *back*, Sound.

BOUNDS—limits, borders, boundaries, frontiers, confines, marches; extent, restrictions. *See* Limited, End, Edge.

BOUNTY—liberality, munificence, beneficence, generosity, benevolence, benignity, kindness; abundance, profusion. *See* Good, Kindness, Generous.

BRACELET—*See* Covering.

BRAVE—courageous, bold, daring, intrepid, undaunted, fearless, gallant, valorous, valiant, heroic, magnanimous. *See* Bold, Courage.

BREAK—*See* Overcome, Fail, Violation, Incursion.

BREATHE——*See* Spirit.

BREED—generate, hatch, engender, produce, occasion, cause, originate; educate, instruct; bring up, nurse, foster. *See* Cause, Fruitful, Race, Foster.

BRIEF—short, concise, laconic, succinct, summary, compendious. *See* Short.

BRIGHT—shining, lucid, splendid, brilliant, luminous, sparkling, animated; glossy, glistering; limpid, transpicuous, translucent, clear, transparent; evident, manifest; resplendent, lustrous, illustrious, glorious, irradiated, illuminated; burnished, furbished, polished. *See* Shine, Strong, Clear, Transparent.

BRING *about*—effect, bring to pass, accomplish, perform, effectuate, achieve, fulfill, attain, do, cause to be, produce. *See* Accomplish, Do, Performance, Effect.

BRINK—margin, edge, verge, border, bank; brim, rim; coast, shore, beach, side. *See* Edge.

BRISKNESS—liveliness, vivacity, quickness, sprightliness, gayety, effervescence; alacrity, cheerfulness, alertness. assiduity; readiness, promptitude, activity, agility. *See* Quickness, Lively, Cheerfulness.

BROAD—*See* Large.

BROADNESS—breadth, latitude, extent, wideness, width. *See* Wide.

BROKEN, *easily*—brittle, fragile, frail, weak, slight, frangible. *See* Weak.

BROTHEL—*See* Lewd.

BRUISE—crush or mangle with blows, contuse; pound, break, mangle, crush, beat, pulverize. *See* Beat.

BRUTAL—beastial, brutish, savage, cruel, inhuman, ferocious, unfeeling, barbarous, merciless, sensual, irrational, senseless. *See* Beastly, Cruel.

BRUTE—*See* Brutal.

BUBBLE—*See* Boil.

BUCKLER—*See* Covering.

BUD—put forth, sprout, germinate, shoot.

BUILD—*See* Found, House, Instruct.

BUILDING—structure, edifice, fabric, erection, construction, pile, shed, house. *See* House, Fabric.

BURDEN—*See* Weight.

BURDEN—load, weight, burden; freight, cargo. *See* Freight.

BURN—*See* Hot, Anger.

BURY—inter, entomb, deposit a corpse, inhume, inhumate; hide, conceal, overwhelm, cover. *See* Unbury, Hide.

BUSINESS—vocation, avocation, calling, profession, trade, art, employment, occupation, engagement, office, duty; matter, concern, affair, point, subject. *See* Office, Trade.

BUTCHER—*See* Kill, Destruction.

BUY—*See* Trade, Redeem.

CAJOLE—flatter, adulate, compliment, praise, fawn, wheedle, coax, soothe. delude, humor, induce, persuade. *See* Fawn, Flatter, Deceive.

CALL *back what one has said or written*—retract, recall, disavow, recant, revoke, reverse; abjure, forswear; reject, renounce, deny; countermand, contradict; rescind, repeal, abrogate, abolish, annul, disannul, nullify. *See* Recall, Disown, Annul.

CALL *out*—evoke; vociferate, utter, cry, exclaim, ejaculate. *See* Utter, Cry.

CALL *together*—convoke, convene; summon, cite, collect, gather, assemble, muster, congregate, amass, accumulate. *See* Gather.

CALLING *together*—convocation, congregation, assembly, gathering; parliament, congress, diet, convention, conventicle, session, presbytery, synod, sanhedrim, senate, council chamber, conference, meeting, company. *See* Council, Interview, Collection.

CALM—serene, unruffled, placid, sedate, gentle, bland, mild, quiet, cool, collected, peaceful, halcyon, composed, still, unmoved, undisturbed, tranquil. *See* Gentle, Even, Silence.

CARE—concern, anxiety, solicitude; heed, caution, circumspection, wariness, attention, regard; charge, oversight, management, direction, economy; trouble, perplexity. *See* Trouble, Caution, Look, Oversight, Thought.

CAREFUL—anxious, solicitous, cautious, wary, mindful, heedful, attentive, intent, observant, circumspect, provident, prudent, watchful, vigilant, diligent, assiduous, sedulous, elaborate. *See* Thoughtful, Wary.

CARELESS—heedless, thoughtless, negligent, unthinking, inattentive, regardless, unmindful, neglectful, unsolicitous, improvident, remiss, listless, reckless, incautious, inconsiderate, inadvertent, unconcerned; hasty, slight, cursory, desultory, superficial, loose, immethodical; roving, wavering. *See* Indifferent, Lazy, Hasty, Loose.

CARRIAGE—chariot, coach, curricle, vehicle, car, omnibus, phaeton, drosky, sociable, gig, cart, wagon.

CASH—*See* Money.

CAST—throw, fling, hurl, drive, thrust, push, sling, jerk. *See* Send, Throw.

CAST *down*—dejected, depressed, grieved, discouraged, disheartened, humiliated. *See* Sad, Dull.

CAST *back* or *off*—reject, retort, echo, reverberate, rebound, report, reflect, rebuff; desert; forsake. abandon, renounce. *See* Bound *back*, Abandon.

CATALOGUE—list, register, muster, roll, record; scroll, schedule. *See* Chronicle, Enlist, Nomenclature.

CATCHING—seizure, caption, capture; apprehension, arrest. *See* Take, Seize.

CATHOLIC—*See* Whole, All.

CAUSE—produce, effect, bring into existence, create, occasion, engender, generate, breed, induce; motive, incitement, inducement, reason. *See* Do, Breed, Effect, Induce, Occasion, Origin.

CAUTION—care, concern, regard, carefulness, circumspection, prudence, solicitude, wariness, watchfulness, vigilance; notice, advice, warning, admonition. *See* Care, Warning.

CAVE—*See* Opening.

CAVIL—carp, censure, catch at, quarrel, object, evade; contest, dispute. *See* Censure, Object, Quarrel, Shift.

CAVIL—*See* Jest, Trick.

CEASING—cessation, truce, leaving off, discontinuance, vacation, intermission, pause. *See* Rest, Agreement.

CENSURE—*See* Blame, Cavil.

CERTAIN—sure, infallible, secure, doubtless. *See* Actual, Doubted, *not to be.*

CHAIN—*See* Band, Covering, Linking *together*.

CHANCE—luck, casualty, fortuity, fortune, accident, incident, occurrence, event, contingency, adventure, hazard. *See* Fortune, Luck, Event, Occasion, Danger.

CHANGE—alter, vary; exchange, substitute, commute; reciprocate, interchange, barter, truck, traffic. *See* Interchange, Trade, Wave.

CHANGEABLE—variable, mutable, fickle, inconstant, versatile, unsteady, irresolute, wavering, uncertain, veering. *See* Undetermined, Always, Lightness.

CHARACTER—mark, figure; reputation, repute, estimation; description, account, representation; person; sort, class, species, kind. *See* Mark, Fame, Sort.

CHARGE—*See* Office.

CHARITY—love, affection; alms; benevolence, beneficence; kindness, goodness, benignity, graciousness, tenderness. *See* Kindness, Mercy, Favor.

CHARM—*See* Amiable.

CHASTE—*See* Modest.

CHASTENESS—chastity, continence; modesty, purity, virtue. *See* Honesty.

CHASTISE—*See* Punish.

CHEAT—deception, finesse, fraud, delusion, imposture, imposition, trick, artifice, deceit, guile, cunning, craft, sleight, stratagem. *See* Hypocrisy. Trick, Cunning.

CHECK—restrain, repress, curb, control, inhibit, stop, hinder. *See* Chide, Put *down*, Keep, Hinder, Damp, Forbid.

CHEER—gladden, exhilarate, animate, enliven, vivify, revive, inspirit, quicken, comfort, encourage, invigorate; incite, excite, stimulate, rouse. *See* Gladden, Animate, Comfort, Encourage, Quicken.

CHEERFULNESS—gayety, liveliness, vivacity, merriment, mirth, sprightliness, blithesomeness, alacrity, jollity, jocundity. *See* Mirth, Pleasure, Briskness.

CHIDE—scold at, reprove, reprimand, rebuke, reprehend, upbraid, reproach. *See* Blame, Abuse, Check, Disgrace, Censure, Gibe.

CHILDREN—offspring, progeny, issue, posterity, descendants. *See* Offspring, Issue.

CHOICE—election, selection, option, preference; *of two things*, alternative. *See* Will, Means.

CHOKE—*See* Kill.

CHOOSE—*See* Wish.

CHRONICLES—annals, archives, records. *See* Chronicle.

CHRONICLE—history, register, record, memoir, narrative, travels. *See* Account, Memoir, Catalogue, Story.

CINDER—*See* Ashes.

CIVILITY—civil behavior, good-breeding, politeness, urbanity, courtesy, courteousness, complaisance, affability. *See* Politeness, Attention.

CIVILIZATION—refinement, culture, cultivation, reclamation. *See* Education, Improvement.

CLASS—rank, order, degree, grade, standing. *See* Kind, Order, Sort.

CLEAR—transparent, translucent, lucid, translucid, diaphanous, pellucid, limpid, pure, unmixed; open; serene, unclouded, luminous, unobscured; sharp, perspicacious; innocent, unspotted, irreproachable; unprepossessed, unpreoccupied, impartial; unentangled, unperplexed, unembarrassed, free; liberated, freed, acquitted. *See* Transparent, Bright, Open, Free.

CLEAR—plain, apparent, evident, undoubted, indubitable, indisputable, undeniable, manifest, visible, unobscure, obvious, open, conspicuous, distinct, perspicuous, express, explicit. *See* Explanatory, Discernable.

CLEAR—purify, clarify, cleanse, purge; liberate, extricate, disembarrass, disentangle, disengage, evolve; elucidate, illume, illumine, illuminate, illustrate; exculpate, exonerate, absolve, acquit, pardon, discharge, relieve; justify, vindicate. *See* Free, Assert, Shine, Explain, Discharge, Forgive,

CLERGYMAN—ecclesiastic, minister, pastor, presbyter, pope, cardinal, archbishop, bishop, archdean, dean, rector, vicar, curate. *See* Ecclesiastic, Minister.

CLEVER—expert, dexterous, adroit, ready, skillful, experienced; intelligent. *See* Able, Ready, Intellectual.

CLIMB—*See* Go.

CLOAK—mask, veil, blind, cover, disguise, pretext, pretense, excuse. *See* Cover, Gloss, Excuse, Pretense.

CLOSE—*See* Thick, Surround, Narrow.

CLOTHE—*See* Invest.

CLOTHES—garments, apparel, dress, clothing, attire, array, vestments, vesture, raiment, robes, garb, habits, habiliments, coverings. *See* Dress, Covering, Beautify.

COARSE—*See* Thick.

COAT—*See* Covering.

COIN—*See* Money.

COLD—*See* Insensibility.

COLLECTION—gathering, muster, assemblage, assembly, group, crowd, congregation; contribution. *See* Crowd, Company, Calling *together*.

COLOR—hue, tint, tinge, dye; false show, pretense, pretext, guise, semblance. *See* Paint, Stain, Pretense, Cloak, Show.

COMBINE—unite *or* join two or more things, link closely, join, unite, coalesce, associate, league, confederate, band. *See* Plot, League.

COME—*See* Go.

COMFORT—strengthen, invigorate, console, cheer, solace, animate, gladden, revive, encourage, support. *See* Animate, Cheer, Encourage.

COMMAND—mandate, order, injunction, precept, charge, behest; edict; bull. *See* Order, Precept, Decree.

COMMANDING—magisterial, imperative, imperious, authoritative. dictatorial, haughty; arrogant, assuming; overbearing, domineering. *See* Proud.

COMMENT—commentary, annotation, note, explanation, exposition, elucidation, notice, remark. *See* Remark, Explanation.

COMMON—ordinary, vulgar, general, public, universal, frequent, usual; not noble, not respected, not distinguished, low, mean; prostitute, lewd. *See* Public, Universal, Mean, Gross, Lewd.

COMMUNION—fellowship, intercourse, converse, association, society, interchange; agreement, concord, alliance. *See* Interchange, Agreement, Concord, Speech.

COMPANION—associate, compeer, equal, comrade, consort, partner, fellow, mate, confederate, ally, accomplice; coadjutor, colleague. *See* Acquaintance, Follower, Accomplice.

COMPANY—collection, association, corporation, society, partnership, community; alliance, confederacy, combination, union, league, coalition; congregation, assembly, assemblage, crowd, group, crew, gang, troop. *See* Collection, Party, Council, Band, Crowd.

COMPARISON—simile, similitude, similarity, likeness; proportion. *See* Likeness.

COMPASS—surround, environ, encompass, encircle, inclose, invest, besiege, beleaguer; obtain, attain to, procure, accomplish; purpose, intend, imagine, plot, contrive. *See* Invest, Surround, Contrive, Accomplish, Embrace.

COMPASSION—*See* Feeling.

COMPENDIUM—*See* Abridgment.

COMPLAIN—*See* Grieve, Mourn.

COMPLAINING, *always*—querulous, querimonious, discontented, dissatisfied, peevish, fretful, ill-humored, testy, petulant, irritable, captious. *See* Cross, Fretful, Angry.

COMPLETION—consummation, perfection, achievement, accomplishment, fulfillment, attainment. *See* Accomplishment, Performance.

COMPRESS—condense, press, squeeze, crowd. *See* Abridge, Squeeze.

CONCEAL—*See* Hide.

CONCEIT—conception, idea, thought, image; notion, imagination, opinion, fancy, freak, whim, maggot. *See* Whim, Pride, Thought, Vain, Opinion.

CONCORD—harmony, agreement, peace, union, unity; harmony, melody. *See* Agreement, Peace.

CONDITION—term, stipulation, article, proviso, provision. *See* Situation, State, Bargain.

CONFIDENCE—trust, reliance, hope, assurance, dependence. *See* Belief, Hope, Trust.

CONFINE—bound, limit, circumscribe, shut up, inclose, imprison, stint, restrain, restrict. *See* Bound, Liberty, *deprived of*.

CONFUSED—disordered, deranged, indistinct, indiscriminate; involved, intricate. *See* Intricacy, Entangle, Order, *put out of*, Promiscuous, Crowd.

CONFUSION—*See* Medley.

CONNECTED—joined, conjoined, linked, united; related, relative, relevant; contiguous, adjoining; consecutive, consequential; allied, confederate. *See* Accompanying.

CONQUER—*See* Overcome.

CONSTITUENT—component, essential, elemental, intrinsic. *See* Necessary, Intrinsic, Formal, Important.

CONSULT—advise with, seek counsel; deliberate, consider, submit to, refer to. *See* Refer.

CONTAIN—hold, comprehend, comprise, embrace, include, inclose. *See* Hold, Embrace.

CONTEMPTIBLE—deserving contempt, despicable, mean, vile, base, paltry, pitiful. *See* Mean, Disdain.

CONTINUE *in a course*—persevere, pursue, prosecute, persist.

CONTRARY—opposite, reverse, adverse, contradictory, inconsistent, repugnant, inimical. *See* Against, Opposite.

CONTRIVE—devise, plan, scheme, invent; machinate, plot, colleague, concert, manage. *See* Design, Discover, Invent, Make.

CONTUMELY—contemptuousness, insolence, contempt, contemptuous language; rudeness, obloquy, reproach. *See* Disdain, Disgrace, Slander.

CONVIVIAL—festal, festival, festive, social, sociable, jovial. *See* Merry.

COOL—refrigerate, refresh. *See* Refresh, Cold.

COPY—*See* Imitate.

CORRECT—set right; proper, right, upright, honest, just, accurate, exact, faultless, nice, precise, punctual, punctilious, strict, scrupulous. *See* Right, Particular, Honesty, Nice.

CORRESPONDENT—answerable to, conformable, agreeable, suitable, adapted. *See* Accordant.

CORRUPT—putrid, rotten, spoiled, tainted, vitiated, unsound, depraved, debased, impure, wicked, sinful; not genuine. *See* Rotten, Wicked.

CORRUPT—become putrid, putrefy, rot; vitiate, deprave, infect, defile, pollute, contaminate, taint, adulterate, debase, sophisticate; waste, spoil, consume; pervert, falsify; bribe; entice, allure. *See* Rot, Stain, Worse, *make*, Waste.

COTTAGE—cot, cabin. *See* House.

COUNCIL—assembly, parliament, congress, diet, senate, sanhedrim, cortes; session, presbytery, synod, general assembly; consistory, college. *See* Calling *together*.

COUNT—number, reckon, compute, estimate, rate, calculate; ascribe, impute, charge; esteem, account, think, judge, consider, repute, hold. *See* Reckon, Accuse, Lay, Value, Think.

COUNTRYMAN—rustic, peasant, farmer, husbandman, agriculturist, cultivator, laborer, villager, cottager, cotter; swain, hind, clown, plowman, churl, boor, bumpkin, lout. *See* Blockhead, Coxcomb, Awkward.

COURAGE—bravery, intrepidity, resolution, fortitude, heroism, boldness, fearlessness, valor, firmness, daring, courageousness, spirit, gallantry. *See* Bold, Brave.

COURSE—running, flowing, passing, race, career, passage, voyage, road, route; series; succession, order, turn, class, train, chain, concatenation, string, link, consecution; system; manner, way, mode, method, line, deportment; bent, propensity, will. *See* Order, Proceeding, Stream, Way, Bent.

COVENANT—*See* Bargain, Alliance.

COVER—*See* Cloak, Hide.

COVERED *with*—Y. *See* Full.

COVERING—cover, covercle, coverlet, lid; shelter, defense, protection, covert; pavilion; veil, coat, tunic, capuchin; clothing, raiment, dress, garment, harness, armor, tackle, tackling, coat of mail, panoply, cap-a-pie, casque, helmet, morion, head-piece, visor, mask, habergeon, cuirass, breastplate, bracelet, gauntlet, buckler, target, shield, greaves, shoe. *See* Clothes, Dress.

COVET—*See* Desire, Wish.

COWARDICE—timidity, pusillanimity, cowardliness, dastardliness, dastardness, timorousness, poltroonery; fear, apprehension, dread. *See* Fear, Afraid.

COXCOMB—vain showy fellow, fop, gay trifling man, macaroni, fribble, finical fellow. *See* Blockhead, Fool.

CRANE—*See* Bird.

CREDIT—*See* Trust.

CRIME—*See* Blame, Sin, Wicked, Debt.

CROOKED—bent, curved, curving, incurvated, bowed, aquiline, hooked; oblique, winding, awry, asquint; devious, froward, perverse; disfigured, deformed. *See* Bent, Winding, Obstinate, Disfigure, Twist.

CROSS—oblique, falling athwart, transverse; adverse, opposite, obstructing; perverse, intractable; contrary, contradictory; perplexing; peevish, fretful, cynical, ill-humored, sour, morose, surly, snappish, crusty; vexatious, froward, untoward, petulant, captious, irritable, angry, splenetic, testy, crabbed, ill-tempered; interchanged. *See* Fretful, Angry, Ill-tempered, Pain.

CROSS—pass over; thwart, obstruct, hinder, stop, embarrass, perplex, oppose, retard, impede, counteract, contravene; clash with, interfere with, be inconsistent with. *See* Hinder, Puzzle, Entangle.

CROWD—collection, multitude, concourse, assemblage, assembly, congregation, throng, group, cluster, swarm. *See* Collection, Company.

CRUEL—inhuman, merciless, unmerciful, pitiless, unrelenting, relentless, ruthless, savage, fierce, ferocious, barbarous, hard-hearted, brutal, inexorable. *See* Brutal, Barbarous, Hard-hearted, Hardened, Unrelenting.

CRUMBLE—*See* Break.

CRY—*See* Call *out*, Noise, Loud, Jingle.

CULPABLE—deserving blame, blameable, censurable, reprehensible, reprovable, reproachable, faulty; sinful, criminal, immoral. *See* Blame, Fault.

CULTIVATE—*See* Countryman.

CUNNING—(knowledge, skill, dexterity, *obs.*); art, artifice, artfulness, craft, craftiness, cunningness, subtility, duplicity, deceit, deceitfulness, fraud, fallacy, cheat, fraudulency, treachery, trickery, stratagem; *in law*, trick, device, collusion, shift, covin. *See* Cheat, Falsehood, Trick, Story.

CUNNING—(knowing, skillful, experienced, well-instructed, dexterous, curious, ingenious, *obs.*); artful, crafty, sly, shrewd, astute, penetrating, designing, wily, arch, subtile, subtle, deceitful, trickish. *See* Sly, Deceitful.

CURB—*See* Check.

CUSTODY—keeping, guarding, guard, care, watch, inspection; imprisonment, confinement, incarceration, restraint; defense, preservation, security. *See* Liberty, *being deprived of.*

CUSTOM—common use, usage, habit, fashion; practice, way, manner, prescription. *See* Use, Way, Tax.

CUT *off*—rescind, abscind, sever, prune, lop; separate, remove, take away, amputate; destroy, extirpate; interrupt, intercept; end, finish; prevent, preclude, shut out. *See* Separate, Part, Maim.

DAGGER—*See* Weapon.

DAINTY—nice, delicious, savory, palatable, squeamish, fastidious, delicate, rare, luxurious; scrupulous; elegant, tender, soft, pure, neat. *See* Nice, Soft.

DAMP—moisten, make humid, humectate, wet, water; chill, cool, deaden, depress, deject, abate; weaken, make dull; check, restrain, make languid, discourage, dishearten, dispirit. *See* Humor, Check, Lower.

DANGER—peril, hazard, risk, jeopardy, venture. *See* Chance.

DARE—have courage, be bold, venture, presume; challenge, provoke, defy, brave, set at defiance. *See* Attempt, Brave.

DARK—*See* Gloom, Dull.

DARKNESS—absence of light, obscurity, opaqueness, opacity, nebulosity, cloudiness, tenebrosity, dimness, dusk, duskishness, eclipse, gloom, gloominess, shade, mistiness, dismalness, mysteriousness, inexplicableness; ignorance; secrecy, privacy; hell; calamities, perplexities, trouble, distress. *See* Gloom, Trouble, Dull.

DART—*See* Cast, Throw.

DASH—*See* Strike.

DAUB—*See* Blot, Stain.

DAY—*See* Time.

DEACON—*See* Clergyman.

DEAD—lifeless, deceased, defunct, inanimate; deep, sound; still, motionless, empty, vacant; unemployed, useless, unprofitable; dull, inactive; gloomy; frigid, cold, unanimated, unaffecting, *used of prayers;* tasteless, vapid, spiritless, *used of liquors.* *See* Lifeless, Inanimate, Dull, Flat.

DEADLY—mortal, fatal, lethal, life-destroying, deleterious, destructive, poisonous; implacable, inexorable, malignant. *See* Mortal, Unrelenting.

DEAL—*See* Trade.

DEATH—*See* Perish.

DEBT—obligation, due, liability, claim, right; *in Scripture*, sin, trespass, transgression, guilt, crime. *See* Obligation, Right, Sin.

DECEITFUL—deceiving, misleading, insnaring, beguiling, cheating, punic, fallacious, delusive, illusive, illusory, fraudulent, trickish, elusive, counterfeit; simulating, feigning, pretending. *See* Cunning, Sly, Corrupt, Spurious.

DECEIVE—mislead, cause to err, impose on, delude, cozen, beguile, cajole, cheat; frustrate, disappoint. *See* Cajole, Abuse, Cheat.

DECIDER *of disputes*—umpire, arbiter, arbitrator.

DECK—*See* Beautify.

DECLARE—*See* Tell.

DECLARE—make known, tell explicitly, exhibit, manifest; proclaim, publish, promulgate, announce; assert, aver, affirm; asseverate, protest. *See* Profess, Discover, Publish, Show.

DECLINE—*See* Waste, Droop.

DECREE—edict, law, order, command, mandate, ordinance, proclamation, rule, prohibition; decision, judgment, sentence, adjudication; purpose, determination. *See* Command, Order, Judgment, Rule.

DEDICATE—*See* Set *apart*, Apply.

DEED—*See* Performance.

DEFAME—*See* Slander.

DEFEAT—frustrate, disappoint, foil, balk, thwart, baffle, render null and void; disconcert, derange, unsettle; overcome. *See* Beat, Baffle, Overcome.

DEFECTIVE—wanting, deficient, imperfect; faulty, bad, blamable. *See* Culpable, Bad.

DEFEND—*See* Protect.

DEFENSE—excuse, apology, plea, justification, vindication. *See* Covering, Excuse, Pretense, Fence.

DEFINITE—limited, bounded, determinate; positive, certain, fixed, precise, exact; defining, limiting. *See* Limited, Settled.

DELAY—put off, prolong, defer, postpone, protract, prorogue, procrastinate; lengthen, continue; retard, stop, hinder, detain, restrain. *See* Prorogue, Hinder, Keep, Pause, Stay, Loiter.

DELIVER—*See* Give *up*.

DELUGE—*See* Water.

DENOTE—mark, signify, express, show, indicate, imply, *See* Betoken, Mean, Mark.

DENSE—thick, close, compact, heavy. *See* Thick, Close, Tight.

DENY—*See* Call *back*.

[illegible]—corruption, depravation, wickedness, vice, profligacy, crime, sin. *See* Iniquity, Crime, Debt.

DESCRIBE—depict, delineate, represent, mark, explain, define, recount. *See* Explain, Relate, Write.

DESERT—*See* Alone, Desolate.

DESIGN—plan, representation, sketch; contrivance, project, plan, scheme; purpose, purport, intention, aim. *See* Intention, Aim, Plan.

DESIGN—delineate, sketch, form an outline; purpose, intend, mean; project, scheme, plan, machinate, plot, colleague, contrive. *See* Mean, Invent, Plot, Plan, Contrive.

DESIRE—*See* Wish, Hope, Avarice, Lust.

DESOLATE—devastated, laid waste, neglected, destroyed; solitary, desert, void, barren; waste, dreary, drear, uninhabited, sad, melancholy, gloomy, destitute, lonely, lone; deserted of God, afflicted, deprived of comfort. *See* Abandoned, Alone, Lonely.

DESPAIR—hopelessness, hopeless state, desperation, despairing; despondency. *See* Lowness, Hopeless.

DESPISE—*See* Disdain, Contumely.

DESPISE—disdain, contemn, scorn, slight, disregard, neglect. *See* Disdain, Neglect.

DESPOT—*See* King.

DESPOTIC—arbitrary, absolute, self-willed, supreme, independent, uncontrolled, unlimited, unrestricted; tyrannical. *See* Arbitrary.

DESTINY—state appointed *or* predetermined, ultimate fate; fate, necessity, lot, doom, appointment. *See* Necessity, Ordain, Fix.

DESTROY—*See* Build, Waste.

DESTRUCTION, *great*—slaughter, carnage, butchery, massacre, havoc, murder, trucidation. *See* Waste, Kill, Slaughter, Hurt.

DETERMINE—ended, concluded, decided, limited, fixed, settled, resolved, directed, resolute, bold, firm, steady, peremptory, decisive. *See* Bold, Firm, Ordain, Undetermined.

DEVIL—*See* Enemy, Adversary.

DEVOTE—*See* Set *apart*.

DEVOUR—*See* Swallow.

DICTION—phraseology, wording, style, expression, manner of expression. *See* Language, Speech.

DICTIONARY—lexicon, vocabulary, nomenclature, glossary. *See* Nomenclature.

DIE—*See* Death.

DIFFERENCE—distinction, discrimination, disagreement, dissimilarity, variation, variety, diversity, dissimilitude, disparity, inequality, contrariety; dispute, variance, debate, contention, quarrel, controversy, dissension, discord. *See* Disagreement, Quarrel.

DIFFERENT—*See* Unlike.

DIFFICULT—not easy, hard to do, laborious, elaborate, arduous; unaccommodating, rigid, austere. *See* Severe.

DIFFICULTY (*opposed to easiness or facility*)—hardship, labor, toil; perplexity, embarrassment, trouble; impediment, obstacle, obstruction, opposition, hinderance, let. *See* Hinderance, Obstacle, Trouble, Ease.

DILIGENCE—*See* Attention.

DILIGENT—assiduous, sedulous, attentive, industrious, careful, laborious, persevering, constant, active. *See* Active.

DIRECTION—aim; course, line; order, conduct, management, disposal, administration, guidance, superintendence, supervision; address, superscription. *See* Bent, Aim, Lead, Show.

DISAGREEMENT—difference, division, dissension, discord, variance, strife, quarrel; unsuitableness. *See* Agreement, Difference, Quarrel.

DISCERNIBLE—perceptible, visible, discriminable, distinguishable, discoverable, ascertainable; manifest, obvious, apparent, evident. *See* Clear, See.

DISCHARGE—*See* Do, Pay, Receipt, Clear.

DISCIPLE—adherent, follower, partisan; learner, scholar. *See* Follower, Scholar.

DISCIPLINE—training, education, instruction, cultivation and improvement; correctness, order, control, restraint, government, rule, subjection; correction, chastisement, punishment. *See* Education, Order, Improvement, Punish.

DISCOURSE—*See* Speech, Dissertation.

DISCOVER—*See* Find *out*, Appear, *make*.

DISCOVER—find out, invent, contrive, design, devise; ascertain, detect; uncover, lay open, disclose, show, make visible, reveal, make known, divulge, manifest, declare, expose; espy. *See* Contrive, Invent, Declare, Publish, Show.

DISDAIN—contempt, contemptuousness, scorn; haughtiness, hauteur, arrogance; indignation. *See* Contumely, Despise, Contemptible.

DISEASE—*See* Illness, Sick.

DISFIGURE—deform, deface, change to a worse form, mar, impair, injure the form of. *See* Injure, Crooked, Form, Order, *put out of*.

DISGRACE—disfavor, disesteem, discredit, dishonor, disrepute, disreputation, scandal, reproach, ignominy, shame, infamy; odium, obloquy, opprobrium. *See* Ashamed, Slander, Contumely, Lower, Shameful, Stain, Blemish.

DISGUST—disrelish, distaste, disinclination, dislike; aversion, repugnance, antipathy, odium, offensiveness, hatred; loathing, nausea, nauseousness. *See* Nausea, Hatred, Displeasure, Disgrace.

DISOWN—disclaim, disavow, not to own, not to allow, deny; renounce, reject; recant, abjure, retract. *See* Call *back*.

DISPEL—drive asunder, disperse, dissipate, banish, scatter. *See* Scatter, Spread *abroad*.

DISPLEASE—dissatisfy, annoy, tease, vex, offend, anger, irritate, worry, provoke. *See* Anger, Offend, Worry.

DISPLEASURE—dissatisfaction, disapprobation, dislike, distaste, vexation, indignation, offense, chagrin, mortification. anger, annoyance. *See* Anger, Disgust, Enmity.

DISPOSITION—disposal, order, method, distribution, arrangement, adjustment; natural fitness or tendency; inclination, bent, bias, propensity, propension; temper, frame, mood, humor. *See* Order, Arrangement, Humor, Bent.

DISSERTATION—treatise, essay, disquisition, discussion, discourse. *See* Argument, Essay.

DISTINGUISH—make or ascertain difference, discriminate, separate, discern, specify; make eminent or known, signalize. *See* Perceive, Separate, Find *out*.

DISTRICT—division, circuit, portion, allotment; quarter, tract, region, territory, country. *See* Part, Country, Kingdom, Dominion.

DIVINE—*See* Clergyman.

DO—perform, effect, effectuate, bring to pass, execute, carry into effect, accomplish, achieve, practice; exert; discharge, convey; finish, transact. *See* Accomplish, Bring *about*, Make, Effect, Finish.

DO *a crime*—commit, effect, perpetrate.

DOCTOR—*See* Scholar.

DOCTRINE—whatever is taught; principle, truth, position; dogma, tenet; postulate; maxim. *See* Truth.

DOLEFUL—sorrowful, expressing grief, mournful, melancholy, sad, afflicted, rueful, woeful, pitiful, piteous, dismal, gloomy. *See* Dull, Sad, Pitiable, Melancholy.

DOMINION—sovereign or supreme authority, rule, sway, authority, control, power; reign, empire, sovereignty, government; territory, region, country, district; an order of angels. *See* Government, Kingdom, District.

DOTE—*See* Madness.

DOUBT—*See* Difficulty.

DOUBTED, *not to be*—indisputable, incontrovertible, incontestible, indubitable, unquestionable, undeniably, irrefutable, irrefragable, doubtless, questionless, evident, certain. *See* Certain, Sure, Actual.

DOZE—slumber, nap, be drowsy, sleep lightly; stupefy.

DRAW *back*—retire, recede, retreat, withdraw; *out* or *from*, extract, extort, exact; derive, deduce; abstract.

DREAD—*See* Fear, Fright, Terrify.

DREAM—*See* Sleep.

DREGS—sediment, lees, grounds, feculence, fæces, waste or worthless matter, dross, scoria, filings, rust, sweepings, refuse, scum, recrement. *See* Remains.

DRESS—apparel, attire, habit, suit, clothes, array. *See* Clothes, Covering, Formality, Beautify.

DRINK—beverage, liquor, tipple; potion, draught, dose.

DRIVE—*See* Force.

DROOP—sink or hang down, languish, pine, fail, sink, decline, fade, faint, grow weak, be dispirited. *See* Faint, Weaken.

DROSS—*See* Remains.

DRUNK—drunken, intoxicated, inebriated, [illegible], intemperate; drenched, saturated with moisture or liquor; tipsy, fuddled, tippled. *See* Intoxication, Luxury.

DRUID—*See* Priest.

DRYNESS—aridness, aridity, drought, siccity, thirst; barrenness, jejuneness, want of ornament *or* pathos; want of feeling or sensibility. *See* Insensibility.

DULL—stupid, doltish, blockish, slow of understanding; heavy, sluggish, without life, spirit *or* motion, vapid, insensate, insensible, insipid, flat, phlegmatic, sleepy, drowsy; saturnine; sad, melancholy, dismal, gloomy, dejected, dispirited, cheerless; gross, cloggy; not bright, clouded, tarnished, dim, obscure, not vivid, cloudy, overcast, not clear; blunt, obtuse. *See* Sad, Doleful, Flat, Lifeless, Dead, Lonely, Pale.

DUMB—mute, silent, not speaking, speechless, taciturn; tacit. *See* Silent.

DWELL—inhabit, reside, live, abide; remain, stay, rest, continue; *for a time*, visit, sojourn, lodge. *See* Abide, Stay.

EAGERNESS—ardent desire, animated zeal, vehement longing, avidity; ardor, ardency, zeal, heat, warmth, fervency, vehemence, impetuosity; forwardness, readiness, promptness. *See* Greediness, Zeal, Heat, Warmth, Quickness.

EASE—facility, easiness, lightness; quiet, rest. *See* Quiet, Difficulty.

EASE *or* Calm—free from pain, etc., relieve, mitigate, alleviate, assuage, allay; calm, appease, pacify, soothe, compose, tranquilize, quiet, still. *See* Calm, Quiet, Allay.

EAT—*See* Swallow.

ECCENTRIC—deviating, anomalous, irregular; departing, wandering, roaming, roving. *See* Odd, Wander.

ECCLESIASTIC—theologian, divine, priest, clergyman, prelate, etc. *See* Clergyman, Divine.

EDGE—margin, brink, border, brim, verge, rim, extremity; sharpness, acrimony, keenness, intenseness. *See* Bounds, Brink, Sharpness.

EDIFY—*See* Build.

EDUCATION—the bringing up, instruction training; formation, tuition, nurture breeding, information. *See* Instruct, Improvement, Discipline.

EFFECT—what is produced, consequence, result, event, issue; purpose, intent; utility, profit, advantage; reality, fact; force, validity; *effects*, goods, movables, personal estate. *See* Issue, Goods, Make, Bring *about*, Operation.

EFFECT, *producing*—effective, efficient, effectual, efficacious, operative, active, causing to be, productive; able, powerful. *See* Make, Active, Able, Powerful.

EFFIGY—image, likeness, picture, resemblance, representation, similitude, portrait, figure, make. *See* Form, Likeness.

ELDER—*See* Old.

ELEMENT—*See* Constituent.

EMBLEM—inlay, mosaic work; type, symbol, figure, allusive picture, painted enigma, typical designation, representation, allusion. *See* Figure, Mark.

EMBRACE—take, clasp *or* inclose in the arms, press, hug, gripe; seize eagerly, lay hold on, receive *or* take willingly; comprehend, include *or* take in; comprise, inclose, compass, encompass, contain, encircle; salute, etc. *See* Take, Kiss, Contain, Compass.

EMPTY *space*—vacuum, vacuity, void, chasm. *See* Void.

EMULOUS—*See* Jealousy.

ENCOURAGE—give courage to, sanction, countenance, abet, foster, support, cherish; embolden, animate, inspire, incite, instigate, inspirit, urge, impel. *See* Animate, Cheer, Foster, Strengthen. Protect, Support.

END—*See* Finish.

END—extreme, point, extremity, limit, termination, close, conclusion, ultimate state; finish, consequence, issue, result; ultimate point, object intended, scope, aim, drift. *See* Aim, Bound, Intention, Issue.

END, *without*—endless, eternal, everlasting, sempiternal, infinite, interminable, perpetual, continual, incessant; boundless, illimitable, unlimited. *See* Unbounded, Bounds, Immense.

ENDOW—gift, indue, invest, supply with, furnish, imbue. *See* Invest.

ENEMY—*See* Adversary, Inimical.

ENGROSS—seize in the gross, take the whole, engage wholly, absorb, monopolize, appropriate. *See* Swallow up.

ENJOYMENT—fruition, pleasure, satisfaction, gratification, agreeable sensations, delight, delectation; possession, occupancy. *See* Pleasure, Sport.

ENLIGHTEN—make light, shed light on, supply with light; lighten, illume, illumine, illuminate; give light to, give clearer views, instruct. *See* Light, Instruct.

ENLIST—enroll, enter in a list, register, record, chronicle; recruit. *See* Catalogue.

ENLIVEN—animate, cheer, exhilarate. *See* Animate, Cheer.

ENMITY—unfriendly disposition, ill-will, malevolence, animosity, hatred, malignity, hostility, rancor, malice, aversion, displeasure. *See* Displeasure, Hatred, Anger, Envy, Malice, Spite.

ENOUGH—sufficiency; abundance, plenty; competence, competency, adequacy. *See* Abounding.

ENTANGLE—twist, entwine, implicate, infold, inwrap, involve, perplex, embarrass, distract, complicate, intricate, puzzle, bewilder; insnare, catch, trepan, entrap, illaqueate. *See* Twist, Cross, Grieve, Puzzle, Intricacy, Confused.

ENTHUSIAST—person of ardent zeal, zealot, fanatic, visionary; bigot. *See* Warm.

ENTIRE—*See* Whole.

ENTRAILS—*See* Bowels.

ENTREAT—beseech, supplicate, importune, exhort, implore. *See* Beg, Ask, Pray, Encourage.

ENTREATY—urgent prayer, earnest petition, prayer, supplication, petition, request, solicitation, suit, exhortation, persuasion. *See* Petition, Beg, Pray.

ENVY—malevolence, ill-will, malice, malignity, pique, grudge; suspicion, jealousy, public odium, ill-repute, invidiousness; rivalry, emulation, competition. *See* Enmity, Malice, Spite.

EQUAL—same, even, uniform, not variable, equable; just, equitable, right; adequate, proportionate, commensurate, equivalent, competent, meet. *See* Able, Suitable, Fair, Like, Even, Inadequate.

ERECT—*See* Right.

ESPOUSED—engaged in marriage, betrothed, affianced, contracted, married, wedded; embraced. *See* Marriage.

ESPY—see, discern, detect, discover, perceive, descry. *See* Perceive, Look.

ESSAY—tract, treatise; essay, trial, etc. *See* Dissertation, Attempt, Try.

ESTEEM—*See* Value, Reckon.

ETERNAL—*See* Lasting.

EVEN—level, smooth, not rough, flat, plain; uniform, equal, calm, equable. *See* Equal, Calm.

EVENT—*See* Chance.

EVERY—*See* All, Whole.

EVIDENCE—proof, testimony, attestation; voucher, certificate, deposition. *See* Prove, Proof.

EVIL—*See* Ill, Bad, Wicked.

EXAMPLE—pattern, model, paradigm, copy, precedent, former instance, exemplar, original, archetype, instance, exemplary person; sample, specimen. *See* Copy, Likeness.

EXCESS—more than enough, superfluousness; superfluity, redundancy; exuberance, superabundance. *See* Extravagance, Much, *too*.

EXCURSION—rambling; expedition, journey, trip, tour, jaunt, ramble. *See* Ramble.

EXCUSE—apology, plea, defense, pretense, pretext. *See* Defense, Cloak, Covering.

EXHORT—*See* Encourage, Entreat.

EXILE—banish, expatriate, expel, proscribe. *See* Banishment.

EXPENSE—money expended, cost, charge, price; dearness, costliness, expensiveness. *See* Lavish.

EXPENSIVE—costly, sumptuous, valuable, dear; given to expense, extravagant, lavish, prodigal, profuse; liberal, generous, *See* Spend, Lavish, Waste.

EXPERIENCE—*See* Trial,

EXPERT—dexterous, skillful, ready. *See* Ready.

EXPIATE—atone for, satisfy, propitiate; compensate, requite. *See* Amends, *make*, Satisfy.

EXPLAIN—make plain, expound, illustrate, explicate, unfold, elucidate, illuminate, interpret, describe, define, solve. *See* Describe, Clear, Relate, Unfold.

EXPLANATION—exposition, illustration, interpretation, explication, definition, description, elucidation, solution. *See* Comment.

EXPLANATORY—serving to explain, exegetical, expository, descriptive, illustrative, elucidatory; explicit, express; circumstantial, minute. *See* Clear.

EXPUNGE—efface, blot out, obliterate, erase, rase, cancel.

EXTRAVAGANT—wandering beyond limits, prodigality, profusion, profuseness, excess; irregularity, wildness, preposterousness, monstrosity. *See* Excess, Waste, Lavish.

EXTREMITY—*See* End.

FABLE—*See* Story.

FABRIC—frame, structure, building, edifice; texture, contexture, web, workmanship. *See* Building, House.

FACTION—junto, clique, cabal, party, coterie; tumult, discord, dissension. *See* Quarreling, Party, Plot.

FADE—*See* Droop.

FAIL—*See* Weakness, Fault, Miscarriage.

FAILURE—failing, deficience, cessation of supply, total defect; omission, nonperformance; decay, defect; bankruptcy, breaking in estate, breaking, insolvency.

FAINT—weak, feeble, languid, exhausted, low; not bright; not loud, low; imperfect, not striking; cowardly, timorous; not vigorous, not active; dejected, depressed, dispirited. *See* Weak, Droop, Low.

FAIR—clear, beautiful, handsome; clear, not cloudy; open, frank, honest; equal, just, equitable, right, reasonable, upright; honorable, mild; civil, pleasing, not harsh, *See* Beautiful, Clear, Art, *without*, Equal, Open, Reasonable.

FAITH—*See* Trust.

FAITHFULNESS—fidelity, fealty, loyalty, trustiness, honesty, firm adherence, strict performance; truth, veracity. *See* Belief, Truth, Honesty.

FAITHLESS—unbelieving, not believing; perfidious, treacherous, punic, disloyal, unfaithful, neglectful; false. *See* Deceitful, Unfaithfulness.

FALL—*See* Tumble.

FALSE—*See* Deceive, Genuine, *not*.

FALSEHOOD—untruth, fabrication, fiction, falsify, lie, fib; mendacity; deceit, fraud, fallacy, duplicity, double-dealing, falseness, counterfeit, imposture. *See* Cheat, Cunning, Invent, Lie, Story.

FAME—public report or rumor, celebrity, renown; reputation, credit, esteem, honor; rumor, report. *See* Character, Respect, Hearsay, Name.

FAMILY—*See* House.

FAMILIAR—acquainted with, conversant, versed in; affable, free, sociable. *See* Free.

FAMILIARITY—intimate acquaintance, intimacy, affability, sociability, courtesy, freedom. *See* Freedom, Acquaintance, Intimacy.

FAMOUS—renowned, celebrated, much-talked of and praised, illustrious, distinguished, eminent; conspicuous; excellent, transcendent. *See* Noted.

FANCIFUL—full of fancies or wild images, fantastical, whimsical, ideal, visionary, chimerical, capricious, humorsome, freakish; imaginative. *See* Odd, Imaginary.

FANCY—*See* Think.

FARCE—*See* Sport.

FASTEN—make fast, lock, bolt, bar, secure, fix; join to, affix, attach, append, annex, conjoin, adjoin, subjoin; adhere, cohere, stick. *See* Fix, Join.

FATE—*See* Destiny.

FATNESS—obesity, obeseness, fleshiness, corpulency, grossness, coarseness; unctuousness, sliminess, richness, fertility, fruitfulness. *See* Bigness, Lusty.

FAULT—*See* Blame.

FAULT—erring, failing, error, mistake, blunder, defect, blemish, imperfection, slight offense, foible, weakness, frailty. *See* Mistake, Blemish, Weakness, Culpable.

FAVOR—kind regard, kindness, countenance, friendly disposition, grace, kind act *or* office, beneficence, benevolence, good-will, lenity; leave, pardon; advantage, convenience; support, defense, vindication. *See* Kindness, Charity, Support.

FAWN—coax, wheedle, cajole, soothe, humor, flatter meanly, blandish, court servilely, cringe and bow to gain favor. *See* Flatter, Cajole.

FEAR—apprehension, alarm, dread, terror, fright, panic, consternation; anxiety, solicitude; slavish dread; filial fear, reverential fear, awe, reverence, veneration; law and word of God. *See* Cowardice, Afraid, Dread, Fright, Terrify, Trembling, Jealousy.

FEARFUL—full of fear, apprehensive, afraid, timid, timorous, wanting courage; impressing fear, frightful, dreadful, tremendous, terrible, terrific, formidable, horrible, horrid, horrific. *See* Afraid, Formidable, Ghastly.

FEAST—banquet, regale, sumptuous entertainment, rich repast, delicious meal, carousal, treat; festival, holiday. *See* Luxury.

FEEBLE—*See* Weak.

FEED—*See* Nourish.

FEELING—sensation, sense; sensibility, susceptibility; excitement, emotion; pathos, tenderness, concern. *See* Sense, Kindness.

FEELING, *want of*—apathy, etc. *See* Insensibility.

FEIGN—*See* Forged.

FELLOW-HELPER—coadjutor, assistant; colleague, partner. *See* Share.

FENCE—wall, hedge, ditch, bank, etc.; guard, security, defense; fencing. *See* Ditch, Defense, Guard

FEVER—*See* Hot.

FIERCE—*See* Cruel.

FIGURE—*See* Form.

FIGURE *of speech*—trope, metaphor, allegory, metonymy, synecdoche, irony, etc. *See* Speech, Emblem.

FIND *out*—discover, invent, detect, ascertain; unriddle, solve; descry, discern, discriminate, distingush. *See* Discover, Invent, Distinguish.

FINE—mulct, amerce, confiscate; pecuniary punishment, mulct, amercement, penalty, forfeit, forfeiture, confiscation. *See* Punish, Pay.

FINISH—complete, perfect, accomplish, conclude, end, terminate, close. *See* Do, Perfect.

FIRM—fixed, compact, hard, solid, sclerotic, stable, steady; constant, unshaken, resolute; strong, robust, sturdy. *See* Determined, Solid, Strong.

FIT—suitable, convenient, meet, becoming, expedient, proper, apt; qualified. *See* Able, Becoming, Suitable, Meet, Necessary.

FIT—adapt, suit, accommodate, furnish, adjust, proportion; qualify, prepare, fit out, furnish, equip, accouter. *See* Qualify.

FIX—make stable, set immovably, destine, establish, settle, confirm, ingraft, implant; resolve, determine, limit; appoint, institute; make fast, fasten, secure, attach; place steadily, direct. *See* Settle, Appoint, Assign, Ordain, Fasten.

FLAT—smooth; level, horizontal; prostrate, fallen; tasteless, stale, vapid, insipid, dead; inanimate, lifeless, inert; dull, unanimated, frigid; dejected, spiritless, depressed; unpleasing; peremptory, absolute, positive, downright; not sharp or shrill, not acute; low, dull. *See* Dull, Inanimate, Lifeless, Taste, Positive, Low.

FLATTER—adulate, fawn, blandish, compliment, soothe, please, gratify, gloze, wheedle, coax. *See* Fawn, Cajole.

FLAY—skin, excoriate, strip off the skin, gall, rub or wear off the skin, abrade.

FLEET—*See* Ship.

FLIRT—pert hussy, jilt, coquette.

FLOOD—*See* Water.

FLOURISH—grow luxuriantly, thrive, prosper, succeed. *See* Prosper.

FLOW—*See* Issue, Overflow.

FLUTTER—move or flap the wings rapidly, hover; palpitate, vibrate, undulate, pant. *See* Palpitate.

FOLD—*See* Entangle.

FOLLOWER—adherent, partisan, dependent, vassal, retainer, imitator; disciple, scholar, learner; pursuer; successor; attendant, companion, associate. *See* Disciple, Companion, Scholar, Villain.

FOLLY—weakness of intellect, imbecility of mind, want of understanding; nonsense, foolery, silliness, inanity, irrationality, unreasonableness; trifling, puerility; weakness, vacuity. *See* Madness, Weakness.

FOOD—diet, regimen; meat, aliment, victuals, provision, eatables, edibles, fare, maintenance; *for beasts*, provender, fodder, litter; pasture, pasturage. *See* Livelihood.

FOOL—natural idiot, driveller, simpleton, changling, trifler. *See* Coxcomb, Mimic, Blockhead.

FOOL-HARDY—daring without judgment, rash, precipitate, hasty, foolishly bold, incautious, daring, adventurous, venturesome, venturous. *See* Bold, Hasty.

FOOLISH—void of understanding *or* sound judgment, weak in intellect; unwise, imprudent; simple, silly, irrational, vain, trifling; ridiculous, absurd, preposterous, unreasonable, despicable; wicked, sinful. *See* Weak, Vain, Insensible, Wicked, Impertinent.

FORBID—prohibit, interdict, bid not to do, proscribe, inhibit; restrain, check, oppose, hinder, obstruct; deny, gainsay, contradict. *See* Gainsay, Keep, Check, Hinder.

FORCE—compel, coerce, constrain, oblige, necessitate; enforce, urge, press, drive, impel; storm, assault; exact, extort. *See* Oblige, Make.

FORCE—strength, active power, power, vigor, might, energy; violence, compulsory power, coercion, compulsion, obligation, constraint, destiny, necessity; momentum *or* quantity of power produced by the action of one body on another; virtue, efficacy; validity, power to bind or hold; strength or power for war, armament, troops, army, navy; *physical force*, or force of material bodies; *moral force*, or power of acting on or influencing the mind; *mechanical force*, or power that belongs to bodies at rest or in motion—as pressure, tension, etc. *See* Power, Obligation, Oblige.

FOREIGN—*See* Outward, Abroad.

FORESIGHT—forethought, premeditation, forecast; prescience, foreknowledge, prognostication; provident care; previous contrivance. *See* Knowledge, Before.

FORETELL—*See* Betoken, Know.

FORGED—hammered, beaten, made; counterfeit, feigned, false, fictitious, invented, fabricated, dissembled, framed, untrue, base. *See* Falsehood, Genuine, *not*, Art, *made by*, Invent.

FORGIVE—*See* Clear, Excuse.

FORLORN—*See* Alone, Solitary.

FORM—shape, figure, mold, configuration, conformation, construction; manner, disposition; model, pattern, draught; beauty, elegance, splendor, dignity; regularity, method, order; empty show, external appearance, semblance; stated method, established practice, ritual, proscribed mode, rite, ceremony, observance, fashion. *See* Appearance, Attitude, Way, Make, Effigy, Order.

FORM—shape, mold, fashion, model, modify; scheme, plan, contrive, invent; arrange, combine; make, frame, cause to be, create, produce, compose, constitute, construct, compile, establish; enact, ordain. *See* Plan, Invent, Make, Ordain.

FORMAL—according to form, regular, methodical; precise, ceremonious, exact, stiff, express; external; constituent, essential, proper. *See* Regular, Constituent.

FORMALITY—practice *or* observance of forms, external appearance, ceremony, mode, method, system, order, rule, precision, decorum, decency, seemliness; mode of dress, habit, robe. *See* System, Order, Dress.

FORMIDABLE—exciting fear *or* apprehension, impressing dread, appalling, terrific, terrible, deterring, tremendous, horrible, frightful, shocking. *See* Fearful, Ghastly, Hideous.

FORSAKE—*See* Leave, Abandon.

FORTUNATE—lucky, successful, prosperous, happy; propitious, auspicious. *See* Lucky, Happy.

FORTUNE—chance, hazard, accident, luck; success, event; chance of life, means of living, wealth; estate, possessions; large estate, great wealth; futurity, destiny, fate, doom, lot. *See* Chance, Misfortune, Riches, Destiny.

FOSTER—feed, nourish, support, bring up; cherish, harbor, indulge, encourage. *See* Breed, Encourage, Harbor, Nourish.

FOUND—lay the basis, set, settle, place, establish, fix; institute, begin, originate; rest, ground; build, construct, rear, erect. *See* Settle, Fix, Begin, Build.

FOUNTAIN—*See* Spring.

FRAME—*See* Make.

FRAUD—*See* Cheat, Deceitful.

FREE—disengage, disentangle, rid, strip, clear; set at liberty, liberate, enfranchise, emancipate, rescue, release, relieve, manumit, loose, save, preserve, deliver, exempt. *See* Clear, Redeem, Liberty, *being deprived of.*

FREE—being at liberty, unconstrained, unrestrained, unconfined, permitted, allowed; open, candid, frank, ingenuous, unreserved; liberal, generous, bountiful, munificent, not parsimonious; gratuitous; familiar. easy; clear, exempt, guiltless, innocent. *See* Open, Clear, Generous, Ready.

FREEDOM—liberty, independence, unrestraint; exemption, privilege, immunity, franchise; frankness, boldness; familiarity; license, improper familiarity; liberation, emancipation, release, enfranchisement. *See* Privilege, Liberty, *being deprived of*, Familiarity.

FREIGHT—cargo, burden, load, lading, transportation of goods; ship's hire. *See* Burden. Ship.

FRETFUL—ill-humored, peevish, testy, easily irritated, splenetic, angry, petulent, captious. *See* Cross, Angry, Complaining, *always.*

FRIGHT—frighten, terrify, scare, alarm, daunt, dismay, intimidate; dishearten, discourage, deter. *See* Fear, Terrify, Dread.

FROLIC—wild prank, flight of levity, or gayety and mirth, game, jest, joke, gambol, fun. *See* Jest, Sport, Whim.

FRUITFUL—fertile, prolific, pregnant, fecund, generating, productive, abundant, plentiful, plenteous. *See* Abounding, Breed.

FURY—*See* Madness.

GAIN—get, win, earn, realize, obtain, acquire, procure, receive; reach, attain to, arrive at;—gain, profit, interest, advantage, emolument, lucre, benefit. *See* Prosper, Profitable, Benefit.

GAINSAY—contradict, oppose, deny, forbid, controvert, dispute. *See* Forbid, Object.

GALL—*See* Anger, Spite.

GAP—opening, breach, break; avenue, passage, way; chasm, aperture, cleft, hiatus; defect, flaw. *See* Opening, Way.

GATHER—*See* Calling *together*, Collection, Council.

GAY—merry, airy, jovial, sportive, frolicsome; fine, showy, fashionable, stylish, gallant; dissipated, profligate. *See* Merry, Showy.

GENERATE—*See* Breed.

GENEROUS—well-born, noble, honorable, magnanimous; liberal, benign, beneficent, bountiful, bounteous, munificent, free to give; strong, full of spirit; full, overflowing, abundant; *overmuch*, profuse, prodigal, extravagant. *See* Free, Abounding, Strong, Full, Bounty.

GENTEEL—polite, well-bred, easy and graceful, gentlemanly, gentleman-like, urbane, courteous, polished, refined, elegant. *See* Polite.

GENTLE—*See* Calm, Soft, Kind.

GENUINE—native, real, authentic, natural, true, pure, not spurious; unadulterated, unalloyed, unsophisticated, unpolluted, pure, unmixed, uncontaminated. *See* Actual, Intrinsic, Sincere.

GENUINE, *not*—spurious, unreal, untrue, supposititious, sophisticated, contaminated, polluted, vitiated, corrupted, adulterated, adulterine. *See* Forged, Spurious, Bastard, Vain.

GHASTLY—like a ghost, pale, dismal, death-like, cadaverous, wan, grim, frightful, hideous, appalling, horrible, shocking. *See* Fearful, Formidable, Hideous.

GHOST—specter, apparition, phantom,

vision, hobgoblin, fairy, fay, elf, demon, evil spirit, devil. *See* Appearance, Vision.

GIANT—*See* Great.

GIBE—reproach, sneer, deride, taunt, scoff, rail at, flout, fleer, jeer. *See* Reproach, Abuse, Jest, Laugh *at*.

GIFT—donation, donative, benefaction, present, gratuity; reward, bribe; power, faculty, talent, endowment; *by will*, legacy, bequest; devise. *See* Reward, Power.

GIMBLET—*See* Bore.

GIRD—*See* Surround, Tie.

GIVE—bestow, confer, impart, communicate, present, grant, allow, transmit, deliver; afford, supply, furnish; produce, show, exhibit; render, pronounce, yield, resign; *back* restore, return. *See* Grant, Allow, Give *up*, Offer.

GIVE *up*—deliver, consign, cease, leave, resign, quit, yield, surrender, relinquish, cede, concede, abandon, addict, devote; renounce, abdicate, forego; forsake, desert. *See* Leave, Abandon, Lay.

GLAD—gratified, happy, pleased, delighted, rejoiced, exhilarated; cheerful, joyous, joyful, exhilarating, exciting joy. *See* Happy, Merry, Lively.

GLADDEN—make glad, cheer, please, gratify, exhilarate, delight, rejoice. *See* Cheer, Rejoice.

GLANCE—glimpse, quick view, short transitory look, peep. *See* Look.

GLEAM—shoot of light, glimmer, beam, ray; brightness, splendor. *See* Beam, Blaze, View, Shine.

GLIDE—*See* Fall.

GLOOM—obscurity, partial *or* total darkness, thick shade, cloudiness, heaviness, dullness, melancholy, sadness, aspect of sorrow, sullenness. *See* Darkness, Dull, Lonely.

GLORY—*See* Honor.

GLOSS—make smooth and shining, varnish, cover; palliate, cover with excuse, extenuate, lessen. *See* Cloak, Lessen.

GLOW—*See* Warm, Hot.

GNAW—*See* Eat.

GO—move, pass, flow, walk, travel, journey, depart; *up*, ascend, mount, rise; *forward*, advance, proceed, forward, promote; *before*, precede, prevent, anticipate; *beyond*, transgress, exceed, surpass, excel, transcend; *back*, recede, return, retreat, withdraw, retire, retrograde, retrocede; *in* or *on*, invade, encroach, intrench. *See* Move, Ramble, Wander, Anticipate, Proceeding, Intrude.

GOAD—*See* Stir.

GODLIKE—resembling God, divine, superhuman; heavenly, celestial. *See* Heavenly.

GODLY—holy, sanctified, righteous, pious, religious, devout, sanctimonious. *See* Spiritual, Heavenly, Holy, Religion.

GOING *before*—preceding, foregoing, antecedent, previous, anterior, prior, former. *See* Introductory, Priority.

GOOD—benefit, interest, advantage, emolument, profit; welfare, prosperity; virtue, righteousness. *See* Interest, Benefit, Kindness, Bounty.

GOODS—movables, effects, chattels, furniture, personal estate; wares, merchandise, commodities, stock. *See* Stock, Merchandise, Property.

GORE—*See* Blood.

GOVERN—*See* Master.

GOVERNMENT—direction, regulation, rule, control, satrapy, jurisdiction, restraint, management, power, dominion, sovereignty; administration, constitution, ministry; empire, kingdom, state; executive power. *See* Dominion, Kingdom.

GRACE—*See* Mercy, Kindness, Becoming, Beautify.

GRAND—great, illustrious, splendid, magnificent, noble, dignified, elevated, sublime, lofty, exalted, majestic, magisterial, stately, pompous, august. *See* Majestic, Great, High, Showy.

GRANT—admit, allow, yield, concede; give, bestow, confer; permit; transfer, convey. *See* Give, Allow, Suffer.

GRATEFUL—thankful, impressed, mindful; agreeable, pleasing, acceptable, gratifying, pleasant, welcome; delicious. *See* Agreeable.

GRATITUDE—thankfulness, gratefulness; thanks, acknowledgments. *See* Pleasure.

GRAVE—low, depressed; solemn; sober, serious, sedate; plain, not gay, not showy; important, momentous, weighty. *See* Low, Sober, Severe, Important.

GREAT—*See* Grand, Large.

GREATNESS—*of size*, magnitude; bulk; corpulence; *of mind*, magnanimity; *of rank*, majesty; *of number*, majority; *of show* or *state*, magnificence, grandeur. *See* Bigness, Size, Fatness, Large.

GREAT *or* GREATER, *make*—magnify, enlarge, amplify, exaggerate, augment, aggrandize; extol, exalt, elevate. *See* Larger, *make*, Praise, Heighten.

GREEDINESS—keenness of appetite, ravenousness, gluttony, voracity, voraciousness, rapacity, rapaciousness; ardent desire, avidity, eagerness. *See* Eagerness, Rapacious, Eat.

GRIEF—sorrow, regret, lamentation, weeping, mourning, affliction, pain. *See* Pain, Repentance.

GRIEVE—mourn, bewail, bemoan, lament, complain, weep, sorrow, cry; afflict, wound, hurt, move, concern, distress, trouble, perplex, vex, disquiet; *for*, deplore, bewail, bemoan, etc.; *with another*, condole, sympathize. *See* Mourn, Complain, Hurt, Entangle.

GROSS—thick, bulky; fat, corpulent; coarse, rude, rough; indelicate, mean, vulgar, impure, unrefined, indecent, obscene, improper, inappropriate, unseemly, unbecoming, shameful; large, enormous, great; dense; unattenuated; stupid, dull; whole, entire. *See* Thick, Common, Mean, Fatness.

GROW—*See* Spring.

GUARANTEE—*See* Answerable *for*.

GUARD—*See* Security, Keep.

GUESS—*See* Think.

GUIDE—*See* Lead, Instruct.

GUILE—*See* Cheat.

HABIT—*See* Dress, Custom.

HAMMER—*See* Beat.

HANDSOME—elegant, nice, beautiful. *See* Beautiful, Nice.

HAPPEN—*See* Chance.

HAPPINESS—beatitude, felicity, bliss, blessedness; welfare, prosperity, success. *See* Prosper.

HAPPY—*See* Glad, Fortunate.

HARBOR—haven, port, bay, inlet; asylum, shelter, lodging.

HARBOR—shelter, secure, secrete, receive, lodge; entertain, cherish, foster, indulge. *See* Hide, Protect, Foster.

HARD—*See* Solid.

HARDENED—made hard, indurated, inured; obdurate, callous, impenetrable, obstinate, unfeeling, insensible, impenitent; remorseless. *See* Insensible, Cruel.

HARD-HEARTED—cruel, pitiless, merciless, unfeeling, inhuman, inexorable, unmerciful. *See* Cruel, Unrelenting.

HARM—*See* Hurt.

HARMLESS—not hurtful *or* injurious, innocuous, innoxious, inoffensive, unoffending; innocent, not guilty; unhurt, undamaged, uninjured. *See* Stain, *without*.

HASTEN—make haste, haste, expedite, speed, dispatch, hurry, press, drive *or* urge forward, push on, precipitate, accelerate. *See* Quicken.

HASTY—quick, speedy, hurried; eager, precipitate, rash, cursory, slight; irritable, irrascible, passionate. *See* Quick, Careless, Fool-hardy, Rashness, Angry, Tumultuous.

HATEFUL—exciting great dislike, aversion *or* disgust, odious, abominable, detest able, execrable; malignant, malevolent. *See* Malicious.

HATRED—great dislike *or* aversion, hate, enmity, rancor, malevolence, malice, abhorrence, detestation, aversion, repugnance, antipathy, dislike. *See* En mity, Malice, Spite, Envy.

HAUGHTY—*See* Proud, Commanding.

HEAD—*See* Behead, Master.

HEAP—*See* Collection, Crowd.

HEAR—listen, hearken, overhear, attend, heed, mark, observe, notice, regard, obey; learn, be told. *See* Mark, Notice.

HEARSAY—common talk, rumor, report, fame, gossip, mere *or* idle talk. *See* Talk, Fame.

HEARTY—from the heart, cordial, sincere, warm, zealous; sound, strong, healthy. *See* Warm, Affectionate, Zealous.

HEAT—*See* Warm, Hot, Anger.

HEAVENLY—celestial; angelic, angelical, spiritual, sublime, divine, supremely excellent, superhuman, supernatural, preternatural. *See* Godlike, Godly, Holy.

HEIGHT *of any thing*—crisis, acme; climax, summit, top, point, apex. *See* Top.

HEIGHTEN—raise higher, lift, raise, elevate, exalt; advance, improve, ameliorate, increase; aggravate, exasperate, irritate, inflame, excite. *See* Greater, *make*, Lift, Anger.

HELMET—*See* Covering.

HELP—*See* Assist.

HERETIC—schismatic, sectarian, sectary, skeptic, infidel, unbeliever, disbeliever, pagan, heathen.

HERO—*See* Brave.

HIDDEN—*See* Secret.

HIDE—keep secret, conceal, abscond, disguise, shelter, secrete, cover, screen, dissemble. *See* Hover, Protect, Bury, Cover.

HIDEOUS—frightful, terrific, ugly, horrible, horrid, dreadful, shocking, detestable. *See* Ghastly, Formidable.

HIGH—tall, elevated, alpine, lofty, exalted, raised; noble, magnanimous; aspiring, proud. *See* Proud, Grand, Majestic.

HINDER—stop, interrupt, intercept, obstruct, impede, prevent, oppose, thwart, embarrass; retard, delay. *See* Oppose, Check, Delay, Interrupt, Prevent, Stay.

HINDERANCE—let, impediment, obstacle, obstruction, retarding, delay, opposition, difficulty. *See* Difficulty, Let, Obstacle.

HINT—suggest, intimate, insinuate, refer to, allude to, glance at—*a hint*, innuendo. *See* Refer.

HIRE—*See* Pay.

HISTORY—*See* Chronicles.

HOLD—*See* Contain, Keep.

HOLINESS—sanctity, sanctitude, piety, devotion, devoutness, godliness, righteousness; sacredness. *See* Religion.

HOLY—whole, entire, perfect; pure, immaculate; sanctified, pious, devout, religious; hallowed, consecrated, sacred, divine. *See* Whole, Godly, Heavenly, Spiritual.

HONESTY—integrity, probity, rectitude, uprightness, justice, purity, sincerity, veracity, virtue; equity, fairness, candor, truth, honor. *See* Justice, Chasteness, Truth, Uprightness, Faithfulness, Correct.

HONOR—*See* Praise.

HONOR—revere, respect, reverence, venerate, dignify, exalt, glorify, render glorious. *See* Respect.

HOPE—expectation, wish, desire, anticipation; opinion, belief, trust, dependence, reliance, confidence. *See* Wish, Belief, Confidence.

HOPELESS—without hope, desperate, irretrievable, irremediable, irrecoverable, lost, gone, abandoned; despairing, despondent. *See* Abandoned, Wicked, Despair.

HOT—calid, fervid, fervent, ardent, burning, feverish, sultry, fiery, piping; excited, exasperated, violent, furious, impetuous, passionate, irritable; eager, vehement, zealous, animated, brisk, keen; acrid, biting, stimulating, pungent. *See* Intense, Boil, Heat, Angry, Passionate, Warm, Keen.

HOUSE—habitation, residence, dwelling, abode, cottage, villa, cot, hut, hovel, cabin, wigwam, shed; mansion, manse, messuage, tenement, edifice, building; temple, church, monastery, college, palace; manner of living, the table; family, household, ancestors, lineage, race, dynasty, stock, tribe; deliberative *or* legislative body of men. *See* Building, Abode, Race, Stock.

HUE—*See* Color.

HUMBLE—near the ground, low; lowly, modest, meek, submissive; unpresuming, unpretending, unassuming, unaspiring. *See* Low, Obedient.

HUMBLE—make low, humiliate, abase, reduce, lower, bring down, debase, degrade, disgrace, deject; crush, break, subdue; mortify; make lowly, make meek and submissive to the divine will; humble one's self, repent, make contrite. *See* Abase, Lower, Lessen.

HUMOR—moisture, fluid; turn of mind, temper, disposition, mood, frame, turn, tendency, bent, bias; freak, whim, maggot, caprice; wit, satire, burlesque, drollery, fun, pleasantry, jocularity, comicality. *See* Damp, Disposition, Bent.

HURT—*See* Injury, Grieve, Maim.

HURT—wound, bruise; detriment, damage, loss, injury, disadvantage, harm, mischief, bane, prejudice, deterioration, depravity, depravation, corruption, vitiation. *See* Bane, Destruction, Injury.

HURTFUL—injurious, mischievous, pernicious, detrimental, prejudicial, baneful, pestilential, harmful, destructive, nocent, noxious, noisome, insalubrious, unwholesome. *See* Inimical, Injure, Abusive.

HYPOCRISY—simulation, dissimulation; disguise, deceit, insincerity, false appearance. *See* Cheat.

IDLE—doing nothing, unemployed, unoccupied, inactive, leisure, vacant; useless, ineffectual, vain, frivolous, trifling; unprofitable, barren, unfruitful. *See* Lazy, Vain, Trifling, Barren.

IGNORANT—not knowing, uninstructed, uninformed, untaught, unenlightened, unlearned, illiterate, unlettered; unacquainted, unapprised. *See* Barbarous, Wise.

ILL—*See* Bad, Wicked, Sick, Malicious.

ILLNESS—indisposition, disease, malady, distemper, disorder, sickness; wickedness, iniquity. *See* Invalid, Sick.

ILL-TEMPERED—sour, morose, crabbed, peevish, petulant. *See* Cross, Fretful.

IMAGINARY—ideal, fancied, visionary, utopian, not real. *See* Fanciful.

IMITATE—ape, mimic, mock, personate, feign, counterfeit. *See* Mimic.

IMMEDIATELY—instantly, presently, directly, instanter.

IMMENSE—unlimited, unbounded, immeasurable, infinite, boundless; vast, very great, huge, very large, prodigious, monstrous. *See* End, *without*, Large.

IMMODERATE—exceeding just *or* usual bounds, excessive, inordinate, intemperate, extravagant, unreasonable, egregious, unrestrained, unbounded, unlimited. *See* Immense.

IMPERTINENT—not pertaining to the matter in hand, irrelevant; rude, impudent, intrusive, meddling, saucy, insolent; trifling, foolish. *See* Bold, Foolish, Officious, Impudence, Affronting.

IMPORT—*See* Mean, Bear.

IMPORTANCE—consequence, weight, moment, significance, significancy, avail. *See* Moment.

IMPORTANT—bearing on *or* to, weighty, momentous, of consequence, significant, consequential, material, essential, forcible, driving. *See* Grave, Constituent, Pressing.

IMPORTUNE—request with urgency, press, urge, tease. *See* Plague, Force.

IMPRESS—imprint, stamp, print, mark; fix on the mind, inculcate, instil, infuse, ingraft, implant, engrave. *See* Mark.

IMPROVEMENT—advancement, progress, advantage, melioration, amendment, reformation, reform; edification, instruction; emendation, correction; good use *or* employment, application. *See* Advancement, Better, Education, Civilization.

IMPUDENCE—shamelessness, immodesty, indelicacy, indecency; assurance, effrontery, boldness with contempt of others, audacity, hardihood, boldness, confidence, insolence, impertinence. *See* Audacity, Shameless, Impertinence.

INADEQUATE—not equal to, insufficient, incompetent, incapable, unable, inefficient, unequal, partial, incomplete, defective. *See* Equal, Able.

INANIMATE—not having life, lifeless, exanimate, dead. *See* Flat, Dull, Dead, Lifeless.

INCENSE—*See* Burn.

INCLINE—*See* Lean.

INCOMMODE—put to inconvenience, give trouble to, molest, trouble, annoy, vex, harass, disturb. *See* Trouble.

INCREASE—augmentation, addition, accession, growing larger, enlargement, extension, aggrandizement, increment; profit, interest; progeny, issue, offspring, produce. *See* Added, *something*, Larger, *make or grow*, Offspring.

INCURSION—running into; inroad, irruption, invasion, attack; expedition. *See* Attack, Battle, Run.

INDICATE—*See* Show.

INDIFFERENT—neutral, careless, heedless, regardless, unconcerned. *See* Careless, Insensible.

INDIVIDUAL—not divided *or* not to be divided, single, one, identical, particular, separate, distinct, undivided, abstract. *See* Particular, Same, Separate.

INDUCE—bring on, produce, cause; persuade, prevail on, influence, bias; incite, move, instigate, actuate, impel; infer. *See* Invite, Lead, Move, Tempt.

INFATUATION—hallucination, stupefaction. *See* Intoxication, Destiny, Mistake.

INFECTION—contamination, taint, pollution, poison, vitiation, defilement; contagion. *See* Pest, Plague.

INFERIOR—lower, secondary, subordinate, subservient. *See* Servant.

INFIDEL—unbeliever. *See* Heretic.

INFLUENCE—flowing in, into, *or* on, power, credit, favor; control, direction. *See* Power, Lead.

INGENIOUS—skillful, inventive, clever, imaginative, witty. *See* Intellectual, Sharp.

NGRATIATE—insinuate, recommend, conciliate, propitiate. *See* Hint, Favor.

NIMICAL—unfriendly, hostile, adverse; hurtful, contrary, opposite, repugnant. *See* Hurtful, Opposite.

NIQUITY—unrighteousness, injustice, nefariousness, sin, crime, wickedness, irreligion, profanity, impiety, depravity. *See* Injury, Depravity, Misdeed, Unjust.

NJURE—hurt, wound; wrong, impair, weaken, damage, make worse, deteriorate, diminish, lessen; tarnish, slander, violate; grieve; *the form*, disfigure, deform, deface. *See* Disfigure, Maim, Hurt, Abuse, Offend, Worse, *make*.

NJURY—wrong, damage, loss, hurt, harm, mischief, detriment, outrage, deterioration, injustice, evil, ill, unfairness, iniquity; insult, affront. *See* Hurt, Iniquity, Affront, Violation.

NSENSIBILITY—want of sensibility, unfeelingness, apathy, indifference, insusceptibility, torpidity, coldness, callousness, unconcern, disregard, dullness, stupidity, torpor. *See* Feeling, Dryness.

INSENSIBLE—that can not be felt *or* perceived, imperceptible, insensate, apathetic, insusceptible, torpid, stupid, dull, foolish, indifferent, unconcerned, regardless. *See* Hardened, Foolish, Dull.

INSTRUCT—teach, inform the mind, edify, educate; direct, enjoin, persuade, admonish, command, inform, advise, give notice to. *See* Guide, Show, Education, Authority, *give*, Enlighten, Build.

INSTRUMENT—tool; dupe, gudgeon.

INSURRECTION—rising against civil *or* political authority, sedition, rebellion, revolt, rising, commotion, mutiny. *See* Tumult.

INTELLECTUAL—mental, talented, gifted, clever, inventive, imaginative, ideal. *See* Ingenious, Spiritual, Mind.

INTENSE—strained, stretched; very close, raised to a high degree, violent, vehement; very severe *or* keen, extreme; ardent, fervent. *See* Hot, Zealous, Warm.

INTENTION—stretching *or* bending of the mind toward an object, close application, earnestness; design, purpose, purport, import, meaning, intent, intendment, view, aim, drift, end, object, scope. *See* Aim, End, Design, Mean, Meaning.

INTERCEDE—plead in favor of. *See* Act *between*.

INTERCHANGE—mutual change, exchange, commutation, permutation, barter, reciprocity. *See* Change, Communion, Trade.

INTEREST—concern, regard, advantage, good benefit; influence; share, portion, part, participation; premium for the use of money. *See* Relate, Benefit, Care, Good, Part.

INTERPRET—*See* Explain.

INTERRUPT—break in upon, stop, hinder, disturb; interfere; divide, separate, break continuity, rescind, disjoin, disconnect. *See* Hinder, Prevent, Act *between*, Separate, Order, *put out of*.

INTERVIEW—mutual view *or* sight, meeting, conference, communication, oral discussion, consultation, convention, parley. *See* Calling *together*, Speech.

INTIMACY—close familiarity *or* friendship, fellowship, acquaintance, familiarity. *See* Acquaintance, Familiarity.

INTOXICATION—drunkenness, inebriety, ebriety, inebriation, tipsiness; infatuation. *See* Drunk, Infatuation.

INTRICACY—perplexity, complexity, perplexedness, complication, involution, entanglement, confusion; maze, labyrinth, meander. *See* Confused.

INTRICATE—entangled, involved, intwined, complicated, perplexed, complex. *See* Confused, Entangle.

INTRIGUE—*See* Plot.

INTRINSIC—intrinsical, inward, internal, innate, true, genuine, real, essential, inherent. *See* Genuine, Constituent.

INTRODUCE—lead or bring in, usher in, present, prepare; begin, open to notice; preface, premise. *See* Begin, Preface.

INTRODUCTORY—serving to introduce, preparatory, initiatory, preliminary, prefatory, proemial, prelusive, prelusory, previous, antecedent, prefixed. *See* Going *before*, Preface.

INTRUDE—thrust one's self in, obtrude, come, go in or enter uninvited or unwelcomed; *unlawfully*, encroach, infringe, invade, intrench. *See* Go.

INVALID—weak, feeble, of no force, weight, *or* cogency, infirm, debilitated, sick, unwell, ill, indisposed; *in law*, having no force, effect, *or* efficacy, null, void:—*Invalid*, a person weak and infirm, sickly, *or* indisposed, valetudinarian. *See* Illness, Sick, Weak.

INVENT—come on by making, find out by making, devise, contrive; fabricate, forge, feign; discover. *See* Contrive, Discover, Find *out*, Lie.

INVEST—clothe, dress, array, adorn; clothe with office *or* authority, endow, endue, authorize; inclose, surround, besiege. *See* Beautify, Authority, *give*, Endow, Compass, Surround.

INVIDIOUS—looking on with an evil eye, envious, malignant, spiteful, rancorous, likely to incur ill-will *or* hatred, *or* provoke envy, offensive, provoking, irritating. *See* Malicious, Affronting.

INVITE—bid, call, ask, summon; allure, draw to, attract, tempt to come. *See* Ask, Bid, Call, Induce.

INWARD—*See* Intrinsic.

ISSUE—passing *or* flowing out, egress, outlet; sending out; event, consequence, effect, result, end, upshot; progeny, child *or* children. *See* Effect, End, Children, Offspring.

ISSUE—pass *or* flow out, emanate, spring, result, proceed, arise, emerge, flow, go out, rush out.

JEALOUSY—suspicion, fear, apprehension, caution, vigilance; rivalry, envy; indignation. *See* Fear.

JEST—gibe, jeer, sneer, scoff, mock, taunt; joke, fun, trick, game, sport, ridicule, laughter, laughing-stock, sportiveness, facetiousness, jocularity. *See* Frolic, Sport, Mirth, Gibe.

JINGLE—clink, ring, rattle, jangle, clang; crackle, decrepitate. *See* Sound.

JOCULAR—jocose, waggish, merry, given to jesting, facetious; sportive, not serious. *See* Merry, Lively.

JOIN—*See* Tie.

JOINT, *out of*—disjointed, dislocated, dismembered, disunited; unconnected, incoherent.

JOURNEY—*See* Excursion.

JOVIAL—*See* Merry.

JOY, *to profess*—congratulate, gratulate, felicitate; greet, compliment. *See* Rejoice.

JOY, *excessive*—ecstacy, rapture, transport, exultation. *See* Pleasure.

JUDGE—*See* Decider.

JUDGMENT—discernment, penetration, discrimination, sagacity, intelligence, discretion, prudence; determination, decision, sentence, award, adjudication; opinion, notion. *See* Decree, Sense, Sharpness, Thought, Understanding, Rule.

JUST—*See* Right, Reasonable.

JUSTICE—law, legality, right; equity, impartiality; retribution; honesty, integrity. *See* Honesty, Correct, Unjust, Law.

KEEN—eager, vehement; sharp, severe, piercing, penetrating; bitter, acrimonious. *See* Severe, Sharp, Eagerness.

KEEP—hold, detain, retain, possess, occupy, reserve; preserve, save; protect, defend, guard; sustain, maintain, board, support; tend, have the care of, feed, pasture; practice, do, perform, observe, fulfill, obey; *back*, reserve, retain, withhold; *in*, conceal, restrain, curb; *from*, abstain, refrain, restrain; forbear, desist; *up*, maintain, continue, hinder from ceasing. *See* Do, Occupy, Maintain, Leave, Abstain, Delay.

KILL—deprive of life, murder, assassinate, slay, massacre, put to death, slaughter, butcher, destroy. *See* Destruction, Behead, Waste.

KIN—relation by birth, consanguinity, relation by marriage, affinity; relatives, kindred; kinsman, relation, relative. *See* Relationship.

KIND—species, sort, class, genus; order, set, rank. *See* Sort, Character, Order.

KIND—mild, tender, bland, indulgent; clement, gentle, compassionate, meek, benign, benignant, generous, benevolent, good; courteous, civil, civilized, obliging, complaisant, affable; gracious, lenient, humane. *See* Affectionate, Loving, Merciful, Obliging, Soft.

KINDNESS—good-will, benevolence, beneficence, benignity, tenderness, humanity; generosity, liberality, goodness; courtesy, politeness, urbanity, civility, complaisance, affability, favor. *See* Bounty, Charity, Affection, Mercy, Favor.

KING—*See* Majestic, Prince.

KINGDOM—realm, state, territory, country; empire; nation, inhabitants *or* population; *in natural history*, division; region, tract; reign of the Messiah, heaven; government, rule, sovereignty, supreme administration. *See* Government, Dominion, Country.

KISS—touch with the lips, salute, embrace, touch gently, caress. *See* Embrace.

KNIT—*See* Tie.

KNOT—*See* Tie.

KNOW—*See* Understand, Wise.

KNOWLEDGE—learning, erudition, letters, science; wisdom, skill; acquaintance, notice; information; *of all things*, omniscience. *See* Learning, Foresight.

LABOR—*See* Work.

LAMENT—*See* Grieve.

LANGUAGE—human speech, tongue, speech; dialect, idiom; solecism; phraseology, diction, expression. *See* Speech.

LARGE—big, great, huge, of great size, spacious, wide, roomy, capacious, extensive, comprehensive, copious, ample, abundant, plentiful, diffusive, broad, extended, liberal. *See* Big, Immense, Abounding, Roomy, Great, Size.

LARGER, *make*—magnify, augment, enlarge, increase, aggrandize, extend. *See* Great, *make*, Increase.

LASTING—continuing, enduring, remaining; durable, permanent, diuturnal; inveterate. *See* Abide, Stay.

LAUGH *at*—ridicule, banter, rally, deride, mock, fleer, grin, leer, scoff, gibe, jeer. *See* Gibe, Scoff, Reproach.

LAUGHABLE—exciting laughter *or* merriment, risible, ludicrous, ridiculous, comic, comical, sportive, odd, droll, burlesque, mirthful. *See* Jocular, Amusing, Odd, Ridicule.

LAVISH—prodigal, wasteful, wanton, profuse, extravagant. *See* Waste, Spend, Extravagance, Expense.

LAW—*See* Decree, Order, Command, Justice.

LAY *hold of*—grasp, catch, snatch, seize, gripe, fasten on, clutch; *open*, open, make bare, uncover, show, expose, reveal; spread out, dilate, expand, extend; *down*, deposit, resign, give up, quit, relinquish, surrender, offer, advance; *up*, hoard, store, treasure, reposit, provide, previously; *out*, expend, plan, dispose in order, exert; *to*, charge upon, impute, set to the account of, attribute. *See* Seize, Swell, Place, Catching, Show, Spread, Give, Count, Reckon, Accuse.

LAZY—sluggish, indolent, slothful, idle, listless, inert, inactive, supine; slow. *See* Careless, Idle, Slow, Dull.

LEAD—guide, conduct, direct; *away*, abduce, draw, entice, allure, attract, decoy, seduce; induce, persuade, prevail on, influence, bias, incline. *See* Induce, Guide, Tempt, Lean.

LEAGUE—confederacy, alliance, national compact, covenant, truce, combination, coalition, union. *See* Alliance, Combine, Band.

LEAN—wanting flesh, meager, not fat, thin, attenuated, wasted, emaciated; not rich, destitute, bare, barren, jejune. *See* Bare, Thin.

LEAN—incline, propend, tend toward, bend. *See* Bend.

LEARN—*See* Scholar, Hear.

LEARNING—erudition, letters, science, literature, acquired knowledge, art. *See* Knowledge.

LEAVE—*See* Remains.

LEAVE—permission, allowance, license, liberty, consent, approval, assent; *a taking*, farewell, valediction, adieu, parting. *See* Approbation, Let.

LEAVE—withdraw, depart from, quit; forsake, desert, abandon, relinquish; bequeath, give by will; *off*, desist, withhold, discontinue, refrain, forbear, hold, cease, stop; *out*, omit, pass by, neglect. *See* Abandon, Give *up*, Ceasing, Keep, Abstain.

LESSEN—make less, diminish, reduce, decrease, abate, liquidate; palliate, extenuate; *in value* or *worth*, depreciate, undervalue, derogate, deteriorate, disparage, detract, decry, traduce, degrade, lower; *become* less, abate, decrease, diminish, shrink; subside. *See* Lower, Gloss, Humble, Slacken, Allay.

LET—*See* Hinderance.

LET—permit, suffer, allow, give leave *or* power; lease, demise; retard, hinder, impede. *See* Allow, Leave, Hinderance.

LEWD—*See* Lust, Loose.

LIBERTY, *being deprived of*—restraint, confinement, imprisonment, incarceration, captivity, bondage, thralldom, slavery, servitude, enslavement. *See* Custody, Privilege, Freedom, Confine.

LIE *or* LEAN—*See* Lean.

LIE—falsehood, untruth, mendacity, fabrication, fiction, fib, invention. *See* Falsehood.

LIFE—vitality, liveliness, sprightliness, vivacity, vivaciousness, animation, spirit. *See* Lightness *of manner*, Spirit, Warmth, Animate.

LIFELESS—deprived of life, dead, destitute of life, inanimate, exanimate; heavy, dull, inactive, vapid; torpid. *See* Dead, Dull, Inanimate, Flat.

LIFT—elevate, raise, erect, exalt, elate. *See* Heighten.

LIGHT—*See* Enlighten.

LIGHTNESS *of manner*—levity, giddiness, gayety, unsteadiness, inconstancy, changeableness, mutability, vanity, freak, flightiness, volatility, buoyancy, elasticity, animation, vivacity, vivaciousness; wantonness, lewdness, unchastity. *See* Life, Whim, Changeable, Loose.

LIKE—alike, identical, equal, similar, uniform, resembling; probable, likely. *See* Equal, Same.

LIKENESS—resemblance, similarity, form, external appearance; similitude, simile; representation, copy, counterpart; image, picture, effigy, statue, *See* Comparison, Effigy, Example, Appearance.

LIMIT—*See* Bound.

LIMITED—bounded, finite, terminable, determinate, circumscribed, restrained, confined, restricted; qualified, narrow. *See* Definite, Narrow, Bound.

LINE—*See* Mark.

LINKING *together*—connection, concatenation, succession, consecution, chain, train, series. *See* Follow, Chain.

LISTEN—*See* Hear.

LIVELIHOOD—means of living, support of life, living, subsistence, maintenance, sustenance, sustentation, support. *See* Food, Living.

LIVELY—brisk, vigorous, vivacious, animated, spirited, sprightly, sportive, blithe, merry, cheerful, mirthful, jocund, gay, airy; humorous, facetious, witty, jocular, jocose; strong, energetic. *See* Active, Gay, Merry, Jocular, Quick, Spirit.

LIVING, *ecclesiastical*—benefice, vicarage, parsonage, rectory; incumbency; preferment, endowment. *See* Livelihood.

LIVING *in the same age with another*—coeval, of the same age, of equal age, coetaneous; *at the same time*, contemporary *or* cotemporary, contemporaneous, coexistent. *See* Time.

LOAD—*See* Burden.

LOFTY—*See* High, Great.

LOITER—linger, move slowly *or* idly, lag, stay behind, delay, be dilatory, spend time idly, saunter. *See* Delay.

LONELY—solitary, retired, sequestered, secluded, ascetic, lone, lonesome, unfrequented, deserted, dull, gloomy. *See* Dull, Alone, Desolate.

LOOK—*See* Appearance.

LOOK—see, behold, view, eye, glance, peep, observe; appear, seem; face, front; *after*, attend, tend, take care of; *for*, expect, seek, search; *into*, inspect, observe, examine, consider; *on*, regard, esteem, consider, view, conceive of, think, be a mere spectator. *See* Glance, Appear, Search, Care.

LOOKER-ON—beholder, spectator, observer.

LOOSE—unbound, untied, unsewed; not tight *or* close, not dense *or* compact; not concise, lax, not precise *or* exact, vague, indeterminate, remiss; unconnected, rambling; dissolute, saturnalian, wanton, lewd, lustful, unrestrained, unchaste, licentious, lax. *See* Abandoned, Lust, Careless, Lightness.

LOP—*See* Cut *off*, Maim.

LORD—*See* Master.

LORD'S SUPPER—communion, sacrament, eucharist.

LOSS—damage, detriment. *See* Injury, Hurt.

LOT—*See* Chance, Clergy.

LOUD—having a great sound, high-sounding, altisonant, obstreperous, streperous, noisy, clamorous, vociferous, vehement, turbulent, tumultuous, blustering; emphatical, impressive. *See* Tumultuous, Noise.

LOVE—*See* Affection.

LOVE, *inclined to*—amorous, fond, doting, loving; *in love*, enamored, smitten; *relating to*, amatory, amatorial, amatorious. *See* Loving.

LOVER—one who loves, wooer, sweetheart, suitor, beau, swain; amateur.

LOVING—enamored, amorous; fond, affectionate, attached. *See* Affectionate, Kind.

LOW—not high, humble; deep; dejected, depressed; mean, abject, grovelling, base, dishonorable; feeble, weak, exhausted; moderate; plain, simple, as *diet*. *See* Humble, Grave, Weak, Flat, Faint.

LOWER—cause to descend, let down, take *or* bring down, reduce, humble, disgrace, humiliate, degrade, debase, abase, depress. *See* Humble, Abase, Lessen, Damp.

LOWLINESS—freedom from pride, humility, humbleness, self-abasement, modesty, unworthiness, penitence, submission, submissivenesss. *See* Humble.

LOWNESS *of spirits*—dejection, depression, despondency, melancholy, hypochondria, low-spiritedness; *in rank* or *state*, humiliation, degradation, debasement, abasement, reduction. *See* Despair, Disgrace.

LUCK—*See* Chance.

LUCKY—fortunate, successful, prosperous, favorable. *See* Fortunate.

LURE—*See* Tempt, Induce, Entangle.

LUST—longing desire, desire, passion, concupiscence, lusting, carnal appetite, unlawful desire, lasciviousness, salaciousness, salacity, lecherousness, lechery, lubricity, incontinence, incontinency, unchastity, evil propensity, depraved affections and desires. *See* Desire, Loose.

LUSTY—fat, corpulent, stout, robust, vigorous, healthful, able of body; bulky, large. *See* Fatness, Strong.

LUXURY—free *or* extravagant indulgence in the pleasures of the table, voluptuousness, sensuality; epicurism, sensual enjoyments; dainty, delicious food *or* drink; any thing delightful to the senses. *See* Glut, Drunk, Pleasure, Feast.

MACHINE—*See* Instrument.

MAD—*See* Foolish.

MADNESS—disorder of the intellect *or* reason, distraction, derangement, insanity, insaneness, lunacy, delirium, mania, phrenzy *or* frenzy, franticness, mental aberration; extreme folly, headstrong passion and rashness; wildness of passion, rage, fury. *See* Folly, Possession, Rage.

MAIM—deprive of the use of a limb, lame, cripple, mangle, mutilate, injure, hurt. *See* Mangle, Cut *off*, Injure, Hurt.

MAINTAIN—assert, vindicate. *See* Keep, Support.

MAJESTIC—august, stately, dignified, magnificent, grand, splendid, pompous, elevated, lofty; princely, royal, regal, kingly, noble; magisterial. *See* Grand, High, Great.

MAKE—constrain, compel; form, fashion, mold, contrive, cause to exist, produce, create, compose, constitute, construct, establish; do, perform, execute, effect, cause; raise, gain, collect; *over*, transfer, convey, assign, alienate; *out*, learn, discover, obtain, prove, evince, find *or* supply. *See* Force, Form, Contrive, Do.

MALICE—extreme enmity, rancor, malevolence, malignity, malignancy, grudge, spite, pique, ill-will. *See* Enmity, Hatred, Envy, Spite.

MALICIOUS—harboring ill-will *or* enmity, malevolent, malignant, malign, evil-minded, evil, wicked, fiendish, fiend-like, diabolical, infernal, hellish, stygian, devilish, spiteful. *See* Hateful, Invidious, Wicked.

MANGLE—lacerate, tear, rend, mutilate, maim. *See* Maim, Worry.

MANNER—*See* Appearance, System, Way.

MANNERS—morals, habits; behavior. *See* Custom, Behavior, Civility.

MANY—manifold, multiform, several, divers, sundry, various, numerous.

MARGIN—*See* Brink, Edge.

MARK—line, incision, impression, print, stamp; note, sign, symptom, indication, token; trace, vestige, footstep, footprint, track; *of disgrace*, brand, stigma, badge. *See* Character, Emblem.

MARK—draw a visible line, stamp, impress, print, imprint; note, notice, observe, remark; heed, attend, regard. *See* Impress, Hear, Denote.

MARKET—*See* Trade.

MARRIAGE—matrimony, wedlock; nuptials, wedding; *relating to*, connubial, conjugal, matrimonial, nuptial, hymeneal, hymenean. *See* Espoused, Relationship.

MARTIAL—warlike, military, soldier-like, brave, given to war; suited to battle.

MASK—*See* Cloak.

MASS—*See* Medley.

MASTER—possessor, proprietor, owner; ruler, director, governor, head, chief, principal, superior, controller, lord; teacher, tutor, instructor, preceptor, professor. *See* Chief, Scholar.

MAXIM—*See* Aphorism.

MAZE—*See* Intricacy.

MEAN—wanting dignity, low, vulgar, low minded, base, spiritless, contemptible, despicable; of little value, humble, poor; sordid, miserly, penurious, niggardly. *See* Low, Gross, Contemptible, Poor, Saving, Sneaking, Miserly, Sorry.

MEAN—have in mind *or* view, intend,

purpose, design, contemplate; signify, indicate, express, imply, import, denote. *See* Design, Denote, Betoken.

MEANING—signification, significance, import, sense, intendment, intention, tendency, aim, purpose, *See* Intention, Aim, Sense.

MEANS, *instrument of effecting any purpose*—income, revenue, resources, substance, estate; organ; *that offer*, expedient, alternative, resource, medium; moyen. *See* Choice, Medium, Way.

MECHANIC—artisan, artist, artificer, operative, workman, journeyman.

MEDITATE—*See* Think.

MEDIUM—middle, mean; mediocrity, moderateness, moderation, temperateness, temperance. *See* Way, Means, Mildness.

MEDLEY—mingled and confused mass, mixture, confusion, mass, hotchpotch, heterogeneousness, diversity, variety, miscellany.

MEET—fit, prepared, suitable, proper, qualified, convenient, adapted. *See* Fit.

MEET—come together, come face to face, confront, encounter, come in contact, join; come to, find, light on, receive; assemble, congregate, collect, concentrate, group, muster, embody. *See* Call *together*, Collection, Crowd, Find.

MELANCHOLY—*See* Sad, Doleful.

MEMOIR—personal history, life, personal narrative *or* chronicle, history, narrative, narration, chronicle, written account, register of facts, recital. *See* Chronicle, Story, History.

MERCENARY—that may be hired or sold, venal, hireling, hired, purchased, sold; greedy of gain, mean, selfish. *See* Mean.

MERCHANDISE—*See* Goods, Trade, Buy.

MERCIFUL—having *or* exercising mercy, clement, compassionate, humane, tender, lenient, benign, benignant, indulgent, not cruel, pitiful. *See* Mildness, Kind.

MERCY—*See* Grace.

MERCY—grace; benevolence, tenderness, mildness, pity *or* compassion, or clemency exercised toward offenders; clemency, lenity, leniency, humanity, benignity, compassion, pity. *See* Kindness, Pity, Mildness.

MERRY—gay and noisy, jovial, exhilarated, cheerful, mirthful, joyful, sprightly, joyous, lively, gay, vivacious, blithe, blithesome, jocund, sportive, festive, convivial, social, sociable. *See* Convivial, Lively, Glad, Gay, Jocular, Cheerfulness.

MESSAGE—verbal *or* written notice sent, errand, mission, commission, embassy, dispatch, communication, mandate, order. *See* Order, Command.

MILD—*See* Kind, Merciful.

MILDNESS—softness, gentleness, suavity, placidity, blandness, tenderness, mercy, clemency; moderateness. *See* Mercy, Kindness, Peace, Medium.

MIMIC—imitator, buffoon, zany, merry-andrew, jester, mountebank, fool. *See* Fool, Blockhead, Coxcomb, Imitate.

MIND—*See* Intellectual, Thoughtful.

MINGLE—*See* Mix.

MINISTER—chief servant, agent, officer, official, magistrate, delegate, embassador, envoy, pastor. *See* Clergyman, Servant, Assist.

MIRTH—social merriment, hilarity, noisy gayety, jollity, jolliness, jocoseness, jocularity, jocundity, jocundness, festivity, joviality, conviviality, sociality, sociability; joy, gladness, cheerfulness. *See* Cheerfulness, Joy, Pleasure, Jest, Sport.

MISCARRIAGE—failure, mishap; ill conduct, evil *or* improper behavior, misbehavior; abortion, untimely birth. *See* Misdeed, Behavior.

MISDEED—evil deed, wicked action, fault, transgression, trespass, offense, misbehavior, crime. *See* Miscarriage, Fault, Iniquity.

MISER—extremely covetous person, sordid wretch, avaricious fellow, very parsimonious creature, curmudgeon, niggard, churl. *See* Money.

MISERLY—very covetous, avaricious, sordid, niggardly, narrow, parsimonious, mean, churlish, curmudgeonly. *See* Mean, Narrow.

MISFORTUNE—ill-fortune, ill-luck, adversity, calamity, disaster, affliction, distress, mischance, evil *or* cross accident, mishap, misadventure. *See* Trouble, Fortune.

MISTAKE—error, misconception, misunderstanding; slip, hallucination, fault; accident. *See* Fault, Oversight, Deceive.

MISUSE—ill-use, use ill *or* improperly, use to a bad purpose, wrong, injure; abuse, treat ill. *See* Abuse, Injure.

MIX—*See* Medley.

MOB—*See* Crowd.

MOCK—*See* Laugh *at.*

MODEST—restrained by a sense of propriety, not forward *or* bold, not presumptuous *or* arrogant, not boastful, bashful, diffident, reserved; not loose, not lewd, chaste, pure, vestal, virtuous; moderate, not excessive *or* extreme, not extravagant. *See* Pure, Chasteness, Shameless, Loose.

MOIST—*See* Soak.

MOMENT—second, instant; importance, etc. *See* Importance, Transitory.

MONEY—coin, stamped metal, gold, silver, copper, cash; specie, bank notes *or* bills, finance, exchequer.

MORALS—*See* Manners.

MORTAL—subject to death, destined to die; deadly, fatal, causing death, bringing death; human, terrestrial, earthly, mundane; perishable, fleeting, evanescent. *See* Deadly, Transitory.

MOUNT—*See* Go.

MOURN—*See* Grieve.

MOUTH—*See* Speech.

MOVE—*See* Go, Stir.

MOVE—impel, carry, convey, draw; excite, affect, touch pathetically, agitate, rouse, incite, instigate, prompt, stir, actuate, urge, persuade, induce, prevail on. *See* Induce, Animate, Stir, Shake, Awaken, Go.

MOVE *round*—revolve, circumvolve, turn, circumgyrate, circulate; wheel, whirl, twirl, twist, reel. *See* Twist, Surround.

MUCH, *too*—excess, exuberance. *See* Excess, Luxuriance.

MURDER—*See* Kill.

MUTUAL—*See* Return *like for like.*

NAKED—not covered, bare, nude, uncovered, unclothed, undressed; unarmed, defenseless, open, exposed; plain, evident, undisguised. *See* Bare, Open.

NAME—appellation, appellative, title, denomination, designation; reputation, repute, character, credit, estimation; renown, fame, honor, celebrity, eminence, praise, distinction; remembrance, memory; authority, behalf, part; appearance only, sound only, not reality. *See* Fame, Praise.

NAME—call, give name to, denominate, entitle, characterize, style, term, designate, nominate. *See* Call.

NARROW—of little breadth, not wide *or* broad, strait, confined, limited, contracted, covetous, not liberal *or* bountiful; close, near, accurate, scrutinizing. *See* Miserly, Limited.

NATURAL—implanted by nature, inborn, innate, ingenerate, inbred; inherent; native, indigenous. *See* Born.

NAUSEA—sea-sickness, sickness, qualm, loathing, disgust, squeamishness. *See* Disgust, Sick.

NEAR—*See* Neighborhood, Narrow.

NECESSARY—that must be, that can not be otherwise, essential, indispensable, requisite, needful, fit; expedient, desirable; wanted, required; unavoidable. *See* Fit, Constituent.

NECESSITY—what must be; irresistible power, compulsive force; want, need, occasion, requirement, indispensableness; extreme indigence, pinching poverty, pressing need, distress, exigency, emergency; unavoidableness, inevitableness. *See* Destiny, Poorness, Want, Occasion, Trouble, Obligation.

NEED—*See* Necessity.

NEEDLE—*See* Sharp.

NEGLECT—omission, forbearance to do, inadvertence, oversight; negligence, inattention, carelessness, disregard, remissness, indifference, recklessness, apathy, unconcern. *See* Oversight, Apathy.

NEGLECT—omit; forbear to do *or* use; slight, contemn, disregard, not to notice. *See* Despise, Shun.

NEIGHBORHOOD—a place near, vicinity, vicinage, proximity, adjacency. *See* Near, Nigh.

NERVE—*See* Strong.

NET—*See* Snare.

NEWS—tidings, recent account, fresh information, intelligence.

NICE—soft, delicate, tender, dainty, fine, sweet, delicious; accurate, exact, precise, methodical, correct, particular, scrupulous, distinguishing. *See* Dainty, Correct, Squeamish, Luxury.

NIGH—*See* Neighborhood.

NIGHT—*See* Darkness.

NOBLE—*See* Generous, Great.

NOBILITY—noblesse, noblemen, nobles, aristocracy, oligarchy, barons, patricians, lords, peers, grandees, optimacy; dignity, grandeur. *See* Grand, Greatness, Government.

NOISE—*See* Sound, Jingle.

NOISE—sound, murmur, creak; cry, outcry, clamor, vociferation. *See* Cry, Loud.

NOMENCLATURE—list *or* catalogue of words, vocabulary, schedule, etc. *See* Dictionary, Catalogue.

NOTED—set down in writing; observed, noticed, notorious; remarkable, conspicuous, eminent, famous, celebrated, distinguished, renowned, illustrious, extraordinary. *See* Famous.

NOTICE—observe, see, regard, attend, heed, mind, remark, mention, mark, note. *See* Mark, Perceive, Hear.

NOURISH—nurture, cherish, foster, support, maintain, encourage; educate, instruct. *See* Support, Foster.

NOVICE—*See* Ignorant.

NUMB—benumbed, deprived of sensation, torpid, chill, motionless, stupefied.

NUMBER—*See* Count.

OBEDIENT—disposed to obey, submissive, obsequious, complaint, humble, tractable, docile, dutiful, respectful. *See* Humble.

OBJECT—oppose, except to, gainsay, deny, controvert, dissent. *See* Oppose, Gainsay, Cavil, Aim, Refuse.

OBLIGATION—duty; compulsion, force, coercion, necessity. *See* Debt, Necessity, Force.

OBLIGE—obligate, engage, constrain, compel, bind, do a favor to, favor, serve, assist, please, gratify. *See* Force, Please, Assist.

OBLIGING—binding, constraining, compelling; kind, complaisant, courteous, civil, affable. *See* Kind, Amiable, Officious.

OBLIQUE—*See* Crooked.

OBSTACLE—what opposes, what stands in the way, obstruction, hinderance, let, impediment. *See* Difficulty, Hinderance, Let.

OBSTINACY—fixedness in opinion *or* resolution, stubbornness, pertinacity, persistence, persistency, inflexibility, contumacy, perverseness, refractoriness, intractableness, obdurateness, obduracy.

OBSTINATE—fixed in opinion *or* resolution, stubborn, inflexible, refractory, contumacious, pertinacious, perverse, obdurate, unyielding, resolute, opiniated, headstrong, heady. *See* Crooked, Unwilling, Averse.

OCCASION—falling, happening *or* coming to, occurrence, casualty, incident; opportunity, convenience, favorable time, season *or* circumstances; incidental need, casual exigency, necessity, need. *See* Cause, Necessity, Chance.

OCCUPY—take possession; keep in possession, possess, hold *or* keep for use; take up, cover *or* fill; employ, use; maintain; invest. *See* Keep, Maintain, Possession.

ODD—not even *or* equal; singular, extraordinary, strange, eccentric, irregular, anomalous, particular, uncommon; fantastic, fantastical, whimsical, comic, comical, droll, queer, ludicrous, funny, laughable, burlesque. *See* Amusing, Fanciful, Laughable, Eccentric.

ODE—*See* Sing.

OFFEND—displease, make angry, affront, vex, insult, mortify, shock, wound; pain, annoy, injure; transgress, trespass, violate. *See* Displease, Affront, Injure.

OFFENDER—one who offends, violator, transgressor, trespasser, criminal, malefactor, felon; culprit, delinquent, defaulter. *See* Crime.

OFFER—bring in the way, bring to *or* before, present, proffer, give, bestow, exhibit, tender; sacrifice, immolate; bid, propose. *See* Give, Kill, Bid.

OFFERING—sacrifice, oblation; presentation, tender; *a burnt*, holocaust.

OFFICE—duty, charge, trust, function, place, post, situation, station, rank, business, employment, occupation, agency. *See* State, Situation.

OFFICIOUS—kind, obliging; excessively forward in kindness; active, busy meddling, intermeddling, intrusive, impertinent, importunate. *See* Obliging, Active, Impertinent.

OFFSPRING—child *or* children, descendant *or* descendants, progeny, young, issue; propagation, generation; production *See* Children, Issue, Increase.

OFTEN—oft, frequently, many times, not seldom, not rarely, repeatedly, constantly, continually.

OINTMENT—*See* Perfume.

OLD—advanced far in years *or* life, aged; decayed, not new *or* fresh; ancient, antique, olden; elderly, senile; antiquated, old-fashioned, obsolete. *See* Ancient, Ancestor.

OMEN—*See* Foretell.

ONE—*See* Alone.

ONSET—rushing *or* setting upon, violent attack, attack, charge, assault, encounter, storming. *See* Attack, Battle.

OPEN—*See* Spread.

OPEN *and free*—ingenuous, frank, fair, candid, sincere, free from reserve, disguise, equivocation *or* dissimulation, unreserved, undisguised, undissembling, artless; communicative. *See* Free, Fair, Art, *without*, Clear.

OPENING—breach, gap, aperture, cleft, rent, crack, crevice, fissure, cranny, chink, slit, chasm; cavity, cave, cavern, grotto, den; orifice, hole, perforation, bore, pore; avenue, passage, way, entrance, dawn, first appearance *or* visibleness. *See* Gap, Way.

OPERATION—working, process, agency, action, effect; manipulation; movement. *See* Work, Proceeding, Effect.

OPINION—sentiment, idea, notion, judgment, settled persuasion. *See* Thought, Judgment, Conceit.

OPPOSE—put *or* set against, act against, resist, withstand, combat, oppugn, controvert, gainsay, contradict, deny, object to, except to. *See* Hinder, Gainsay, Object, Refuse.

OPPOSITE—*See* Cross, Inimical.

ORDAIN—set, settle, establish, institute, constitute, appoint, decree, order, prescribe; adjudge, adjudicate. *See* Fix, Appoint, Destiny, Form.

ORDER—regular disposition *or* methodical arrangement, regularity, rule, method, system, settled mode; rank, degree, class, division, species; series, succession, consecution, consecutivenesss; religious fraternity; regular government *or* discipline. *See* Command, Decree, Arrangement, Order, System, Discipline, Kind, Course, Formality, Message.

ORDER—regulate, methodize, put in order, systemize, adjust, dispose, digest, class, classify, range, rank, arrange; direct, command. *See* Command, Class.

ORDER, *put out of*—disorder, break order, derange, confuse, disarrange, disturb, perplex, confound, displace, unsettle, ruffle, discompose, interrupt; *change the*, invert; reverse. *See* Unsettle, Disfigure, Interrupt, Confused.

ORDERLY—regular, methodical, systematic; well-regulated, not tumultuous; not unruly, peaceable. *See* Regular.

ORIGIN—first existence, original, commencement, beginning, rise, source, first cause, fountain-head, descent; grounds, foundation, base, basis; rudiments, elements; primitive, etymon, etymology. *See* Begin, Cause, Rise.

OUTRAGE—*See* Affront.

OUTWARD—outer, external, exterior, extrinsic, adventitious; extraneous; *in theology*, carnal, fleshly, corporeal, not spiritual. *See* Abroad.

OUTWEIGH—exceed in weight, overbalance, preponderate; exceed in value, influence, *or* importance. *See* Go.

OVERBEAR—bear down, overpower, subdue, oppress, overwhelm, suppress. *See* Conquer, Overcome.

OVERCOME—conquer, vanquish, subdue, subjugate, overpower, suppress; surmount, get the better of. *See* Beat, Defeat, Overbear.

OVERFLOW—flow over, inundate, cover with waters, deluge, overwhelm, cover. *See* Flow, Overbear, Water.

OVERRULE—influence *or* control by predominant power, dispense with, supersede, annul, reject. *See* Annul, Refuse.

OVERSIGHT—superintendence, watchful care, supervision, inspection; mistake, overlooking, omission, error, inadvertence, inattention, slight, accident. *See* Care, Mistake, Neglect.

OWN—acknowledge, avow, confess, not to deny, admit, recognize. *See* Recognize, Profess, Allow.

PACE—step, gait, stride; amble. *See* Step.

PAIN—uneasy sensation, uneasiness, distress, suffering; anguish, agony, torture, pang, torment; disquietude, anxiety, solicitude, grief, sorrow, remorse, compunction; *pains*, labor, work, toil. *See* Grief, Trouble, Bear, Repentance, Work.

PAINT—form a figure *or* likeness in colors, depict, represent, delineate, color, besmear, sketch, describe. *See* Color, Stain.

PALACE—*See* House.

PALATE—*See* Taste.

PALE—white *or* whitish, fair, wan, cadaverous, pallid, ghastly, deficient in color, not ruddy; not bright, not shining, dim. *See* Dull, Ghastly.

PALPITATE—beat gently, beat, flutter, pant, heave, gasp. *See* Beat, Flutter.

PARCH—*See* Burn, Hot.

PARDON—*See* Forgive.

PART—portion, piece, fragment, share, division, section, species, sort, class, member; concern, interest; side, party, faction; *parts*, qualities, powers, faculties, accomplishments; quarters, regions, districts. *See* Party, Interest, Rate, District.

PART—divide, parcel, separate, break, sever, disunite. *See* Separate, Cut *off*.

PARTICULAR—not general, individual, distinct, single, minute; special, especial, peculiar, exclusive, specific, principal, chief; odd, singular. *See* Correct, Odd.

PARTY—*See* Company, Faction, Plot.

PARTY—faction, clique, set, cabal, junto; side, company. *See* Company, Faction, Plot.

PASS—*See* Go, Way.

PASSED *or* PIERCED, *not to be*—impassable, impenetrable, impervious.

PASSIONATE—irrascible, choleric, angry, irritable, hasty, impetuous; highly excited, vehement, warm; animated. *See* Angry, Hasty, Hot.

PASSIVE—suffering, enduring, patient, resigned; submissive, unresisting, not opposing, quiescent; unmoved, unprovoked. *See* Sufferance, Peaceable.

PATTERN—*See* Copy, Example.

PAUSE—make a short stop, stop, cease, intermit, delay, wait, forbear; *in uncertainty*, demur, hesitate, deliberate, waver, fluctuate. *See* Delay, Waver.

PAWN—*See* Pledge.

PAY—compensation, recompense, reward, remuneration, equivalent, wages, salary, allowance, stipend, hire. *See* Amends.

PEACE—quiet, tranquility, calm, calmness, quietness, ease, repose, rest, peacefulness, serenity, stillness, peaceableness, mildness. *See* Quiet, Mildness, Calm, Concord.

PEACEABLE—tranquil, quiet, undisturbed, unagitated, calm, serene, peaceful, mild, still, pacific. *See* Calm, Passive.

PECULIAR—*See* Particular.

PEER—*See* Nobility, Equal.

PEEVISH—*See* Fretful.

PENALTY—*See* Fine.

PENCIL—*See* Paint.

PERCEIVE—*See* See.

PERCEIVE—know by the senses, feel, see, discern, distinguish, know, understand, notice, regard, observe. *See* Distinguish, Notice, Espy.

PERFECT—bring to perfection, complete, finish, consummate, fulfill, accomplish, achieve. *See* Finish, Bring *about*, Accomplish.

PERFORMANCE—execution, completion, doing, action, act, deed, thing done; composition, written book; *of some note*, exploit, achievement, feat, heroic act, deed of renown, great *or* noble achievement. *See* Accomplishment, Production, Work, Thing *done*.

PERFUME—*See* Smell.

PERISH—die, lose life, expire; wither, fade, decay, waste away, pine, *See* Die, Dead, Wasting.

PERPLEX—*See* Entangle, Worry.

PEST—plague, pestilence, epidemic, infection, bane, worrying, nuisance, annoyance. *See* Infection.

PETITION—request, supplication, prayer, suit, entreaty, solicitation. *See* Beg, Entreaty.

PILE—*See* Heap.

PIOUS—*See* Godly.

PITH—*See* Strength.

PITIABLE—exciting pity, piteous, pitiful, miserable, doleful, woeful, rueful. *See* Doleful, Unhappy.

PITY—commiseration, compassion, fellow-suffering. sympathy, condolence, mercy, humanity. *See* Feeling, Mercy.

PLACE—spot, site, position, situation, station; rank, order; seat, residence, mansion; office, employment; calling, occupation, condition; ground, room, stead; portion. *See* Office, Situation.

PLACE—put, set, lay, locate, posit, deposit, reposit; appoint, induct, establish, fix; invest, lend. *See* Order, Fix, Lay.

PLAGUE—*See* Pest.

PLAGUE—infest with disease, etc.; vex, tease, harass, trouble, embarrass, annoy, molest, torment, torture, tantalize, importune. *See* Worry, Weary, Importune.

PLAIN—*See* Clear.

PLAN—draught, form; scheme, project, design, device, contrivance, stratagem. *See* Design, Invent, Plot.

PLEASURE—joy, delight, gratification, luxury, enjoyment, comfort, delectation, agreeable sensations *or* emotions; will, choice, purpose, intention, command;

favor. *See* Enjoyment, Gratitude, Joy, Mirth, Satisfaction, Luxury, Sport.

PLEASURE, *one given to*—voluptuary, epicure, sensualist. *See* Luxury.

PLEDGE—pawn, surety, hostage, security, mortgage, caution. *See* Security.

PLEDGE—*See* Answerable *for*.

PLENTY—*See* Enough.

PLOT—conspiracy, intrigue, confederacy, combination, cabal, junto, party clique, set, coalition; device, machination, contrivance, scheme, stratagem. *See* Design, Contrive, Party, Plan, Combine.

PLOW—*See* Till.

PLUNDER—pillage, rapine, prey, booty, spoil; ruin, ravage, waste. *See* Rapacious, Waste.

POISON—*See* Deadly.

POLISH—*See* Beautify.

POLITE—polished, refined, well-bred, elegant, graceful; courteous, complaisant, obliging, civil, urbane, affable, genteel, deferential. *See* Genteel, Awkward, Becoming.

POLITENESS—polish *or* elegance of manners, gentility, good breeding, good manners, refinement, civility, courteousness, [illegible], [illegible], [illegible], complaisance, obliging attentions. *See* Civility, Attention.

POMP—splendid procession, magnificence, parade, splendor, grandeur, state. *See* Procession, Show, Grand.

POOR—needy, indigent, destitute, necessitous, distressed; barren, mean, jejune; depressed, low, dejected; *in spirit*, humble, contrite, abased in one's own sight by a sense of guilt. *See* Bare, Barren, Mean, Sorry.

POORNESS—destitution, indigence, poverty, want, need, distress, necessity, exigency; meanness, lowness; barrenness, sterility. *See* Necessity, Want.

POPPY—*See* Sleep.

PORE—*See* Opening.

PORTER—*See* Bear.

PORTION—*See* Part.

POSITIVE—set, laid down, expressed, direct, explicit; absolute, real, express, peremptory, arbitrary, despotic, dogmatical, confident. *See* Actual, Arbitrary, Flat.

POSSESSION—occupancy, occupation, tenure, tenancy; thing possessed, land, estate, goods, etc.; madness, lunacy. *See* Occupy, Goods, Madness.

POUR—*See* Melt, Flow.

POWER—ability, strength, potency, force, energy, capacity, capability, puissance, cogency, efficacy, efficaciousness, efficiency; influence: command, rule, sway, authority, right of governing, dominion, domination, ascendancy; *royal*, royalty, scepter, crown. *See* Ability, Force, Influence, Dominion, Gift.

POWER, *want of*—inability, disability, impotence, impotency, weakness, incapacity, inefficacy, inefficiency, insufficiency, inadequacy, incompetency, imbecility. *See* Weakness.

POWERFUL—mighty, potent, strong, puissant, forcible, efficacious, influential, cogent, energetic, vehement, emphatic, intense. *See* Effect, *producing*, Prevailing, Strong, Able, Almighty.

PRAISE—commendation, approbation, applause, encomium, eulogy, panegyric. *See* Approbation, Name.

PRAISE—commend, approve, applaud, laud, extol, magnify, glorify, eulogize, panegyrize, do honor to. *See* Great, *make*.

PRAISEWORTHY—deserving praise, commendable, laudable, approved.

PRATTLE—*See* Talk.

PRAY—*See* Beg, Entreat, Entreaty, Petition.

PRECEPT—command, rule, doctrine, maxim, principle. *See* Command, Order.

PREFACE—introduction, proem, preliminary, prelude. *See* Introductory, Introduce.

PRESENT—*See* Gift, Reward, Give.

PRESERVE—*See* Keep, Free.

PRESS—*See* Embrace, Force.

PRESSING—urging with force *or* weight, squeezing, constraining, crowding, embracing, distressing, forcing; urgent, importunate, emergent. *See* Important, Squeeze.

PRETENSE—false appearance, pretext, excuse, delusion, imposture. *See* Color, Defense, Cloak.

PRETTY—*See* Beautiful.

PREVAILING—gaining advantage, superiority *or* victory, having effect, persuading, succeeding; predominant, prevalent, superior in power, efficacious; most general, epidemic, epidemical. *See* Powerful.

PREVENT—go before, precede, anticipate; hinder, obstruct, intercept, impede, obviate, preclude. *See* Anticipate, Go, Hinder, Interrupt.

PREY—*See* Plunder.

PRICE—*See* Value, Sell.

PRICK—*See* Stir.

PRIDE—inordinate self-esteem, self-conceit, conceit, arrogance, haughtiness, hauteur, presumption, assumption, insolence, vanity; splendid show, ostentation. *See* Conceit, Proud, Show.

PRIEST—*See* Ecclesiastic.

PRINCE—sovereign, monarch, potentate, king, emperor, chief, ruler.

PRIORITY—precedence, preference, preeminence. *See* Going *before*.

PRISON—*See* Liberty, *being deprived of*.

PRIVATE—*See* Secret.

PRIVILEGE—immunity, exemption; benefit, advantage, favor, prerogative, right, claim, liberty. *See* Freedom, Benefit.

PROCEEDING—process, procedure, movement, course, progress, progression; affair, matter, concern, transaction, suit, measure, step. *See* Course, Operation, Go.

PROCESSION—cavalcade, triumph, ovation; train, retinue, suite. *See* Pomp, Victory.

PROCLAIM—*See* Publish.

PRODUCE—*See* Beget.

PRODUCTION—that which is produced, produce, product; performance, composition, work. *See* Performance, Offspring.

PROFESS—make open declaration of, avow, acknowledge, declare, asseverate. *See* Declare, Own.

PROFIT—*See* Gain.

PROFITABLE—yielding *or* bringing profit *or* gain, gainful, lucrative; beneficial, useful, advantageous. *See* Gain, Use.

PROJECT—*See* Plan, Design.

PROMISCUOUS—mingled, mixed, confused, undistinguished, indiscriminate, common. *See* Mixed, Confused, Common.

PROMISE—binding declaration, assurance, guarantee, engagement, undertaking. *See* Warrant.

PROOF—trial, essay, experiment, test; demonstration, conviction, satisfaction; testimony, attestation, evidence, certification; firmness, hardness, impenetrability. *See* Evidence, Trial.

PROPERTY—quality, attribute; wealth, possessions, paraphernalia. *See* Quality, Goods, Riches.

PROPHESY—*See* Foretell.

PROROGUE—protract, prolong, defer, adjourn, delay, postpone. *See* Delay.

PROSPER—favor, render successful; be successful, succeed; grow, increase, thrive, make gain. *See* Gain, Favor, Increase, Flourish, Happiness.

PROTECT—cover, shield, defend, guard, preserve, secure, support, harbor, shelter, foster, cherish, countenance, patronize, encourage, sanction. *See* Covering, Defend, Harbor, Foster, Encourage.

PROTECTION, *place for*—asylum, sanctuary; shelter, defense, refuge, retreat. *See* Defense, Security.

PROUD—having inordinate self-esteem, self-conceited, conceited, vain, arrogant, haughty, supercilious, assuming, insolent; daring, presumptuous; grand, lofty, splendid, magnificent, ostentatious. *See* High, Grand, Pride.

PROVE—try, test; evince, establish, ascertain, verify, demonstrate, manifest; certify, attest, evidence. *See* Proof, Evidence.

PROVIDE—procure beforehand, get, furnish, supply. *See* Give.

PRUDENT—*See* Wise.

PRUNE—*See* Cut *off*.

PRYING—inspecting closely, inquisitive, scrutinizing, searching, curious. *See* Search.

PUBLIC, PUBLISH—*See* Common.

PUBLISH—make known, divulge, disclose, promulgate, proclaim, discover, expose, declare, reveal, impart, communicate. *See* Discover, Public, Declare, Spread, Utter, Blaze.

PUFF—*See* Swell.

PULL—*See* Draw, Tear.

PUNISH—*See* Discipline, Fine.

PURGE—*See* Clean.

PURSE—*See* Money.

PUSH—*See* Drive.

PUT—*See* Place.

PUT *down*—baffle, repress, crush, quell, suppress, subdue, reduce, restrain; degrade, deprive, depose; confute, silence. *See* Baffle, Check, Delay.

PUZZLE—perplex, embarrass, put to a stand, gravel, confound; bewilder, entangle. *See* Cross, Entangle, Worry.

QUACK—empiric, charlatan, mountebank.

QUAKE—*See* Shake, Fear.

QUALIFICATION—endowment, acquirement; legal *or* requisite power; modification, restriction, limitation. *See* Accomplishment, Endow.

QUALIFY—fit for, furnish with; moderate, modulate, temper, humor, restrain, limit, modify, regulate. *See* Bound, Fit.

QUALITY—*See* Property.

QUARREL—wrangle, scold, petty fight, scuffle, dispute, contest, contention, brawl, broil, jar, jangle, altercation, tumult, feud, fray, affray, variance, difference, disagreement, breach. *See* Difference, Disagreement, Tumult, Insurrection.

QUARRELING—contention, dispute, disputation, caviling, discord, dissension, strife, faction, controversy, altercation, wrangling, debate, variance, difference, disagreement. *See* Difference, Quarrel, Faction.

QUESTION—*See* Ask, Search.

QUICK—alive, living; swift, hasty; speedy, prompt, expeditious, ready; active, nimble, agile, brisk, vigorous, lively, vivacious. *See* Hasty, Active, Lively, Ready, Sharp.

QUICKEN—make alive, vivify, revive, resuscitate; hasten, accelerate, expedite, dispatch, sharpen, stimulate, incite; cheer, reinvigorate. *See* Cheer, Animate, Hasten.

QUICKNESS—speed, velocity, swiftness, celerity, fleetness, rapidity, rapidness, nimbleness, briskness, alertness; expedition, dispatch; activity, promptness, agility, dexterity; acuteness, keen sensibility; sharpness, pungency; *of intellect*, acuteness, sharpness, sagacity, penetration, acumen, shrewdness. *See* Briskness, Sharpness, Eagerness.

QUIET—rest, repose, stillness, peace, ease, tranquility, calm, quietness. *See* Peace, Ease, Still, Silence, Subside.

QUOTE—*See* Adduce.

RACE—running, rapid course *or* motion, course, progress, movement; breed; lineage, family, house, descent; stock, dynasty, generation. *See* Course, Stock, House, Breed.

RAGE—violent anger, passion, fury, excitement, extreme violence; enthusiasm; extreme eagerness *or* passion. *See* Madness, Anger, Boil.

RAISE—*See* Lift.

RAMBLE—rove, wander, stroll, range, walk, ride *or* sail at random. *See* Excursion, Stray, Go, Wander.

RANK—*See* Order.

RAPACIOUS—given to plunder, seizing by force, greedy on seizing, ravenous, voracious, greedy, devouring. *See* Plunder, Greediness.

RARE—uncommon, not frequent, scarce, singular, choice, precious, usually excellent, incomparable, unique; thin, porous, not dense; nearly raw, imperfectly roasted *or* boiled. *See* Uncommon, Thin.

RASH—*See* Foolhardy.

RASHNESS—temerity, precipitance, precipitancy, precipitation, hastiness. *See* Hasty.

RATE—proportion, standard, ratio, quota, degree; price, amount; tax, sum. *See* Tax, Value, Count, Part.

RAVE—*See* Madness.

RAW—*See* Rare.

RAY—*See* Beam.

READ—*See* Collect.

READY—quick, apt, prompt, not hesitating; acute; expert, dexterous; prepared, fitted; willing, free, cheerful, disposed; being at the point, near, not distant; easy, facile, opportune, short. *See* Quick, Active, Clever, Free, Sharp, Briskness.

REASONABLE—rational, equitable, just, fair; not immoderate, moderate, tolerable, not excessive. *See* Fair, Just.

REBELLIOUS—seditious, mutinous. *See* Tumultuous.

RECALL—revoke, repeal. *See* Call *back*.

RECALLED, REGAINED *or* REMEDIED, *not to be*—irrevocable, irretrievable, irreversible, irrecoverable, irreparable, incurable, irremediable. *See* Call *back*, Recover.

RECEIPT—act of receiving, acceptance, acceptation, reception; discharge, acquittance; recipe, prescript, prescription. *See* Take, Pay.

RECKON—count, number, compute, calculate, estimate; esteem, account, repute. *See* Count, Pay.

RECOGNIZE—remember, notice, recollect. *See* Own, Mark.

RECOVER—get *or* obtain what was lost, regain, retrieve; restore, repair, recruit. *See* Recalled, *not to be*, Redeem.

REDEEM—purchase back, ransom, liberate, relieve, rescue, affranchise, manumit, recover, deliver from, save; compensate, make amends for. *See* Free, Buy, Recover.

REDRESS—relief, remedy, deliverance from wrong, injury *or* oppression; reparation. *See* Cure.

REDUNDANT—*See* Abounding.

REFER—relate, regard, respect; appeal, apply; allude, glance at, hint; direct; reduce. *See* Relate, Appeal, Hint, Apply, Consult.

REFRESH—cool, allay heat; reinvigorate, give new strength to, revive, renovate, renew. *See* Cool, Animate.

REFUGE—*See* Protection.

REFUSE—reject, deny, decline, oppose, repel, rebuff, object. *See* Object, Oppose, Overrule, Remains.

REGARD—*See* Respect, Interest.

REGULAR—*See* Rule.

REGULAR—conformed to a rule, methodical, systematic, orderly, exact, periodical. *See* Orderly, Formal.

REIGN—*See* Govern.

REJOICE—make joyful, gladden, exhilarate; exult, joy; gratulate, congratulate, felicitate. *See* Joy, Gladden.

RELATE—tell, recite, rehearse, repeat, narrate, recount, recapitulate, detail, enumerate; refer, concern, respect, regard, appertain, interest, affect. *See* Tell, Explain, Describe, Refer.

RELATIONSHIP—kindred, relation, alliance; affinity, consanguinity. *See* Kin, Marriage.

RELIGION—godliness, piety, devotion, sanctity; system of faith and worship. *See* Holiness.

REMAIN—*See* Dwell.

REMAINS—that which is left, leavings, raspings, scrapings, relics, remnant, remainder, residue, refuse, scoria, dross; dead body, corpse, carcass. *See* Dregs.

REMARK—notice, observation, annotation, note, comment, commentary. *See* Explanation, Comment.

REMEMBER—*See* Recognize.

RENOWN—*See* Fame.

REPEAT—*See* Seek,

REPENTANCE—sorrow, pain, grief, regret, penitence, contrition, compunction, remorse. *See* Pain, Grief.

REPORT—*See* Fame.

REPLY, *smart or witty*—repartee, retort.

REPROACH—censure, find fault with, chide, reprove, upbraid, cast in the teeth, scold, rail, brawl, rate. *See* Blame, Abuse, Disgrace, Gibe.

RESPECT—regard, attention, deference, consideration, esteem, estimation, honor; veneration, reverence. *See* Refer, Honor.

RESPECT—hold in respect *or* estimation, esteem, value, regard, relate to; venerate, revere, reverence. *See* Refer, Value, Honor.

REST—*See* Ceasing.

RESTORING *or* RETURNING, *the act of*—restoration, rendition, restitution, retribution. *See* Amends.

RETURN *of like for like*—retaliation, requital, reciprocation, reciprocity, mutuality, alternation. *See* Each, Other.

REWARD — remuneration, recompense, compensation, requital, satisfaction, amends, guerdon; bribe; punishment. *See* Amends, Satisfaction, Gift.

RICHES—wealth, opulence, affluence, possessions, mammon, substance. *See* Possession, Fortune.

RIDICULE—contemptuous laughter, derision, burlesque; satire, irony, sarcasm. *See* Censure, Laughable.

RIGHT—straight; just, equitable, fair, honest; fit, proper, suitable, becoming; lawful; true; correct; not left. *See* Fair, Fit, Correct.

RIGID—*See* Severe.

RING—*See* Surround, Jingle.

RISE—*See* Go, Issue, Origin.

RITE—*See* Form.

RIVER—*See* Water.

ROAD—*See* Way.

ROLL—*See* Catalogue.

ROOM—space, compass, extent, place, stead; apartment, chamber. *See* Place.

ROOMY—spacious, large, wide, capacious. *See* Large, Immense.

ROT—putrefy, corrupt, decay. *See* Corrupt.

ROTTEN—putrid, putrefied, carious, decayed, corrupt; unsound, defective, treacherous, deceitful; fetid, stinking, rancid, ill-smelling. *See* Corrupt, Deceitful.

ROUSE—*See* Stir.

RUDE—*See* Barbarous, Impertinent.

RULE—*See* Precept, Order, Decree.

RUN—*See* Course.

SACRED—*See* Holy.

SAD—sorrowful, melancholy, mournful,

dull, downcast, dejected, depressed, cheerless, doleful, trist, gloomy. *See* Dull, Doleful, Mourn, Cast *down*.

SAFE—*See* Sure.

SALUTE—salutation, greeting. *See* Kiss.

SAME—*See* Equal, One, Individual.

SANCTION—*See* Fix, Ordain.

SATISFACTION—contentment, repose of mind; conviction; pleasure, gratification; amends, recompense, compensation, indemnification, atonement; payment, discharge. *See* Pleasure, Reward, Amends.

SATISFY—suffice, content, gratify, please; pay to content, recompense, indemnify; free from doubt, suspense, *or* uncertainty; convince; pay, discharge. *See* Amends, *make*, Pay.

SAUCY—*See* Fretful.

SAVE—*See* Free, Redeem.

SAVING—preserving, sparing, frugal, not lavish, economical, thrifty, parsimonious, excepting. *See* Mean.

SAW—*See* Cut.

SAY—*See* Speech, Tell, Aphorism.

SCALE—*See* Climb.

SCARCE—*See* Rare.

SCARCITY—scarceness, deficiency, penury, dearth, famine; rareness, infrequency. *See* Want.

SCATTER—*See* Spread, Dispel.

SCENT—*See* Smell.

SCHOLAR—learner, pupil, disciple, tyro; man of letters, doctor. *See* Follower, Master.

SCIENCE—*See* Knowledge.

SCOFF—*See* Laugh *at*, Disdain.

SCOPE—*See* Aim.

SCROLL—*See* Catalogue.

SCRUPLE—*See* Doubt.

SCULPTURE—*See* Carve.

SEA—ocean, main, deep, wave, billow, surge. *See* Wave.

SEAMAN—seafarer, sailor, mariner, tar, marine, sea-soldier; sea-robber, pirate, sea-freebooter.

SEARCH—seeking, looking for, scrutiny, investigation, inquiry, examination, research, rummage, quest, inquest, pursuit. *See* Prying.

SEARCH—look over *or* through, explore, rummage, examine, scrutinize, investigate, inquire, seek for, probe, pry. *See* Look.

SECRET—hid, hidden, concealed, clandestine. unrevealed, occult, unseen, private, unknown, secluded, latent, mysterious, mystic. *See* Hide.

SECT—*See* Heretic.

SECURITY—protection, guard, defense, palladium, guarantee, fence, safety, certainty, deposit, pledge, mortgage. *See* Guard, Sure, Protection, Pledge.

SEDIMENT—*See* Dregs.

SEE—*See* Look.

SEEK—*See* Look.

SEIZE—*See* Take, Catching.

SELL—*See* Buy, Merchandise, Trade.

SEND—throw, cast, thrust, impel, drive, cause to go *or* pass, commission; *away*, dismiss, discard, discharge, dispatch, cause to depart; *forth* or *out*, produce, put *or* bring forth, emit, exhale; *on a special commission*, depute, delegate. *See* Cast, Throw.

SENSE—sensation, perception, apprehension, discernment, judgment, faculty, intellect, reason, understanding; consciousness, conviction; meaning, import, signification. *See* Feeling, Judgment, Understanding, Meaning.

SEPARATE—divided from, disjoined, disconnected, unconnected, not united, distinct, different, detached, disunited, apart, asunder. *See* Part, Individual, Unlike.

SEPARATE—disunite, divide, sever, part, sunder, disconnect, detach, disjoin, disengage. *See* Part, Cut *off*, Distinguish, Interrupt.

SERENE—*See* Calm.

SERMON—*See* Speech, Dissertation.

SERVANT—*See* Minister.

SERVANT—one who serves, domestic, menial, drudge; help, assistant; *in Scripture*, slave, bondman, one used as an instrument. *See* Minister, Inferior, Instrument.

SET—*See* Fix, Appoint.

SET *apart*—dedicate, devote; consecrate, hallow, sanctify. *See* Apply.

SETTLE—make permanent, fix, establish, determine, corroborate, confirm; marry; adjust, compose, tranquilize; regulate, arrange; colonize; liquidate, balance *or* pay. *See* Fix, Found, Still, Pay.

SEVERE—rigid, harsh, stern, austere, not mild *or* indulgent, strict, hard, rigorous; grave, sober, sedate; afflictive, distressing, sharp, violent; biting, extreme; exact, critical, nice. *See* Rigid, Sharp, Difficult, Grave.

SHADE—*See* Darkness, Dull.

SHAKE—agitate, move, tremble, shudder, shiver, quiver, quake, totter. *See* Move, Trembling.

SHAME—*See* Disgrace.

SHAMEFUL—what brings shame *or* disgrace, scandalous, disgraceful, infamous, opprobrious, ignominious, injurious to reputation. *See* Disgrace.

SHAMELESS—destitute of shame, wanting modesty, impudent, brazen-faced, immodest, audacious, insensible to disgrace; indecent, indelicate. *See* Impudence, Modest.

SHAPE—*See* Form.

SHARE—*See* Part.

SHARP—keen, acute, not blunt, not obtuse; discerning, penetrating, sagacious, shrewd, quick, witty, ingenious; sour, acid, piercing, shrill; severe, harsh, rigid, cruel, biting, sarcastic, taunting, satirical; fierce, ardent, fiery, violent; keen, severe, pungent, painful, pricking, piquant. *See* Keen, Quick, Active, Severe, Ready.

SHARPNESS—keenness, acidity, sourness, acrimony, pungency, painfulness; acuteness, penetration, shrewdness, sagacity, discernment, quickness, ingenuity; keenness, edge, severity. *See* Sourness, Quickness, Judgment, Edge.

SHIELD—*See* Covering.

SHIFT—change, turning; expedient, resource, refuge, alternative; fraud, artifice, chicane, evasion, subterfuge, trick, turn. *See* Cheat, Trick.

SHINE—*See* Light.

SHINE—emit rays of light, radiate, give light, beam, glitter, coruscate, glisten, gleam, glare, sparkle. *See* Gleam, Blaze, Bright.

SHOOT—*See* Sprout, Bud.

SHORE—*See* Brink, Edge.

SHORTER, *made*—shortened, abridged, abbreviated, epitomized, condensed, contracted, curtailed, lessened, diminished. *See* Brief, Abridgment.

SHOUT—*See* Call.

SHOW—spectacle, exhibition, sight, representation; ostentation, parade, display, array, pomp; appearance, semblance, seeming, speciousness, plausibility. *See* Pomp, Appearance, Color.

SHOW—exhibit, present, display; make to know, direct, point out, indicate, manifest, prove, inform, instruct, teach, explain; disclose, discover, bestow, confer, afford. *See* Instruct, Discover, Declare, Direction.

SHOWY—making a great show, ostentatious, splendid, fine, gay, gaudy, glaring, pompous, sumptuous, grand, magnificent, stately. *See* Gay, Grand, Vain.

SHUDDER—*See* Shake, Fear.

SHUFFLE—prevaricate, equivocate, evade, quibble, cavil, sophisticate.

SHUN—avoid, keep clear of, eschew; evade, escape, elude; decline, neglect. *See* Neglect.

SHUT—*See* Close, Surround.

SHY—fearful of near approach, coy, reserved, not familiar; cautious, wary, careful; suspicious, jealous. *See* Careful, Jealousy.

SICK—sickly, ill, diseased, morbid; disgusted. *See* Illness, Invalid.

SIDE—*See* Edge.

SIFT—*See* Separate, Judge.

SIGHT—*See* See, Look.

SIGN—*See* Mark.

SILENCE—taciturnity; stillness, calmness, quiet, calm, repose, cessation; dumbness, muteness. *See* Calm, Quiet, Still.

SILENT—*See* Calm, Dumb.

SILVER—*See* Money.

SIMPLE—*See* Bare.

SIN—*See* Wicked, Crime, Violation, Debt, Depravity.

SINCERE—real, unfeigned, genuine, true, honest, undissembling, upright, uncorrupt; unvarnished, plain; frank. *See* Genuine, Honesty.

SINGLE—*See* Alone, Particular.

SITUATION—position, seat, location, site, state, condition, predicament, plight, case; place, office. *See* Place, Condition, State, Office.

SIZE—bulk, bigness, magnitude, greatness, extent. *See* Bigness, Fatness, Greatness.

SKILL—*See* Ability.

SKIN—*See* Flay.

SLACKEN—slack, make less tense, tight *or* severe, relax, remit; mitigate, diminish, abate, lower, relieve, unbend. *See* Lessen, Lower.

SLANDER—defamation, detraction, scandal, calumny, backbiting, aspersion; disgrace, reproach, disreputation, ill-name. *See* Disgrace, Contumely, Asperse.

SLAUGHTER—massacre, carnage, murdering, butchery. *See* Destruction, Kill.

SLAVE—*See* Liberty, *being deprived of.*

SLEEP—*See* Doze.

SLEEPY—drowsy, lethargic, inclined to sleep; causing *or* inducing sleep, soporific, soporiferous, narcotic, opiate, dormitive, somnific, somniferous, anodyne, sedative, composing. *See* Doze.

SLENDER—*See* Thin.

SLIP—*See* Deceive, Mistake.

SLOW—tardy, dilatory, sluggish, tedious. *See* Lazy, Dull.

SLY—cunning, deceitful, artful, insidious, crafty, wily, circumventive, subtle, subtile. *See* Cunning, Deceitful.

SMELL—*See* Sweet-smelling.

SMOOTH—*See* Soft, Beautify.

SNAKE—*See* Serpent.

SNARE—*See* Entangle.

SNARLING—growling, grumbling angrily, cynical, snappish, waspish.

SNATCH—*See* Seize.

SNEAKING—creeping away slily, stealing away; crouching, cringing, servile, obsequious, mean, pitiful; meanly, parsimonious, covetous, niggardly. *See* Mean, Miserly.

SOAK—steep, imbrue, macerate, imbue, wet, moisten, drench.

SOBER—temperate; steady, serious, solemn, grave. *See* Abstaining, Grave.

SOFT—easily yielding to pressure, easily to be bent *or* led, flexible, supple, lithe, limber, flaccid, pliant, yielding, ductile, pliable, compliant, tractable, docile; malleable; gentle, mild, meek, kind, civil; smooth, flowing; easy, quiet. *See* Kind, Dainty, Allay, Ease, Weak.

SOIL—*See* Stain.

SOLE—*See* Alone.

SOLEMN—*See* Grave.

SOLID—hard, firm, compact, stable, strong, massive; real, substantial, sound, valid, true, just; entire, whole. *See* Firm, Strong, Thick.

SOLITARY—living alone, desolate. *See* Alone, Desolate. Lonely.

SOPHISTRY—fallacious reasoning, chicane, chicanery, sophism, fallacy. *See* Falsehood.

SORRY—grieved, pained, afflicted, affected, hurt, mortified, vexed, chagrined; poor, mean, vile, worthless. *See* Mean, Poor, Grieve.

SORT—*See* Kind, Character.

SOUL—*See* Spirit, Mind.

SOUND—*See* Jingle, Bound *back.*

SOUND—*See* Whole.

SOUR—*See* Sharp.

SOURNESS—acidity, acidness, tartness, sharpness; *of manner*, asperity, harshness, acrimony. *See* Sharpness.

SOURCE—*See* Origin.

SPARING—*See* Saving.

SPEAK—*See* Tell.

SPEAK *to*—accost, address; *with*, talk, converse, discourse, commune. *See* Talk, Utter, Unspeakable.

SPEECH—language; oration, philippic, harangue, address, discourse; solecism. *See* Language, Speech, Talk, Interview.

SPEND—lay out, dispose of, part with; expend, consume, waste, squander, exhaust, drain; pass; harass, fatigue. *See* Expensive, Waste.

SPIRIT—*See* Life, Lively, Active.

SPIRITUAL—immaterial, incorporeal; mental, intellectual; sacred, ecclesiastical; ethereal, ghostly; godly, holy. *See* Intellectual, Godly, Holy.

SPITE—hatred, spleen, rancor, malice, malignity, malevolence, gall; grudge, pique. *See* Malice, Hatred, Enmity, Envy.

SPLEEN—*See* Spite.

SPOIL—*See* Plunder.

SPOKE—*See* Beam.

SPORT—what diverts and makes merry, play, game, diversion, fun, drollery, frolic, waggery, waggishness; pastime, recreation; amusement, entertainment; mock, mockery, contemptuous mirth; diversion of the field, as fowling, hunting, fishing. *See* Mirth, Jest, Frolic, Pleasure, Amusing, Lively.

SPOT—*See* Stain, Blemish, Blameless.

SPREAD *abroad*—scatter, disperse, distribute, diffuse, dispense, circulate, propagate, divulge, publish, disseminate; *out*, open, expand, unfold, unfurl. *See* Dispel, Publish, Open, Lay, Swell, Unfold.

SPRING—*See* Issue.

SPROUT—*See* Bud.

SPUR—*See* Stir.

SPURIOUS—not genuine, counterfeit, supposititious, false, fictitious, deceitful, adulterate; illegitimate, bastard. *See* Genuine, *not*, Bastard, Vain, Law.

SPURN—*See* Despise.

SQUEAMISH—fastidious, over-nice, over-scrupulous. *See* Nice.

SQUEEZE—press, gripe; oppress, harass,

crush; hug, embrace closely; *out*, extort, express, extract. *See* Compress, Press.

STABLE—*See* Strong.

STAGGER—walk unsteadily, reel, totter, vacillate; fail; hesitate. *See* Doubt, Wave, Stammer.

STAIN—discolor, maculate, blot, spot, foul, soil, pollute, blemish, sully, tarnish, taint; dye, tinge. *See* Blot, Blemish, Corrupt, Disgrace, Color.

STAIN, *without*—immaculate, pure, spotless, untainted, innocent, unstained, unblemished, unpolluted, irreproachable, unsullied, untarnished. *See* Disgrace, Harmless.

STAMMER—stutter, falter, hesitate in speaking. *See* Stagger.

STAMP—character. *See* Mark.

STAND—*See* Stay.

STATE—*in life*, condition, circumstances, situation, station; political body, *or* body politic, body of men; rank, post, degree, quality, dignity, grandeur. *See* Condition, Situation, Order, Grand.

STATUE—*See* Stand.

STAY—remain, continue, abide; endure, last; wait, attend; rest, rely, confide in, trust; stop, restrain, withhold, delay, obstruct, hinder. *See* Abide, Dwell, Delay, Hinder.

STEP—*See* Go, Pace, Mark.

STICK—*See* Follower, Attachment.

STIFF—*See* Formal.

STILL—stop, check, restrain, calm, allay, assuage, lull, pacify, compose, appease, quiet; silence, suppress, subdue. *See* Settle, Calm, Ease, Peace, Allay, Silence.

STINK—*See* Rotten.

STIR—move, agitate; *up*, incite, instigate, prompt, excite, raise, animate, stimulate, provoke, rouse, begin, quicken, enliven, disturb. *See* Move, Animate, Awaken, Agitation, Anger.

STOCK—stem, body; family, lineage; fund, capital, store, magazine, supply, accumulation, hoard, provision; *live stock*, as cattle *or* sheep. *See* Body, House, Race, Goods, Lay.

STOP—*See* Hinder.

STORE—*See* Stock.

STORY—tale, narration, narrative, history, memoir, recital, relation; fiction, fable; incident, anecdote; floor, loft. *See* Memoir, History, Chronicle, Falsehood.

STRANGE—*See* Odd, Outward.

STRATAGEM—*See* Plan, Trick.

STRAY—wander, deviate, err, swerve, rove, ramble. *See* Ramble, Wander.

STREAM—current, course, tide; river, rivulet, brook, streamlet, rill; drift. *See* Course.

STRENGTH—*See* Strong, Power.

STRENGTHEN—make strong *or* stronger, fortify, invigorate, animate, encourage: enforce; establish, confirm, corroborate *See* Encourage, Animate, Strong.

STRICT—*See* Severe.

STRIFE—*See* Quarrel.

STRIKE—*See* Beat.

STRONG—powerful, vigorous, robust, stout, sturdy, hardy, firm, solid, sinewy, muscular, able; mighty, potent, cogent, forcible, efficacious; ardent, eager, zealous; violent, vehement, earnest; bright, glaring, vivid. *See* Powerful, Firm, Solid, Able, Lusty, Bright, Zealous.

STUDY—*See* Think, Attention.

STRUGGLE—*See* Unwilling.

STUPID—*See* Blockhead.

SUBJECT—placed *or* situate under; exposed, liable, obnoxious; prone, disposed. *See* Accountable.

SUBSIDE—sink *or* fall to the bottom, settle; abate, intermit, assuage, allay, become tranquil. *See* Calm, Ease, Quiet, Settle.

SUCCESS—*See* Prosper, Lucky.

SUCKLE—*See* Nourish.

SUDDEN—without notice, abrupt, unexpected, unlooked for, unanticipated; emergent. *See* Abrupt.

SUFFER—undergo, feel *or* bear pain, endure, support, sustain; allow, tolerate, permit. *See* Support, Allow.

SUFFERANCE—bearing, endurance, patience, moderation; toleration, permission, suffering, allowance. *See* Bear, Suffer, Allow, Passive.

SUITABLE—fitting, accordant, agreeable, conformable, adapted, convenient, befitting, proper, becoming, adequate. *See* Agreeable, Becoming, Fit.

SUPERFICIAL—being on the surface; shallow, flimsy, not deep *or* profound, slight, cursory, desultory.

SUPPORT—bear, sustain, uphold, stay, prop, second, forward, assist, countenance, favor, patronize, promote, encourage, nurture, nourish, cherish, foster; maintain, protect, shield, defend; verify, make good, substantiate, vindicate. *See* Bear, Suffer, Assist, Stay, Favor, Encourage, Nourish, Foster, Protect.

SURE—certain, unfailing, infallible, indubitable; safe, secure, firm. *See* Certain, Doubted, *not to be*, Firm, Security.

SURROUND—encompass, compass, environ, inclose on all sides; inclose, encircle, invest, besiege.

SURVEY—*See* Look.

SWALLOW *up*—take into the stomach; engulf, absorb, engross, engage wholly; imbibe, exhaust, consume, devour. *See* Engross.

SWEET—*See* Amiable.

SWEET-SMELLING—odoriferous, odorous, fragrant, perfumed, sweet-scented, ambrosial.

SWELL *out*—dilate, distend, expand, extend. *See* Lay, Spread.

SWIFT—*See* Quick.

SWING—*See* Stagger.

SYSTEM—method, order, mode, manner. *See* Manner, Order, Formality.

TAKE—receive, accept; *from*, deprive of, deduct, subtract; detract, derogate; *to or upon one's self*, appropriate, assume, adopt, undertake; arrogate, usurp. *See* Seize, Embrace, Catching.

TALENT—*See* Ability.

TALK—*See* Speak.

TALK—converse, speak, confer, discourse, commune, hold intercourse, chat, confabulate. *See* Speak.

TALK—converse, conversation, colloquy, dialogue, discourse, conference, confabulation, chat. *See* Speech, Hearsay.

TALKATIVE—speaking much, loquacious, garrulous.

TAME—*See* Overcome.

TART—*See* Sour.

TASTE—gustation, savor, relish, flavor, palate; judgment, genius, discernment, perception, sensibility. *See* Palate, Flat, Judgment.

TAX—impost, tribute, duty, contribution, custom, toll, rate, sum imposed, assessment; burden; charge, censure; task. *See* Custom, Rate.

TEACH—*See* Instruct.

TEASE—*See* Trouble, Incommode.

TELL—*See* Relate, Declare.

TEMPER—*See* Abstaining, Cool, Cross, Ill-tempered, Sourness, Qualify.

TEMPT—allure, entice, attract, solicit, incite, provoke, decoy, seduce, inveigle, coax, persuade, induce, draw; *in Scripture*, try, prove, put to trial for proof. *See* Allure, Induce, Lead, Try.

TEND—*See* Lean.

TERRIFY—frighten, appal, alarm, intimidate, dismay. *See* Fright, Fear.

TEST—criterion; standard; trial. *See* Trial.

THICK—dense, not thin, compact, close, solid; gross, coarse; turbid, muddy, feculent; inspissated; frequent; *make thick*, incrassate; consolidate. *See* Dense, Close, Solid, Gross.

THIN—rare, attenuated, not dense, not close; slim, small, slender, lean, meager, slight. *See* Rare, Small, Lean.

THING *done*—fact; act, action, deed; feat, exploit, achievement. *See* Performance.

THINK—judge, conclude, imagine, suppose, conceive, opine, fancy, muse, ruminate, meditate, reflect, call to mind, cogitate, consider, deliberate, contemplate, ponder; believe, deem; guess, conjecture, surmise, divine. *See* Fancy, Count.

THOUGHT—idea, conception, imagination, perception, notion, fancy, conceit; reflection, consideration, contemplation, meditation, cogitation, deliberation, opinion, judgment, supposition; design, purpose; solicitude, care, concern. *See* Conceit, Judgment, Opinion, Care, Whim.

THOUGHTFUL—full of thought, contemplative, meditative, reflective, mindful, considerate, deliberate, deliberative, attentive, careful, circumspect, wary, advised, discreet. *See* Careful, Watchful, Mind.

THROW—*See* Cast, Send.

THRUST—*See* Intrude.

TIDINGS—*See* News.

TIE—*See* Gird, Band, Knot.

TIME—period, age, date; duration, season, era, epoch; repetition, doubling.

TIMELY—seasonable, opportune. *See* Untimely.

TIRE—*See* Weary.

TIRED—fatigued, wearied, harassed, exhausted. *See* Weary.

TONGUE—*See* Language, Speech.

TOOL—*See* Instrument.

TOP—*See* Height.

TRACE—*See* Mark.

TRADE—business, traffic, barter, dealing,

commerce, merchandise, exchange, truckage; occupation. *See* Business, Interchange, Merchandise, Change.

TRANSITORY—passing, fleeting, temporary, transient, evanescent, momentary, speedily vanishing, quickly passing away, fading. *See* Time, Vanish, Mortal.

TRANSPARENT—pervious, pellucid, diaphanous, translucent, transpicuous, limpid. *See* Clear, Bright.

TRAVEL—*See* Go.

TREATMENT—management, manipulation; usage; entertainment. *See* Use.

TREMBLE—*See* Shake, Fear.

TREMBLING—tremor, trepidation, quaking, shaking with fear, shivering. *See* Fear, Shake.

TRIAL—experiment; experience; test. *See* Test, Attempt, Proof, Try.

TRICK—*See* Entangle.

TRICK—artifice, chicane, stratagem, cheat, cheating, wile, fraud, cozenage, juggle, finesse, sleight, legerdemain, deception. *See* Cheat, Cunning, Shift, Jest.

TRIFLING—trivial, petty, frivolous, futile, unimportant, insignificant, immaterial, useless, inept, unfit, inconsiderable, light, slight, worthless. *See* Idle, Vain.

TROUBLE—*See* Grieve, Hurt.

TROUBLE—TROUBLES—disturbance, agitation, commotion, perplexity, distress, affliction, suffering, adversity, calamity, misfortune; molestation, inconvenience, annoyance, uneasiness, vexation; difficulties, embarrassments, perplexities, vexations, cares, anxieties, disquietudes; sorrow, misery. *See* Agitation, Misfortune, Care, Difficulty, Pain, Vexation, Darkness.

TROUBLESOME—molesting, annoying, irksome, disquieting, disturbing, harassing, perplexing, afflictive, vexatious. *See* Wearisome.

TRUE—*See* Sincere.

TRUNK—*See* Body.

TRUST—*See* Belief, Confidence.

TRUTH—veracity; honesty, virtue, faithfulness, fidelity, constancy; fact, realty, conformity. *See* Faithfulness, Honesty, Maxim, Doctrine.

TRY—*See* Trial, Attempt, Tempt.

TUMBLE—roll, fall, roll down, drop, sink.

TUMULT—commotion, disturbance, agitation, riot, broil, row, affray, uproar, confusion, bustle, stir, convulsion. *See* Insurrection, Quarrel, Trouble.

TUMULTUOUS—disorderly, tumultuary, agitated, restless, unquiet, irregular, noisy, disturbed, confused, promiscuous, unruly, ungovernable, turbulent, violent; seditious, mutinous, rebellious, insurgent, riotous. *See* Insurrection, Rebellious, Confused, Loud, Hasty.

TURN—*See* Change, Shift.

TWIG—*See* Shoot.

TWIST—contort, writhe; wreathe, wind, encircle, twine, twirl, form, weave, bend, turn, wrest, wrench, swing; pervert, distort. *See* Entangle, Move *round*, Crooked.

TYPE—*See* Mark, Letter.

UMPIRE—*See* Judge.

UNBELIEF—incredulity, infidelity, disbelief, distrust. *See* Belief.

UNBOUNDED—boundless, infinite, unlimited, interminable, unchecked, uncontrolled, unrestrained. *See* End, *without.*

UNBURY—exhume, exhumate, disinter. *See* Rise, Bury.

UNCERTAIN, *be*—waver, fluctuate, undulate, oscillate, vacillate; doubt, hesitate. *See* Wave, Doubted, *not to be.*

UNCOMMON—not common, not usual, rare, scarce, unique, choice, singular. *See* Rare.

UNDERSTAND—comprehend, know, conceive, apprehend, appreciate. *See* Know.

UNDERSTANDING—intellect, intelligence, judgment, faculty, knowledge, comprehension, apprehension, conception, perception. *See* Judgment, Knowledge, Sense.

UNDETERMINED—not determined, unsettled, undecided, indeterminate, irresolute, unresolved, unsteady, wavering, fluctuating, doubtful, hesitating. *See* Changeable, Uncertain, *be.*

UNEASINESS—restlessness, want of ease, disquiet, disquietude; solicitude, anxiety, care. *See* Care, Trouble.

UNEQUAL—*See* Equal.

UNFAITHFUL—faithless, perfidious, treacherous; undutiful, disloyal; neglectful. *See* Faithless, Neglect.

UNFOLD—open folds, unravel, expand, spread out; develop; disclose, reveal, divulge, declare, tell. *See* Explain, Spread, Declare.

UNHAPPY—wretched, miserable, unfortunate, unlucky, calamitous, evil, distressed, afflicted. *See* Pitiable.

UNIMPORTANT—immaterial, insignificant. *See* Trifling.

UNIVERSAL—*See* Whole, All.

UNJUST—not just, inequitable, unfair, dishonest, iniquitous, knavish, roguish, wrongful. *See* Iniquity, Wicked, Honesty, Justice.

UNLIKE—not like, dissimilar; different, diverse; separate, distinct. *See* Separate.

UNRELENTING—relentless, implacable, inexorable, hard, cruel. *See* Appeased, *not to be*, Cruel, Deadly.

UNSETTLE—unfix, unhinge, make uncertain *or* fluctuating, disconcert. *See* Order, *put out of*.

UNSPEAKABLE—that can not be uttered *or* expressed, ineffable, inexpressible, unutterable. *See* Speak.

UNTIMELY—premature, inopportune, unseasonable, ill-timed. *See* Timely, Time.

UNWILLING—not willing, loth, disinclined, reluctant, backward, averse. *See* Obstinate, Averse.

UPRIGHT—*See* Right.

UPRIGHTNESS—perpendicular erection; rectitude, integrity, honesty. *See* Honesty, Justice.

USE—usefulness, utility, advantage, benefit, profit, avail, service, serviceableness; employment, practice, custom, usage. *See* Benefit, Profitable, Custom, Treatment, Apply.

USURP—*See* Assume *falsely*, Take.

UTTER—speak, pronounce, articulate, express; disclose, discover, divulge, publish. *See* Speak, Publish, Call *out*.

UTTERED—spoken, pronounced; disclosed, published; *by mouth* or *voice*, oral, verbal, vocal.

VAIN—empty, unreal; worthless, idle, useless, abortive, fruitless, ineffectual; conceited, proud, self-conceited, opinionative, opiniated, opinioned, self-opinioned, egotistical; showy, ostentatious; light, inconstant; unsatisfying; false, deceitful, spurious. *See* Proud, Idle, Empty, Foolish, Conceit, Showy, Spurious.

VALE—valley, dale, dell, dingle.

VALOR—*See* Courage.

VALUE—worth, price, rate; estimation, account, importance, efficacy, appreciation; appraisement *or* apprizement, valuation, assessment. *See* Rate, Worth.

VALUE—estimate, rate, apprize *or* appraise, assess, compute, calculate; prize, esteem, respect, regard, appreciate. *See* Rate, Respect.

VALUABLE—having value *or* worth, precious, costly, estimable, worthy. *See* Worthy.

VANISH—disappear, pass away from sight; flit. *See* Transitory.

VANQUISH—*See* Overcome.

VAUNTING—boasting, glorying, vainglory, ostentation, display, parade, vapor, vanity, arrogance, rodomontade. *See* Boaster.

VEIL—*See* Hide.

VENGEANCE—*See* Punish, Assert.

VEST—*See* Covering.

VETERAN—*See* Old.

VEX—*See* Incommode.

VEXATION—chagrin, mortification, teasing trouble, uneasiness. *See* Wearisome, Trouble.

VIBRATE—*See* Shake.

VICE—*See* Crime.

VICTUALS—*See* Food.

VIE—*See* Emulous.

VIEW—*See* Look, See, Glance.

VIGOROUS—*See* Active, Strong.

VILLAGE—*See* Countryman, House.

VILLAIN—vassal, servant, subject, dependant; wretch, scoundrel, rascal. *See* Follower, Blockhead.

VIOLATION—law-breaking, infringement, infraction, transgression, trespass; rape. *See* Sin, Injury.

VIOLENT—forcible, vehement, outrageous, boisterous, turbulent, fierce, furious, impetuous, passionate, assailant, *See* Cruel, Hot, Force.

VIPER—*See* Serpent.

VISION—sight; appearance, apparition, phantom, specter, ghost. *See* Ghost, Ghostly.

VOICE—*See* Uttered.

VOID—*See* Empty *space*.

VOTE—suffrage, voice.

VOW—*See* Pray.

VOWEL—*See* Letter.

WAGES—*See* Pay, Reward.

WAIL—*See* Mourn, Grieve.

WALK—*See* Go.

WANDER—rove, ramble, stroll, roam, range; leave home, depart, migrate; digress, diverge, deviate, err, stray; be delirious. *See* Ramble, Go, Eccentric, Joint, *out of*.

WANT—deficiency, defect; need, lack, necessity; poverty, penury, indigence. *See* Scarcity, Necessity, Poorness, Poor.

WANTON—*See* Lust, Loose.

WARM—*See* Heat.

WARM—cordial, hearty, sincere, zealous, ardent, fervent, intense; keen, irritable. *See* Affectionate, Hearty, Zealous, Keen, Hot, Enthusiast.

WARMTH—warmness, gentle heat, fervency, fervor, zeal, ardor, intensity, cordiality, vehemence, heat, glow; earnestness, eagerness; excitement, animation. *See* Heat, Eagerness, Life.

WARNING—previous notice, monition, admonition, caution. *See* Caution.

WARRANT—*See* Answerable *for*, Promise.

WARY—cautious, circumspect, watchful, guarded, scrupulous, timorously prudent. *See* Watchful, Careful, Aware.

WASTE—devastation, spoil, ravage, desolation, havoc, destruction; squandering, dissipation; consumption, loss, useless expense; desolate or uncultivated country; ground or space unoccupied. *See* Plunder, Loss, Destruction.

WASTE—cause to be lost, expend uselessly, squander, dissipate, lavish, consume, spend, use; destroy, desolate; wear out, exhaust. *See* Lavish, Spend, Destroy, Desolate, Corrupt.

WASTING—lavishing, dissipating, desolating, laying waste; decay, consumption, decline, phthisis; perishing, fading, decadence.

WATCHFUL—vigilant, attentive, careful, heedful, observant, cautious, circumspect, wakeful. *See* Careful, Thoughtful, Wary, Aware.

WATER—*See* Soak.

WAVE, WAVER—*See* Pause, Uncertain, *be.*

WAVE—billow, surge, breaker. *See* Sea.

WAY—passing; passage, road, highway, lane, street; method, system, mode, course, means, manner, form, fashion. *See* System, Gap, Opening, Means, Course, Custom.

WEAK—feeble, infirm, piping, weakly, enfeebled, debilitated, enervated, flaccid, limber, lax; easily broken; soft, pliant; low, small. *See* Broken, *easily*, Low, Foolish.

WEAKEN—debilitate, enfeeble, enervate, effeminate, invalidate. *See* Droop.

WEAKNESS—feebleness, debility, languor, infirmity, unhealthiness, imbecility, frailty, frailness; foolishness; *in the plural*, defeat, failing, fault, foible. *See* Power, *want of*, Fault, Folly.

WEAPON—*See* Arm, Covering.

WEARISOME—causing weariness, tiresome, tedious, prolix, fatiguing, exhausting, reducing, troublesome, annoying, vexatious. *See* Troublesome.

WEARY—reduce, exhaust, tire, fatigue, harass, dispirit, jade, wear out, subdue; annoy, vex. *See* Worry.

WEEP—*See* Mourn.

WEIGH—*See* Think.

WEIGHT—*See* Burden, Importance, Heavy.

WELL—*See* Good.

WET—*See* Moist, Soak.

WHEAT—*See* Food.

WHIM—sudden turn *or* start of the mind, freak, fancy, maggot, caprice, prank. *See* Conceit, Thought, Frolic, Lightness.

WHITE—*See* Pale.

WHITEN—bleach, blanch.

WHOLE—all, total, integral; complete, entire, perfect, sound, well, undivided; full. *See* All, Wholly.

WHOLLY—totally, completely, entirely, perfectly, fully.

WICKED—evil, sinful, immoral, impious, profane, irreligious, depraved; unjust, iniquitous, nefarious; *in a high degree*, atrocious, heinous, flagrant, flagitious, facinorous, villainous, enormous, monstrous. *See* Abandoned, Corrupt, Unjust, Iniquity, Sin.

WIDE—*See* Large.

WIFE—*See* Marriage.

WILD—*See* Cruel.

WILL—*See* Disposition, Pleasure, Choice, Kindness, Malice.

WILL—testament; codicil.

WINDING—*See* Crooked.

WIPE—*See* Clean.

WISE—having knowledge, sage, sagacious, sapient, discerning; discreet, judicious, prudent; learned, knowing, skillful, dexterous; godly, pious. *See* Godly, Ignorant.

WISELY—prudently, judiciously, discreetly, with wisdom, sagely, sagaciously, skillfully, cautiously, circumspectly.

WISH—*See* Hope, Choose.

WISH *for*—desire, covet, long for, hanker after, sigh for; request, entreat, solicit, beg, ask; aspire to. *See* Beg, Aim.

WITTY—*See* Odd.

WONDER—surprise, amazement, astonishment, admiration; miracle, marvel, prodigy, strange thing, monster.

WONT—*See* Custom.

WORK—employment, occupation, labor, toil, drudgery, operation; fabric, manufacture; action, deed, feat, achievement; composition, book. *See* Operation, Accomplishment, Performance, Pain.

WORRY—bore, tease, trouble, vex, harass, perplex, distract, disturb, annoy, confuse, confound; fatigue; tear, mangle; taunt, tantalize, torment. *See* Trouble, Mangle, Displease, Plague.

WORSE, *make*—deteriorate, impair; injure, damage. *See* Corrupt, Injure.

WORTH—value, excellence, perfection; merit, desert, goodness, usefulness; virtue, morality. *See* Value, Morals.

WORTHY—*See* Valuable, Praiseworthy.

WRATH—*See* Anger.

WRETCH—*See* Miser, Unhappy.

WRITER—penman, scribe, clerk, copyist, transcriber, secretary, amanuensis; lawyer; author, classic, editor.

WRITHE—*See* Twist.

WRONG—*See* Wicked, Ill.

YEAR—*See* Time.

YIELD—*See* Give *up*.

YIELDING—producing, affording; conceding, resigning, surrendering, allowing; flexible, accommodating; compliance, submission, deference.

YOUNG—youthful, juvenile, infantile, infantine; puerile, boyish, childish.

YOUTH—juvenility, adolescence, puerility; boyhood, childhood, infancy.

ZEAL—ardor, heat, fervency, fervor, earnestness, warmth, intensity, eagerness, avidity, enthusiasm. *See* Eagerness, Warmth, Heat.

ZEALOUS—ardent, earnest, warm, fervent, solicitous, anxious, intense. *See* Warm, Affectionate.

EXPLANATION OF MARKS

USED IN THE SPECIMEN PROOF-SHEET.

A WRONG letter in a word is noted by drawing a short perpendicular line through it, and making another short line in the margin, behind which the right letter is placed. (See No. 1.) In this manner whole words are corrected, by drawing a line across the wrong word and making the right one in the margin opposite.

A turned letter is noted by drawing a line through it, and writing the mark No. 2 in the margin.

If letters or words require to be altered from one character to another, a parallel line or lines must be made underneath the word or letter: namely, for capitals, three lines; small capitals, two lines; and Italic, one line; and in the margin opposite the line where the alteration occurs, *Caps*, *Small Caps*, or *Ital.* must be written. (See No. 3.)

When letters or words are set double, or are required to be taken out, a line is drawn through the superfluous word or letter, and the mark No. 4 placed opposite in the margin.

Where the punctuation requires to be altered, the correct point, marked in the margin, should be encircled. (See No. 5.)

When a space is omitted between two words or letters which should be separated, a caret must be made where the separation ought to be, and the sign No. 6 placed opposite in the margin.

No. 7 describes the manner in which the hyphen and ellipsis line are marked.

When a letter has been omitted, a caret is put at the place of omission, and the letter marked as No. 8.

Where letters that should be joined are separated, or where a line is too widely spaced, the mark No. 9 must be placed under them, and the correction denoted by the marks in the margin.

Where a new paragraph is required, a quadrangle is drawn in the margin, and a caret placed at the beginning of the sentence. (See No. 10.)

No. 11 shows the way in which the apostrophe, inverted commas, the star, and other references, and superior letters and figures, are marked.

Where two words are transposed, a line is drawn over one word and below the other, and mark No. 12 placed in the margin; but where several words require to be transposed, their right order is signified by a figure placed over each word, and the mark No. 12 in the margin.

Where words have been struck out that have afterward been approved of, dots should be marked under them, and *Stet* written in the margin. (See No. 13.)

Where a space sticks up between two words, a horizontal line is drawn under it, and the mark No. 14 placed opposite in the margin.

Where several words have been left out, they are transcribed at the bottom of the page, and a line drawn from the place of omission to the written words (See No. 15); but if the omitted matter is too extensive to be copied at the foot of the page, *Out, see copy*, is written in the margin, and the missing lines are inclosed between brackets, and the word *Out* is inserted in the margin of the copy.

Where letters stand crooked, they are noted by a line (see No. 16); but where a page hangs, lines are drawn across the entire part affected.

When a smaller or larger letter, of a different fount, is improperly introduced into the page, is is noted by the mark No. 17, which signifies wrong fount.

If a paragraph is improperly made, a line is drawn from the broken-off matter to to the next paragraph, and *No* ¶ written in the margin. (See No. 19.)

Where a word has been left out, or is to be added, a caret must be made in the place where it should come in, and the word written in the margin. (See No. 19.)

Where a faulty letter appears, it is marked by making a cross under it, and placing a similar one in the margin (see No. 20); though some prefer to draw a perpendicular line through it, as in the case of a wrong letter.

SPECIMEN PROOF-SHEET.

EXHIBITING THE MARKS USED IN THE CORRECTION OF ERRORS.

[1] *a/* THOUGH a v*e*riety of opinions exist as to
the individual by w*h*om the art of printing was [2] *ꝺ*
first discovered; yet all authorities concur in
admitting Peter Schoeffer to be the person [3] *Caps*
who invented *cast metal types*, having learned
ꝺ the art ~~of~~ of *cutting* the letters from the Gut-
[5] :/ tembergs/ he is also supposed to have been
[6] # the first who engraved on copper plates. The [7] /-/
following testimony is presered in the family, [8] *v/*
[9] ‿ by‿Jo.‿Fred.‿Faustus,‿of‿Ascheffenburg: <# [6]
[10] □ >'Peter Schoeffer, of Gernsheim, perceiving *S. Caps.*
[11] V his master Fausts design, and being himself
[12] *tr.* (desirous\ardently) to improve the art, found
out (by the good providence of God) the
method of cutting (~~incidendi~~) the characters [13] *stet.*
in a *matrix*, that the letters might easily be
[5] ,/ singly *cast*/ instead of bieng *cut*. He pri- [12] *ei/*
[14] ⊥ vately *cut matrices*| for the whole alphabet: ^ [15]
Faust was so pleased with the contrivance,
/that he promised Peter to give him his only [17] *wf.*
[16] /daughter Christina in marriage a promise [3] *Ital.*
/which he soon after performed.
[19] *as/* (But there were many difficulties at first [18] *no* ¶
with these *letters*, as there had been before [3] *Rom.*
[20] + with wooden ones, the metal being too soft [3] *Ital.*
to support the force of the im pression: but [9] ⁀/
this defect was soon remedied, by mixing
a substance with the metal which sufficiently *tr.* [12]
[5] ⊙ hardened it/

and when he showed his master the letters cast from these matrices,

SPECIMEN PROOF-SHEET.

AS CORRECTED.

Though a variety of opinions exist as to the individual by whom the art of printing was first discovered, yet all authorities concur in admitting PETER SCHOEFFER to be the person who invented *cast metal types,* having learned the art of *cutting* the letters from the Guttembergs: he is also supposed to have been the first who engraved on copper-plates. The following testimony is preserved in the family, by Jo. Fred. Faustus, of Ascheffenburg:

'Peter Schoeffer, of Gernsheim, perceiving his master Faust's design, and being himself ardently desirous to improve the art, found out (by the good providence of God) the method of cutting (*incidendi*) the characters in a *matrix,* that the letters might easily be singly *cast,* instead of being *cut.* He privately *cut matrices* for the whole alphabet: and when he showed his master the letters cast from these matrices, Faust was so pleased with the contrivance, that he promised Peter to give him his only daughter *Christina* in marriage, a promise which he soon after performed. But there were as many difficulties at first with these letters, as there had been before with *wooden ones,* the metal being too soft to support the force of the impression: but this defect was soon remedied, by mixing the metal with a substance which sufficiently hardened it.'

www.ingramcontent.com/pod-product-compliance
Lightning Source LLC
LaVergne TN
LVHW010145110826
845151LV00002B/428

* 9 7 8 1 4 2 5 5 3 7 1 8 0 *